HUMAN SEXUALITY

Prepared by
American Medical Association
Committee on Human Sexuality

Second Printing

HUMAN SEXUALITY *is an exclusive publication of the*
AMERICAN MEDICAL ASSOCIATION

0139-177J-8/73;10M   OP-139

ACKNOWLEDGMENTS

The Association is grateful to members of the Committee on Human Sexuality who gave graciously of their time and talents to outline the general content and to review the final manuscript of this volume. The members of the Committee are as follows:

ROBERT C. LONG, M.D., Chairman . . . . Louisville, Kentucky
Associate Professor of Obstetrics & Gynecology
University of Louisville School of Medicine

MILDRED MITCHELL—BATEMAN, M.D. . . Charleston, West Virginia
Director
West Virginia Department of Mental Health

SPRAGUE H. GARDINER, M.D. . . . . Indianapolis, Indiana
Professor of Obstetrics & Gynecology
Indiana University School of Medicine

HAROLD I. LIEF, M.D. . . . . Philadelphia, Pennsylvania
Director
Division of Family Study
University of Pennsylvania

FREDERICK J. MARGOLIS, M.D. . . . . Kalamazoo, Michigan
Assistant Professor of Medicine
Wayne State University School of Medicine

HERBERT C. MODLIN, M.D. . . . . Topeka, Kansas
Director
Department of Preventive Psychiatry
The Menninger Foundation

DAVID M. REED, PH.D. . . . . Philadelphia, Pennsylvania
Assistant Professor of Family Study in Psychiatry
University of Pennsylvania School of Medicine

PHILIP M. SARREL, M.D. . . . . New Haven, Connecticut
Assistant Professor of Obstetrics & Gynecology
Yale University School of Medicine

i

The preparation of the initial manuscript for this book was carried out by Richard C. Lemon of New York, a freelance author who worked under the editorial supervision of the Committee on Human Sexuality.

The Association expresses its appreciation to the following distinguished consultants, representing a diversity of disciplines bearing upon human sexuality, for their cooperation and assistance in the preparation of this book:

CARLFRED B. BRODERICK, PH.D. . . .University Park, Pennsylvania
Department of Child Development and Family Relationships
Pennsylvania State University

MARY S. CALDERONE, M.D. . . . . .New York, New York
Director
Sex Information and Education Council of the U.S.

PAULINE CARLYON . . . . .Lansing, Michigan
Bureau of Maternal and Child Health
Michigan Department of Public Health

WARREN M. COX, M.D. . . . . Louisville, Kentucky
Assistant Clinical Professor of Psychiatry
University of Louisville School of Medicine

ROBERT S. DANIELS, M.D. . . . . Chicago, Illinois
Professor of Psychiatry and Social Medicine
University of Chicago School of Medicine

STEPHEN ETTENSON, M.D. . . . . Philadelphia, Pennsylvania
Department of Psychiatry
Philadelphia Naval Hospital

RAYMOND FELDMAN, M.D. . . . . Boulder, Colorado
Director — Mental Health Division
Western Interstate Commission for Higher Education

EVALYN S. GENDEL, M.D. . . . . Topeka, Kansas
Director — Kansas State Department of Health
Divison of Maternal and Child Health

JERROLD LOZNER .... Louisville, Kentucky
Medical Student
University of Louisville School of Medicine

WILLIAM H. MASTERS, M.D. .... St. Louis, Missouri
Director
Reproductive Biology Research Foundation

THE REV. PAUL B. McCLEAVE . ... Blue Rapids, Kansas

THE REV. MSGR. JAMES McHUGH, S.J......... Washington, D.C.
Director — Family Life Bureau
National Catholic Welfare Conference

JOHN MONEY, PH.D. .... Baltimore, Maryland
Associate Professor of Medical Psychology and Pediatrics
The Johns Hopkins Hospital

LONNY MYERS, M.D. .... Chicago, Illinois
Director of Medical Education
Midwest Population Center

MICHAEL A. NELSON, M.D. .... Albuquerque, New Mexico
U.S. Public Health Service Hospital
United States Army

JEAN PAKTER, M.D. .... New York, New York
Director, Bureau of Maternity Services and Family Planning
New York Department of Health

C. ALVIN PAULSEN, M.D. .... Seattle, Washington
Professor of Medicine
University of Washington School of Medicine

WILLIAM L. PELTZ, M.D. .... Philadelphia, Pennsylvania
Institute of Pennsylvania Hospital

LOWELL F. PETERSON, M.D. .... Hinsdale, Illinois
Assistant Professor of Obstetrics & Gynecology
University of Illinois School of Medicine

HARRIETT F. PILPEL ....New York, New York
General Counsel
Planned Parenthood — World Population

DAVID SANDERS, M.D. ....Los Angeles, California
Associate Director — Division of Psychiatry
Mount Sinai Hospital

JAN SCHNEIDER, M.D. .... Ann Arbor, Michigan
Associate Professor — Obstetrics & Gynecology
University of Michigan Medical Center

JAMES P. SEMMENS, M.D. ....Charleston, S. Carolina
Associate Professor — Obstetrics & Gynecology
Medical University of South Carolina

ROBERT A. SENESCU, M.D. ....Albuquerque, New Mexico
Chairman — Department of Psychiatry
University of New Mexico Medical School

RICHARD E. SHANTEAU .... Kansas City, Kansas
Medical Student
University of Kansas Medical School

THE REV. A.W. RICHARD SIPE, S.J. ....Baltimore, Maryland
Director of Family Services
The Seton Psychiatric Institute

JOSEPH B. TRAINER, M.D. .... Portland, Oregon
Professor of Medicine and Physiology
University of Oregon Medical School

ROY M. WHITMAN, M.D. ....Cincinnati, Ohio
Professor of Psychiatry
University of Cincinnati School of Medicine

Finally, the Association expresses its appreciation for the contributions of the following members of its staff in the preparation of this book:

John C. Ballin, Ph.D.
William R. Barclay, M.D.
Richard P. Bergen, J.D.
Asher J. Finkel, M.D.
Kathryn S. Huss, M.D.
Hugh H. Hussey, M.D.

Marilyn A. Krause
Charles W. Macenski
Karl Mayer, D.V.M.
Emanuel M. Steindler
Walter Wolman, Ph.D.

v

Preface

In 1968, the AMA Committee on Human Reproduction submitted a report to the Board of Trustees recommending that the American Medical Association provide written source material for the physician to improve his understanding and knowledge of human sexuality.

An ad hoc committee from the Board of Trustees met with representatives of certain AMA Councils and Committees to study this recommendation. It was agreed that physicians should assume a major portion of the responsibility for dealing with problems of human sexuality and for family counseling.

Evidence was presented, however, that physicians often are not prepared to meet this responsibility. Therefore, in 1969, the Board of Trustees authorized the publication of this book, *Human Sexuality*.

Human sexuality is a subject of infinite complexity; counseling in this area is subject to a variety of interpretations. Therefore, the purpose of this book is to focus the physician's attention on medicine's current views of this complex facet of human behavior. Comments, criticisms and recommendations will be welcome.

ERNEST B. HOWARD, M.D.
Executive Vice President
American Medical Association

Foreword

The past decade has seen a proliferation of literature on the subject of human sexuality. Although much of this material is sensational, there remains a substantial body of scholarly literature. Why, then, another book on the subject?

For the medical profession a book such as this is certainly needed. From surveys of physicians and medical students, publications in the medical literature and the nature of inquiries to the American Medical Association, it is apparent that many physicians believe they are unprepared for the task of providing counsel and advice on sexual matters.

The physician must feel hard pressed to select from the bewildering stream of books, manuals and articles appearing in both the lay and professional press, those few publications in which he can have confidence and which meet his special needs as a practitioner of medicine. The AMA Committee on Human Sexuality, its consultants, and the staff have reviewed, judged and selected from the plethora of sources the material which they think will best meet the needs of the medical profession.

Most physicians possess thorough knowledge of reproductive anatomy and physiology. Such knowledge does not, however, constitute a large part of human sexuality and, therefore, does not of itself make a physician an effective counselor. However, the physician gains greater insight into human behavior in the course of his practice. Together, his knowledge of anatomy and physiology along with his insight gained by experience do provide the background to make the physician an effective counselor on sexual matters.

Every practicing physician is aware of the patient who masks sexual problems with organic complaints, but who desperately seeks the counsel and guidance of an understanding physician to cope with an underlying psychosexual disorder. Too often the physician does not follow up on this opportunity for counseling because he lacks training in this area. If he does give counseling, he may project his own personal experiences and biases instead of offering professional advice.

The need for better training of physicians in human sexuality has become increasingly apparent. More and more medical schools have recognized this need by incorporating the subject into their curricula. This book is intended to augment the efforts of the medical schools and to provide, in concise form, an overview of the subject for medical students, interns and residents as well as for practicing physicians. Although the central theme of the book is the counseling of patients on those aspects of sex which are of most practical concern, there is an attempt to place human sexuality in a rational perspective within the totality of interpersonal relationships.

This book was written primarily for a medical audience, but it is hoped that it may also prove useful to clergymen, marriage counselors, psychologists, sex educators and other personnel in the allied health professions. There was no intention to produce another marriage manual or textbook on human sexuality. For readers who wish more detailed information, references at the end of each section and an annotated bibliography are provided.

Many aspects of human sexual behavior are governed by religious doctrine and standards of morality. This book attempts to present facts in an objective fashion without making moral judgments. It assumes that each physician will act on his professional and ethical judgment within the context of his own conscience and beliefs in extending medical advice to his patient.

The book is organized into sections which trace sequentially normal sexual development, common problems of a sexual nature seen in medical practice and the societal aspects of human sexuality. The knowledgeable physician-counselor is a key figure in each area, but he cannot function adequately as a counselor unless a proper doctor-patient relationship has been established.

It is hoped that this book will facilitate a comfortable dialogue between physician and patient, an essential first step in overcoming problems and in achieving the fullest measure of that which is human in human sexuality.

Robert C. Long, M.D., Chairman
AMA Committee on Human Sexuality

TABLE OF CONTENTS

ACKNOWLEDGMENTS i

PREFACE vii

FOREWORD ix

PART I

THE PHYSICIAN AND HUMAN SEXUALITY 1

Chapter I   The Meanings of Human Sexuality 3
             Sexual Attitudes and Codes 3
             Concepts of Masculinity and Femininity 5
             Sexual Anxiety 6

Chapter II   The Role of the Physician 7
             Counseling 7
             The Management of Sexual Problems 7
             The Physician's Preparation 8

Chapter III The Doctor-Patient Relationship 9
             The Physician's Attitude 9
             The Patient 10
             Doctor-Patient Roles 11
             Discussing Sexuality 12
             The Sexual History 14
             The Physical Examination 17

References 18

PART II

THE PHYSICIAN AND HUMAN SEXUAL DEVELOPMENT 19

Chapter IV   Patterns of Sexual Development 21
             The Family 21
             Male and Female Roles 23

Chapter V   The Sexual System 24
             Biologic Sex 24
             Sexual Identity 25
             Gender Identity 25

Chapter VI   Childhood 28
             Sexual Development in Childhood 28
             Normal Development 28
             Variant Sexual Development in Children 30
             The Role of the Physician 33
             Prevention and Parental Counseling 33
             Management of Problems 36

Chapter VII Puberty and Adolescence 39
             Normal Sexual Development 39
             Masturbation 40
             Social and Sexual Attitudes 41
             Homosexual Episodes 43
             The Role of the Physician 44
             Prevention and Adolescent Counseling 44
             Management of Problems in Puberty
             and Adolescence 46

Chapter VIII Early Adulthood 60
             Sexual Development 60
             Heterosexuality 60
             Homosexuality 61
             The Role of the Physician 63
             Prevention and Counseling 63
             Management of Problems 74

Chapter IX   Late Adulthood 81
             Normal Sexual Development 81
             The Role of the Physician 83
             Prevention and Counseling 83
             Management of Problems 83

References 85

PART III

THE PHYSICIAN AND HUMAN SEXUAL RESPONSE 89

Chapter X   The Sexual Relationship 91
             Sexual Attitudes in Marriage 93

Chapter XI   The Sexual Response System 95
             Excitement 96
             Plateau 96
             Orgasm 99
             Resolution 100
             The Female Orgasm .100

Chapter XII Methods of Coitus 103
             Foreplay 103
             Coital Positions 103

Chapter XIII Evaluating Sexual Complaints 106
             Goals of Treatment and Counseling 106
             The Premarital Examination and Counseling . .108

Chapter XIV Problems of Male Sexual Response 111
             Impotence 111
             Premature Ejaculation 114
             Other Ejaculatory Problems 115

Chapter XV   Problems of Female Sexual Response 117
             Non-orgasmic Response 117
             Vaginismus 120
             Dyspareunia 120
             Complaints of Frequency and Method
                of Coitus 121

Chapter XVI Disease and Surgery 123
             Diabetes 123
             Neurologic Diseases .123
             Surgical Procedures 125

Psychosexual Reactions to Illness 126
Venereal Disease 129

Chapter XVII **Variations of Sexual Response 135**
Nymphomania 135
Satyriasis 135
Homosexuality 135
Transvestitism and Transsexualism 136
Fetishism 136
Voyeurism and Exhibitionism 136
Masochism and Sadism 136
Pedophilia 137
Sexual Assault on Adult Females
(Forcible Rape) 138

Chapter XVIII **Referral and Allied Professionals 141**

References 142

PART IV

THE PHYSICIAN, SEX AND SOCIETY 145

Chapter XIX **Sexual Standards 147**
Laws on Sex 147
Changing Standards in America 148

Chapter XX **Social Class and Sexual Counseling 150**

Chapter XXI **Sex Education in the Community 151**

Chapter XXII **The Multiplicity of Roles of the Physician 154**

References 158

Appendix I **Evaluation, History and Attitudes 161**

Appendix II **Sex Education Reading List 184**

Appendix III **Genetic Counseling Units 189**

Appendix IV Sex and the Law 194

Glossary...277

Bibliography...284

Index...289

PART 1

THE PHYSICIAN AND HUMAN SEXUALITY

THE PHYSICIAN AND HUMAN SEXUALITY

CHAPTER I—THE MEANINGS OF HUMAN SEXUALITY

Human sexuality is no longer a taboo subject in our society, but increased discussion has not resulted in a proportionately greater understanding of the meaning of sex and human sexuality. Since problems of sexuality are often a significant component of a patient's ills, it is important that the physician have a basic orientation in this complex field.

Sex is understood to mean biologic gender, but it also involves the self-image, or feelings of maleness or femaleness. It is both an appetite and the behavior which is oriented toward satisfaction of that appetite. What we call "sex" has many meanings and shadings and is only a part of the collective differences that mark an individual as male or female.

Human sexuality is not confined to the bedroom, to the night time, or to any single area of the body. It involves what we do, but it is also what we are. It is an identification, an activity, a drive, a biological and emotional process, an outlook and an expression of the self. It brings great fulfillment, but it also engenders problems that undermine and unbalance entire lives. It is strongly influenced by social and personal beliefs and in turn strongly influences both beliefs and behavior. It is an important factor in every personal relationship and in every human endeavor from business to politics. Human beings see, hear, feel, think, act and react in masculine and feminine ways and parents, in so doing, influence their children in similar directions.

SEXUAL ATTITUDES AND CODES

Many persons view human sexuality too narrowly and often with distorted vision; they overemphasize its biologic features and underestimate its psychologic and social aspects. Until recently, in this country, sex was considered a purely private and somewhat shameful matter that might be referred to jokingly but was unacceptable as a topic for open discussion. Because of these strictures, few persons with sexual problems sought professional help to better understand themselves and the important role that sexuality played in their lives.

In the large body of sexual mythology some of the prevalent misconceptions are: that men and women respond to sexual activity very differently; that masturbation is physically damaging; that intercourse is always harmful during the last three months of pregnancy and first six weeks postpartum; that women can achieve two different types of orgasm, clitoral and vaginal; that women can experience only one orgasm during an act of coitus; that persons who have had coronary occlusions should severely curtail or abstain from sexual activity; that simultaneous orgasm is the indication of sexual competency; that multiple orgasms in the female should be achieved to provide sexual satisfaction; that sexual performance is governed mainly by physical factors; that sex drive is reduced after the menopause; that ability to have intercourse disappears in old age in both sexes; that sexual pleasure is reduced by hysterectomies and vasectomies; and that orgasm is debilitating. All of these false beliefs cause much needless anxiety and suffering.

To relieve a patient of a specific, defined misconception is relatively easy for the physician. By contrast, it is a challenging task to treat sexual neuroses and to help a patient develop a "healthy attitude toward sex." Unfortunately, or perhaps fortunately, there is little agreement on what a "healthy" attitude is or, if such an attitude does exist, whether anybody has it. There are no universally recognized norms for sexual attitudes and behavior, because what is "healthy" or "unhealthy" is usually decided on social and moral rather than on scientific and medical grounds.

Individuals within American society have profoundly divergent views on sexuality. Some men and women believe a "healthy" sex life means having intercourse with a number of persons before marriage and occasionally thereafter. Others feel it is "healthy" to remain virginal until the honeymoon and monogamous after marriage; while among the sons and daughters of these same individuals, many consider it healthy to have intercourse with anyone they love——in and out of marriage. One American couple will regard oral-genital contact as a basic part of loveplay, while the couple next door may consider anything except coitus in the male-superior position as a perversion.

Sexual taboos have emerged in the course of every civilization, some prohibitions being based on biologic[1] convictions and others on socioeconomic factors. These sexual codes vary from society to society, from group to group and from time to time. The Puritans prohibited intercourse on Sunday because it was believed to cause spontaneous abortion, and this belief was translated into law in Massachusetts. Unfortunately, the laws that result from "current" sexual codes may remain in existence long after underlying concepts have been proved invalid or socio-economic changes have made them useless or even detrimental. Laws are much slower to change than are attitudes and customs.

Nevertheless, laws concerning sexuality are undergoing revision. The press has given much publicity to the revisions of laws governing contraception and abortion. However, physicians are not always aware of the complex laws in each state that relate to coitus and sexual practices. While these laws are largely unenforceable because they relate to acts usually performed in private, it would be appropriate for physicians to make themselves aware of the various laws in their states. It has been estimated that if all the laws regulating sexual activity in America were strictly enforced, 90% of the population would be jailed as sex offenders, and this estimate may be conservative.

CONCEPTS OF MASCULINITY AND FEMININITY

Man has traditionally divided society into masculine and feminine components, and he has usually seen the two as opposite, or even antagonistic. Biologically, this is an exaggerated view, for the fact is that the male and female genitalia develop from the same embryonic tissue and both men and women secrete both androgens and estrogens. Moreover, orgasm in both sexes is an analogous experience.

Biological, environmental and emotional influences all contribute in important ways to the individual's feelings of gender. A boy develops certain male mannerisms partly because he has been taught that he should. In a case of ambiguous genital development, if both parents assign a particular gender, that gender is likely to be the one with which the grown child feels comfortable, even though, as occasionally happens, it turns out to be biologically incorrect.

Today men and women engage in activities that, a few years ago, would have been considered inappropriate for their particular sex. Masculine and feminine roles may shift even more in the future, and create difficulties for those whose sexual self-concept is insecure or tenuous. One man may lift bar bells or climb mountains and not feel securely male, while another will feel comfortably male despite wearing long hair and doing the dinner dishes. The critical factor is not what a man or woman does but whether the individual feels comfortable about his own sexuality.

SEXUAL ANXIETY

Many factors in our society generate sexual anxiety: misconceptions concerning sexuality, taboos, laws, changing attitudes and insecurity of sexual identity. Some ambiguity about sexuality begins during childrearing. An infant responds to physical stimulation of its erotic zones. The mother's caresses induce sensual pleasure, yet she may rebuke the child if he masturbates. Eventually, the child discovers that all bodies are not alike and this may initiate sexual anxiety. Many parents unnecessarily bring on sexual anxiety in their children by treating the subject as something which is mysterious, unpleasant or dirty. Most persons have encountered some echo of these views in their parents, their friends or even themselves.

As a result of such muddled and anxious views of human sexuality, many persons today do not lead fully gratifying sexual lives, and almost everyone at one time or another experiences some kind of sexual stress. Since few individuals exchange personal sexual information, it is easy to erroneously assume that others are leading uniformly pleasurable, or at least satisfying sexual lives. When sexual difficulties develop, therefore, the individual often considers himself unusual or even freakish. Many marriages are blighted for a lack of discussion of the problem. Even temporary failures of sexual response are emotionally traumatic and may threaten the marriage itself.

CHAPTER II—THE ROLE OF THE PHYSICIAN

COUNSELING

The physician is in an advantageous position to carry out preventive counseling and to intervene to prevent a self-perpetuating cycle of sexual anxiety. Physicians see patients at every stage of life; each juncture furnishes opportunities to provide appropriate information on the varieties of normal sexual development and behavior. The pediatrician can inform parents about their importance in shaping sexual character, and he can instruct the growing child about sexual development. The obstetrician-gynecologist has opportunities to provide information to his patients throughout their adult life, to invite and answer questions, and to help them become confident and loving parents and spouses. The general practitioner can be important, especially to his male patients, who are often neglected in counseling. The surgeon has a crucial role in preventing sexual problems in his patients: certain operations (eg, hysterectomy, prostatectomy, vasectomy) have spelled the end of sexual activity simply because the patient was not informed that the surgery would have no lasting organic effect on sexual ability.

THE MANAGEMENT OF SEXUAL PROBLEMS

When an actual sexual problem arises the physician must be ready to serve as a counselor. Sexual problems are sometimes associated with disease or organic change. A person recovering from a coronary occlusion may be shocked and frightened by continuing sexual desire, and the resultant anxiety may be far more dangerous to health than is intercourse. When a woman who has often avoided coitus during her childbearing years experiences a rejuvenation of sexual interest following menopause, she may become anxious and irritable. The physician who has the patient's confidence is in a position to uncover and ameliorate such problems through counseling and discussion.

The sexual problems that physicians encounter most commonly in their patients are those of sexual response. Such problems revealed in a survey by Golden[2] included failure of orgasm, frigidity, impotence, dyspareunia and premature ejaculation. Some of these problems may be resolved by a brief explanation and discussion; others require more extended counseling but still fall within the physician's capabilities. In the remaining cases the physician can uncover the problem, assess its severity, and then send the patient to an appropriate resource for additional help.

THE PHYSICIAN'S PREPARATION

The physician has several assets for dealing with human sexuality. His position of authority in the patient's eyes enables him to dispel deeply ingrained misconceptions and to give needed reassurance. Patients are usually more comfortable discussing sexuality with a physician than with anyone else and initial reticence or embarrassment dissipate with a little encouragement. The physician also can determine if there is any physical basis for the problem.

Until recently, physicians received very limited or no training in human sexuality. In 1961, only three medical schools in the United States offered courses in human sexuality[3]; today many medical schools offer such courses and the number is increasing. Courses in sexuality and family counseling in some communities are now being taught by medical students. Thus, the recently graduated physician has received more extensive instruction in the physiology of coitus, the psychologic aspects of sexual development and behavior, the psychologic and moral problems of contraception, and the social, psychologic and sexual aspects of marriage, than the older physician who has been forced to rely primarily on personal observation, intuition, and common sense.

The physician's personality is a crucial factor in his effectiveness as a counselor. Lief[4] found that the medical student who has come to terms with his own problems is likely to be a more effective counselor than the seemingly adjusted student who appears poised, outgoing, competent and makes a good impression on fellow students and faculty, but is out of touch with his own feelings.

Even though much important sexual research has been mechanistic, it has provided a body of physiologic knowledge that has been badly needed. Some physicians have rebelled, believing that sex should be "natural" rather than taught or contrived. Naturalness in sexuality is desirable, but much sexual counseling is in fact directed at clearing away the impedimenta that childhood training and society have put in the way of natural sexual expression.

CHAPTER III—THE DOCTOR—PATIENT RELATIONSHIP

THE PHYSICIAN'S ATTITUDE

In general, sexuality is not discussed during an office consultation unless the physician introduces the subject or the patient is under tremendous pressure to talk about something that is sexual in nature. Burnap and Golden[5] conducted a survey in which they interviewed physicians about the sexual problems of their patients and how they dealt with them. They found that physicians who said they routinely asked about sexuality, encountered sexual problems in 14% of their patients, those who asked only when it seemed indicated reported an incidence of about 8%. The investigators rated the behavior of the physician as to whether he behaved naturally to sexual material during their interview or whether he fidgeted, blushed, conspicuously avoided sexual terms, grew angry or was otherwise uneasy. Physicians who were rated as acting naturally reported finding sexual problems in a mean proportion of 15% of their patients. Physicians who reacted with discomfort found sexual problems in only 2.7% of patients. The authors concluded that the uncomfortable physicians might have reacted similarly when patients began to present sexual problems and that this discomfort might have effectively silenced many patients.

The physician affects the course of a sexual dysfunction by his words and his attitudes. Mathis[6] has described several examples:

> A young married woman consulted her family physician about a sexual problem. During the interview, she mentioned that she had seen the word "fellatio" and didn't know what it meant. The physician defined it and remarked that "only homosexuals and perverts did that." But the couple had practiced fellatio until then with pleasure. The wife eventually saw a psychiatrist because of overwhelming feelings of guilt and shame about her "perversion." As Mathis concluded, the physician should always assume that any sexual question has some personal relevance for the patient, and it should not be answered casually.

> A 37-year old woman was advised to have a tubal ligation. She refused, then consented but grew very

DOCTOR—PATIENT   9

depressed. The physician postponed the operation, and the husband and wife were interviewed. It developed that both of them were convinced that a woman became promiscuous once she was sterilized. Two brief counseling sessions relieved their fears and her depression.

Golden believes that a physician may fail to identify a sexual dysfunction in a patient for any of three basic reasons: a need to deny the existence of any sexual problems of his own; a lack of confidence that he can do anything about sexual problems; and a concern that patients or colleagues will consider his interest prurient. In addition, the physician often fails to recognize that, even when no specific problem exists, there is much he can do in the course of his practice to help prevent sexual problems from arising.

THE PATIENT

The patient who consults a physician because of a sexual dysfunction differs in some ways from other patients. A man who is impotent may have strong guilt feelings about his disability, which he can only vaguely define. Even if he is sophisticated about the subject of sex in general, he may have some trouble broaching his problem. A patient may have no idea what the real nature of his trouble is, because sexual problems are often masked by real or imaginary ailments. Unfortunately, the physician usually has no direct evidence of the patient's sexual impairment since only the patient is in a position to make observations, and he is not likely to be objective.

A patient's beliefs and attitudes about sexuality are often an intimate part of his problem; in fact, his moral standards may interfere with his treatment. His reading about sex also may complicate treatment. Books on how to play tennis seldom suggest that if the reader follows instructions dutifully, he will get to Wimbledon, but books on love-making often suggest that championship sex is within everyone's reach.

The presenting patient is almost always only part of the problem, because sexuality usually involves interpersonal relationships. Cuber[7] noted that practical advice may be either good or bad depending on the expectations and habitual interrelationships of the patient to whom it is given. For example, it may make matters worse to tell a couple to spend more time together if intuitively they have found that the way to a reasonably harmonious life lies in avoiding one another much of the time.

DOCTOR—PATIENT ROLES

Patients usually have one of four basic attitudes toward physicians:

1) *The Magic Model:* The physician is an authority figure in realms beyond comprehension and is expected to pull a solution out of a hat.

2) *The Parent-Child Model:* The physician is a parent figure who is expected to give the patient instructions for his own good, and the patient, like a child, will do as he is told.

3) *The Peer Model:* The physician is a fellow adult with special knowledge, who can help him solve his problem.

4) *The Self-Help Model:* The physician is a guide to the development of a patient's own resources; the patient expects to become largely self-reliant.

In some instances the physician temporarily must take an authoritarian approach in order to help with a sexual problem. In dealing with most sexual problems, however, the physician should guide the patient to eventually reach the self-help model. Usually an authoritarian approach will be the least productive on a long term basis. Although the physician may find it difficult to abandon his accustomed role of knowledgeable authority, it is necessary that he do so because he must have the patient's active help if treatment is to succeed. It is essential that the physician gain a good knowledge of the patient's background, history and attitudes. Therefore, he must establish trust and a relaxed and productive mutual working relationship.

The physician dealing with sexual problems of patients may find his own feelings involved more than is usual or comfortable. Sexual information may bring forth unwelcome erotic thoughts and reactions. By recognizing, understanding and accepting his own sexual feelings, the physician can keep personal reactions in the treatment process to a minimum. If a physician finds it difficult or impossible to bring the same objectivity to sexual problems that he brings to other clinical problems——if he cannot overcome a feeling of discomfort when dealing with sexual matters——it is better to refer the patient to another physician. A special challenge occasionally arises when a patient's behavior becomes seductive. The patient's involvement of the physician in such a case may be very gradual and therefore go unnoticed unless the physician keeps alert for signals of a seductive approach.

DISCUSSING SEXUALITY

Eliciting information and uncovering the patient's sexual difficulties are often a difficult problem. Some physicians begin a discussion of sexuality with a general question: "Is there anything else that's bothering you that you haven't talked about?" Many prefer to begin with a question about the family: "What significant problems do you have within the family? You know everyone has family problems that can affect health. Let's look into your marriage a little bit. Do you feel satisfied with it? What do you like about your marriage? What do you dislike about your marriage?" If specific sexual material does not emerge spontaneously, the physician can proceed to more direct questioning. "You haven't said anything about how you're getting along sexually."

However the subject is approached, it is important that the patient understand that questions about sexuality are a natural part of medical history taking. Any suggestion in the physician's manner that he is straying into a "private" matter will reinforce any anxieties that the patient has about sex. A relaxed manner lets the patient know that sexuality is as appropriate an area for medical consideration as any other. If the patient seems embarrassed, the physician may observe that it is often difficult for patients to talk about these things, especially for the first time. It may be necessary to discuss the patient's difficulties in talking about the subject before getting into the details of his problems. Many patients protest that they have never been able to talk about sex with anybody. The physician should then point out that the doctor is not "anybody" but a professional person qualified to deal with problems of sexuality on the same basis as other health matters.

In all interviews about sexuality, the physician should be careful to leave the door open for subsequent discussion. As much as possible, his questions should be open-ended ones that cannot be answered with a simple yes or no. It is more effective to ask, "How satisfied do you think your wife is with your sexual relations?" than "Do you think your wife is satisfied with your sexual relations?" Even if a problem seems unimportant, the physician should be careful not to dismiss it. If a new bride confesses that she and her husband seem to be having a sexual problem, a response such as, "Don't worry, time will take care of that," effectively closes the door. If the patient cannot bring himself to talk about the subject, the physician should let him know that he believes sexual problems are medically important and that he will be available for consultation at any time the patient is ready.

The terminology the physician uses in discussing sexuality with patients should be carefully selected. Lansing[8] has noted that Latinized terms inappropriately suggest a process of disease and therapy, and more common words, such as "impotence" and "frigidity," are often loaded for the patient. The terminology which the physician uses in discussing sexuality with the patient should be the terminology the patient understands without being offensive. The tone of the interview should be clinically objective, matter-of-fact and frank. Chez[9] has noted that some women tend to lower their voice in such conversations, and the physician often unconsciously lowers his voice in response. The resulting hush is apt to be disturbing; a normal tone is far more reassuring. The male physician should also be careful to avoid any suggestion of male superiority which will engender resentment in the female patient.

Judgments based on the patient's appearance will influence questioning, and thus should be avoided. Castelnuovo-Tedesco reported[10] that an interviewer of a prim, mousy-looking woman skipped past a question as to whether the patient had ever had a venereal disease. When asked why, he said that the patient obviously would have been too embarrassed. "Who would have been too embarrassed?"

At first, patients may consciously mislead the physician about their sexual problems through the use of denial and avoidance, or they may simply lie. Specific words and phrases (eg, normal, frigid, my privates) often need to be questioned, because they may have a different meaning for the physician than for the patient. Occasionally, it may be useful to direct the conversation away from any specific sexual complaint that emerges into the broader subject of sexuality. Discussing the patient's feelings about sex openly, often helps the patient to recognize their importance and clarifies the specific complaint. "I get the impression that you were brought up to think that sex was something shameful. It sounds as though you feel guilty about some of these things."

Gardiner suggests[11] that if the patient is especially reluctant to discuss his feelings, the physician may recommend that both husband and wife make a list of their sexual and marital assets and liabilities to be brought in at the next interview. The lists would demonstrate the patients' interest and cooperation, and establish items for further discussion. Another technique is to use a rating scale of some pertinent dimensions of marital interaction, wherein each spouse rates a particular area according to the degree of problem it presents in the marriage. Each spouse's perception is then checked against his mate's to see if there is congruence of perception. This then becomes a focal point for discussing marital interaction. The Marriage Counsel of Philadelphia has designed the "Marital Problem Questionnaire" for this purpose (Appendix I).

When a new patient voices specific sexual complaints, it may be wise to postpone discussing them until a history and physical examination have been completed. The physician should let the patient know that he is interested in and unembarrassed by the specific sexual problem, but considers a history and an examination essential first steps in his investigation. With some patients, the physician will need to follow up specific leads more quickly, so as not to impede the flow of information. In such cases, the examination and history should be postponed. The art of medicine has been defined as the ability to respond effectively to clues.

THE SEXUAL HISTORY

A few questions about sexuality should be a part of every general medical history. In many cases, the patient's initial reaction to questions about sexuality furnish a clue to the advisability of further exploration.

A suggested form for taking a sexual history can be found in Masters and Johnson's *Human Sexual Inadequacy*. However, each physician should work out the specific method of gathering information with which he is most comfortable. Not only will physicians differ in their methods, but these methods will need to be adjusted to individual patients. The same questions obviously are not appropriate for a young girl, a middle-aged bachelor, a happily-married man, and an elderly widow, but all pertinent questions should be asked, even if the physician believes he knows the answer. Similarly, there are inappropriate times to obtain a sexual history: during an acute illness and whenever emergency care is rendered.

When obtaining a complete sexual history, usually the easiest way to begin is to ask when the patient first acquired information about birth and reproduction, and what were his or her reactions to it. The physician should also ask about the patient's earlier notions concerning sexuality and the age at which he acquired his first accurate information. The history should include chronological information about sexual training and experiences, the amount of affection in the family, family attitudes toward sex, the patient's attitudes about sex, the role of sex in his life, and the nature of the relationship between husband and wife.

On the subject of sexual intercourse, patients expect the physician to ask about frequency, sexual drive and the degree of satisfaction obtained, so it is best to start with those items. If the patient is married or has a quasi-permanent relationship, the impact of the relationship on sexual behavior should be explored. It is relatively easy then to proceed to the special problems encountered, such as difficulty in obtaining an orgasm, premature ejaculation, impotency, conflicts over desired frequency of coitus, the frustration of desires for affection and the boredom resulting from mechanical and routinized sexual behavior. After this it is comfortable for the patient to be asked about premarital or extramarital sexual encounters. (See Appendix I for a sexual evaluation test and a sample interview.)

Variant sexual behavior, including homosexuality and lesbianism, usually is upsetting to both patient and doctor. Wahl[12] suggests introducing the subject with a reference to variant behavior in the opposite sex, which puts the matter in a more general framework. Thus, a patient might be asked, "How old were you when you first found out that women are sometimes attracted sexually to other women and men to men? How did you react to this knowledge?" The physician may then note that although homosexual approaches to children are uncommon, they are often upsetting, and ask whether the patient ever had any such experiences. Finally, he may comment that homosexual experimentation is common in childhood and early adolescence, and ask whether the patient has ever had any homosexual experiences.

The physician should be honest, consistent, nonjudgmental, and sensitive to the patient's feelings and attitudes. He should be aware that he can elicit or suppress information by his manner as well as by his words. If a patient contradicts himself by revealing something he had previously denied, the new information should be accepted as readily as if there had been no denial and interpreted as a step forward in overcoming his resistances.

Masters and Johnson[13] have concluded, "Almost ten years of investigation in the broad areas of human sexual response has brought conviction to the writers that if the interviewing physician can project sincere interest in the patient's problem and, even more important, exhibit no personal embarrassment in an open sexual discussion, almost any individual's sexual history will be reported with sufficient accuracy and adequate detail for treatment purposes."

Wahl[14] lists three general principles that the physician should follow in taking a sexual history:

> "1) The history progresses from those topics that are easier to discuss to those that, in our culture, are more difficult to discuss.
>
> "2) The patient is asked first about how he acquired sexual information before he is asked about sexual experience.
>
> "3) When appropriate, questions are preceded by informational statements on the generality of the experience. These reassure the patient as well as supply information; they significantly reduce his shame, anxiety, and evasiveness."

A well-taken sexual history can in itself be beneficial to a patient. The history offers the patient an opportunity to ask about anything that has been bothering him, and offers the physician an opportunity to dispel misconceptions which may be a source of trouble in the future. Most patients have at least a few such questions and concerns, and the simple opportunity of discussing them often helps the patient become more relaxed about sex.

16

It is important to develop skills in interviewing couples as well as individual patients. The physician has an invaluable opportunity to evaluate the impact of a sexual problem on the marital relationship by watching how the husband and wife interact, how effectively they communicate, and whether the sexual problem is secondary to marital discord. It usually is. Reed and Lief[15], in a series of teaching films on aspects of sexual interviewing, note differences between taking a history from a "frigid" wife alone and an impotent husband who is seen with his spouse. In addition to the components of an interview including rapport, appraisal, and therapeutic response, they note that the patient is likely to be in a time of crisis and in need of a review of his or her own coping patterns. This, together with some education from the doctor as to the reasons for the sexual dysfunction, can prove to be quite beneficial.

THE PHYSICAL EXAMINATION

A careful examination of the external genitalia should be done at birth. Many intersex problems have been exacerbated by the fact that they went undiscovered until late childhood or early adolescence, at which time the information is highly upsetting to the child's self-concept.

A physical examination should precede treatment of every sexual complaint, regardless of the patient's sex. If the presence of an organic illness or abnormality can be ruled out, the physician can reassure the patient that he has no apparent relevant anatomic or physiologic defects. The physician also may get revealing clues to the patient's sexual attitudes during the physical examination.

A pelvic examination should be a part of every adult female patient's medical management. Allen[16] reported that approximately 30% of all the important diseases in women occur in the reproductive organs. A pelvic examination should be performed before puberty or during adolescence only when indicated. The premarital examination should include a pelvic examination and a Papanicolaou smear.

REFERENCES — PART I

1. Evans DK: Sexual attitudes, norms and practices in cross-cultural perspective, in Vincent CE (ed): *Human Sexuality in Medical Education and Practice.* Springfield, Ill, Charles C Thomas Publisher, 1968, pp 157-183.

2. Golden JS: Varieties of sexual problems in obstetrical and gynecological practice, in Wahl CW (ed): *Sexual Problems, Diagnosis and Treatment in Medical Practice.* New York, Free Press, 1967, p 59.

3. Lief HI: What medical schools teach about sex. *Bull Tulane Med Fac* 22: 161-168, 1963.

4. Lief HI: Preparing the physician to become a sex counselor and educator. *Pediat Clin N Amer* 16: 452-453, 1969.

5. Burnap DW, Golden JS: Sexual problems in medical practice, in Vincent CE (ed): *Human Sexuality in Medical Education and Practice.* Springfield, Ill, Charles C Thomas Publisher, 1968, pp 52-53.

6. Mathis JL: Iatrogenic sexual disturbances. *Med Aspects Human Sexuality* 1: 49-51, 1967.

7. Cuber JF: Three prerequisite considerations to diagnosis and treatment in marriage counseling, in Klemer RH: *Counseling in Marital and Sexual Problems.* Baltimore, Williams & Wilkins Co, 1965, p 58.

8. Lansing C: Exploring sexual complaints. *Med Aspects Human Sexuality* 1: 36, 1967.

9. Chez RA: The female patient's sexual history, in Wahl CW (ed): *Sexual Problems, Diagnosis and Treatment in Medical Practice.* New York, Free Press, 1967, p 5.

10. Castelnuovo-Tedesco P: Talking with patients about their sexual problems. *Med Aspects Human Sexuality* 2: 21, 1968.

11. Gardiner S: Oral communication.

12. Wahl CW: Psychiatric techniques in the taking of a sexual history, in Wahl CW (ed): *Sexual Problems, Diagnosis and Treatment in Medical Practice.* New York, Free Press, 1967, pp 17-18.

13. Masters WH, Johnson VE: Counseling with sexually incompatible marriage partners, in Klemer RH (ed): *Counseling in Marital and Sexual Problems.* Baltimore, Williams & Wilkins Co, 1965, p 127.

14. Wahl CW: Psychiatric techniques in the taking of a sexual history, in Wahl CW (ed): *Sexual Problems, Diagnosis and Treatment in Medical Practice.* New York, Free Press, 1967, p 15.

15. Reed DM and Lief, HI: *Aspects of Sexual Interviewing,* a series of films under the auspices of the Center for the Study of Sex Education in Medicine, University of Pennsylvania, Philadelphia Pennsylvania. Available from Ortho Pharmaceuticals, Raritan, New Jersey, 08869.

16. Allen ED: Examination of the genital organs in the prepubescent and in the adolescent girl. *Pediat Clin N Amer* 5: 26-27, 1958.

PART 2
THE PHYSICIAN AND HUMAN SEXUAL DEVELOPMENT

THE PHYSICIAN AND HUMAN SEXUAL DEVELOPMENT

CHAPTER IV—PATTERNS OF SEXUAL DEVELOPMENT

"Is this normal?" Implicit in this frequent question is the assumption that there is a pattern of natural sexual behavior against which the individual's pattern can be measured. The range of customary human sexual behavior is greater than most patients realize. One of the physician's tasks is to find out what each patient means by "normal" and to indicate in which ways this definition may be limited. The real question is whether the behavior is harmful, and that, in turn, most often depends on what the patient thinks is harmful. Most common sexual dysfunctions result not from abnormality but from anxiety about abnormality and misconceptions about normality. The physician has a major role as educator, listener and counselor. His understanding of the various patterns of sexual development is essential, not to provide a yardstick of acceptability, but to provide an understanding of the many factors which influence concepts of sexuality.

Contemporary American society has more than one code of acceptable sexual behavior, different for the young, the old, the wealthy, the poor, the black and the white. All the codes of the various segments of society together have an influence on the attitudes of parents, who, in turn, shape the attitudes of their children, at least until adolescence, when friends and peer groups become more influential. The prevailing sexual code of any given person, therefore, is the result of numerous variables during development.

THE FAMILY

The family is the preschool child's predominant influence. Regardless of variation in family structure, it is here the child gets his first impressions of who he is and what is expected of him. In the family, as usually constituted, the child learns that he has a parent of one sex and a parent of another and that he is supposed to behave in the manner of one or the other. He may or may not conclude, from the way his father and mother treat one another, that women are valued by men and vice versa. Of course, these lessons are not learned in absolute terms. Nonetheless, it is through the family that the young child forms his impressions of masculinity, femininity, himself, his role, his value and the value of other persons. Quite literally, everything his parents do influences his views and, therefore, his views about human sexuality. It is widely accepted that families hand down certain characteristics from generation to generation, but it is less widely recognized that families also tend to hand down basic male and female roles. A boy who fails to get his father's approval is likely to grow into an insecure man, who is still trying to win praise from his father while neglecting his own son. The son is then likely to grow up to neglect his son, and so on.

Generally speaking, the nuclear or immediate family plays an intense but an increasingly isolated role in the emotional life of its members. Relations between the nuclear family and relatives are not as close as they used to be and many family traditions have been lost. In the past, the growing child gradually moved from the nuclear family into the expanded family of grandparents, aunts, uncles, and close family friends. Today, the expanded family has virtually ceased to function as a unit, and the child moves from the nuclear family directly into the community. In addition, many family functions, including work, education, religious instruction, and care of the sick and the old, are performed outside the home or have been taken over by the community. Unfortunately, because families frequently move, ties with communities are often feeble and fragmented. At a time when the adolescent is trying hard to demonstrate his independence from his parents, the peer group of the community becomes the strongest influence on his thinking.

These changes in the family's role have inevitably affected the roles of the family members. Adults have become unsure of what is expected of them as parents, and what to expect of their children. As a result, children are often unclear about what they should do. Not long ago, marriage was an arrangement in which each partner was assigned specific tasks so that both could survive, and any emotional gratification which husband and wife got from one another was considered a secondary benefit. Today, with survival assured for most persons, husbands and wives have come to expect more emotional gratification. With less time demanded for the chores of existence, they also have more time to worry about emotional needs. All interpersonal relations, therefore, have a greater potential for both reward and disruption.

MALE AND FEMALE ROLES

In most societies, there are more or less clearly differentiated roles for men and women. These roles may vary greatly from one culture to another. Mead[1] has demonstrated that even the responsibility for child rearing is not universally assigned to females, and that in some societies, men raise the children. It does not matter what these roles are as long as they are understood and accepted.

Within American society, the roles of men and women have changed significantly during the past 30 years, as society and the family have changed. Women constitute a growing proportion of the work force, and many earn more than their husbands. Because the husband is frequently away from home, in many families the wife has taken over as the true head of the household. External signs of gender have become blurred: women wear pants, and men grow long hair.

Sexual behavior also has changed. Since improved methods of contraception have freed women to enjoy sex without fear of pregnancy, there has been a more apparent interest in sex on the part of many women. The old, culturally dictated gender roles in which the man was aggressive and the woman passive are no longer generally accepted. "The prevailing female attitude seems to be a righteous demand for sexual satisfactions," Greenson[2] has written. "In the past, one had the impression that it was an acceptable female trait to disclaim any sexual passion; today, my female patients seem to demand the right to equal orgasms."

Mead states that in societies in which all women marry, the woman is likely to resolve any questions about her proper role, but the man in every society is under considerable pressure to demonstrate his masculinity. He is, therefore, likely to be unsettled by things that confuse or obscure his role. Today, Americans are re-evaluating their feelings about what is man's role and what is woman's role. But uncertainty has made men uncomfortable about their roles. Today's boy may be told to "act like a man," but is given conflicting models of how a man is supposed to act. This confusion, which increases stress, would not arise if clear models of both sexes were available to help pattern behavior.

Sexuality may be described in terms which define the subunits that constitute the total concept of sexuality:

Biologic sex is the sum total of the chromosomal configuration (genotype), the gonads (ovary or testis), the hormonal environment and its effect on the end organs. These factors determine the internal and external reproductive structures.

Sexual identity or *core gender* is the sense of maleness and femaleness, which develops from the sex of rearing (psychobiologic sex);

Gender identity is the sense of masculinity or femininity;

Sexual role behavior is activity with masculine or feminine connotations and physical sexual activity.

BIOLOGIC SEX

A child's biologic inheritance is contained in 46 paired chromosomes—23 from the sperm cell and 23 from the ovum. Only one of these 46 paired chromosomes (44 autosomes and 2 sex chromosomes) determines sex (genotype); it is from the sperm cell. The spermatozoon contains either one X sex chromosome or one Y sex chromosome. The ovum contains a single X sex chromosome. An XY combination produces a male, an XX combination a female. Abnormalities of sex differentiation are frequently associated with the absence of one of the sex chromosomes or the presence of one or more additional sex chromosomes. Nondisjunction or failure of paired sex chromosomes in the spermatozoon or egg to separate to the opposite poles during meiosis is the most common genetic mechanism involved in these abnormalities.

During the first five weeks of gestation or the neutral stage, the fetus has a common "indifferent" group of structures which form the germinal ridge. Sexual differentiation of the reproductive organs begins in the sixth week of fetal life. The chromosomal constitution determines whether ovaries or testes will develop.

During early development the fetus possesses the anlage of both male and female urogenital tract structures. The anlage consists of the Wolffian and Müllerian ducts. The Wolffian ducts differentiate to form parts of the male reproductive tract and parts of the urinary bladder in both the male and the female. The Müllerian ducts develop into the uterine-vaginal canal and tubes. In the presence of functioning fetal testes, the Müllerian ducts regress while the Wolffian ducts develop. If testes are absent, the Müllerian ducts will form the uterus and tubes even if no ovaries are present. The differentiation of the Wolffian duct and the formation of the male external genitalia are under the influence of androgen produced by the fetal testes.

SEXUAL (CORE GENDER) IDENTITY

In the vast majority of children, the various components that comprise biologic sex are in concert, eg, all female or all male. Abnormalities of the sex chromosomal patterns or of hormonal exposure during gestation can result in mixed internal reproductive systems, ambiguous external genitalia or both. In the newborn, it may be difficult to differentiate between a small penis and a large clitoris. Core gender identity is based on sex assignment and rearing and can be established independently of biologic sex. Abnormalities of biologic sex, particularly when the external genitalia are ambiguous, may make a child vulnerable to errors in core gender identity. In the vast majority of these cases, the sex of assignment and rearing will prevail. When there is doubt in an infant's biologic sex, the physician should defer judgment until the appropriate laboratory studies are completed.

At birth a child is capable of acquiring either a male or a female identity. Money[3] in a study of more than 100 hermaphrodites and pseudohermaphrodites, found that those who had been reared as boys behaved and thought as boys, and those raised as girls thought and acted as girls, even though they may have been incorrectly assigned. Fewer than 5% of the individuals Money studied acted and thought in ways which were at odds with their assigned sex. Of nine subjects whose gender assignment had been changed before the age of two years, only three had even mild symptoms of psychologic disturbance, but of five children whose gender was reassigned after the age of two, four were found to have psychologic disturbances.

GENDER IDENTITY

Imitation is a powerful force in the establishment of gender identity. Children copy the clothing and even the mannerisms of their parents, and parental approval reinforces such mimetic behavior. If, for any reason, this kind of imitation does not seem desirable or profitable to the child, the basic formulation of gender identity will be impaired.

Every child needs a parent figure of the same sex upon whom he can model his behavior, a parent figure of the opposite sex whom he can trust, and acceptance of his assigned sex by both. Broderick[4] has set forth three conditions which are needed for heterosexual development: 1) the parent figure of the same sex must not be so punishing or weak as to make it impossible for the child to identify with him or her; 2) the parent figure of the opposite sex must not be so seductive, so punishing, or so emotionally erratic as to make it impossible for the child to trust members of the opposite sex; 3) the parents must not systematically reject the child's biologic sex and attempt to teach him cross behavior. Money suggests that normally a child establishes identification with the parent of the same sex and a complementary role with the parent of the opposite sex.

Lack of suitable role models is a factor in many cases of homosexuality, transsexualism, and other variations of sexual expression. Although the etiology of homosexuality is not known, clinical impressions suggest that among male homosexuals who have sought psychiatric help, many have had overly protective, affectionate, seductive mothers and weak, hostile, or absent fathers. The seductive mother appears to create a revulsion toward heterosexuality by arousing incestuous feelings, which produce excessive guilt. The weak father, obviously, provides no model on which the child can pattern himself. Adult homosexuals who become parents are handicapped by their dual sexual inclination because they are unable to create firm gender models for their children. Similarly, the blurred gender identities of transsexuals and transvestites can interfere with their performance as parents.

Parents teach gender identification in subtle but specific ways, with the most direct indoctrination aimed at boys. A boy is prompted to prove himself on the athletic field; aggressive and manly behavior is actively encouraged. Boys are often overtly discouraged from pursuing interests in certain of the arts. While girls may be discouraged from developing interests in engineering and physics, considerable latitude is allowed in their behavior. Girls become tomboys with little or no criticism; many easily accept masculine nicknames. Vincent[5] has noted that a girl in a pretty dress who smiles sweetly usually will be admired by all the adults present. Little else appears to be needed to establish acceptance as a feminine person.

The role models have a bearing on actual sexual behavior later in life. Loeb[6] concluded that teenagers who felt comfortable in their sexual roles were the least likely to become indiscriminate in their sexual behavior. Schofield[7] drew similar conclusions from a study of British teenagers: girls who got along well with their parents were less likely to be sexually experienced than those who did not, and boys who got along poorly with their mothers were more likely to be sexually experienced. The establishment of gender identity is an important area of parental responsibility. Presentation of accurate sex information by parents in a relaxed manner is one of the many factors which contribute to the establishment of this identity, but probably the most critical factor is the role models they provide in their own interaction as man and woman.

If the etiology of homosexuality is not known, the etiology of heterosexuality is equally unknown. The homosexual male identifies himself as *male,* the homosexual female as *female.* Where heterosexual and homosexual oriented individuals differ is in the gender of the individual they chose as a sex object. In trying to understand the etiology of homosexuality and its possible relationship to parental role models, the Kinsey[8] 0-6 heterosexuality-homosexuality scale is useful.

CHAPTER VI——CHILDHOOD

SEXUAL DEVELOPMENT IN CHILDHOOD (PREPUBERTAL PERIOD)
Normal Development

Freud's pronouncement that all children have sexual feelings brought storms of disapproval and denial. Today, it is accepted that all children experience forms of physical pleasure which can be described as sexual. Males sometimes develop erections during the first weeks of life; some have five erections a day and others have as many as 40. Kinsey et al[8] reported that about one-third of all boys exhibited signs of orgasm, without ejaculation, between two and twelve months of age, that more than half did so between two and five years of age, and that almost 80% of boys ten to thirteen years did so, either with or without ejaculation. However, childhood sexual activity is not heterosexual in the adult sense, but basically self-referrent. Most children manipulate their genitalia and if observed are reprimanded for it. Ironically, the rebuke is often the child's first lesson in sex education.

The development and resolution of oedipal conflicts crucially affect subsequent sexual behavior. A child's sexual fantasies focus on the parent of the opposite sex and hostile fantasies of rivalry on the parent of his own sex. In families where sexual privacy is valued and protected, this is played out primarily in the child's rich fantasy life, but to some degree also spills over into his behavior.

Eventually, this highly sexualized phase wanes. The oedipal fantasies are repressed, and the consequence is a kind of reversal. Identification with the parent of the same sex is increased, and interest in the other parent is diminished and repressed. Both parents then come to be loved equally but in different ways, and the child patterns himself on the parent of the same sex. However, echoes of both competitive and oedipal feelings may linger on through adolescence and even into marriage.

Until the age of five or six, children largely ignore gender in picking their playmates. After that, they become aloof and then openly hostile toward members of the opposite sex until near puberty, when the aloofness becomes shyness. Freud believed that the libidinal drive decreases during this "latency period." Most psychiatrists today view this "latency" stage as a time of change of direction, not loss of sexual drive. Between five and eleven, the child develops new interests in the outside world; while this interest in worldly affairs receives encouragement at home, his curiosity about sex is generally discouraged. Furthermore, he is inclined to play with children of his own sex, whose interests are nearer his own and with whom he is likely to feel more comfortable. In this age group boys are struggling to shake free from the dominance of women.

Nonetheless, boys and girls both continue to have a good deal of interest in the opposite sex throughout the prepubertal period, but their mutual interest is usually camouflaged. Only about one boy in five has been found to have genuinely negative feelings about either girls or romance,[9] and children of both sexes make firm and early commitments to heterosexuality. Broderick[10] has reported that by age five most children have already thought about getting married some day. Such an expectation seems to be a necessary step in healthy heterosexual progress.

Throughout childhood, the child learns about sex from his parents, both directly and indirectly. The parents' discussion or lack of discussion of sex, their reactions and answers to the child's questions, their behavior toward one another, the amount of parental nudity, and their emotional and physical reactions to the child collectively shape the child's sexual consciousness. Bryant,[11] in a study of marital relationships found that 87% of the children showed problems in the same areas as their parents. A child's chances for growing up without undue sexual anxiety may be improved by a family in which sex is discussed frankly and without embarrassment, but attitudes are shaped more by the atmosphere of the home and behavior of the parents than by words.

Explicit or implicit, parental education about sexuality is usually influential for a longer period of time than their instructions about other areas of life. Communications in nonsexual areas are subject to early verification. When a child is told that a hot stove is dangerous, he can confirm the finding immediately. As his experience grows, the taboo against touching the stove will be modified. Sexual commandments may not be tested and modified so easily because sexual experiences are rarely objective. Also, the growing child is able to evaluate his parents' judgment in most other areas by means of independent criteria. He discovers, for example, that all adults do not share his parents' political and religious views. In contrast, little comparative data about sexuality is available to him. This lack of comparative data makes the parents' sexual instruction a fiat that goes largely unchallenged until the child is well into adolescence. Thus, the parent must be the focus of any attempt to improve the sex education and sexual health of children.

The facts are that most children cannot give names to their sexual feelings and have little idea why such feelings often have an aura of danger or shame. The fabled father-son talk about sex usually does not take place in real life; fathers are even less inclined to discuss sex with their daughters. Usually, mothers discuss sex only with their daughters, and the discussion is limited to menstruation and pregnancy. About half of all children are told nothing about sex by either parent. In questioning high school students, Margolis[1 2] found that fewer than one in ten had had open discussions with their parents about sex, and these few indicated that the discussion had been limited or superficial. This failure to teach creates considerable guilt among parents and the lack of communication, in itself, is harmful to the children. Young people feel bitter and angry when their parents have failed to be truthful and open with them. Parents who do give their children sex instruction often pass along their sexual fears and ambivalences at the same time.

Variant Sexual Development in Children

a) Sex Errors of the Body

Two commonly occurring disorders of gonadal development associated with sex chromosome anomalies are Klinefelter's and Turner's syndromes. In the general population, the incidence of XXY seminiferous tubule dysgenesis (typical Klinefelter's syndrome) is 1 in 500. In institutions for the mentally retarded, the incidence may be as high as 1 in 100 males. These patients are phenotypic males, chromatin positive, with small firm testes, and are sterile. During puberty, gynecomastia and signs of androgen deficiency occur in about one half of these patients. An XY cell line in XXY/XY mosaics may lead to the development of testicular function and fertility. Other chromosomal abnormalities and mosaics involving supernumerary X chromosomes lead to clinical variants of chromatin positive seminiferous tubule dysgenesis.

The absence of a second sex chromosome (XO) in typical gonadal dysgenesis (Turner's syndrome) is associated with a female phenotype of short stature with sexual infantilism due to rudimentary "streak" ovaries and somatic manifestations, such as distinctive facies and webbing of the neck. This syndrome occurs in about 1 infant in 5,000. Clinical variants of the classical gonadal dysgenesis syndrome occur frequently with XO/XX mosaicism.

The chromosomal abnormality XXX, with two chromatin bodies in peripheral cells, is not associated with gonadal defects; mental retardation is the characteristic feature. Affected women may bear genetically normal children. Other sex chromosome abnormalities without typical gonadal defects but with a high incidence of mental retardation are XXXX, XXXXX, XYY and XYYY. Extra Y chromosomes are reported to be associated with tall stature and antisocial behavior.

True hermaphroditism requires the presence of both ovarian and testicular tissue: a testis on one side and an ovary on the other; ovarian and testicular tissue on both sides; or an ovary or testis on one side and ovarian and testicular tissue on the other. The development of the ducts usually is in accord with the gonad on that side. With both ovarian and testicular tissue, the development of the ducts on that side is predominately female. The external genitalia may be male, female or ambiguous. Most true hermaphrodites are reported as buccal smear sex chromatin positive (XX); undoubtedly, many of these have sex chromosomal mosaicism with a Y-bearing cell line internally.

Pseudohermaphrodites are persons whose somatic development is not in harmony with the gonads. A female pseudohermaphrodite has ovaries, but the genital development has some male characteristics. The masculinization of the genitalia is due to androgens or progestogens administered to the mother during pregnancy, or to congenital virilizing adrenal hyperplasia of the fetus. A male pseudohermaphrodite has testes but the ducts or external genitalia lack full masculinization or are not masculinized at all. These are sex chromatin negative patients whose androgens do not exert an effect on the body because of end organ resistance to androgen stimulation (testicular feminizing syndrome).

STEPS IN THE DIAGNOSIS OF INTERSEXUALITY IN INFANCY AND CHILDHOOD

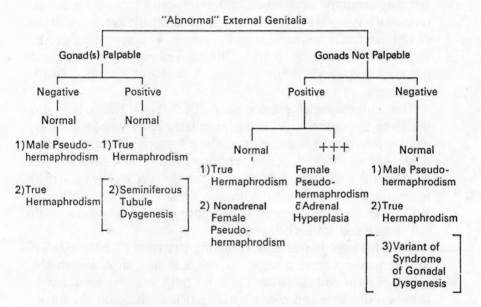

A. Family History, Pregnancy (Hormones), "Crises," Virilization

B. INSPECTION

C. PALPATION OF INGUINAL REGION & LABIO-SCROTAL FOLDS and Rectal Examination

D. ORAL MUCOSAL SMEAR Sex Chromatin Pattern

E. EXCRETION OF 17-KETOSTEROIDS and Pregnanetriol

F. PROVISIONAL DIAGNOSIS

G. VAGINOGRAM (Urogenital Sinus) Selected Cases

H. ENDOSCOPY, LAPAROTOMY, GONADAL BIOPSY
Restricted to Suspected Male Pseudohermaphrodites and True Hermaphrodites and Selected Instances of Nonadrenal Female Pseudohermaphrodism

Brackets around seminiferous tubule dysgenesis and variants of the syndrome of gonadal dysgenesis indicate that in these conditions the appearance of the external genitalia may be normal. In congenital adrenal hyperplasia due to a defect in 3–beta hydroxydehydrogenase the urinary 17-ketosteroids are elevated.

Reprinted with the permission of Melvin M. Grumbach, M.D., *Pediatrics,* 14th Edition

b) Variant Sexual Identity

Most children without genetic or gonadal defects grow up secure in their identities as a male or a female; however, a few grow to adulthood with no firm conviction about the sex to which they want to belong, and some are convinced they should belong to the other sex.

If the individual belongs biologically to one sex but has a strong dislike for the sexual equipment of that gender and wants to function socially and sexually as a member of the opposite sex, he is a transsexual. Cross-gender behavior includes an avoidance of play typical of his sex, cross-dressing, and an openly stated wish to belong to the other sex. This behavior is not diagnostic since it may appear transiently at some stage in the development of children who have no fundamental problem of sexual identity.

The parents of transsexual children often have a history of sexual and psychologic problems. The father of a transsexual boy is frequently meek or rejecting, and the mother dominant, overprotective or seductive. A transsexual girl may be overly close to her father and remote from the mother. The parents of transsexual children may also insidiously reward, early in life, the very cross-gender behavior that they subsequently find alarming.

THE ROLE OF THE PHYSICIAN

Prevention and Parental Counseling

The physician's role in counseling is to help parents reach a mature attitude toward their own sexuality, and to call their attention to the many ways in which they communicate with their children which foster sexual development. The basic role of the parent is to develop the child's capacity to love and be loved. Finch[13] gives the case history of a nine-year old girl whose highly intellectual parents had carefully taught her the physiology of reproduction; the girl could explain the process accurately and in detail. Yet she was terrified of sexual feelings and ideas because her parents never showed affection toward one another or toward her.

An excellent starting point for counseling is to discuss the parents' own sex education. It is hardly surprising that parents have difficulty in discussing sex openly with their children when they have had no such discussions with their own parents;

moreover, few adults have received the kind of sex education which is desirable to teach to children. By recognizing these difficulties, the physician will be relieving the parents' discomfort and emphasizing the importance of the parents in shaping the sexual attitudes of their children. At the same time, it is equally important to let the parents know that they probably will not make any more mistakes in the rearing of their children than everyone else.

Counseling on child development should begin soon after the birth of the first child. When counseling begins early, the parent comes to understand that the physician is available for consultation about all subjects, and questions about sexuality will follow automatically. As the child grows the parent is likely to be asked a wide variety of questions. The parents' ability to discuss sexual behavior with the physician almost inevitably makes it easier for them to discuss sexual behavior with their child. Such discussions usually improve communications in other areas as well.

An important subject for discussion is the effect of parental acceptance and approval of the child. The new mother should be encouraged to express her love in many ways: holding her baby, talking to it and singing to it. The child who has been fully accepted and has received a wide variety of sensory stimuli is usually the child who is best equipped to deal with the complexities of later life. The loved child is capable of love; the valued child values others, and the respected child respects others. It is important to respect both the child and his rights. A child whose own body and property have been respected will be less likely to violated the rights of others.

It is especially important that parents accept their child even if he is not of the sex which they had preferred. If the physician finds a new mother crying in her hospital room because she wanted a girl and had a boy, it is imperative that he spend some time explaining the importance of accepting the child for what he is. Even subtle hints or a single comment that a child was "supposed to be" of the opposite sex can be highly damaging to the child's self-concept. At the least, he is likely to feel unvalued, and at the worst, he may feel unwanted.

The physician will often get clues about sexual communication within a family during examinations of children in his office. If a small girl faces the corner while her infant brother is being examined, it may show that the family has considerable anxiety about sex. If a mother slaps her child's hand because he is fondling his genitalia, the physician may later take the opportunity to point out that the child's behavior was usual and that the mother's action was inappropriate. While he is examining a small child, the physician can name the genitalia and other parts of the body to indicate to the parent that these areas are not unfit to mention.

Much childhood sexual behavior, including some which shocks parents, is the result of simple curiosity. Even when the behavior needs to be discouraged, the parents' job is not to punish or criticize, but to satisfy the child's curiosity while instilling respect for the body.

Parents who have considerable anxiety about their children should be informed about the range of human sexual development and the likelihood that their child will develop normally. They should recognize that their own attitudes influence their children's attitudes and behavior. Reassurance about the importance of love and acceptance may be especially valuable for parents separated from their spouses. In divorce, it is essential that the parent having custody avoid giving the child a feeling that all men or women are worthless or that the child had anything to do with causing the separation.

The physician who has counseled a parent about a child's sexual development since birth will usually find it simple to help the parent answer explicit sexual questions with equanimity. When children first ask about sex, their attitude is remarkably matter-of-fact. Parents who have learned to answer questions simply and honestly usually have few difficulties. The young child's satisfied acceptance and the older child's respect for his parents outweigh any embarrassment the parents may have. The physician can recommend reading material to the parents and child, but ordinarily should not assume the parents' responsibility for instructing the child.

Considerable evidence indicates that sexual knowledge tends to reduce the likelihood of undesirable sexual behavior and experimentation caused by curiosity. Sex education in the home should be a part of every child's upbringing. A few simple facts about reproduction should be given the child at about three years of age. Before he is ten, he should have a reasonably complete understanding.

Honesty and consistency are essential. Parents should try to tell the child what he wants to know——no more and no less. That means that the first questions about sex should not be greeted with a lecture on human reproduction but with a simple, clear, and specific answer. It is not necessary to tell a young child as much as the parents and physician know, but everything he is told should be true, and the answers should be sufficiently complete to avoid misconceptions. Attempts to soften or disguise the facts by giving incomplete or inaccurate information often have adverse results. The parents should use terminology the child understands and explain the meaning of technical terms such as penis, vagina, semen, etc. The simplest answer for a particular question is usually the best.

For those children who never ask questions about sex, parents should introduce the subject. It is helpful for the parents and the child to sit down together and read a book on the subject. Books appropriate for instructing children about sex are listed in Appendix II.

When a child inquires about sex, it may be useful to ask him about what he believes so that mistaken ideas can be corrected. Parents should impress upon their children that some information they receive about sex from television, movies, and friends will be misleading or incorrect. Popular fictions promote many distorted impressions about the nature, purpose, and uses of sexuality; children need help to distinguish between fact and fantasy.

Management of Problems

a) Sex Errors of the Body

A careful examination of the external genitalia of every newborn child is important. Where abnormalities create ambiguity about the child's sex, assignment should not be made until sufficient investigation is done to make a firm decision about sex of rearing. (See chart on page 32.)

In the diagnosis and management of developmental errors certain aspects of the history, physical examination and laboratory work-up are especially pertinent. A family history may reveal similar abnormalities. Congenital adrenal hyperplasia and the syndrome of testicular feminization are both determined genetically. The mother should be questioned about drugs, especially progestogens such as norethindrone, she received

36

during pregnancy. Buccal smears for sex chromatin determination may be followed by a chromosome analysis if indicated.

In congenital virilizing adrenal hyperplasia, hormonal assays show elevated levels of urinary 17-ketosteroids and pregnanetriol. Female pseudohermaphrodites with adrenal hyperplasia, if recognized at birth, can be assigned as females. Adrenal corticosteroid therapy is indicated. Babies who do not have adrenal hyperplasia but whose mothers received androgens or progestogens during pregnancy or whose mothers showed signs of maternal virilization can likewise be assigned as females. They need no hormonal treatment because they will usually feminize at puberty. In either syndrome, surgical correction may be done for psychologic reasons if the masculinization of the external genitalia is extreme.

Male pseudohermaphrodites with the syndrome of testicular feminization should be reared as females because androgen therapy will not produce male secondary sex characteristics. If the phenotype of other sex chromatin negative patients is not clearly male or female, assignment of sex should be based on the possibilities for surgical correction of the external genitalia. Some cases may require a surgical exploration before puberty to determine the nature of the gonads and genital duct structures. Klinefelter's syndrome is usually not recognized in infancy or early childhood since the patient is a phenotypic male. Patients with Turner's syndrome have other somatic stigmata which may be recognized during childhood. Substitution therapy with estrogens is needed to achieve feminization of the patient with Turner's syndrome.

If a wholly inappropriate assignment of sex has been made at birth, a change in the sex rearing is feasible before 18 months. Between 18 and 30 months a change is sometimes possible without serious psychiatric consequences. After puberty some patients may request a change of sex assignment since it may be difficult for the parents and for the patient to accept a sex of rearing which is not the chromosomal or gonadal sex. It then is essential for the physician to give assurance that "true sex" is based on many more factors than biologic sex and that the patient is being reared in his "true sex." Firm acceptance of sex of rearing, surgical repair of the external genitalia, removal of heterologous gonadal tissue when possible and eventual hormonal therapy to achieve secondary sex characteristics all contribute to developing an adult capable of normal sexual relations. If female hermaphrodites are properly treated they are usually fertile.

When disorders of sex differentiation result in sterility, this information should be given as tactfully as possible early in childhood. Money[14] suggests that the physician put the diagnosis in terms of probability during a discussion of pregnancy: "On the basis of experience with cases like yours, doctors expect that you will achieve motherhood by adoption. When you decide you would like a child, do not, therefore, wait too long for a pregnancy." The approach does not remove the goal of parenthood, but refocuses the child's attention on the means of achieving it. The general concept of adoption should be introduced early, and put in personal terms later. Sterile males can be informed that in addition to adoption there is the option of artificial insemination of their wives.

b) Problems of Sexual Identity

Children are vague about the differences between the sexes, and cross-gender behavior during childhood generally is not a cause for concern. However, if childhood cross-gender behavior lasts too long and appears intense, a basic disturbance may be present. If parents are concerned about inappropriate behavior in a child, the first task is to identify the reasons for their alarm. The physician should obtain a clear definition of the behavior; where, when and in front of whom it took place; whether concern was expressed to the child and what his reaction was; when the behavior began; and which parent is most concerned.

The physician should try to get the child's view of the family: which parent he considers most authoritarian and which he prefers. Neuter cut-out figures and draw-a-person tests may be helpful as diagnostic tools, but they should be administered by a person trained in such testing methods.

In cases where the identity problem is minimal, counseling will usually suffice. Where the cross-gender behavior indicates significant problems, early referral to a psychiatrist is indicated. Psychotherapy with young children, combined with counseling of the parents, often proves effective. A strong male therapist may be helpful to a boy and a warm female therapist to a girl. If psychiatric techniques over a long period of time prove ineffective and it appears the patient will continue to look at life through the eyes of the opposite sex, surgical reassignment may ultimately be considered.

CHAPTER VII—PUBERTY AND ADOLESCENCE

SEXUAL DEVELOPMENT

Normal Development

During preadolescence, sexual curiosity reappears openly. The boy shows more interest in girls, although his interest may appear as teasing or aggression. The girl may temporarily reject her own femininity while trying to catch the boy's attention by acting like a tomboy. There is interest in genital examination. At this same time conflict between independence and dependence within the family is intensified, and preadolescents may become sloppy, crude, defiant and unruly.

The time and nature of pubertal growth are influenced by genetics, hormones, environment and psychologic factors. Puberty normally occurs between 9 and 16 years of age, at which time pituitary gonadotropin secretion begins to stimulate the ovaries to secrete estrogen and progesterone, and the Leydig cells to secrete testosterone. The seminiferous tubules begin spermatogenesis. Estrogen in the female promotes growth of the breasts, as well as the appearance of other secondary sex characteristics, and initiates menstruation. Ovulation may not occur until a few months or even years after menstruation has begun.

In the boy, testosterone secretion is essential to the development of secondary sex characteristics such as growth of facial and body hair, enlargement of the penis and scrotum, lowering of the voice and recession of scalp hair.

While puberty is generally regarded as the time of sexual awakening, many children have had their first exploratory sexual experience much earlier. Samplings by the Kinsey Institute indicate that 57% of American men and 48% of American women engage in some form of sexual play before puberty. More than one-fourth of the women in a Kinsey sample had experienced sexual arousal at least once before adolescence.[15] Kinsey et al found that almost 10% of all white Americans had had coital experience by 13.

Puberty is a time of inspection and introspection. Girls are concerned about the size of their breasts, the growth of body hair, the beginning of menstruation and their emerging figures. Menstruation usually has great impact and many women apparently attach deep symbolic significance to it. Lidz[16] has reported that a group of pseudohermaphroditic women, who had neither breast development nor other secondary sexual characteristics, expressed the hope that estrogen therapy would enable them to menstruate even if it did nothing else. Some girls welcome the beginning of menstruation as proof of maturity, and others attempt to deny that the change has taken place either by acting more tomboyish or by showing no apparent interest in the change.

Boys worry about the size of their penis, the appearance of body hair and the changes in their physique. The appearance of gynecomastia is likely to be a major source of worry for adolescent boys. It occurs in 50% or more boys and is usually transient.

The sudden upsurge of sexual feelings usually takes the adolescent by surprise. The sexual urges of the oedipal period could be easily repressed; the new urges are much more imperative. A child sees a parent or sibling of the opposite sex undressing and the eruption of sexual feelings throws him into a confused state of pleasure and guilt. These feelings may create an urge for self-gratification through masturbation, which in turn can result in guilt. He finds it impossible to tell anybody about these strange new feelings and, until they are mastered, the adolescent experiences alternating periods of chaos and calm. He may fall in and out of love in the space of a few hours. His struggle with his sexual feelings is often waged at the expense of his performance in other areas. Adolescence is a time in which to act peculiarly is to be normal.

Masturbation

Studies indicate that as many as 90% of males and 60% of females masturbate at some time, and regardless of how often it is practiced, it is neither physically nor mentally harmful. Although it may produce some feelings of guilt, masturbation is a normal part of adolescent sexual development and requires no medical management. Many adults still believe that masturbation reduces sexual potency but there is evidence that the opposite may be true. Hutton[17] has reported that women who have practiced regular self-stimulation over a period of years are actually more heterosexually responsive than those who have given up masturbation. Kinsey et al found that men and women who had made the most satisfactory adjustments in their marriage had a history of more masturbation than those who had adjusted less well. Kinsey et al also found that women who had not experienced orgasm before they were married took longer to become sexually adept than those who had reached orgasm, by whatever means, including masturbation.[18]

Social and Sexual Attitudes

Society's attitude toward the adolescent varies considerably from culture to culture, and the adolescent may be under great pressure or very little. The Plains Indians of America set such great store by aggressiveness in warfare that many young Indians became social dropouts, creating a class called the "berdache," or "not man." Berdache could hunt, marry, and sire children, but they had to wear women's clothing and could not take part in warfare. In the Samoan Islands, on the other hand, adolescence was a relatively serene period, apparently partly because the society permitted considerable sexual activity among adolescents.[19]

American society's attitude toward the adolescent is paradoxical. Society is increasingly lascivious in its entertainments and advertising, and even the most moralistic parents may push their children toward early dating, use of make-up and seductive clothing. A report from the Group for the Advancement of Psychiatry observes that many parents demand obedience, dependency and sexual abstinence from their children while adults are expected to be just the opposite——innovative, independent and sexually capable. The report concludes, "It is possible that our social norms are not as well-suited for training children to become adults as for training them to become successful children."[20] One result of this kind of double standard is that the adolescent has both the tremendous task of controlling his sexual feelings and urges, and the heavy burden of guilt arising from his almost inevitable failure to do so. Both society and the adolescent pay a high price for these contradictory pressures. Many young people resolve their conflicts through early marriage, sexual revolt, rejection of accepted morality or neurotic suppression of sexual feeling.

impulse; = passion, etc.

Adolescent impetuosity takes different forms for the two sexes. For boys, delinquency and recklessness are the most extreme forms of defiance. For girls, premarital sexual intercourse may serve the same function. Data available in 1965 indicate that over 40% of all brides are teenagers and about half of the teenage brides are pregnant when they stand at the altar.[21] Fifty percent of teenage marriages terminate in divorce within two years.[22] These sobering statistics reflect, in part, the confused and conflicting sexual attitudes which many young Americans develop.

Many parents view the arrival of puberty with misgivings, partly because of their own conflicts about sexuality and partly because they feel uneasy about sexual attraction toward their children. A father is likely to withdraw from a developing daughter out of a feeling that distance is more seemly or out of alarm at the sexual feelings which she arouses. Since he does not feel free to explain his reasons and may not even recognize them, the daughter may mistakenly conclude that her father has lost interest in her. Lidz[23] has written that women in psychoanalysis frequently are amazed to realize that their father's withdrawal was not caused by repulsion but by attraction; the discovery is sometimes a significant turning point in treatment.

In their turmoil, most adolescents seek solace from their friends. However, the adolescent recognizes that he is not ready to "fly the nest" completely. His partiality for the telephone represents an ideal compromise: he can escape his parents to be with his friends without ever leaving the security of home. Nonetheless, the influence of the adolescent's friends (most of whom are as confused as he) becomes dominant.

Because girls grow and develop sooner than boys, and because they usually prefer to go out with older boys, it is often assumed that girls are more sexually advanced than boys their own age. In terms of sexual drive and behavior, the opposite appears to be true. In our society, the young girl's preference for older boys seems to be far more social than sexual. The socially maladroit 14-year old boy is usually packed with sexual feeling, while the seemingly socially sophisticated and mature girl of 14 may have hardly any sexual feelings whatever. Boys experience their first erotic arousal earlier and they seek relief earlier. Kinsey determined that by 15, 80% of boys while only 20% of girls have masturbated. All such studies have the limitations of using

42

selected samples. Moreover, the disparity in sexual drive between the sexes seems to have decreased since the Kinsey studies were made, and the disparity, while it still exists, may not be physiologic, but social or cultural. In a different culture with different sexual attitudes, the sexual drive of girls and boys might be equally strong.

The feelings which adolescent boys and adolescent girls have about sexual activity differ in our culture. For many young men, sex is a form of pleasure and also a proving ground. The boy who has coitus with several girls is considered to have proved his masculinity. For men love often arrives in the context of sex. The opposite is true for most women—sex arrives in the context of love. Even after marriage, sex remains a form of pleasure and recreation for the man and primarily an expression of love for the woman. A boy may experience strong sexual arousal simply by being near an attractive girl. There is no equivalent experience for most girls. Their reaction depends on their particular feelings for the male in question.

Attitudes of young men and women toward sexual experiences are reflected in the frequency of premarital pregnancy. The boy who is only enjoying himself often feels little responsibility for the use of contraceptives; they are the girl's responsibility. The girl who sees sexual activity as the spontaneous expression of love dislikes the idea of coldly preparing herself before the event. She may also fail to use contraceptives out of desire to create a family with the boy.

Homosexual Episodes

One of the most upsetting events for parents is the discovery that their adolescent child is taking part in homosexual experiments. Such practices, although quite common, are generally considered unacceptable and even perverse by society. What represents expected experimentation and what represents emergence of homosexuality is difficult to define. Mutual masturbation may be practiced by adolescent boys; adolescent girls may hold hands, kiss, fondle each other's breasts and masturbate each other. Since sexual development during these years produces curiosity, anxiety and self-consciousness, many teenagers turn for relief to the friends with whom they feel most secure. Such adolescent behavior is usually temporary; however, in our society taboos against homosexuality are so severe that even a single episode can cause considerable anxiety in an adolescent. A boy may develop fears that he is "not normal" as the result of an isolated homosexual episode occurring during a period of loneliness or frustration, or following excessive use of alcohol, or other drugs. Anal intercourse and oral-genital contact are especially threatening to an adolescent's stability.

Homosexuality is fairly widespread in many societies. In one study of 193 cultures,[24] 28% were found to accept male homosexuality and only 14% rejected it. Fifty-eight percent of these cultures were equivocal about homosexuality, and in these, bisexuality was common among men. Ten percent of the cultures accepted female homosexuality, 11% rejected it and 79% were partially accepting or equivocal. Among world religions, Judaism and Christianity are most harsh in condemnation of homosexuality. Among countries, America has been one of the most condemning, although there is evidence that this attitude is now changing.

There are divergent medical opinions about the causes and nature of homosexuality. However, much homosexual activity, particularly during adolescence, is not a symptom of homosexuality but the result of curiosity and temporary psychosexual need. Only about 13% of American males and 8% of females react erotically to members of their own sex.[25] Nonetheless, Kinsey et al found that 37% of the total male population and 13% of the female population had at least some homosexual experience leading to orgasm.[26]

THE ROLE OF THE PHYSICIAN

Prevention and Adolescent Counseling

Many adolescents seek an opportunity to talk to someone outside the family about sex, and the physician is often a logical choice. Others come to the physician with vague somatic complaints in order to be reassured that they have not done themselves any damage by masturbating. These opportunities to disseminate accurate information to adolescents can be used to good advantage by the physician, but he should not attempt to conduct a complete course in sex education. Several brief sessions are usually better than one long one since they give the patient time to digest information, realign his thinking and get over his embarrassment. The physician may wish to refer his adolescent patients and their parents to reading material. A list of recommended books is provided in Appendix II.

The questions most commonly asked by pubescent girls center around birth, birth control and boys. The physician should ask all young female patients whether they have begun to menstruate, and, if so, whether they understand the process. Some adolescent girls are not clear about the difference between the vagina and the urethra. When a pelvic examination is performed, the results should be explained to both the girl and her parent, if present, in a way that is both thorough and comprehensive. Words which may be misinterpreted, such as "infantile," should be avoided. A young woman may become sexually anxious if she is told that her uterus is infantile and erroneously concludes that she will never be able to have a child. If the patient will be able to reproduce normally, assurance of this is important.

The most common questions[27] asked by adolescent boys concern the genitalia, masturbation, homosexuality, intercourse, venereal disease, and the female sex organs. When giving factual information, the physician should be alert for signs of anxiety concerning a specific subject area, which may indicate the need for more careful explanation and reassurance. With adolescents of both sexes, it is often helpful to explain the variations in normal sexual development that occur at the age of the patient. Assuring the patient that he is normal will relieve anxiety.

The physician should encourage parents to discuss their own adolescent development with the child. A father's casual comment that he was late to mature can greatly relieve a son whose puberty is delayed. Adolescent boys need to be reassured that the size of the genitalia is not important to sexual function and that their own sex drive is normal. Prepubertal girls should know that one breast will probably begin to develop before the other, and that this is entirely normal. Parents should be advised that silence on the part of their children is no sign of lack of concern. If a 14-year old boy never asks about sex, it does not mean that he has no interest, but rather that he has sensed his parents' reluctance to talk about sex.

Signs of sexual tension in an adolescent may be unwelcome reminders to the parents of their own sexual tension at that age. Parents should be reminded that the teens are the years of great sexual drive, but if communication is genuinely established, the child can get through the stresses of adolescence very well.

Management of Problems in Puberty and Adolescence

a) Physical Anomalies

Puberty usually occurs at about 12 years of age for girls and 14 for boys. The development of pubertal changes before the age of 9 for girls and 11 for boys is designated precocious puberty and merits consultation. True precocious puberty includes development of the gonads as well as secondary sex characteristics. In some cases, intracranial lesions (eg, tumors, hydrocephalus, encephalitis, encephalomyelitis following measles) cause involvement of the hypothalamic center, which triggers the release of pituitary gonadotropins, which in turn causes the gonads to start secreting. In most cases, however, the cause is not pathologic.

Precocious puberty occurs rarely, but when it does, it is found much more frequently in girls than in boys. It has been reported in infants under two years of age. Most cases in girls seem to occur between four and seven years. In some persons a systemic illness may stimulate the hypothalamus; in others some event makes the gonads more sensitive to minute amounts of gonadotropins. Rarely, a granulosa cell tumor of the ovary is the cause. Breast development is the first sign in girls followed by growth of body hair and rounding of the figure. Menstruation may start, be irregular at the onset and then occur at monthly intervals. Ovulation may occur and pregnancy is possible. Pregnancy as early as five years has been reported. Both boys and girls have a spurt in growth, but their ultimate height is usually below the average because the steroids cause premature closure of the epiphyses.

These children are of normal intelligence and psychologic difficulties are uncommon. The parents need to be reassured that the development is precocious and not abnormal. Adequate sex education is necessary to protect the child from emotionally traumatic situations with the peer group and from sexual involvements with older persons. Occasionally psychiatric help may be indicated. Anti-estrogenic drugs for the treatment of precocious girls are being investigated.

Precocious pseudopuberty involves early development of only the secondary sex characteristics, not the gonads. Production of sex steroids is caused by adrenal hyperplasia or tumors, or by testicular or ovarian tumors.

Some adolescents come to the attention of the physician because puberty has not occurred by age 16. Factors to be considered are heredity, nutrition and chronic diseases, as well as genetic and gonadal defects. If for some reason secretion of gonadotropins by the anterior pituitary fails, the testes and consequently the secondary sex characteristics will not develop. Males exhibiting the typical form of hypogonadotropic eunuchoidism are usually tall with testes of prepubertal size and consistency. The patient will remain eunuchoidal (infantile genitalia, high pitched voice, lack of adult male hair distribution, poor muscular development, and excessive long bone growth) unless treatment with gonadotropins or testosterone is instituted. Patients with incomplete forms of hypogonadotropic eunuchoidism show varying degrees of development: puberty proceeds slowly and full maturation is not obtained.

Klinefelter's syndrome, caused by the presence of extra X chromosomes is the most common type of hypogonadotropic syndrome seen at puberty. In the classic form (XXY), the testes are small and firm, azoospermia is found, gynecomastia is present and the boy exhibits varying degrees of eunuchoidism depending on the amount of impairment of Leydig cell function. Testosterone secretion in Klinefelter's syndrome is usually low but may be normal even though the patient is eunuchoidal. In mosaicism, the testes may be almost normal in size and spermatogenesis may be active. Subnormal intelligence of varying degrees is common. It tends to be mild in the classic form and severe when more than one supernumerary sex chromosome is present.

In functional prepubertal castrate syndrome, there is complete atrophy of the testes. Because the patient is a phenotypic male, the damage to the testes occurs after somatic differentiation of the fetus or during the prepubertal period. These patients have absent testes, sometimes misdiagnosed as cryptorchidism, and do not attain puberty. The etiology of this syndrome is not determined although infections and trauma have been suggested. Testosterone treatment is indicated.

In the female, ovarian hypofunction can be primary or secondary to the failure of production of pituitary gonadotropic hormones.

Turner's syndrome (gonadal dysgenesis) is a genetic abnormality (XO) which may be diagnosed during childhood because of failure of adequate growth with or without the characteristic stigmata, such as webbing of the neck. However, failure of development of secondary sex characteristics and primary amenorrhea most often bring the patient to the physician's attention. The diagnosis can be entertained clinically if the hypogonadism is associated with short stature and other stigmata and is confirmed by chromosomal analysis (karyotype). Atypical cases of girls of normal size or with some breast development or with a history of secondary amenorrhea always need a buccal smear or chromosomal analysis. Substitution therapy with estrogens induces development of the breasts and secondary sex characteristics and some growth of the genital tract, usually enough to permit normal sexual activity.

b) Homosexual Behavior

In dealing with homosexual episodes during adolescence, the physician's first task is to try to determine whether the activity is merely experimental, which is quite common during this period or is indicative of emerging homosexual orientation. In talking with the patient, it is essential to listen without putting in too many questions. The adolescent will be vastly relieved to find a nonjudgmental adult but will be frightened by too much interrogation. As in all counseling, a rhetorical or leading question is likely to bring an expected answer, not an honest one. The physician should remember that the patient is probably feeling considerable embarrassment and is under contradictory pressures both to deny and to talk about the behavior.

Information about the frequency of homosexual episodes in normal development is often reassuring to the parents and the child, especially in cases where the homosexual behavior does not seem significant. Both the patient and his parents should be told that homosexuality is not created at birth and that there remains considerable chance of changing the behavior pattern. When explaining the environmental factors, however, it is important not to create or increase feelings of guilt in the parents. Most parents of homosexuals feel a strong sense of personal responsibility for the condition and the physician should try to reduce their guilt by pointing out that the etiology is uncertain.

If the homosexual behavior appears significant rather than

48

experimental, the physician should ascertain the patient's attitude toward his parents. It may be helpful to interview both parents to get an impression of the home environment. If the parents are not providing suitable role models, their attitude can sometimes be influenced and they can be encouraged to spend more time with the child. If the home environment cannot be managed effectively, the physician should suggest outside activities that offer the adolescent other appropriate role models. If evidence suggests a serious basic personality disturbance, psychotherapy should be recommended.

c) Premarital Sexual Counseling

One of the most difficult areas of premarital sexual counseling is the subject of premarital coitus. The physician's role is to talk about the subject with his patients, point out the possible consequences, and try to help the patient reach the best possible decision. In every case it is the patient who finally decides. A simple analogy for the physician's role in counseling on premarital sex is that of a travel agent: he can explain how to reach various destinations; he can point out what will probably happen if various routes are taken; he can even say which course he personally favors; but the traveler charts his own journey.

This is a role to which the physician may not be accustomed and which may be uncomfortable for him. However, only by learning to counsel with patients rather than unilaterally directing them, can the physician be truly effective. He does not have to withhold his personal views from patients, but he should not try to impose them. He must try to be as objective about his own views as about those held by patients. His primary task is to reveal the considerations involved in deciding about coitus, help the patient examine his or her motives and feelings, and assist the patient's understanding of these feelings. The patient must finally make his or her own decision, and most of the time, if counseled well, will decide responsibly.

In counseling adolescents, the physician should be aware that attitudes and standards are changing now. For many young people permanence is not the hallmark of every satisfactory sexual relationship. Many today do not expect permanence in personal relationships or in general. They emphasize the quality of a relationship, not its duration. The dominant standard has been defined by Reiss[28] as "permissiveness with affection," and it gives greater emphasis to affection and less to behavior than that held by most parents. A young person today is inclined to approve of coitus when love or strong affection is felt. Physicians should not lose sight of the fact that sexual activity is pleasurable and that this is the primary motivation for most people.

A number of questions may be asked by the physician who is exploring with the adolescent girl her reasons for engaging in premarital coitus.

1. Do you have one boyfriend?
2. How close and intimate are you and your boyfriend?
3. What kind of commitment do you feel toward each other?
4. Do you prefer sex play that stops short of intercourse?
5. Do you derive pleasure from intercourse with your boyfriend?
6. Do you feel any regrets at having established this sexual relationship?
7. What method of birth control do you use?

It would appear that usually, but by no means always, a girl who is sexually active has established a close and warm relationship with one boy, and the fact that she is having intercourse may say a great deal about her commitment to him. In the absence of love or strong attachment, few girls will be able to engage in coital activity without guilt and feelings of worthlessness which may complicate their future sexual life.

An adolescent may enter into a sexual relationship with considerable self-delusion, in effect playing at being sexually progressive, then feel overwhelmed by the experience, which may seem to represent the irrevocable termination of childhood. It is always easier to reach an intellectual decision about coitus than it is to resolve one's emotional conflicts about it. If the girl, is experiencing emotional problems which result from coital activity, the physician should point out that she is harming rather than benefiting herself and try to persuade her to examine her motives.

Persons may enter sexual relationships to appease loneliness or to prove their desirability. Some engage in coitus to determine sexual compatibility. However, the special tensions involved in premarital coitus do not make it an ideal proving ground for compatibility. Some girls agree to engage in coitus to preserve a relationship with a boy. Some adolescents whose childhood needs for closeness were thwarted or overindulged may seize on sexual activity as a way of being close to someone.

The dissolution of a sexual relationship may also create problems. Some adolescents withdraw from all heterosexual activity and others throw themselves into indiscriminate sexual activity. If the relationship being terminated is the girl's first sexual experience, her sense of loss and depression and her need for reassurance may be great. The physician should point out that repetitive sexual activity based on temporary needs will not be reassuring, and that few girls can sexually "play the field" successfully.

Other considerations should be kept in mind when counseling adolescent boys. A boy who feels he needs to demonstrate his dominance may use coitus for that purpose. Some boys use sex exploitively, and then experience considerable guilt. Others, feeling obliged to demonstrate their masculinity, may place great emphasis on technique and performance. If self-consciousness inhibits sexual performance, panic and depression can result.

The practical importance of contraception is not obvious to many adolescents engaged in premarital coitus. Many girls simply do not believe that pregnancy will happen to them, and do not use contraceptives. Other girls feel that using the pill or a diaphragm entails a greater commitment to permissiveness than they care to make; such precautions seem to introduce an element of cold calculation into what they feel should be a spontaneous act. As Vincent[29] has asked, "How does she prepare herself psychologically to begin taking the pill regularly on the assumption that next week, next month or next year the boy will want to sleep with her? What will he think of her if she is so prepared?"

Effective female methods of contraception have made many males feel even less responsible in sexual relationships. Although the man is expected to show responsibility in virtually all other situations, he commonly feels little responsibility for the consequences of sexual activity. In counseling adolescent boys, the physician should stress that pregnancy is the responsibility of both partners, and that the boy must be prepared for the girl's emotional commitment and her possible emotional dependence on him.

For the teenage girl whose sexual behavior exposes her to the risk of pregnancy, the AMA has adopted the following policy statement:

Physicians are greatly concerned about the medical and health problems of the sexually involved adolescent, the school-age pregnant girl, the teenage mother and father, and the child of adolescent parents. In 1967 in the United States, 197,000 school-age girls under the age of 18 gave birth to a child. Of these, 78,000 were unmarried at the time. In the past five years, there has been an average annual increase of about 4,000 such births. These figures do not take into account the number of premarital pregnancies which have forced early marriages or the number of abortions among teenagers. In one state in which figures are available, 48 per cent of teenage marriages involved a premarital pregnancy. Approximately one-half of these marriages end in divorce within the first four years.

It is common knowledge that involved teenagers come from all social strata. In many instances, the most responsible parents and families have been unable to guide teenage behavior, and their need for help appears clear.

In or out of marriage, such pregnancies may create serious medical, psychological, social and educational problems for the teenage parents. The problems for the unwanted child may be tragic. For mother and child, teenage pregnancy is often the critical initiating factor and, later, a continuing major contributory factor in the development of psychosomatic, psychoneurotic, and even occasional psychotic illnesses.

Consistent with responsible preventive medicine and in the interest of reducing the incidence of teenage pregnancy, the American Medical Association recommends that:

(a) The teenage girl whose sexual behavior exposes her to possible conception have access to medical consultation and the most effective contraceptive advice and methods consistent with her physical and emotional needs; and

(b) The physician so consulted should be free to prescribe or withhold contraceptive advice in accordance with his best medical judgment in the best interests of his patient.

The foregoing is also the recommendation of the American Academy of Pediatrics, the American Academy of Family Physicians and the American College of Obstetricians and Gynecologists.

A sexually active girl presents both a social and a medical problem. Because she is clearly exposed repeatedly to pregnancy, contraceptive advice generally should be given as a part of a broad program of preventive therapy. Counseling may play a key role in contraceptive effectiveness. A group in Baltimore has instituted a required course in sex education for all unmarried girls who wish oral contraceptives, and the program has greatly reduced the pregnancy rate among the teenage participants. Through counseling, the group has helped its clients understand the meaning and importance of family life and, in many cases, has improved the quality of the client's own life. In this study group, prescribing contraception combined with education has proven acceptable to society and to the patient, and has not increased sexual activity.

The importance of dealing with the patient's basic sexual pattern and not merely with the presenting complaint is illustrated by a patient seen in a clinical setting on a college campus:

A girl requested a "morning-after pill" (estrogen) because her partner's condom had perforated during coitus the night before. She informed the physician that she and the boy were beginning an important relationship. The physician advised her that the condom was not the most suitable contraceptive in her case. She did not want to take oral contraceptives as he suggested, but agreed to the use of a diaphragm. After fitting her the physician asked her to return in a few weeks.

Six months later, the girl returned. She had seen a program about venereal disease and was worried that she might be infected. When the physician asked whether she had had any problems with the diaphragm, she said she had never used it because "it was always some place else." The patient related that since her visit she had engaged in coitus with two other men and was worried about venereal disease.

Further questioning revealed her real concern, which was not contraception or venereal disease. "I guess I realized I'd slept with three men," she said, "and I never expected to sleep with any one before I got married." She was examined and assured that she did not have venereal disease. More importantly, her sex behavior and its meaning were discussed. Additionally, she was referred to a course on human sexuality being given in the community. This course gave her the opportunity to understand her behavior and provided further insight into her problems.

A crisis is usually an isolated event superimposed upon a sexual pattern. If the physician looks below the crisis at the pattern itself and is receptive to discussions of sexual feelings, he may uncover problems which he can help solve or he may refer the patient to an appropriate source of therapy.

One of the most neglected subjects in adolescent sexual counseling is the consequences of early pregnancy which strains the marital relationship and often leads to divorce. Lief[30] has stated "young people are attracted to each other at this time in their lives, and are motivated for marriage for many maladaptive reasons; to obtain illusory security, status, or sexual pleasure, to make a pregnancy legal, to rebel against parental wishes, to overcome loneliness, to become one of the crowd, to attain independence before being emotionally ready for it, or to find a romantic lover." Another common reason is an unhappy home situation. In some cases postponing the marriage may offer a couple time to develop more maturity and inter-personal sensitivity. The counselor should not try to create fear, defend a besieged position, or prescribe his own concept of the best solution for the patient, but encourage the patient to find the best course of action for himself or herself.

d) Nonmarital Pregnancy

In dealing with a nonmarital pregnancy, the physician has three basic objectives: to care for the physical needs of the mother; to assist the patient to arrive at the most suitable decision about abortion, adoption, marriage, or keeping the baby without marriage and to help the patient understand the factors that led to her situation. There are three critical junctures in this treatment process: the first visit, choosing a program of care and the mother's decision regarding the baby.

Confirming the fact of pregnancy is one of the critical moments of treatment, because it obviously marks a turning point in the patient's life. At such a time, the physician's every word and expression is subject to interpretation, which is often inaccurate. The identical remarks of the physician have been interpreted by some girls as condemning them for their predicament while other girls have felt the remarks condoned their situation.[31] Since it is important that physicians appear to be nonjudgmental, some make it a point to ask the patient specifically what she thinks his attitude is.

It is also important for the physician to let the girl know that she is the patient and the one with whom he will deal. In a survey of several hundred unwed mothers in California,[32] the chief complaint was that the physician had not treated the girl herself as the primary patient. The parents, if present, should wait outside the office until the interview is completed and the girl, not her mother, should be the one first informed that pregnancy exists. A young, unmarried girl already may have complicated feelings of guilt and resentment toward her parents; if the physician appears to be on their side, his attempts to help her will suffer.

After confirming the pregnancy, some physicians leave the patient with a nurse or receptionist for 10 or 15 minutes to compose herself. The physician may see another patient, then return to the girl to begin discussing the problem. This discussion constitutes another critical point for the girl, because it sets the stage for the whole program of care.

At the beginning of treatment, there are four basic questions which the physician should ask:

1) "Did you suspect that you were pregnant?" The patient may or may not have anticipated her condition and the physician needs to have an idea of her state of preparedness.

2) "Whom have you told about your condition and what was the response?" The answer to this question will throw considerable light on the girl's own feelings, her relationship with her family, and her relationship with the child's father. If she did not know about her condition or has not told anybody about it, the physician himself may be needed to play the important role

of confidant and friend. The girl's family is a critical element and many families react in damaging ways. Some parents take all the blame and others none of it. Some so severely castigate the daughter that there is little chance that they will ever be considered as a source of help again. The physician can serve as a lightning rod in many cases, and draw out the parents' anger and bitterness before they say things to their daughter which they will regret for life. Communication with the parents is often difficult for the pregnant teenager; in fact, lack of effective communication may be among the precipitating factors in her pregnancy.

3) "Have you had time to think about what this means to you?" Like some parents, some girls blame others for everything and take no responsibility themselves. Some see the pregnancy as a minor slip. Some feel crippling guilt, which they may or may not show. Vincent[33] has noted that it may be important to define the specific context in which the child was conceived. If the girl had sexual relations with a boy she planned to marry and the marriage was later cancelled, she may unnecessarily add to her feeling of guilt by viewing the father as a man who did not love her. It may be helpful to remind the girl that when conception took place, the context of loving and marriage was planned. The physician's task is to help the patient see her situation as realistically as possible, with sufficient concern but without excessive guilt.

4) "Do you understand what the alternatives are?" It seems to be a reflex action of many male physicians, when confronted with an illegitimate pregnancy, to ask whether the girl plans to marry the father. Marriage must certainly be discussed, but later, and it must be presented as one of several alternatives. The patient often interprets instant talk of marriage as a rebuke. ("Now that you've got yourself in this fix, what are you going to do about it?") The unmarried girl who has just found out that she is pregnant is in no condition to decide anything. She is acutely aware that she has not acted wisely, and many girls at such a moment feel obliged to show their maturity by providing an answer. The answer, in turn, may start the girl on the road to carrying out the plan, especially if she feels there are pressures from both the physician and her parents. The visit in which pregnancy is confirmed is the worst possible time to start such a chain of events in motion. Promoting an unwanted marriage to

justify an unwanted baby may be the poorest solution; the physician can help greatly by telling his patient that there is still plenty of time to reach a decision.

Contraception should be discussed in depth, but not immediately after pregnancy has been confirmed. To discuss contraceptive methods during the first visit is as appropriate as offering skiing lessons to a man who has just broken his leg on the slopes. Besides being momentarily irrelevant, the discussion inevitably sounds like a lecture to the patient.

In an attempt to insure proper care, the physician can provide information on appropriate resources in the community and help arrange for the patient to make use of these resources in cases where referral is appropriate. He may inform the patient where she can obtain a legal abortion if such action does not conflict with his own beliefs and standards and state laws. The patient should be made aware that the physician is available to help her prevent another unwanted pregnancy.

Sarrel[34] observed that pregnant teenagers are high risks——medically, socially, and educationally——and they often require the attention of professionals from several fields. The pregnant adolescent often drops out of school. Without proper medical care, the incidence of toxemia, prematurity, infant mortality and morbidity are all significantly increased. She is ill-equipped to take on the demands of parenthood; if she marries, divorce is likely. One study of 100 unwed, pregnant teenagers showed that within five years, 95% had had repeated pregnancies, 91% were still unmarried, and 60% were living on welfare.[35] The 100 girls accounted for a total of 249 repeat pregnancies.

The unwed teenager who repeatedly becomes pregnant constitutes a problem for herself and for society, and treatment requires a combination of approaches from a variety of disciplines. Such a program may require many coordinated services: maternity home care, therapeutic abortion, medical aftercare of illegal abortion, special education, family counseling, psychiatric care, social work, and well-baby care. The physician can provide only a limited amount of the services needed and he should refer the girl to the appropriate sources whenever indicated. The Young Mothers Program in New Haven, Conn. is based on such an approach. The program was created for the poor, but it is now used by the patients of many private physicians as well. The teenage patients in New Haven can continue their education throughout pregnancy in a special center set up within the city school system, which offers vocational training, a summer recreation program and family counseling for the patient, the child's father and the family. Throughout pregnancy, the girl is cared for by a team consisting of a nurse-midwife, obstetrician, pediatrician and social worker. The program stresses that the girl must try to become self-sufficient, that the baby is her responsibility and she must not abdicate the responsibility to others. Marriage is rarely recommended. In most cases, it is suggested that marriage be postponed until the baby has been born, by which time the girl may have developed a better concept of herself and be able to plan her own future. Girls are offered birth control material if their parents give permission.

The success of this program has been dramatic. The cycle of repetitive pregnancy has been broken, and there is sufficient data to indicate, now that the program has served over 400 teenagers, that the approach leads to a fuller and more meaningful life for the girl. Similar results have been witnessed in other comprehensive teenage pregnancy programs.

Even if she has decided tentatively on her course of action, she should be urged to reconsider it in light of the alternatives available. It is important that she should understand that she has four choices, and that each choice will probably involve emotional difficulties:

1) The girl who does not want to bear the child can have the pregnancy terminated by a legal abortion which involves very little risk. If the physician himself does not perform abortions, he should refer the patient to a physician who does or to a voluntary or public agency which can make the appropriate referral. The appropriateness of this option depends on the individual's attitude toward abortion, on the one hand, and toward having the baby, on the other. The psychologic effects of abortion may be less severe than those of adoption for many women, some of whom never seem to get over the trauma of bearing and then losing their child.

2) Adoption permits the mother to bear her child without becoming involved in an unwanted marriage. Nonetheless, many young girls who elect to have their child adopted are forced to move from home during the last months of pregnancy, and a feeling of stealth and guilt is often created. A decision to give the

baby up may also have an adverse effect on the child's father, whose feelings are often not taken into consideration.

3) If the girl plans to marry the father of her child, the physician should see him as well as the girl. If they seem to be uncertain about their decision, he should urge them to try to clarify their feelings, and help them by raising the other alternatives, including postponing a decision about marriage until the baby has been born. The disadvantages of early marriage and the special handicaps which face a marriage in which the bride is pregnant should be discussed. There will be little time for the couple to get used to each other and married life before the baby arrives. The couple will inevitably wonder whether they would have married if she had not been pregnant. If marriage is chosen, it should probably be open, not secret.

4) The girl may decide to keep the child, accept responsibility for its care, but not marry. This alternative is not explored often enough by adoption agencies and those groups dealing with unwed pregnant girls. It has the advantage of keeping mother and child together and may produce the fewest feelings of guilt for some girls. Eventual marriage obviously remains a strong possibility.

CHAPTER VIII—EARLY ADULTHOOD
SEXUAL DEVELOPMENT

Heterosexuality

Many societies have developed irrational sexual fears, but Western culture "is unique in strictly isolating the individual in the fears that society has devised."[36] This isolation is imposed by taboos on the discussion of sexual matters and by sharp restrictions on exploration of beliefs and practices. "In most areas of social activity a reality check upon individual fantasies is provided either by interaction with other persons or by contact with the mass media; but the sexual area lacks such checks, and the proportion of fantasy probably outweighs the proportion of reality."[37] The individual's dilemma is also compounded by a sexual moral code which is accepted but not actually observed by most persons. We doubt the code enough to violate it but many of us feel intense guilt about the violation. The physician has opportunities to help interrupt this cycle of misinformation, unrealistic expectation and guilt through counseling adolescents, young adults and parents.

Most men reach a peak of sexual drive before the age of 20, followed by a gradual decline with the passage of years. Female sexual responsiveness generally increases until age 30, then levels off until the woman is 50 or older. Sexual drive in both is probably controlled by physiologic and cultural factors. Masturbation is practiced by men and women of all ages, often as a supplement to marital coitus, and women tend to masturbate more often as they grow older.[38]

A sense of responsibility for others seems to increase sexual conservatism. Reiss[39] found that married people at 40 have less permissive sexual standards than unmarried people the same age. People with children are even less permissive, and married persons with adolescent children are the least permissive, thereby confirming the old definition of a conservative as a liberal who has a teenage daughter.

Although ninety-five percent of all Americans marry, the American ideal of marriage is not the way people actually live. One of every five first marriages ends in divorce. Of the first children born to American women in the mid 1960's, one-third were conceived out of wedlock, and one-seventh were born out of wedlock. Early marriage and pregnancy decrease the chance of marital continuity. Much of the sex education, which is received in the home, in the school and in the streets, is inadequate. Therefore, at the time they marry, many Americans are poorly informed about sexuality and much of what they believe is false. Like the child, the adult who is poorly educated about sexuality has little opportunity to correct the failure. Undoubtedly, failure to establish a satisfactory sexual relationship accounts for much marital unhappiness and sometimes divorce; ignorance about sex is often the basic problem.

Almost 50% of all husbands and 30% of all wives have had an extra marital sexual affair by the time they reach their mid-forties, with the highest rate among the most educated. Among married partners who remain together, Rubin[40] has estimated that after age 60, one in four is enthusiastic about the marriage, one in four is quite satisfied, and two in four are dissatisfied.

Homosexuality

Whereas isolated homosexual incidents during adolescence are experimental and not significant, adult continuation of homosexual behavior is a sign of fixed homosexual orientation. Anal intercourse and homosexual oral-genital contact are more likely to be continued into adulthood than other forms of homosexual behavior, although male homosexual activity often takes the form of caressing, kissing and fondling, not necessarily accompanied by genital manipulation.

Homosexuality does not have a known genetic or hormonal basis. Although the precise etiology is not known, studies of homosexuals who have sought psychiatric treatment quite consistently point to disturbed relations between the child and the parents. Childhood seduction by an adult of the same sex does not seem to be a common cause. Male homosexuals may have feelings of revulsion, varying in intensity, toward coitus with a female, and the feeling may result in impotence.

The stereotype of the homosexual is highly inaccurate; most are productive people who actively participate in their community affairs and have no distinguishing physical characteristics. Although there appears to be more homosexuality among residents of cities than of rural areas, considerable homosexual activity is practiced by lumbermen, cattlemen, miners and other outdoor workers. There seems to be little difference in the amount of homosexuality practiced by manual and non-manual workers.

There is little agreement about whether homosexuality should be classified as a social deviation, a mental disorder, or simply an alternate sexual preference. Some experts have concluded that homosexuality should not be considered a mental illness, and suggest that when psychologic abnormalities are observed in a homosexual, these are often caused by society's pressures. In fact, some psychiatrists believe that the homosexual's resistance to these pressures creates strong neurotic fears about heterosexuality.

Most male homosexuals form no lasting relationships with other men and the number of partners is often high. It is believed that only about 4% of white males are dominantly or exclusively homosexual.[41] Non-dominant homosexual behavior is more common. At 35, more than half of all single males reportedly have had homosexual experience to the point of orgasm. Some men are disturbed that they may be "latent homosexuals" because of homosexual thoughts and fantasies, even though they have never acted on them. Because homosexual urges are present in some form in almost everybody, such fantasies are of no significance.

Society is more tolerant of female than of male homosexuality. Lesbianism is often associated with a poor parental relationship, especially with the father. In a study by Bene,[42] few lesbians wished to pattern themselves after either parent, and they especially rejected their fathers, who were seen as weak or frightening. In many instances, the mother may have been overly affectionate, frequently sleeping with and caressing the child. On the other hand, she may have abused the daughter, who then sought a loving, older woman to provide the maternal affection not given at home. Homosexual relations between women are generally more affectionate and long-lasting than those between men. The most common sexual activities are kissing and body contact, mutual masturbation and cunnilingus, but simulated coitus seems to be rare. Kinsey found that the incidence of lesbianism increased among the well educated. More than three-fourths of the homosexual women in his sample expressed no regret. The stereotype of the manly lesbian is even less accurate than that of the effeminate male homosexual. The incidence of dominant female homosexuality is lower than the incidence of dominant male homosexuality: only about 2 to 3 percent of females are exclusively homosexual[43] throughout their lives.

THE ROLE OF THE PHYSICIAN

Prevention and Counseling

a) Contraceptive Counseling

During the early adult years, the physician functions as counselor and educator on many levels; he deals with his patients as parents, as husbands, as wives and as sexual partners (see Chapter III). The physician's goal in all sexual counseling is to help his patients to be not only sexually responsive but also sexually responsible men and women. An important part of that process is contraceptive counseling with single men and women who are sexually active, and family planning with engaged and married couples.

The importance of providing contraceptive information to single men and women who are having sexual intercourse is obvious. It is also obvious from the large number of out-of-wedlock pregnancies that such information is infrequently sought or used when it is available.

The role of the physician and other members of the health team is apparent: to ensure that contraceptives are available to all persons throughout the community; to advocate sex education as a part of general health education in the home, the school, the church and other areas.

Finally, the importance, indeed the necessity, of taking a sexual history on singles is again emphasized. Few patients will volunteer information of a sexual nature to a physician or other member of the health team. Once the subject is introduced by the interviewer, however, most patients will respond appropriately, and may well indicate relief that they have found someone with whom they can discuss their sexual activity or lack of it.

The advisability of any given method of contraception finally depends upon its acceptability to the individual couple, so that one of the responsibilities of the physician is to inform the couple of the safety and effectiveness of the various contraceptives now available. In most real life situations, it is the woman, rather than the man, who assumes the responsibility of contraception.

There are many ways to prevent pregnancy, so that the patient has a wide selection of contraceptives from which to choose. It is the counselor's role to explain the advantages and disadvantages of each method in terms of safety and effectiveness, and it is useful to inform the patient that the perfect, wholly ideal contraceptive has not yet been found.

In terms of effectiveness, the oral contraceptive is the method of first choice. When taken as directed, pregnancy occurs so rarely that many physicians tell their patients that its effectiveness is one hundred percent if used as directed. Confidence in a contraceptive reinforces peace of mind for the couple, especially the woman, for fear of pregnancy occurs commonly, and when present, often interferes with sexual responsiveness and diminishes the frequency of intercourse.

The oral contraceptive is, by far, the contraceptive most frequently prescribed by obstetricians and gynecologists. A poll of the membership of the American College of Obstetricians and Gynecologists as early as 1967 indicated this.

In terms of acceptability of the patient, the oral contraceptive rates are very high indeed. In terms of undesirable effects, however, the oral contraceptive is not ideal. The AMA in cooperation with the American College of Obstetricians and Gynecologists, the Food and Drug Administration and the Pharmaceutical Manufacturers Association have prepared a pamphlet for patients entitled, *What You Should Know About "The Pill"* which is available from the AMA on request.

Andrews,[44] in a recent extensive review of the reported physiologic and pathologic effects of the oral contraceptive, concluded that 1) use of oral contraception incurs an increased risk of thromboembolism; this risk is small and probably comparable to the risk of death in pregnancy occurring as a result of contraceptive failure with other methods. A slightly greater risk is present with the use of the sequential regimen. Relationship of risk to estrogen dosage is not yet clear, but since combined compounds with 50 μg give virtually complete protection from pregnancy, it would seem prudent to employ the lower dose compound unless other dosages are required for control of menstruation. Occlusion of cerebral or coronary arteries in the reproductive age group is rare, and a causal relationship to oral contraceptives has not been established.

2) Oral contraceptives lower glucose tolerance in initial months of use. These changes are only clinically significant in patients with latent diabetes; hence, women with a family or clinical history predisposing to diabetes should have at least a postprandial blood glucose determination before using this method of contraception.

3) Hypertension may be produced by oral contraception in an occasional susceptible individual. These changes are usually reversible, but all patients employing these agents should have regular blood pressure determinations, with discontinuance if significant hypertension is found.

4) No significant change in liver function has been found in women without an inherited or acquired defect in hepatic excretory function.

5) Ophthalmological abnormalities are no more frequent in users than in nonusers.

6) Thyroid function is not altered, although the results of some tests of thyroid function are changed by oral contraception; a similar conclusion is made in regard to adrenal function.

7) Etiologic relationships of subjective symptoms such as headache, nervousness and depression are difficult to assess. Oral contraceptives apparently do initiate or aggravate migraine headache in some patients, and when this complaint, or increased nervousness or depression, is reported, oral contraceptives should be discontinued at least temporarily to allow the patient to act as her own control.

8) Subsequent fertility is rarely altered by oral contraceptives, with the occasional exception of a patient previously showing evidence of gross ovarian deficiency.

Into the overall equation of side effects, and remote possibilities of significant ones, must be placed the positive value of totally reliable control of conception, and the prevention of certain dangers thereby. Also, some value must be assigned to the important embellishment provided in the exercise of one of nature's most rewarding privileges, by the removal of fear of pregnancy, and the elimination of mechanical intervention and interruption.

The intra-uterine device (IUD) is a contraceptive device which is effective, safe and acceptable to a large number of women. It is a plastic device of varying size and shape, which is inserted into the uterine cavity, preferably during menstruation. Insertion is performed in the physician's office without anesthesia, and insertion is usually not a painful procedure. Once inserted, it need not be removed for several years unless the couple desires another pregnancy.

The way in which an IUD prevents conception (or implantation) is not known. Its effectiveness as a contraceptive, however, is known, and while not as effective as the oral contraceptive, it is very effective indeed. Failure rates reported vary from 0.50% to 2.0%. Those pregnancies which do occur are not harmed by the IUD, as it is extra-ovular, and no attempt should be made to remove the IUD during pregnancy. It is usually expelled from the uterine cavity at the time the placenta is removed. When it is not expelled spontaneously at this time, manual removal is carried out.

The disadvantages, or side effects of the IUD are uterine cramping, expulsion and excessive bleeding. The first two do not occur very often. Excessive bleeding, however, is common and frequently necessitates removal of the device. The presence of myomas which distort the uterine cavity also preclude the use of the device.

Another disadvantage of the IUD is perforation of the uterine wall, so that the device ends up not in the uterine cavity, but in the abdominal cavity. While such occurrences are relatively rare, they are serious, and require laparotomy for the removal of the IUD.

The risk of perforating the uterine wall is always present at the time of insertion of an IUD; it follows then that great care should be taken at the time of insertion. Determination of the position of the uterus, the use of a cervical tenaculum, sounding of the uterine cavity, gentle dilatation of the cervical canal, and the insertion of the device during menstruation, will reduce the incidence of perforation very nearly to zero.

In summary, the IUD is an excellent contraceptive which is gaining ever-wider acceptance by physicians and patients alike. Recent changes in the shape of the device, and the inclusion of copper filament, still experimental and not available for general use at this time, indicate increased effectiveness with diminished side effects.

The use of the diaphragm-jelly combination by the woman, or

a condom (rubber, rubber sheath, prophylactic) by the man, is still another effective contraceptive. It has the added advantage of being almost entirely free of side effects. However, neither method has wide acceptability, so that neither method is widely nor consistently practiced. For the woman, the diaphragm-jelly combination is inconvenient and often messy. For the man, the condom dulls his pleasure of the act, and occasionally breaks.

In addition to contraception, the condom has one property which no other contraceptive has: protection against venereal disease during intercourse. In these times, when an epidemic of gonorrhea exists throughout the land, its unacceptability by most men is unfortunate.

Spermatocidal vaginal foams have become very popular (a high rate of acceptability), readily available (no prescription needed), quite safe (allergic reactions are rare), but are not nearly as effective a contraceptive as those described in the preceding pages. These aerosol foams have largely replaced vaginal jellies, creams, and suppositories, because they are believed to be more effective.

The rhythm method of contraceptive practice is based on the observation that most women menstruate cyclically every twenty-six to thirty days and that a high percentage of these women ovulate between day twelve and day seventeen of their cycle. If basal body temperature is employed to more accurately determine the time of ovulation, the rhythm method becomes more effective. The problem of course is that most couples will not abstain for 10 out of 28 days, nor go to the trouble of employing basal body temperature when other more effective measures are available.

Finally, in a discussion of various contraceptive practices, there remains coitus interruptus and douching immediately following intercourse. The former is possibly the most commonly employed method of contraception throughout the world. Hopefully, the frequency with which coitus interruptus is practiced will diminish as the dissemination of accurate information of contraceptives and their availability increases.

Douching immediately following intercourse is not recommended, as it is ineffective as a contraceptive.

b) Abortion

Until January 22, 1973, abortion was illegal in most states

when the physical life of a mother was not threatened by the pregnancy. The Supreme Court in a landmark decision presented on January 22 overturned virtually all state laws on abortion, even the least restrictive New York statute, with its opinion on the Texas abortion statute in the case of Jane Roe, et.al., Appellants, v. Henry Wade. The Court's own summary of its decision follows:

"1. A state criminal abortion statute of the current Texas type, that excepts from criminality only a life saving procedure on behalf of the mother, without regard to pregnancy stage and without recognition of the other interests involved, is violative of the Due Process Clause of the Fourteenth Amendment.

"(a) For the stage prior to approximately the end of the first trimester, the abortion decision and its effectuation must be left to the medical judgment of the pregnant woman's attending physician.

"(b) For the stage subsequent to approximately the end of the first trimester, the State, in promoting its interest in the health of the mother, may, if it chooses, regulate the abortion procedure in ways that are reasonably related to maternal health.

"(c) For the stage subsequent to viability the State, in promoting its interest in the protentiality of human life, may, if it chooses, regulate, and even proscribe, abortion except where it is necessary, in appropriate medical judgment, for the preservation of the life or health of the mother.

"2. The State may define the term "physician," as it has been employed in the preceding numbered paragraphs of this Part XI of this opinion, to mean only a physician currently licensed by the State, and may proscribe any abortion by a person who is not a physician as so defined."

"This holding, we feel, is consistent with relative weights of the respective interests involved, with the lessons and example of medical and legal history, with the lenity of the common law, and with the demands of the profound problems of the present day. The decision leaves the State free to place increasing restrictions on abortion as the period of pregnancy lengthens, so long as those restrictions are tailored to the recognized state interests. The decision vindicates the right of the physician to administer medical treatment according to his professional judgment up to the points where important state interests provide compelling justifications for intervention. Up to those points the abortion decision in all its aspects is inherently, and primarily, a medical decision, and basic responsibility for it must rest with the physician. If an individual practitioner abuses the privilege of exercising proper medical judgment, the usual remedies, judicial and intra-professional, are available." (For full text see Appendix IV.)

While abortion should not be considered an acceptable primary method of fertility control, no longer can it be summarily dismissed as a factor in family planning.

The first full year of experience with New York's liberal abortion law produced the events documented in the following four tables. The data were made available through the courtesy of Jean Pakter, M.D., Director, Bureau of Maternity Services and Family Planning, Department of Health, New York City.

TABLE 1.

Number and percent of induced abortions compared to number and percent of live births to New York City residents by age of woman, July 1, 1970—June 30, 1971.

	Abortion					Ratio of total
		Estimated				abortions
	Number	Total		Live Births		per 1,000
Age of Woman	Reported	Number	Percent	Number	Percent	live births
Under 20	8,197	10,081	16.1	18,651	13.8	540.5
20-24	17,936	22,060	35.2	46,492	34.4	474.5
25-29	12,125	14,912	23.8	40,410	29.9	369.0
30-34	7,210	8,868	14.2	19,056	14.1	465.4
35-39	3,820	4,698	7.5	8,381	6.2	560.6
41-44	1,241	1,526	2.4	2,162	1.6	750.8
45 and over	130	160	0.3	135	0.1	1,185.2
Not stated	260	320	0.5	14	*	*
Total	50,919	62,625	100.0	135,301	100.0	462.9

Source: Weekly Abortion Reports
*Less than .05

TABLE 2.

Complications following abortion, by type and period of gestation numbers and rates per 1,000 abortions, New York City, July 1, 1970—June 30, 1971.

Type of Complication	Total Number	Rate	Period of Gestation			
			12 weeks and under		13 weeks and over	
			Number	Rate	Number	Rate
Hemorrhage	192	1.5	84	0.8	108	4.7
Infection	248	1.9	102	0.9	146	6.3
Perforated uterus	192	1.5	168	1.5	24	1.0
Anesthesia	12	0.1	7	0.1	5	0.2
Shock	9	0.1	2	*	7	0.3
Retained tissue	289	2.2	56	0.5	233	10.1
Failure	67	0.5	5	*	62	2.7
Lacerated cervix	31	0.2	24	0.2	7	0.3
Other	66	0.5	42	0.4	24	1.0
Unspecified	11	0.1	7	0.1	4	0.2
Total Complications	1,117	8.5	497	4.6	620	26.8
Total abortions	131,956		108,817		23,139	

TABLE 3.

Complication rates per 1,000 abortions by type and method of termination, New York City, July 1, 1970—June 30, 1971.

Type of Complication	Total	Method of Termination				
		Dilation and Curettage	Suction	Saline	Hysterectomy	Other
Hemorrhage	1.5	1.3	0.8	5.0	4.9	1.2
Infection	1.9	1.1	0.8	7.6	13.7	2.3
Perforated uterus	1.5	1.8	1.6	0.1	6.9	0.6
Anesthesia	0.1	0.1	0.1	0.2	1.0	*
Shock	0.1	0.1	*	0.3	1.0	*
Retained tissue	2.2	0.6	0.5	13.4	2.0	0.6
Failure	0.5	*	0.1	3.6	*	*
Lacerated cervix	0.2	0.3	0.2	0.1	1.0	0.6
Other	0.5	0.4	0.4	1.0	3.9	1.2
Unspecified	0.1	0.2	*	0.2	*	0.6
Total	8.5	5.9	4.4	31.6	34.3	7.0

Source: Weekly Abortion Reports
*Less than 0.05

TABLE 4.

Maternal deaths, total and due to abortions, New York City, 1960-1971.

	Number of deaths		Rates per 100,000 live births		Percent maternal deaths due to abortions
Year	Total	Due to Abortions	Total	Due to Abortions	
1960	115	46	69	28	40.0
1961	130	55	77	33	42.3
1962	121	53	73	32	43.8
1963	116	42	69	25	35.2
1964	74	34	45	21	45.9
1965	104	41	66	26	39.4
1966	80	31	52	20	38.8
1967	76	20	52	14	26.3
1968	66	21	47	15	31.8
1969	77	24	53	16	31.2
1970	68	22	46	15	32.4
Jan.-June	37	12	51	17	32.4
July-Dec.	31	10	43	13	32.3
Jan.-June 1969	38	11	53	15	28.9
Jan.-June 1970	37	12	51	17	32.4
Jan.-June 1971	14	3	21	4	21.4

c) Surgical Sterilization

Vasectomy: A disadvantage of vasectomy is the common although unwarranted fear of subsequent impotence. Vasectomy causes no physiologic change in the ability to have intercourse or to ejaculate semen; the only difference is that the ejaculate contains no spermatozoa. Nonetheless, many males fear that their sexual functions will change and are reluctant to consider surgery which terminates their ability to impregnate. A more valid concern is that of the unknown future. Should the marriage end through either death or divorce, there is a possibility that the male might remarry a woman who might wish to have children. This prospect of a new situation and a recurrent desire for children is more likely for the male than for the female. Although there are operations performed to reestablish continuity of the vas deferens, fewer than half of these are successful at this time and, therefore, those considering vasectomy should be advised that the resulting sterility may be permanent.

Tubal Sterilization: Division of the fallopian tubes requires more extensive surgery than division of the vas; general or regional anesthesia is virtually always required and the peritoneal cavity must be entered. While tubal sterilization is performed most commonly in the immediate postpartum period, there has been a marked increase in the number of sterilizations performed months or years after pregnancy (interval sterilization).

The major disadvantages of tubal ligations are the risks of surgery itself and the absence of any method of testing the effectiveness of the procedure. Failures are known to occur, but there is no way of accurately identifying patients with either reanastomosis or incomplete division of the tube. The advantage of sterilization of the female is that if the marriage should fail, almost always the children stay with the wife; it is less likely that she will wish to start another family later.

These factors must be discussed with the marriage partners as they set about making their decision. The process of decision is painful for many; the couple needs support and full information concerning the procedures of surgical sterilization.

The advisability of any given method of contraception finally depends upon its acceptability to the individual couple, so that one of the responsibilities of the physician is to inform the couple of the safety and effectiveness of the various contraceptive methods now available.

d) Family Planning

Family planning with engaged or married couples, in addition to contraception, includes such subjects as timing of the marriage, timing of the first child, child-spacing, deciding about total family size and the sexual adjustment of the couple. It is usually wise to advise delaying the arrival of the first child, particularly when the couple is young, until both partners want a child and are emotionally ready for it. The Committee on Human Reproduction of the American Medical Association has recommended that,[45] "In almost every marriage (even when the couple strongly desire children) it is generally advisable to postpone pregnancy for at least a few months until some of the basic adjustments have been made." At the same time, an unreasonably long delay is inadvisable since a fertility problem may remain undiscovered.

Child-spacing should be discussed during every premarital consultation and examination.

The obstetrician has the opportunity to discuss child-spacing[4][6] as a matter of routine during pregnancy and the six-week postpartum period, when a woman's motivation for family planning is usually highest. After delivery, the attitudes of the family are of basic concern to the obstetrician, the pediatrician and the family physician. It is important for the physician to know the mother's attitude and the father's attitude towards the child, and both parents' attitudes toward having additional children. A few questions may shed considerable light on these matters: "Does your husband ever take care of the baby?" "How are you managing at home?" "When did you first feel like a mother to this child?" "Was this baby a surprise?"

e) Sexual Adjustments During Pregnancy

For the overwhelming majority of women, there is no reason to avoid coitus during pregnancy. The main exceptions are patients who have habitually aborted and even in these cases, the prohibition is more empirical than objective.

Masters and Johnson[4][7] found that the principle change in coital response during pregnancy is that the resolution (See page 98) phase lasts longer and is less complete due to the vasocongestion of pregnancy. Sexual tension returns rather quickly after coitus. Many women are more responsive than usual during the first and second trimesters of pregnancy, and less responsive as they approach term. Some primigravida women reported severe breast pains during the advanced stages of sexual tension.

The same authors reported little change in sexual response in multiparas during the first three months of pregnancy, but a marked increase in eroticism and effective performance during the second trimester regardless of parity. During the last trimester, about two-thirds of the women were advised by their physicians to avoid coitus for varying periods prior to delivery. Many women lost interest in coitus during the last trimester but reported a return of sexual interest within the first two or three weeks after delivery. A few had no interest after more than two months.

Of the 77 women whose physicians warned them against coitus during the last trimester and postpartum, 68 said they were worried about their husband's reaction. Of the 71 affected husbands who took part in the study, 18 admitted that they had extramarital sexual activities during the period. Only 21 said they understood, accepted and agreed with the reasons for the ban. Almost one-third said that they did not understand the prohibition on coitus or that they doubted that the physician ever made such a recommendation. Sexual prohibitions during pregnancy may increase the instability of a marriage relationship.

Pugh and Fernandez,[48] in 1953, reported no ill effects among 600 women who had intercourse during the final weeks of pregnancy. Based on this data they did not believe abstinence is necessary as long as intercourse is physically comfortable. Masters and Johnson[49] found no increased risk of vaginal or cervical infection during the last trimester.

Resumption of coitus after the delivery should be based on the couple's sexual feelings, the healing of the episiotomy, and the presence of uterine bleeding. For many, there are no physical contraindications, although physicians empirically advise patients to avoid coitus for six weeks or more after delivery.

After childbirth, a few women desire an early return to sexual activity for general reassurance. Occasionally sexual harmony is disrupted by the presence of the new child, although serious disruption undoubtedly has deeper roles. Some women are absorbed in their new roles as mothers and have relatively little interest in sex; the husband may therefore feel like a relic from an earlier era. Nursing mothers are particularly likely to resume interest in sexual performance. Mothers who breast feed experience considerable sexual stimulation during nursing, and three of Masters and Johnson's subjects reached orgasm on such occasions. Because many women feel guilty about these erotic reactions and may refuse to nurse as a result, physicians should open this topic for discussion.

In discussing child-spacing with a nursing mother, the physician should emphasize that pregnancy may occur during lactation.

Management of Problems

a) Infertility

Infertility may be the result of sterility, anatomical abnormalities, faulty technique, misinformation or marital problems. At least half of all couples achieve pregnancy within a month of regular coitus without contraception, and more than three-fourths achieve pregnancy within six months.[50] If a couple under age 30 has failed to achieve pregnancy within a year, professional help should be sought. If the woman is over 30, help should be sought even sooner, since fertility declines with aging. Ten percent of all couples are unable to achieve pregnancy, and at least ten percent of all pregnancies end in spontaneous abortion.

The investigation of a sterility problem involves a study of both husband and wife. In taking a history from the husband, the physician should ask about the frequency of coitus, the character of ejaculation, previous illnesses (especially mumps and radiation exposure), surgical history, methods of contraception, and any previous treatment for infertility.

Physical examination of the male should include palpation of the prostate, testicles and vas deferens. A semen analysis should be performed. Many men are hypersensitive to any implication that they may be to blame for the infertility; however, the physician should explain the importance of the husband's full cooperation.

The physician should follow the same general line of questioning with the wife. He should obtain a complete history, and perform a thorough physical examination. Basal body temperatures should be determined, endometrial biopsy and tubal insufflation should be performed unless semen analysis demonstrates male sterility. In addition, hysterosalpingography, culdoscopy and laparoscopy should be performed when indicated.

The best coital position for achieving conception is that of the man above, with a pillow placed under the wife's buttocks to help prevent the escape of semen; the ballooning of the vagina during coitus creates a natural receptacle for semen. Masters and Johnson[51] believe that the likelihood of fertilization may be increased if the woman achieves plateau-phase levels of response but not orgasm, because orgasm causes the vagina to return more rapidly to its normal state and the receptacle flattens out.

Although douching is not an effective contraceptive measure, it is generally considered unwise for the woman to douche when attempting to achieve pregnancy. Remaining in bed for 35 to 40 minutes immediately after intercourse may be helpful.

Masters and Johnson[52] found that in some cases of infertility sperm from the husband and from male donors (placed with the cervix capped to prevent possible conception) were quickly inactivated in the wife's vagina. An unidentified "lethal factor" was assumed, which was avoided by introducing the husband's semen directly into the uterus, through the cervix. Several wives treated in this fashion became pregnant.

If tests reveal that the wife's blood contains antibodies to the husband's spermatozoa, the husband should wear a condom during coitus until such time as the antibodies disappear, usually six to eight weeks. When antibody titers become negative, the couple should have intercourse twice monthly without the condom at or near the time of ovulation as determined by basal body temperature. The man should then resume use of the condom, since further introduction of antigen may result in an antibody response. Where male infertility has been clearly established artificial insemination may be offered as an alternative to adoption.

An estimated 50,000 babies have been born in the United States as a result of artificial insemination. This procedure should not be recommended unless both partners who want the child favor the procedure, and are emotionally stable. The donor should, if possible, be of the same physiotype as the husband. A donor whose blood is Rh positive should be avoided for a woman who is Rh negative. The technical aspects of the procedure, including such decisions as combining the husband's semen with that of the donor, are best managed by a specialist in this field. A model consent form for artificial insemination can be found in Appendix IV.

b) Genetic Counseling

Adults with a history of disease in the family will be concerned about the likelihood of transmitting defects to their children. It may be advisable to refer such patients to available genetic counseling centers (see Appendix III). Some genetic or congenital defects may be detected in the fetus in the second trimester of pregnancy by amniocentesis,[53] and the couple can then make a more rational decision regarding continuation or interruption of the pregnancy.

c) Homosexuality

Most homosexuals who come to the physician do not consult him about their homosexuality. When a patient's homosexuality is reported in a history, it is important that the physician be nonjudgmental and avoid labeling as a problem that behavior which the patient accepts. If such a patient seeks treatment for gonorrhea, he should not necessarily be referred to a psychiatrist for treatment of his homosexuality. Even if his homosexual activity is a problem, he may not want to change his behavior pattern but may simply want to become a better-adjusted homosexual. Under such circumstances counseling by the physician may be adequate.

When referral is indicated, treatment of either men or women is best handled by a psychiatrist who is knowledgeable about the condition. Bieber[54] studied 106 male homosexuals who received psychoanalytic therapy and found that 29 of the men had become heterosexual.

In assessing the likelihood of amending homosexuality in those seeking therapy, Wahl[55] has suggested a number of critical factors:

1) The later the onset, the lesser the frequency, and the greater the conflict aroused by the homosexual behavior, the better are the chances for change.

2) Any heterosexual experience improves the chances for change.

3) If the patient shows self-discipline in other areas of his life, improvement is more likely.

4) Those who are comfortable with their own gender have a better prognosis than those who are envious of the opposite sex.

5) If the patient has a good work history, the prognosis is improved.

6) Any history of heterosexual dreaming improves the prognosis——even if the patient reacted with disgust to the dreams.

7) If the patient is strongly motivated to change, the prognosis is improved.

On the other hand, if the patient is frightened or repelled by the opposite sex, if homosexual activity seems compulsive, if the patient has little capacity for affection, if he takes great risks in seeking out homosexual partners, if there are persistent homosexual fantasies, or if there are other sexual deviations, the chances of amending the behavior are poor.

d) Extramarital and Nonmarital Sexual Behavior

In more than half of all marriages at least one partner engages in extramarital intercourse. Anything that can create personal and sexual frustration and tension within a marriage can also encourage infidelity: boredom, the fear of aging, the pressures of a job change, the pressures of moving to a new community, frustration because of abstinence during a wife's pregnancy, protracted or repeated separation from the spouse because of business or military service, overwork, anxiety caused by illness, retirement or the failure to give or receive satisfaction during marital coitus. Extra-marital sexual activity seldom can be traced to simple sexual indulgence. The partner who has an affair may feel intense guilt, which is personally destructive. The spouse, in turn, may feel a deep sense of bitterness and rejection. Yet, infidelity does not prove that the partners no longer love one another, or that the marriage is a failure. Counseling should be aimed at helping the partners assess their relationship, clarify their feelings about themselves and each other, and develop a satisfying relationship.

It is important to understand the true assessment of the infidelity in the couple's mind. The partner who engages in coitus outside of marriage may be led by guilt and self-rebuke to accept all the blame or, conversely, to put too much of it on the spouse. Occasionally, premarital coitus can create a problem in a marriage many years after the activity actually took place. The patient of 45 may be an unrealistically severe judge of actions taken 10 or even 20 years earlier and may view activities of the past as though they had taken place in the context of the present.

Male infidelity is about twice as common as female infidelity. Mace has identified five common types of such males:[5][6]

1) The libertine——The man who regularly engages in coitus outside of marriage and often gets away with his exploits. The chances of "reform" are very poor. His sexual activity is usually compulsive, and he seldom cares for women as individuals.

2) The bored husband——Many marriages grow monotonous and the husband may become involved in an extra-marital affair impetuously or by accident. A business trip or sudden temptation may be the precipitating factor. The man may love his wife and be bewildered by his behavior. In such cases, the infidelity may provide a needed jolt to a marriage which is going stale, and force husband and wife into a mutual re-assessment.

3) The curious husband——While the bored husband is trying to escape something, the curious husband is driven toward something. A man who has been faithful to his wife and reasonably happy may begin to wonder what he has missed, and, especially during his forties, be driven to find out while time remains. He may have an affair without feeling any animosity toward or loss of affection for his wife. Such affairs should probably be treated relatively lightly, because undue recrimination may lead to far more serious marital problems.

4) The disturbed husband——Men plagued by feelings of insecurity and inadequacy may try to attain a feeling of importance through the attentions of another woman. The wife is usually a contributing factor. If she can be counseled to recognize the feelings which led to her husband's infidelity, the marriage may be repaired and even improved.

5) The sexually frustrated husband——The wife who sexually starves her husband is equally responsible for his infidelity; both partners must carefully reexamine their relationship.

Wives who have been unfaithful to their husbands can be categorized in the same manner. A female's situation is complicated by the possibility of pregnancy. If pregnancy results from an illicit relationship, most women do not tell their husbands, but some inform their physicians because they need counseling. The physician should assure the patient that her confidence is secure with him. She might also appreciate knowing that people rarely disclose information under anesthesia during delivery.

Widowed and divorced persons have special counseling needs which are often not met. Divorced women are more likely than widows to engage in postmarital coitus. Kinsey found that both widowed and divorced men tended to have almost as active a coital life as they had when they were married. It is important that divorced or widowed patients resolve any feelings of guilt created by a resumption of sexual activity.

Vincent[57] observed that divorcees tend to be less conservative in their sexual behavior than other women, only partly out of a desire to find a new husband. Many men assume that the divorcee misses coitus and are quick to do her a "favor" by providing it. The divorcee may unwittingly reinforce this notion, since any discussion of sex may be taken as an invitation. Some divorced couples continue having intercourse; if the wife did not want the divorce, she may neglect contraception in the hope of getting her husband back. *After Divorce,* a book by William Goode, treats these and other problems in detail and may be usefully recommended to many divorced patients.

The physician should inform the divorcee or the widow that there is a stronger chance she will remarry than if she had never married. However, the percentage of widowed or divorced males who remarry is higher at all age ranges.

PROBABILITY OF MARRIAGE

Age	Never Married	Widow	Divorcee
35	50%	67%	94%
40	20%	50%	84%
45	12%	34%	69%

CHAPTER IX—LATE ADULTHOOD

NORMAL SEXUAL DEVELOPMENT

Some of the most mischievous myths conceived by man concern sexuality in old age: that sexual interest and ability decline after the menopause, that hysterectomies and prostatectomies reduce libido, and that both interest and ability vanish completely before or soon after sixty. These myths often have the strength of self-fulfilling prophecies. The aging man becomes anxious about his ability to perform and his anxiety diminishes or destroys his ability.

Kirkendall and Rubin[58] believe that "The premature cessation of sexual functioning may accelerate physiological and psychological aging, since disuse of any function usually leads to concomitant changes in other capacities." "The most important factor in the maintenance of effective sexuality for the aging male," according to Masters and Johnson,[59] "is consistency of active sexual expression."

Menopause, the most specific sign of sexual aging, now arrives about ten years later in life than it did at the turn of the century: the average age of onset is 50, but it may occur any time between 35 and 55. Some women anticipate the menopause with dread and many go through some period of depression. For some, the menopause is evidence that age is beginning to take its toll. For others, the end of menstruation represents the loss of a symbolic badge of femininity. Even for the woman who does not wish to bear more children, the end of fertility may be felt as a loss. For many others, the end of the possibility of pregnancy and the end of menstruation are welcome.

Menstruation ceases as the production of estrogen diminishes, the uterus and ovaries gradually atrophy, the width and length of the vagina are reduced, the introitus becomes smaller because of shrinkage of the labia majora and the clitoris may eventually be reduced in size. In the absence of estrogen, the vaginal epithelium becomes thin and the vagina becomes dry. This may result in dyspareunia.

Despite these changes, neither sexual drive nor capacity is reduced for many years. Many women report that they became more interested in sex than they had been before menopause, possibly because of the removal of all fear of pregnancy. About 60% of all women continue to have coitus at 60, and Masters and

Johnson[60] have concluded that "there is no time limit drawn by the advancing years to female sexuality."

Gonadal failure in the male is not generally related to age. Spermatogenesis and testosterone production usually decline only if a pathologic process intervenes. Adult Leydig cell failure ascribed to such causes as mosaic Kleinfelter's syndrome, mumps orchitis, surgical impairment of testicular blood supply or systemic disease results in decreased libido and potency. However, psychologic rather than organic problems account for most of the complaints of impotence in males over 40. The man may become bored with marital coitus; his wife may become bored; he may become so preoccupied with business interests that he has little time for sex; or he may reduce his potency by overindulging in food and alcohol.

Myths about sexuality in old age have interfered with the enjoyment of sex activity for centuries. The belief that a man has a limited amount of semen available in his lifetime can be traced to the ancient Chinese, who held that woman's essence, yin, was inexhaustable while man's essence, yang, was limited. The man was taught to help his wife reach orgasm whenever she desired, but to permit himself orgasm only two or three times out of ten. Loss of semen was considered a loss of the life force itself.

Fear of failure is the most powerful influence of all. Any lessening of sexual capacity can create anxiety, then fear and further reduction of capacity. Thus, a vicious cycle is established. A man already rationalizing other signs of aging, or refusing to think about them is vulnerable. When the reduced ability to reach and maintain erection is evidenced, he interprets it as the expected end of his sexually active days, and it strikes at the core of his manhood. As a result, many older persons go through an identity crisis as severe as that of adolescence.

While young persons may assume that sexual needs simply steal away or that coitus is inappropriate for older persons, good physical condition, good mental adjustment, and continued regularity of sexual activity keep the aging man or woman sexually active into the 80's or even longer. The male may remain fertile to an advanced age; men in their 80's and even 90's have produced children. In fact, some persons enjoy sex most in their old age. Kleegman[61] has reported that a woman who was frigid through two marriages began having extramarital relations at 72, and experienced orgasm for the first time at 74.

Victor Hugo at 82 told the French Senate: "Gentlemen of France, it is difficult for a man of my years to address such an august body. Almost as difficult as it is for a man of my years to make love three—no, four—times in one afternoon to a woman." Victor Hugo, of course, was a generally exceptional man, but ordinary people do maintain their sexual powers well into old age. In 1960, Newman and Nichols[62] interviewed 250 persons whose ages ranged from 60 to 93. Of the total, 149 were still living with their spouses. Fifty-four percent of these married people were sexually active, with frequency of sexual relations ranging from six times a year to three times a week. Only those over 75 reported any significant decline in activity. In 1961, Freeman[63] reported on 74 men whose average age was 71; more than 75% said they felt sexual desire; 55% were potent. Of those 80 years old, 22% reported sexual desire and 17% were capable of sexual relations.

THE ROLE OF THE PHYSICIAN

Prevention and Counseling

When coitus has been abandoned for a long time, older men and women can be helped to return to satisfying sexual activity. Treatment of all older patients should first include therapy for any physical problems, followed by counseling, preferably of both partners. Counseling should be directed toward relieving anxieties and tensions and toward educating the couple about coital methods appropriate for their changed capacities. Usually, the physician must introduce the subject of sexuality with older patients, since few of them will introduce it on their own.

Management of Problems

In the aging woman, dyspareunia at the time of penetration can result from lack of lubrication, reduction in the size of the introitus, vulvitis due to bacterial or mycotic infections, long-standing anxiety, or male ineptness. Dyspareunia after penetration may be caused by perineorrhaphy scars, senile vaginitis and vaginal atresia. If a man is already having trouble maintaining an erection, his awareness that the vagina is dry and the introitus painfully sensitive will further inhibit him.

Estrogen therapy, either systemic or local, will correct vaginal dryness. Estrogen replacement also may help maintain the elasticity of the vagina. Relaxed precoital sexual play will help some older women to develop adequate vaginal secretions. A gel lubricant also may be useful. The reduction in the size of the clitoris, which may occur at age 60 or 70, seems not to be accompanied by a loss of clitoral responsiveness.

An effective means of improving erectile ability in the aging man is to alter the pattern of sex activity. Facilitation of potency usually can be accomplished with no more than changes in the amount and the methods of stimulation. If the penis is pushed downward, pressure and stimulation are increased. Stimulation of the base of the penis puts pressure on the major blood vessels to retain blood. The couple should be counseled that potency may be improved with the cooperation of both partners, and that the male, who once could be quickly aroused cerebrally, probably would be helped by manipulation of his penis. The problem is not that the aging man cannot respond, but that he requires more stimulation and more time for response. He can reach and maintain erection on most occasions. If full erection is not reached, intromission still can be successfully accomplished with a partially erect penis; full erection will usually be attained after the first few strokes. The aging man need not expect to ejaculate during each act of coitus.

In all sexual problems, it is important for the physician to learn whether the problem is of recent origin or a chronic one which has been aggravated. If a condition has existed for many years, the prospects for improvement may appear relatively poor. Nonetheless, when simple misunderstanding is a primary factor, the effect of counseling may be dramatic. Many aging couples have developed habits based on conditions which no longer exist. A wife may have been anxious about coitus early in the marriage because of fear of pregnancy, and the husband may have concluded that she didn't enjoy sex. When her fear of pregnancy ceased to exist, she may have developed a new interest in coitus which she has been unable to communicate to her husband. All couples, young and old, should be encouraged to conduct their sex lives in terms of the conditions of the present, and to regard relaxed and pleasurable sexual activity as a fitting part of marital life throughout their lives together.

The sexual activity of residents of homes for the aged often shocks and upsets staff members, who are uncertain how to handle such situations. If residents are discovered masturbating or petting or having intercourse, the proper approach for staff personnel is to close the door and insure the privacy of the individual(s) involved.

REFERENCES—PART II

1. Mead M, cited by Greenson PR: Masculinity and femininity in our time, in Wahl CW (ed): *Sexual Problems, Diagnosis and Treatment in Medical Practice.* New York, Free Press, 1967, p 44.

2. Greenson PR: Masculinity and femininity in our time, in Wahl CW (ed): *Sexual Problems, Diagnosis and Treatment in Medical Practice.* New York, Free Press, 1967, pp 40-41.

3. Money J, cited by Coombs RH: The socialization of male and female: Sex status and sex roles, in Vincent CE (ed): *Human Sexuality in Medical Education and Practice.* Springfield, Ill, Charles C Thomas Publisher, 1968, pp 250-251.

4. Broderick CB: Preadolescent sexual behavior. *Med. Aspects Human Sexuality* 2:28, 1968.

5. Vincent CE: Sexual interest in someone older or younger. *Med. Aspects Human Sexuality* 2: 7, 1968.

6. Loeb MB, cited by Kirkendall LA, Libby RW: Sex and interpersonal relationships, in Broderick CB, Bernard J (eds): *The Individual, Sex and Society.* Baltimore, Johns Hopkins Press, 1969, p 123.

7. Schofield M, cited by Kirkendall LA, Libby RW: Sex and interpersonal relationships, in Broderick CB, Bernard J (eds): *The Individual, Sex and Society.* Baltimore, Johns Hopkins Press, 1969, p 124.

8. Kinsey AC, Pomeroy WB, Martin CE: *Sexual Behavior in the Human Male.* Philadelphia, WB Saunders Co, 1948, p 176.

9. Kirkendall LA, Rubin I: Sexuality and the life cycle. *SIECUS Study Guide* No. 8: 16, 1969.

10. Broderick CB: Preadolescent sexual behavior. *Med Aspects Human Sexuality* 2: 28, 1968.

11. Bryant FT, cited by Sacks SR: Marital interactions: Insights for physicians' roles in sex education. *Pediat Clin N Amer* 16: 461, 1969.

12. Margolis FJ: Preparing parents and the community. *Pediat Clin N Amer* 16: 472, 1969.

13. Finch SM: Sex education: The role of the physician. *U Mich Med Center J* 33: 208, 1967.

14. Money J: Sex errors of the body, in Broderick CB, Bernard J (eds): *The Individual, Sex and Society.* Baltimore, Johns Hopkins Press, 1969, p 289.

15. Kinsey AC, Pomeroy WB, Martin CE: *Sexual Behavior in the Human Female.* Philadelphia, WB Saunders Co, 1953, p 103.

16. Lidz T: *The Person.* New York, Basic Books, 1968, p 308.

17. Hutton L, cited by Rubin I: *Sexual Life After Sixty.* New York, Signet Books, New American Library Inc, 1965, p 223.

18. Kinsey AC, Pomeroy WB, Martin CE: *Sexual Behavior in the Human Female.* Philadelphia, WB Saunders Co, 1953, p 390.

19. Group for the Advancement of Psychiatry: *Normal Adolescence: Its Dy-*

namics and Impact. New York, Charles Scribner's Sons, 1968, p 35.

20. Ibid, pp 44-45.

21. Calderone MS: The married teen-ager. *J Int Coll Surg* 43: 442-447, 1965.

22. Reed DM: What is the norm for sexual relations in marriage? *Med Aspects Human Sexuality* 1: 6, 1967.

23. Lidz T: *The Person.* New York, Basic Books, 1968, p 311.

24. Pomeroy WB: Homosexuality, transvestism and transsexualism, in Vincent CE (ed): *Human Sexuality in Medical Education and Practice.* Springfield, Ill, Charles C Thomas Publisher, 1968, pp 368-396.

25. Ibid, p 372.

26. Kinsey AC, Pomeroy WB, Martin CE: *Sexual Behavior in the Human Female.* Philadelphia, WB Saunders Co, 1953, p 475.

27. Calderwood DD: Teen-age sex questions, in Rubin I, Kirkendall LA (eds): *Sex in the Adolescent Years.* New York, Association Press, 1968, p 56.

28. Reiss IL: *The Social Context of Premarital Sexual Permissiveness.* New York, Holt Rinehart & Winston Inc, 1967, pp 28-30.

29. Vincent CE: The pregnant single college girl. *J Amer Coll Health Assoc* 15: 51, 1967.

30. Lief HI: The Physician and Family Planning. *JAMA* 197: 128, 1966.

31. Vincent CE: Unmarried mothers and pregnant brides, in Vincent CE (ed): *Human Sexuality in Medical Education and Practice.* Springfield, Ill, Charles C Thomas Publisher, 1968, p 465.

32. Ibid, p 464.

33. Ibid, p 467.

34. Sarrel PM: Teen-age pregnancy. *Pediat Clin N Amer* 16: 347, 1969.

35. Ibid, p 349.

36. Trilling L, cited by Gagnon JH: Sexuality and sexual learning in the child, in Vincent CE (ed): *Human Sexuality in Medical Education and Practice.* Springfield, Ill, Charles C Thomas Publisher, 1968, p 220.

37. Ibid, p 221.

38. Kinsey AC, Pomeroy WB, Martin CE: Masturbation: *Sexual Behavior in the Human Female.* Philadelphia, WB Saunders Co, 1953, pp 142-143.

39. Reiss IL: *The Social Context of Premarital Sexual Permissiveness.* New York, Holt Rinehart & Winston Inc, 1967, pp 141-156.

40. Rubin I: *Sexual Life After Sixty.* New York, Signet Books, New American Library Inc, 1965, p 179.

41. Pomeroy WB: Homosexuality, transvestism and transsexualism, in Vincent CE (ed): *Human Sexuality in Medical Education and Practice.* Springfield, Ill, Charles C Thomas Publisher, 1968, p 372.

42. Bene E: On the genesis of female homosexuality. *Brit J Psych* 3: 818-821, 1965.

43. Pomeroy WB: Homosexuality, transvestism and transsexualism, in Vincent CE (ed): *Human Sexuality in Medical Education and Practice.* Springfield, Ill, Charles C Thomas Publisher, 1968, p 372.

44. Andrews WC: Oral contraception: *Obstetrical and Gynecological Survey.* Baltimore, Williams & Wilkins Co, 1971, pp 477-499.

45. Control of fertility: Committee on Human Reproduction of the American Medical Association. *JAMA* 194: 462-470, 1965.

46. Calderone MS: *The Manual on Family Planning and Contraceptive Practice.* Williams & Wilkins Co, 1971, Second Edition.

47. Masters WH, Johnson VE: *Human Sex-*

ual Response. Boston, Little Brown & Co, 1966, pp 141-168.

48. Pugh WE, Fernandez FL: *Coitus in Late Pregnancy.* Obstetrics and Gynecology 2: 636, 1953.

49. Masters WH, Johnson VE: *Human Sexual Response.* Boston, Little Brown & Co, 1966, pp 141-168.

50. David ME: Management of infertility. *JAMA* 201: 1030, 1967.

51. Brecher R, Brecher E: *An Analysis of Human Sexual Response.* New York, Signet Books, New American Library Inc, 1966, pp 96-99.

52. Ibid, pp 96-99.

53. Nadler HL, Gerbie AB: Role of amniocentesis in the intrauterine detection of genetic disorders. *New Eng J Med* 282: 596, 1970.

54. Bieber I: Advising the homosexual. *Med Aspects Human Sexuality* 2: 34-39, 1968.

55. Wahl CW: Advising the homosexual, in Wahl CW (ed): *Sexual Problems, Diagnosis and Treatment in Medical Practice.* New York, Free Press, 1967, pp 201-203.

56. Mace DR: Problems of marital infidelity, in Klemer RH (ed): *Counseling in Marital and Sexual Problems.* Baltimore, Williams & Wilkins Co, 1965, pp 161-166.

57. Vincent CE: Illicit pregnancies among married and divorced females, in Vincent CE (ed): *Human Sexuality in Medical Education and Practice.* Springfield, Ill, Charles C Thomas Publisher, 1968, p 475.

58. Kirkendall LA, Rubin I: Sexuality and the life cycle. *SIECUS Study Guide* No. 8: 24, 1969.

59. Masters WH, Johnson VE: *Human Sexual Response.* Boston, Little Brown & Co, 1966, p 262.

60. Ibid, p 247.

61. Kleegman S, cited by Rubin I: *Sexual Life After Sixty.* New York, Signet Books, New American Library Inc, 1965, p 34.

62. Newman G, Nichols CR, cited by Rubin I: *Sexual Life After Sixty.* New York, Signet Books, New American Library Inc, 1965, p 34.

63. Freeman JT, cited by Rubin I: *Sexual Life After Sixty.* New York, Signet Books, New American Library Inc, 1965, pp 35-36.

PART 3

THE PHYSICIAN AND HUMAN SEXUAL RESPONSE

PART III

THE PHYSICIAN AND HUMAN SEXUAL RESPONSE

CHAPTER X—THE SEXUAL RELATIONSHIP

Sex, one of man's primary pleasures, is also a target for a variety of physical and psychologic dysfunctions. It has been estimated that less than half of all Americans lead sex lives which they consider satisfactory. Most persons experience a sexual difficulty at some point during their lives. The few studies which have been made indicate that physicians in office practice discover sexual problems in roughly one patient in seven. Sexual problems may present themselves in all medical fields. Many physicians have been insensitive to them, perhaps because they felt that they had neither the training nor the experience to deal with such problems. It should now be clear that physicians can relieve some sexual dysfunction by counseling their patients about the basic nature of human sexual response, and that they have a responsibility to be sensitive to sexual problems.

Human sexuality should not be viewed narrowly in terms of sexual response, and sexual response should not be regarded as primarily a physiologic activity. Masters has said that, "there is no such thing as the pure physiology of sexual response." Human beings function sexually as whole persons and anything which is capable of undermining them personally is capable of undermining their sexual response. A young wife may be sexually unresponsive because her husband cannot make their income cover their expenses. A wife who always tears her husband down may undercut his confidence sufficiently to create premature ejaculation or even impotence. Relatives in a home may create enough tension to produce impairment of sexual response.

Mistaken beliefs about the roles of the sexual partners also create disturbances. Both men and women commonly assume that a man is instinctively able to sense what a woman wants in the way of sexual stimulation. As a matter of fact the woman's desires depend on many variables, and they cannot be conveyed in a subliminal or mystic way. Communication is vital to sexual satisfactions, and sexual performance cannot be memorized or programmed and remain a pleasure. It is a common assumption that sexual expertise is the man's responsibility, and yet the female's sexual response, though analogous, is different from the male response, and is something he can never experience. Therefore, he must be guided by the woman herself.

Seventy-five percent of the married couples who seek counseling at the Marriage Council of Philadelphia at the University of Pennsylvania have a significant sexual problem. In 15% of the total cases, a sexual problem is the primary cause of the marital problem. While it is possible that some couples who are sexually incompatible lead satisfactory married lives, usually marital compatibility and sexual compatibility go closely together. Coitus is one of the deepest forms of marital communication, and when there is a failure to communicate sexually, there usually is a communication failure in other areas as well. Sexual response, therefore, cannot be compartmentalized or mechanized if the physician is to treat the whole patient effectively. No sexual dysfunction within marriage is the problem of one person alone. As Masters and Johnson[1] aptly observed, "there is no such thing as an uninvolved partner in any marriage in which there is some form of sexual inadequacy."

Many common stress situations can create sexual problems. The pressures of business may so absorb the man that he does not pay enough attention to his wife, who may retaliate, consciously or unconsciously, in the marital bed. Separations because of business or military service are a common cause of strain. Retirement can undermine a man's self-respect and he may demand increased attention from his wife for reassurance about his own worth. Too much leisure time after the children have grown can have a similar effect on a wife. Simple boredom can also interfere with the sexual relationship: some people lose so much interest in each other, or allow their sexual activity to become so monotonous, that they simply abandon coitus for work, reading or even television. Auerback[2] has reported that when a cable TV strike shut down all TV broadcasts in a West Virginia city in early 1968, the birth rate nine months later was triple the usual. The same thing was true of the New York City blackout in 1965.

Differences in social or family background can create conflicting ideas about what is acceptable in foreplay and coitus. A wife with a conservative background may be shocked and repelled if her husband suggests oral-genital contact. He may be hurt and puzzled by her reaction, or conclude that she is sexually inhibited.

Shulman[3] has listed six basic and healthy uses of sexual activity: reproduction, pleasure, a feeling of belonging, sharing, consolation (loss or humiliation often increase sexual appetite), and self-affirmation. To Shulman's surprise, a female patient once doubled the list by adding encouragement of the partner, relaxation, distraction, physical closeness, physical rejuvenation, the pleasure of giving and, more questionably, "for getting acquainted." Shulman listed several misuses of sex: rebellion, distance (as in exhibitionism), domination, suffering and martyrdom.

SEXUAL ATTITUDES IN MARRIAGE

In general, sex is a more important force in married life for the man than for the woman, although this may be changing rapidly because of the emergence of different attitudes and demands on the part of the wife. Sexual enjoyment apparently has a strong effect on marital satisfaction for the male, while marital satisfaction has an effect on sexual enjoyment for the female. Gebhard[4] has reported a statistical correlation between marital satisfaction and female orgasmic ability in both highly successful and highly unsuccessful marriages; in all intermediate categories, the correlation was unclear. Gebhard has suggested that marital happiness may be the extra factor needed to enable a mildly responsive woman to reach orgasm, while marital unhappiness may prevent a mildly responsive woman from reaching orgasm.

Husbands who believe that their wives enjoy sex as much as they do tend to report more satisfaction with their marriages than those who believe that their sex drives are stronger than their wives'. Sexual frustration damages the marital relationship much less for the wife. Wallin and Clark[5] found that women who were unsatisfied sexually but were deeply involved in religious activities were about as content with their marriages as wives who were sexually satisfied. Men who were sexually unsatisfied and religiously involved were generally unhappy about their marriages.

In some marriages, the wife's sexual drive is stronger than the husband's, although it may be difficult for either to admit it. In a survey[6] of middle class couples one wife in six reported a greater desire for coitus than that reported by the husband. These wives reported that both they and their husbands liked to engage in coitus about 12 times a month. The husbands of these wives reported that both they and their wives liked to engage in coitus about six times a month. If a couple is happy in their sexual relationship, it makes no difference whether they have the same attitude toward sex. Whenever a patient has a sexual problem, it is important for the physician to learn the attitudes of both husband and wife toward the problem, toward one another, and toward sex itself.

CHAPTER XI—THE SEXUAL RESPONSE SYSTEM

The anatomy and physiology of human response to sexual stimuli have been investigated during the past decade by Masters and Johnson by direct observation and measurements of the physical changes which develop as males and females respond to effective sexual stimulation. The clinical investigations were accompanied by interrogation of the laboratory study-subjects and clinical research populations to obtain material of significant behavioral content. The extensive statistics compiled by direct interrogation by Kinsey et al reflect patterns of sexual behavior between the years 1938 and 1952, but they were not intended to interpret physiologic and psychologic responses to sexual stimulation.

Masters and Johnson established the anatomy of human response to sexual stimulation and observed and recorded physiologic variables such as intensity and duration of individual reaction patterns. In order to provide structuring and a continuum of response, these investigators arbitrarily divided the cycle of sexual response into four specific phases: (1) the excitation phase, (2) the plateau phase, (3) the orgasmic phase and (4) the resolution phase.

Although there are many variations in the male response, the variations are related to duration rather than intensity and one basic pattern exists for the male. Intensity as well as duration of response are variable factors in the female.

The two basic responses to sexual stimulation are widespread vasocongestion and increase in muscle tension. These reactions are more severe in the plateau and orgasmic phases. Masters repeatedly demonstrated that, although there are anatomical differences in the male and female reproductive organ systems, direct parallels exist in the sexual response of both sexes to a great extent. It is the similarities and not the differences in the anatomy and physiology of response in the male and female that are emphasized by the observations and measurements done on the study-subjects.

The four separate phases of anatomic and physiologic reaction have been summarized briefly.[7]

EXCITEMENT

Men may attain erection either from cerebral imagery or direct stimulation of erogenous areas. There is considerable lengthening of the urethra during erection, the testes are elevated in the scrotal sac and there is notable tensing and thickening of the scrotal integument.

In a female, lubricating fluid, a mucoid transudate, appears in the vagina within 30 seconds of somatic or psychic stimulation. This "sweating" reaction begins on the walls of the vagina, where tiny beads of moisture coalesce to create a film of lubrication. Under stimulation, both the glans and shaft of the clitoris swell because of vascular engorgement. The rapidity and degree of response of the clitoris depends upon whether stimulation is direct or indirect and on individual variations. The nipples also become erect and enlarge. Late in the phase, the breasts increase in size as a result of deep vasocongestion. The labia minora also swell, and in nulliparous women the labia majora flatten and undergo anterolateral elevation; in parous women they become markedly distended with venous blood and move away from the midline to a slight degree. The vaginal barrel expands and lengthens, while the uterus is elevated, creating a chamber of the inner two-thirds of the vagina. The vagina eventually lengthens from 8 or 9 cm. to 11 or 12 cm. At the level of the cervix, the width increases from about 3 or 4 cm. to 6.75 or 7.25 cm. Muscles become tense in both men and women, and a faint flush may begin over the epigastrium and then spread.

PLATEAU

During the plateau phase, the corona glandis increases in diameter slightly, and the elevation of the testes continues; complete elevation of the testes is characteristic of impending orgasm. The testes also increase in size. The penis may emit a few drops of fluid from the Cowper's glands. The fluid is not semen, its function is unknown, but it may contain a few spermatozoa.

The woman's vagina becomes more engorged during the plateau phase, and the outer third of the lumen shrinks in diameter as much as 50%, so that the vagina actually grips the penis. Stimulation of the male is thereby greatly increased. The gripping action makes the size of the penis of minor importance in coitus. The uterus continues to be elevated and may increase in size from 50 to 100 percent as a result of vasocongestion. The

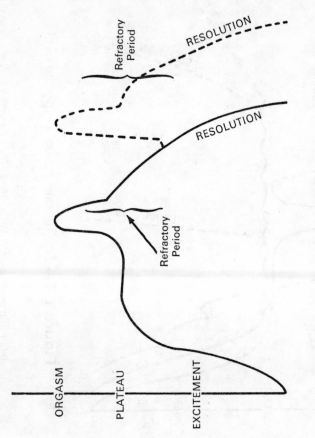

Figure 1-1——The male sexual response cycle

98

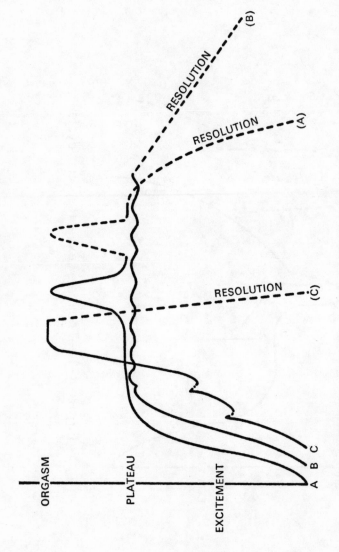

Figure 1-2—The female sexual response cycle

Reprinted with permission of Little, Brown & Co.: *Human Sexual Response*

inner portion of the vagina continues to expand. The clitoris retracts from the vaginal entrance, and its previously elongated shaft shrinks again. The labia majora may continue changes begun in the excitement phase, but do not change in late plateau. The labia minora noticeably change color——from red to deep wine color in parous women, and from pink to bright red in nulliparous women. This "sex skin" coloration signifies intense sexual tensions and is characteristic of impending orgasm if effective stimulation techniques are maintained.

ORGASM

Orgasm for the male begins with a series of contractions of the periurethral musculature. As fluids collect in the prostatic urethra near the base of the penis, the man may experience the first sensation of orgasm. Men may be aware of the beginning of orgasm a few seconds before the contractions actually take place. Thereafter, the urethral bulb and the penile urethra both undergo a series of rhythmic contractions which expel the seminal fluid from the penis. The ejaculate consists of prostatic fluid and the contents of the ampulla accompanied by simultaneous expulsion of seminal-vesicle content. The contractions then gradually decrease in frequency and intensity.

During orgasm, the female experiences a series of muscular contractions in the outer third of the vagina. The first contractions are four-fifths of a second apart. Subsequent contractions are less intense and come at greater intervals. The number of contractions may range from three to twelve. The uterus also contracts rhythmically.

Muscles of the neck, face and abdomen sometimes contract severely enough to produce muscular aches the next day. In a relatively mild orgasm, the woman's introitus, labia minora, clitoral area and vaginal passage experience contractions. In more intense orgasm, many adjacent pelvic structures also contract. In very intense orgasm, all the voluntary muscles of the abdomen may contract.

During orgasm, pulse rate, blood pressure and breathing speed up in both sexes, and the sex flush becomes widespread and intense. Respiration is often 40 per minute or higher. Heart rate is usually from 110 to 180 beats per minute. Systolic blood pressure rises by 40 to 100 mm Hg in males and 30 to 80 mm Hg in females. Diastolic pressure rises 20 to 50 mm Hg in males and 20 to 40 mm Hg in females.

RESOLUTION

After orgasm, the man quickly loses erection in two stages. The first stage is rapid but incomplete. A second, longer stage brings the penis back to normal size. The testes and the scrotum descend to their normal positions at varying rates of speed; pulse, blood pressure and breathing gradually return to normal; and any sex flush quickly disappears.

A light film of moisture appears over the body of about one-third of both men and women, sometimes it is limited only to the hands and feet; the cause is not known.

Following orgasm, the male goes through a refractory period during which he is unable to ejaculate. The length of this period varies greatly, and increases with aging.

After orgasm, the woman's areolas, clitoris, uterus and vaginal barrel return to normal usually within half an hour. Unlike the man, the woman requires no restorative period and is capable of a second orgasm almost immediately. Some women are able to achieve as many as a dozen orgasms during coitus without respite.

THE FEMALE ORGASM

That a "decent" woman could enjoy coitus at all was considered unthinkable for many years, and echoes of that attitude have persisted. Today, attitudes have changed, perhaps too far in the other direction: many members of both sexes are overly concerned about the frequency and intensity of the female orgasm.

Several studies suggest that the female's ability to reach orgasm is closely related to the length of both foreplay and intromission. Gebhard[8] has reported that three-fifths of the women he studied almost always reached orgasm if foreplay lasted longer than 20 minutes; half almost always reached orgasm after 15 to 20 minutes of foreplay, and two-fifths almost always reached orgasm when foreplay lasted one to ten minutes. When foreplay continued for more than 20 minutes only 7% of the women never experienced orgasm.

Gebhard concluded that intromission of less than one minute was too brief to permit most women to reach orgasm; that intromission of one to 11 minutes would bring about half of all women to orgasm almost all the time; and that intromission lasting more than 16 minutes would bring almost all women to "the limits of their orgastic capacities." Since Kinsey et al found that three out of four men reach orgasm in less than two minutes after entry, and many within 10 to 20 seconds,[9] the obvious cause of much female inadequacy is the male.

Studies indicate that about 10% to 15% of married women never achieve orgasm during coitus, while about 40% achieve it virtually every time they have coitus. The intensity of the orgasmic experience varies from woman to woman and from occasion to occasion. Occasionally, orgasm is the explosive sort memorialized in some fictional works. More often, it is quieter and less intense. Masters and Johnson suggest that there is little short-range concern about failure to reach orgasm, but that repeated failure may result in chronic pelvic congestion.

Female responsiveness and sexual drive are much more variable than in the male. Kinsey et al found that the average college man had some sexual outlet two or three times per week, and 10% had as many as seven orgasms a week. About half the college women in his sample experienced orgasm only a few times during their four years, while a few averaged more than 50 orgasms per week throughout college.

Research has demonstrated that women are more likely to reach multiple orgasm through self-stimulation than through coitus, when the man's inability to maintain erection and postpone ejaculation is a limiting factor. During self-stimulation, a woman may experience as many as 20 orgasms before becoming satiated and exhausted. Some subjects found stimulation by electric vibrators less tiring than manual stimulation. Masters and Johnson concluded that the average woman could continue such stimulation for an hour or more and reach as many as 50 orgasms; the ability to reach multiple orgasm is not limited to a few women. Further, they found wives who had never achieved orgasm by any means were able, after short-term therapy, to achieve intense multiple orgasm. Having experienced this once, they were able to achieve orgasms more easily and rapidly thereafter.

There may be unfortunate consequences as well as benefits in the newly discovered wonders of multiple orgasm and the greatest danger is that it will be enshrined, as simultaneous orgasm has been, as the "proper goal of all enlightened husbands and wives." In actuality, fewer than 15% of all women do reach multiple orgasm. Multiple orgasms should not be sought as a right or a duty, and the husband who is determined to achieve it for his wife may well experience unnecessary feelings of inadequacy.

Simultaneous orgasm is not a useful goal, and there are even some arguments against it. At the moment of climax, the male's tendency is to plunge deep into the vagina and remain there, with perhaps one or two more deep thrusts at the end of orgasm. The female's tendency at climax is to continue her rhythmic motions, perhaps increasing the rate of the thrusts and the pressure on the vulval area.[10] The two tendencies are obviously incompatible.

Enjoyment of coitus, however, is not necessarily an indication of the strength of the woman's sexual drive. "A woman who has been sexually responsive during coitus may have no specific afterthoughts of sex or desires for sexual intercourse for a period of weeks, months, or even longer" Kephart[11] has written. "Extended periods without coitus may well have no adverse effects. In short, although she actively enjoys coitus when it occurs, her sexual needs remain low as compared with most men." The woman's sexual drive is also cyclical, unlike the man's. The peak of sexual interest usually comes at the time of ovulation and at the time before menstruation. Coitus during menstruation is not harmful, although it may be unesthetic to some persons.

CHAPTER XII——METHODS OF COITUS

Undue concentration on coital technique is always inhibiting and creates more problems than it solves. Moreover, technique alone can never produce satisfying sexual response just as giving a man a dictionary does not make him a poet. Nonetheless, basic information about coital technique may be helpful to many patients who have allowed coitus to become routine or who are ignorant or misinformed about sexual arousal.

FOREPLAY

There is no precise moment when love play can be said to begin: the mood for sexual activity at midnight may have been set over breakfast, and the act of undressing may inaugurate sexual stimulation. Sight, sound, smell, touch and fantasy all have roles in sexual arousal, and men are particularly amenable to sexual fantasy. Men are twice as likely as women to have erotic dreams resulting in orgasm. About nine out of ten men fantasize when masturbating, and their fantasies are usually more bizarre than the female's.

During foreplay, many erogenous zones of both sexes are stimulated by touching, fondling, kissing, squeezing or licking: the mouth, nose, eyes, ears, vagina, clitoris, breasts, penis, anus, mons area, inner thighs, lower abdomen and scrotum. Touching or kissing almost any area of the body can produce purely sensual pleasure and the ability to accept relaxed pleasure from physical stimulation contributes greatly to one's ability to enjoy coitus. Several erotic areas, however, may become overly sensitive from prolonged stimulation. The woman's breasts, the clitoris and the glans penis are particularly sensitive. Lengthy manipulation of the clitoris can actually make the glans painful and cause the woman to lose sexual excitement. When the clitoral shaft shrinks and retreats from the entrance to the vagina during the plateau phase, it may be hard to locate. If the man is convinced that the clitoris must be found and manipulated, the woman may lose interest while he is conducting his search. In recent years, there has been a steady increase in the acceptance and use of oral-genital contact as part of foreplay.

COITAL POSITIONS

The man above: In the most commonly used position, the man's thighs may be either inside or outside those of the woman, and the woman may elevate her pelvic region by using a pillow. The man generally controls the pace of movement, and the woman synchronizes with him. With the man's thighs outside the woman's, clitoral contact is increased, but the closing of the woman's thighs also increases the pressure of the labia on the penis and increases the erotic stimulation for both partners, which will be undesirable if the man tends to reach orgasm too rapidly. The raising of the woman's pelvic region, by use of a pillow or by the woman putting her legs over the man's shoulders, reduces clitoral contact to a minimum and permits deep penetration by the penis. The disadvantages of the position are that the man must support his weight on his legs, arms and hands and so is unable to caress the woman, and the man cannot pause for very long in order to slow down his response.

The woman above: The woman's thighs may be inside or outside the man's, or the woman may bring her knees alongside the man's hips and take a sitting position. She controls the movements of coitus and the pressure on the penis and clitoris, leaning backward to increase pressure on the penis, or leaning forward, to increase pressure on the clitoris. By leaning all the way forward and pressing against the man, she can reduce the movement of the penis and slow the man's response, while moving her hips for clitoral stimulation. As she nears orgasm, she can raise her hips and allow the man to set the pace to his own level of response. The man is free to caress the woman's breasts, hips, clitoris and buttocks. The disadvantage of this position is that the greatest physical demands are made on the woman, whose ability to caress the man is limited.

The lateral position: This is a variation of the woman-above position, and it is recommended by Masters and Johnson[12] as the most effective position for mutual satisfaction. The woman lies partly above the man, with her head beside his, with her lower leg extending between his legs, and her upper leg over his upper one. His lower leg is bent at the knee flat on the bed to cradle her as they face each other. This position offers the greatest control of male ejaculation: he can stop pelvic thrusting at any time, and the woman has total freedom of pelvic movement against the erect penis. Both are relaxed, and have a free hand for caressing.

To assume it most easily requires converting from the woman-above position. Masters and Johnson report that the position can be learned fairly easily, and couples who become comfortable with it use it as least 75% of the time.

Side by side: In this position, the man and woman lie facing each other. The woman may put one or both legs outside the man's. Each is free to caress the other, and there is a minimum of physical strain for both. The position offers great control, and it is often recommended for couples who are having coital problems or are just beginning to have intercourse together. Because of the lack of strain, it is recommended during pregnancy.

The disadvantage is that movement, clitoral contact and penetration are quite limited.

Other positions include the *rear-entry position:* The man kneels or lies behind the woman, and the penis enters the vagina from below her buttocks. The partners may lie side by side, with the man leaning slightly backward and curving his pubic region under hers. The partners may also kneel, with the man's hips being lowered beneath the woman's buttocks. Or they may kneel with the woman resting her chest on her knees and her head on the bed, and the man kneeling behind her in an upright position, which is called the *knee-chest position.*

These positions are usually used for variety. The man's hands are free to caress the woman, but there is little or no clitoral contact and penetration is limited.

Several standing and sitting positions also have the appeal of variety but are probably too gymnastic for most people. In the simplest of the sitting positions, the man sits on a chair or bed, and the woman faces him and lowers herself into a sitting position high on his flanks. There is maximum clitoral pressure, the penis is fully caressed, the woman can control the movements and the degree of arousal, and each partner is free to caress the other. The disadvantages are that movement is restricted, penetration may be too deep, and the position is tiring.

There are three basic questions which the physician should ask in evaluating a sexual problem:

1) Did the problem precede the present relationship? If a problem stems from childhood, the patient probably should be referred for psychiatric treatment. If the response is a conditioned one, such as premature ejaculation associated with a history of petting to orgasm, it may be treatable by the general physician.

2) Is the problem part of the relationship? If a problem is traceable to guilt, fear or any other emergency emotion, and if the physician can get both partners to his office, there is a reasonable chance that counseling will be effective. If the problem is chronic and deep-seated, referral to a psychiatrist, other physician or marriage counselor may be indicated.

3) Is the problem a function of ignorance? Many patients are factually uninformed, and others are unaware of important factors in sexual response. Many women and older men are unaware that they require extensive stimulation for arousal, and some patients do not realize that the response of the partner is itself an important source of stimulation. When a problem is traceable to inadequate preparation, ignorance, bias or insensitivity to the needs of the partner, the physician can effectively help with information and counseling.

GOALS OF TREATMENT AND COUNSELING

Once the problem has been evaluated, the physician may proceed with treatment and counseling. Whenever possible, both partners should be included in therapy. If the spouse is reluctant, it may be useful to point out that his help is needed ("Come in and help me and your wife deal with this problem"). Masters and Johnson[13] believe that isolating one partner from therapy "may actually destroy or negate much therapeutic effort, initially from lack of knowledge and understanding and finally from frustration." If the wife of an impotent man is not involved in therapy, she will not know what she should and should not do during sexual activities. Similarly, a wife may be sustaining a symptom which she complains about; a frigid, masochistic wife may need her husband's unfaithfulness to keep up her sense of victimization. Many authorities believe that counseling a wife alone is, in Vincent's words,[14] "waving a red flag to the husband reared in a society wherein masculinity is equated with knowing all about sex."

Sexual response is unique among physiologic drives in that it can be delayed or denied, even for a lifetime. Thought and action may be separated in the sexual act, and the participant then assumes the additional role of a spectator. Under these circumstances, fears about performance are very likely to come to the fore. Sexual performance cannot be willed successfully and attempts to do so only remove the activity ever farther from its natural context. It may also be beneficial to point out to the patient that the state of passion usually heightens any existing fear and anxiety. The physician's goal, therefore, is to put sexual activity back into the context of a natural expression. In trying to help his patients reach this state of sexual self-acceptance, the physician should bear several basic principles in mind.

Sexual response is more than mechanics, and problems of sexual response usually require more than a mechanistic approach to therapy. However, instruction in some specific techniques may improve sexual response. The usefulness of any technique is directly related to its ability to make coitus more, not less, natural.

No sexual dysfunction within a relationship is the concern of one person; both sexual partners are always involved. When one person in this reciprocal process has a difficulty, the other is inevitably affected, and the partner's response will further affect the dysfunction. Sexual problems may either spring from or create other problems in a relationship, but whether they are cause or effect, they are almost always accompanied by other failures within the relationship.

In counseling patients with sexual dysfunctions, the physician should neither dismiss a problem nor attempt to go beyond his competence. In determining whether to suggest any approach, the physician should always keep in mind his patients' feelings and attitudes, the suitability or unsuitability of the approach for the particular couple, the advantages and limitations of any technique, and the possibility that the patients may require help from a more specialized source.

Touch is the most important sense involved in sexual activity and dysfunctional partners may need to learn or relearn how to touch each other. Masters and Johnson begin all forms of sex therapy by asking their patients to explore each other's bodies while they are nude, avoiding the genital areas and the woman's breasts. Thus, partners learn to enjoy sensuous, but not specifically sexual pleasure, relaxed and naturally. No specific goal can be set for any point in the treatment program. It is important to emphasize that touch is not a textbook exercise which can be assigned and completed; it is an activity to be rediscovered.

Throughout counseling, the physician should discover the patient's feelings about the subject under discussion. If the patient seems afraid to acknowledge or discuss his feelings, questions requiring factual material may elicit his feelings or undercut his denial of them. A discussion of the specific influence of emotions on sexual function will reassure the patient that he is not unusual because his feelings affect his sexual performance. One of the important tasks in sexual counseling is to help the patient to understand the environmental influences and experiences that produced these feelings.

THE PREMARITAL EXAMINATION AND COUNSELING

The overwhelming majority of young people welcome the reassurance of a physical examination and information about sex in marriage, sexual adjustment and contraception.[15] Ideally, counseling should be conducted in three sessions, the last of which should take place after the wedding. Although it is often difficult to get the prospective groom to appear, he should be seen at least once, both alone and with his fiancee. Whether the examination consists of one visit or three, a physician's premarital counseling has the same goals: to assess the patients' general health and their sexual attitudes in particular; to discuss their attitudes toward marriage, sexual activity and parenthood; to encourage them to examine and discuss these attitudes between themselves; to provide them with basic information about family planning, including child-spacing and contraception; to provide them with basic information about the marital and sexual relationships; to discuss their sexual experiences and counsel them about any existing anxieties, fears and inhibitions; to answer their questions; to encourage them to develop open sexual communication between themselves and to encourage them to feel free to return if any difficulties or questions arise.

Each physician must choose his own approach to premarital counseling, but it is almost impossible to cover all the appropriate material with just one session before the wedding. Scheduling a second session gives the patients time to digest new information, do further reading at home and become comfortable about discussing sexuality. The second visit is almost always more relaxed and productive than the first. The post-marriage visit also has beneficial possibilities. Concepts which once may have been abstract will have become far more real and understandable, and experience will have created many questions. The three-session format, therefore, is considered a model for premarital counseling.

If a couple is not sexually experienced, it is especially important that they be encouraged to discuss sex with one another. Both should be told that relaxation is important for sexual enjoyment. The girl is usually more anxious about her sexual behavior and responsibilities than is her future husband. It may be necessary to unlearn a pattern of sexual response in which the key factor was stopping in time. Many young couples expect to experience the sexual equivalent of the San Francisco earthquake the first time they have coitus. If, as is usual, the experience is a shade milder, many head for the nearest technical manual to see what they are doing wrong; Mark Twain noted that, on the typical honeymoon, "The second biggest disappointment is Niagara Falls."

The future husband should be advised that his wife's sex drive may not be as strong as his at first, and emotional preparation for each act of coitus is important to her. Because most women respond more slowly than men, tactile stimulation of the clitoris or general mons area during a relaxed period of foreplay will usually help to increase her response. The vagina is a somewhat insensitive passage; the clitoris and labia minora are the primary sources of sensation for most women. It should be emphasized to the prospective husband that, along with the physical methods of arousal, a woman needs a loving mood; she cannot be "started" by means of a checklist, like an airplane. No man can become coitally adept without experimentation and open communication.

If the couple has been having intercourse, they still may be in need of counseling since their experiences may not have been satisfactory. If one or both partners did not enjoy their experiences together, they may feel guilt and anxiety. If the girl has not reached orgasm, she may wonder whether something is wrong with her. Even if the experiences have been pleasant, deep feelings of guilt occasionally occur. Every sexual disturbance which can occur inside marriage is also possible outside marriage. The couple may not ask for help, but it is never safe to assume that they do not need counsel and would not welcome it. It is easier to correct disturbances before they have acquired the force of habit. Good premarital counseling is good preventive medicine.

CHAPTER XIV—PROBLEMS OF MALE SEXUAL RESPONSE

Males have a difficult time functioning sexually while they are under pressure; consequently, the most common male sexual dysfunctions are of psychologic origin.

IMPOTENCE

The man whose problem is impotence can be expected to be tense and anxious when he visits a physician, and the physician should begin therapy by trying to win the patient's confidence and by assuring him that impotence usually can be corrected. A great many men suffer temporary impotence, which is virtually always psychologic in origin. Even prolonged impotence is psychologic 90% of the time.[16]

Primary impotence is not usually attributable to a single factor but to a cluster of influences. The most common pressures are the family environment, adolescent social associations, adverse maternal influences, psychosocial restrictions, religious orthodoxy, homosexual involvement and personal devaluation from negative experiences with prostitutes. If the first unsuccessful coital attempt is associated with a traumatic episode, a pattern of failure may be established.

Etiologic factors such as drug and alcohol dependence, diabetes and diffuse arteriosclerosis may be involved in some cases of secondary impotence, but fear is undoubtedly the most frequent cause. Since reaching and maintaining an erection is largely a psychologic process, it often suffers when the man has lost confidence in himself. A man who has been repeatedly criticized by his wife for ejaculating prematurely may subsequently fail to achieve erection. Any failure can create fear about performance, and fear can make successful performance virtually unachievable. Similarly, overindulgence in alcohol or even simple fatigue may lead to a single episode of impotence which is capable of arousing self-perpetuating fears. A single failure is taken in stride by a secure man, but one who is pressured and anxious about his performance in other areas of life may see such a failure as a confirmation of his inadequacy. The demands of a sexually aggressive woman also can create or contribute to doubts and fears in a man about his ability to perform.

Guilt feelings may impair or eliminate potency. Guilt can result from masturbation or shame over the act of coitus if a partner or place seem shameful. Divorced men often have potency problems with their nonmarital partners because of guilt over the broken marriage, and a widower may become impotent because of guilt at having intercourse after his wife's death. A sexual partner who does not appear to enjoy or desire coitus can also interfere with potency. A man will lose erection rather swiftly if his wife starts talking about the laundry bills in the middle of love-making. Repeated failures can establish a pattern.

Impotence is not necessarily pervasive. A man may be impotent with his wife and fully capable with his mistress. Some are impotent only with young, pretty girls, and others with older women. Some men are potent with women they consider degraded but impotent with any woman they respect. Such a man is often unable to function sexually with a woman he loves because he associates his love with incestuous fantasies; he very often experiences erection before and after unsuccessful attempts at coitus. "When such men love, they have no desire," Freud wrote, "and when they desire, they cannot love." If a wife discovers that her husband is potent with prostitutes or other women, the blow to her already damaged ego is often severe. Yet, there is little that she can do for her husband without psychiatric assistance; some wives try imitating a prostitute's behavior but this seldom succeeds in resolving the problem.

Whatever the cause, impotence is usually reinforced by a man's attempts at correction. The impotent man approaches coitus in an anxious and distracted state, tries to achieve erection through will power, and inevitably takes sexual performance completely out of its pleasurable context. Willful direction of one's own sexual activities is not only ineffective, it is harmful. Tension and distraction are infectious and the responsiveness of both partners is predictably affected.

Occasionally, impotence is reinforced by incompetent professional advice. About 10% of the persons complaining of secondary impotence who were referred to Masters and Johnson had been advised that nothing could be done for them when they first sought help.[17] That advice came from physicians, clergymen, psychologists, a marriage counselor and a psychoanalyst. The condition had been variously attributed to aging, a single homosexual experience, masturbation, penance for past adultery and penance for a past abortion.

Masters and Johnson attributed six cases of impotence to direct suggestion by a consulted authority. Two of these cases are instructive about the influence of anxiety on male erective ability:

"A couple unable to accomplish intercourse consulted a gynecologist who diagnosed an impervious hymen and recommended surgery. Following surgery, the physician told the husband that the wife was now fine and that if they should still be unable to have intercourse, 'the fault is certainly yours.' Penetration still proved impossible. After two weeks of failure, the husband began to have difficulty achieving and maintaining erection. Within three months, he was impotent. More than five years after their marriage, the wife was found to be suffering from vaginismus, and the husband from secondary impotence.

"A husband and wife who had been having intercourse almost daily consulted a psychologist on the advice of friends who said that such frequency was unusual. The psychologist said that such a coital rate would wear out the husband, and expressed surprise that he had not been worn out already. He advised them to cut down, and added that he hoped they had come to him in time. Two nights after this consultation, the husband's response was noticeably slowed. Within three days, he was impotent. Except for an ability to perform coitus with a partial erection six or eights times a year, he remained impotent for seven years before seeking help."

Primary impotence is more likely to require psychiatric referral than secondary impotence, but many cases of both can be treated by the family physician. In regard to secondary impotence, the sexual history should answer the following questions: is the impotence of long duration or of recent origin, and, if recent, what specific events coincided with its appearance; have there been any masturbatory difficulties; is the impotence total or does it appear only with certain partners; is there any important homosexual background; what is the man's attitude toward his partner and her attitude toward him and what are the wife's sexual demands.

Because most impotence is a maladaptive reaction, the treatment is one of unlearning, not learning. Treatment is specifically directed at removing the man's fear of failure, the wife's fear concerning the man's performance, and the man's desperate attempts to will his own reactions. Sexual performance should be reestablished out of the context and trial of the coital act. Both husband and wife should be encouraged to engage in sex play not intended to culminate in coitus. Once the man is able to relax and enjoy non-coital sex play, he is likely to be able to proceed to successful coitus, because the pattern of failure will have been broken and a pattern of relaxing and accepting sexual pleasure, initiated.

Masters and Johnsons' therapy consists of permitting the husband to establish erection as a result of manual manipulation by the wife, then extending the range of sexual activity through repetitive erection, erective experimentation, and non-demanding intromission with the wife in the superior position. Manual manipulation is practiced throughout, and at no point is coitus or ejaculation a goal. The man simply learns to enjoy continuous, relaxed stimulation without demand, and he is assured that when he becomes comfortable during intromission, ejaculation will eventually occur spontaneously.

PREMATURE EJACULATION

Premature ejaculation is often the result of conditioning. The rapid completion of coitus encouraged by such activities as intercourse performed in cars or with prostitutes establishes the pattern; petting to orgasm may also contribute to a pattern of premature ejaculation. Infrequent coitus often aggravates the condition; the man might have some control when coitus is frequent, while having almost none when coitus takes place only two or three times a month. If the wife's demands and rebukes are frequent, premature ejaculation may lead to impotence; the man increases his conscious efforts to delay ejaculation and becomes increasingly more of a spectator and less of a participant. Masturbation has not been found to be a cause, and no specific environmental background has been associated with premature ejaculation.

114

Some men ejaculate if their genitalia are touched; others upon viewing a naked woman or looking at pornography. Most men who suffer from premature ejaculation, however, ejaculate during or immediately after intromission.

The wife may be understanding at first, and she may assure her husband that time and love will cure the problem. But when failure persists, her frustration usually grows. She may rebuke the man for just using her, or accuse him of selfishness and a lack of feeling for her. Eventually, she may seek sexual activity with another man.

Since psychologic difficulties often accompany premature ejaculation, tranquilizers may prove beneficial, but retraining procedures will be the primary treatment for most patients. The prospects for therapeutic success are excellent when the partners have not lost all mutual interest and are motivated to change their sexual pattern. The wife should be brought into therapy and given appropriate information about the most effective methods of assisting her husband. Short periods of manual manipulation should be tried, with stimulation stopping whenever ejaculation seems imminent. If ejaculation occurs, it should not be considered a failure; the stimulation should simply be reduced until the man is able to postpone ejaculation. Masters and Johnson have described a technique, pioneered by Semmens, and report a success rate of 97.8% with 180 patients. The man is stimulated until ejaculation is imminent. The wife then squeezes the glans of the penis to the point of pain. This causes the man to lose the urge to ejaculate. To perform the squeeze technique properly, the woman places her thumb on the frenulum and the first two fingers on the superior surface of the coronal ridge and squeezes them together for three or four seconds. The squeeze technique can be used by the man himself, but it will have no relevance or value for his sexual activity with a woman when the pace of activity is not entirely within his control.

OTHER EJACULATORY PROBLEMS

In cases of non-emissive erection, the problem is basically one of fertility, not incompatability. The history should reveal whether the patient has nocturnal emissions, especially after sexual activity, and whether the condition exists with all sexual partners.

Ejaculatory incompetence, the inability to ejaculate into a vagina, is a relatively rare condition which is a clinical entity separate from impotence. Ejaculatory incompetence may have numerous causes, but they are all psychologic. The problem is most common among young adults and is usually transitory. Unlike the treatment for impotence, the partner's approach must be demanding. She should first attempt to induce ejaculation manually; several attempts may be necessary. After ejaculation is achieved, the next step is to manipulate the male to a high level of sexual stimulation and, continuing manual manipulation, rapidly accomplish intromission in the female-superior position. If demanding pelvic thrusting does not lead to prompt ejaculation, manual manipulation should be resumed. When ejaculation is imminent, intromission is accomplished again. The procedure will be beneficial even if ejaculation takes place before penetration, since even a few drops of ejaculate within the vagina will serve to reduce the male's psychologic block.

CHAPTER XV—PROBLEMS OF FEMALE SEXUAL RESPONSE

NON-ORGASMIC RESPONSES

Frigidity is the inability to reach orgasm and does not necessarily indicate any lack of sexual responsiveness, let alone a deliberate refusal to try. However, Hastings[18] has observed that men frequently and incorrectly assume frigidity to be a willful condition. The causes are usually psychologic or environmental, and past social attitudes toward female sexuality are probably important. Frigidity represents an incompletely developed capacity to respond fully to sexual stimulation.

Surveys indicate that 5% to 15% of all women enjoy or have coitus without reaching orgasm. The incidence of non-orgasmic response decreases markedly with coital experience. An estimated 2% to 3% of all married women engage in coitus willingly but derive no pleasure from it, while about 1% of married women are actually repelled by coitus. If these figures are typical, the great majority of non-orgasmic women would like to achieve orgasm, but are unable to do so. Common causes of this inability are fear, a disturbed marital relationship and negative influences during early sexual development. Frequently, non-orgasmic women grew up in households where sex was never mentioned and where the mother failed to provide a suitable model of female sexuality. In many other cases, the parental influence was explicitly negative: the mother deliberately indoctrinated her daughter with the attitude that men are untrustworthy or foolish, and that sex is a disgusting appetite. Fear of penetration, fear of pain during the coital act and fear of disease are common causes of non-orgasmic response. Attachment to the father or, less commonly, the mother may interfere with a woman's sexual responsiveness; incestuous wishes toward a father are common, and even incest itself is not as rare as is often assumed. Women who retain a libidinal attachment to their fathers may have normal sexual relations before marriage but become non-orgasmic thereafter, when the male, in his new roles as husband and parent, begins to remind the woman of her father.

Some women develop an aversion to coitus because of what they consider excessive sexual demands, or because of feelings of personal inadaquacy brought on by the husband's treatment and attitude. Loss of respect, disappointment in the husband's earning capacity or preference for another man may disrupt the marital relationship. Anything which interferes with the husband's positive masculine image, including excessive drinking or an affair with another woman, may create orgasmic insufficiency in the wife. The wives of men who ejaculate prematurely commonly are non-orgasmic, at least with their husbands.

A female's sexual response is affected by many cyclical and variable factors such as menstrual periods, pregnancy, the life cycle, and intangible factors. Although sexual response is cyclical, the reaction to cyclical factors will vary from patient to patient. Fear of pregnancy is a common cause of female orgasmic insufficiency. Many women become more responsive after the menopause because they are free from worry about becoming pregnant, while others associate coitus closely with child-bearing and lose interest when there seems to be no more reason for intercourse.

Pelvic pathology such as endometriosis or pelvic inflammatory disease may be the cause of reduced coital pleasure; every non-orgasmic woman should receive a thorough physical examination. Orgasmic insufficiency caused by a traumatic experience, such as a rape, is rare. Homosexual experiences, however, may interfere with basic heterosexual orientation and expression. Rigid religious upbringing is also associated with primary orgasmic insufficiency. Masters and Johnson have reported that of 193 women patients who had never experienced orgasm, 41 had backgrounds of rigid religious control.[19]

In taking a sexual history from a non-orgasmic woman, special attention must be given to interpersonal relationships. The sexual history should also determine the patient's attitude toward sex and her concept of the role of sex in marriage; her view of her husband's attitude toward women as sexual partners and toward male-female differences in sexual drive; fear of pregnancy; early sexual training and experience; the degree and nature of parental affection; any homosexual history; any traumatic sexual episodes; past orgasmic experiences, and their circumstances; experiences of sexual arousal, and if so, under what circumstances; awareness of sexual arousal from dreams, fantasies or from erotic material and the patient's usual reactions during foreplay and coitus. If the patient is indifferent toward her husband, there is a strong possibility that the marriage was not desired or was entered into hastily, and referral to a marriage counselor may be warranted.

Occasionally, a female patient does not know whether she is orgasmic or not, but if there is any uncertainty, she probably is not. If organic causes are not present, the non-orgasmic woman should be counseled on how to increase her sexual responsiveness. First she should be instructed on the body areas and the methods of stimulation to which she is the most responsive. Distractions or anxieties which may interfere with her responsiveness should be dispelled. She should be encouraged to develop her sexual feeling and thinking through open communication with the male. Mutual pleasure, not orgasm, should be the goal of intercourse, and the male should be non-demanding. As in cases of male orgasmic dysfunction, the partner plays a critical role in the treatment program and should be included in therapy.

The physician should emphasize that sexual activity is an essential part of the meaningful interpersonal relationship. The woman must learn to feel and express herself sexually, and her partner must concern himself with giving her sexual pleasure. The sexually unresponsive woman should be urged to explore her own body to learn what areas are most responsive. She may benefit from consciously thinking about erotic subjects and images, especially if she was brought up to avoid such thoughts. The removal of inhibitions may bring an increased willingness to partake in coitus even though sexual feeling has not changed appreciably. In selected cases, masturbation leading to orgasm may be helpful in this learning process, and may reduce the woman's anxiety. However, if excessive guilt would be associated with masturbation, the practice should not be recommended.

Carefully selected techniques and training sometimes can increase the sexual responsiveness of patients. It may be appropriate to suggest that the patient read erotic literature or think about erotic subjects, then stimulate herself manually to orgasm. As this process is repeated, she may gradually reduce the amount of time required to reach orgasm during the act of coitus. Some women have been able to develop the capacity for multiple orgasm with this technique. Desensitization may result if the woman is able to picture mildly erotic scenes, and then to move on to progressively more erotic fantasies. She should be advised to keep her muscles relaxed during her fantasies, since acceptance of erotic thoughts is the key to the desensitization process.

Orgasm cannot be willed, and must never be the ultimate goal of sex activity. Both partners must recognize the importance of relaxed mutual pleasure. Since three-quarters of all men reach orgasm within two minutes of penetration, the delaying methods recommended for premature ejaculation may also be of benefit in other marriages where delaying the husband's ejaculation would improve the female's response.

VAGINISMUS

Vaginismus, or reflex spasm of muscles about the introitus, is a particularly disruptive problem. The involuntary spasms are psychologically induced and cause resistance to penetration. Vaginismus often occurs in association with primary impotence in the sexual partner, and in such cases it may be either cause or result. Strict religious training and social control are common causes. Sexual trauma in the form of assault, or a coital attempt which was interpreted as an assault, is also a cause. Dyspareunia and homosexual orientation are less frequent etiologic factors.

The condition is readily detected with a pelvic examination and its cure is relatively simple. Once the condition has been detected and the psychologic cause identified, the anatomic and psychologic processes involved should be explained in detail to both partners. Information about sexual anatomy and the physical effects of anxiety usually dispels the patient's fear and tension. Once both partners understand the condition, the woman should be advised to dilate the vaginal orifice with her fingers or Hegar dilators in the home. Correction often can be accomplished within five days.

DYSPAREUNIA

Dyspareunia or painful coitus may be of either organic or psychologic origin, and the effect on both the sexual partners is obviously great. In about one-fifth of all women who have undergone operations for prolapse of the uterus, the resultant vaginal narrowing and scarring are sufficient to cause a loss of feeling or pain during coitus.[20] Jeffcoate[21] has reported a 30% incidence of apareunia and dyspareunia following combined anterior and posterior colporrhaphy. Vulvovaginitis, endometriosis, and pelvic infection[22] are frequent causes of painful coitus.

Vaginal sensitivity to intravaginal chemical contraceptives or the rubber of a diaphragm or condom cause dyspareunia occasionally. Frequent alkaline douching may change normal vaginal flora and lead to secondary infection; sensitivity to products used in douching may develop. Other causes include: an intact hymen, irritated remnants of the hymenal ring, episiotomy scars, excessive manipulation of the clitoris, shortening of the vagina following hysterectomy, and carcinoma of the reproductive tract. If estrogen replacement therapy is not instituted postmenopausally, dyspareunia may result from senile changes in the vagina. Lack of lubrication is probably the most common cause of dyspareunia. Despite these many organic causes, dyspareunia in younger women is psychologic in origin the majority of the time.

There are three types of dyspareunia: pain on entry, pain during coitus, and pain after coitus. Pain on entry may be caused by vaginismus which is most often due to apprehension. Pain during deep thrust may be caused by post inflammatory scarring or by endometriosis in the pelvic region. If not corrected, this condition can almost completely incapacitate a female sexually. The patient may continue to have intercourse for a while out of a sense of obligation to her husband, but her aversion to coitus inevitably grows. Pain after coitus is most commonly a vague ache in the lower abdomen and pelvic region. It is often associated with inadequate sexual response which may result in chronic pelvic congestion.

Painful intercourse is a less common complaint in the male,[2][3] but also can be sexually crippling. Lack of proper hygiene may lead to irritation and infection in uncircumcised males. Phimosis, a foreskin which cannot be retracted, causes pain. A few men suffer from true hypersensitivity of the glans penis. Peyronie's disease can make coitus difficult or impossible. Penile irritation also may result from hypersensitivity to contraceptive chemicals.

COMPLAINTS OF FREQUENCY AND METHODS OF COITUS

The physician often is consulted by patients who are unhappy about the frequency of sexual intercourse. Sexual drives vary among people, but a weak sexual drive usually reflects psychologic disturbances, marital difficulties, or poor technique. Misperception about the partner's sexual drive may be a factor; husbands sometimes underestimate their wives' sexual interest. Therefore, when consulted about coital frequency, the physician should ask patients what their expectations are.

There are no safe chemicals which can be given to a patient to increase libido; there is no such thing as an aphrodisiac. Cantharides, or "Spanish Fly," a legendary sexual stimulant, is in fact, a powerful corrosive poison. Most investigators believe that sex hormones have[24] no established aphrodisiac qualities. However, androgen ingestion in the female frequently is beneficial. People sometimes take drugs like heroin, cocaine, LSD, and marijuana under the impression that they are aphrodisiacs; they are not. There is evidence that these drugs have a variable effect on sexual feeling, increasing it for some, but more commonly decreasing it.

Heroin in sufficient doses produces a marked reduction in sexual activity, and in males can lead to non-emissive erection. Excessive use of alcohol can reduce the sexual drive, and even lead to impotence. If loss of desire is due to mild depression, medicinal therapy may be beneficial. If the sexual problem is part of a complex neurotic problem, psychotherapy is indicated.

Complaints about coital methods may reflect differences in family or social background, or a simple desire to find out whether a practice is normal and acceptable. Information about the prevalence of such practices as oral-genital contact is often reassuring; however, there should be no attempt to convert a patient who has a genuine dislike for any practice. The husband and wife should be urged to respect the other's feelings. The most important factors in a good sexual relationship are the capacity for sexual feeling and the desire to share. These factors can be developed, but not willed.

CHAPTER XVI—DISEASE AND SURGERY

Disturbances of sexual function may be caused by an acute illness or a chronic disease. Some disorders which commonly have an effect on sexual function are diabetes, neurologic disorders, gynecologic disorders, prostatitis, castration, rectal surgery and heart attacks. In all cases where the physical disturbance will have an effect on sexual function or where the patient may fear such an effect, the physician should provide accurate information and reassurance when appropriate. He should also encourage the patient to consult him as questions arise.

DIABETES

Joslin et al[25] have estimated that half of all diabetic men complain of impotence. Potency depends on the integrity of the autonomic nervous system, which is frequently involved in diabetic neuropathy. A high percentage of impotent diabetic males have been shown to have neurogenic bladder abnormalities and signs of peripheral neuropathy. The results suggest a significant neuropathic factor in diabetic impotence. No correlation was noted between the severity or duration of the disease and the impotence.[26] In a controlled study, a significantly greater number of diabetic women suffered secondary orgasmic dysfunction than non-diabetic females. Duration of the disease in this study appeared to correlate with the onset of the sexual dysfunction.[27] All patients complaining of impotence or the appearance of orgasmic dysfunction should be examined for diabetes since impotence is known to often be the first clinical manifestation of the disease. There is no indication that psychogenic impotence occurs more frequently in diabetic than in non-diabetic males.

NEUROLOGIC DISEASES

Multiple sclerosis and tabes dorsalis are also commonly associated with impotence. Nutritional neuropathies have been associated with disturbances of sexual function, although the general debility of the patient may be a more important factor. Diseases of the cerebellum and brain stem usually produce impotence. Loss of libido reported in patients with pituitary tumors may be the result of pressure on the hypothalamic area. Hormonal derangement resulting from pituitary tumors may cause other disturbances in sexual function. Lesions in the temporal lobes appear to affect sexual function but the relationship has not yet been defined.

Spinal cord lesions may cause loss of ability to sustain erection. Depending on the location of the lesion, erection and ejaculation may be maintained through a spinal reflex mechanism. Transection does not invariably cause loss of erectile ability even if it effects loss of sexual satisfaction,[28] and each patient must be viewed as an individual case. Even when impotence results, many paraplegics use non-coital stimulation to bring the partner to orgasm. In the paraplegic man, reflex erection may be produced by manipulation of the penis, or by pinching the inner thigh. Once insertion has been made, the erection is likely to be maintained, especially if the woman's pelvic thrusting is vigorous, but ejaculation may or may not take place. Many paraplegic men report considerable psychologic satisfaction from coitus, even though they are unable to have the normal sensations. Their sexual desires are based on mental imagery, and the act of coitus usually has a beneficial effect on their egos.

Female paraplegics can become reasonably good sexual partners, either through petting or coitus. The paraplegic woman may be able to conceive and deliver.

Sexual behavior may be influenced by a number of gynecologic illnesses which bring real or anticipated pelvic pain, or in some way damage the woman's self-esteem. Melody[29] has listed the most common: congenital or developmental anomalies, genital infections, lower urinary tract infections, rectosigmoid suppurative processes, trauma, retrodisplacement of the uterus, endometriosis, ovarian lesions, estrogen deficiency and ectopic pregnancy.

Diseases of the prostate affect sexual function only when they cause pain during erection and ejaculation. Inflammation, benign enlargement and cancer rarely interfere with sexual potency. Removal of prostatic tissue for benign enlargements generally does not affect potency. Nerves and blood vessels involved in maintaining an erection may be damaged in radical prostatectomy for cancer. After prostatic surgery, ejaculation may be retrograde and not visible and this can be the reason for the misconception that prostatic surgery destroys potency. The patient, therefore, should be informed and reassured that he is not impotent.

SURGICAL PROCEDURES

Vasectomy——sterilization of the male——does not impair potency physiologically; the physician should reassure his patient to avert possible psychologic complications. Even following orchiectomy, men retain some degree of sexual functioning, but their desire for sexual activity is often greatly reduced.

Colostomy and rectal surgery are likely to have far-reaching effects on the patient's sexual life. In men, surgical damage to pelvic nerves may lead to erectile difficulty or impotence. However, rectal surgery does not always reduce potency or erectile ability, and many men emerge from such surgery sexually unaffected, but there may be a loss of self-esteem which can affect sexual performance. Some men become so afraid of rejection that they will not allow their wives to look at the colostomy.

Hysterectomy produces more unnecessary sexual disruption for women than any other surgical procedure, and the potential psychologic effects should never be underestimated. Some women fear that they will lose their sexual drive, their sexual attractiveness, or their femininity. The duration of recuperation is often far out of proportion to the severity of the operation. The physician can help dispel fears and misconceptions with anatomic and biologic facts, and he will find that most patients are eager to discuss the subject if given the chance.

If hysterectomy is to be accompanied by a bilateral salpingo-oophorectomy, estrogen replacement therapy is indicated for the surgical menopause which results.

In discussing hysterectomy with his patients, the physician should try to anticipate concerns which the patient may be too timid to bring up or of which she may not be aware. Loss of the ability to bear children seems to many a loss of basic femininity, and many patients report that they feel "less like a woman" afterward. Many women fear that the removal of the uterus will age them or effect their sexual capacity in other ways. Some women view the operation as a punishment for past sins. Others have a nearly mystical belief that the uterus and ovaries are a source of strength and the loss of any one will make them weaker and less womanly. These feelings may be hard for the male physician to understand, but they are real and he should not underestimate their depth. "What do you need the uterus for?"

one physician asked a 42-year old patient. "What do you need that thing for?" she demanded bitterly, pointing to his genital area.[30]

The husband may also experience sexual reaction to his wife's hysterectomy. Some men become impotent, apparently from the belief that coitus is no longer enjoyable for the woman. Their potency with other women is often unaffected.

Breast cancer, which affects 4% to 5% of American women, is the most common cancer in women; sympathetic counseling is always required. In a study[31] at Memorial Hospital in New York, all patients who had undergone mastectomy suffered from loss of self-esteem, and an impaired sexual self-image.

PSYCHOSEXUAL REACTIONS TO ILLNESS

The most neglected sexual problems are those created by psychologic reactions to physical illness. Golden[32] has observed that many people feel a vague sense of guilt when they get sick. Patients sometimes suspect that illness is punishment for past sins. They try to determine where their guilt lies, and since sex is a leading producer of guilt, they may consciously or unconsciously avoid sexual activity. Golden has written: "It is as if they say, 'My sexual sins may have led to my getting cancer, so I will undo my misfortune by avoiding sexual activity;' and they do."

In other cases, illness restricts sexual life not because restriction is necessary but because the physician failed to inform his patients that restriction is not necessary. Ford and Orfirer[33] have reported the following illustration:

> Following the diagnosis of multiple sclerosis in a young woman, her husband assumed that she should rest and that sexual relations would be harmful and moved to a different bedroom. Eventually, he discussed his resultant sexual frustration and conflicts with her physician and was assured that coitus would do her no harm. He also was able to discuss feelings of guilt about his wife's illness and shame at feelings of abhorrence which he had experienced during one phase of the illness. As he was able to verbalize his feelings, he could return to the basic love and tenderness that had existed between them. Sexual activity was resumed and became an important part of readjustment for both partners.

For the woman, a return to sexual activity after illness may be emotionally difficult. She may be embarrassed at finding herself with sexual feelings and needs which she assumed had been lost and which she is not sure her husband will welcome. For the man, the return to sexual health represents the recovery of masculinity. Resumption of sexual activity may be difficult and he is likely to have fears about whether he is ready for the exertion. He should be prepared to accept occasional failure and be willing to try coital positions which do not tire him. The wife's understanding acceptance of his failures and his need to change coital patterns is critically important to his self-respect. Reassurance by the physician is particularly needed by aging men who require surgery, and the failure to provide it will often bring an unnecessary end to the patient's sex life.

In all cases of illness, sexual activity should be resumed at the earliest possible moment consistent with the patient's health to avoid unnecessary hardship and the risk of far-reaching effects on the marriage. Believing such questions trivial and inappropriate at the time of illness, sexual partners are generally reluctant to ask questions about coitus. Some patients withdraw from all sexual activity after a chronic illness, but some try to reassure themselves of their continuing sexual ability by increasing their activity, to the dismay of a spouse who was content with the way things were before the illness. If a sexual attempt fails for any reason, the patient's frantic reaction may lead to more attempts, more failure, and possible sexual dysfunction.

In a study[34] of 105 patients under the age of 60 who had had cerebrovascular accidents, 60% said that their sexual appetite was either unchanged or increased. However, frequency of coitus for these same patients had decreased in 43% and had stayed the same or increased in only 22% (information was inadequate on 35%). Most of these patients had as much sexual desire after recovery as before their illness but had less opportunity to satisfy it, mostly because of misunderstanding.

Heart disease undoubtedly causes more needless sexual tragedy than any other major illness. A 1964 survey[35] of men who had suffered coronary occlusion found that only about one-third had resumed full sexual activity; that one-tenth had become impotent; and that the pattern of resumption of activity bore no relation to either the age of the patient or the severity of the attack. Two-thirds of these patients reported that they had received no advice about sexual adjustment from their physicians, and the other third reported only vague advice.

Most patients can safely resume coitus six to eight weeks after an acute coronary occlusion if there has been no subsequent anginal pain. Hellerstein and Friedman[36] have reported a study of sexuality in 48 post-coronary men and 43 men who had not experienced heart disease but were assessed as coronary-prone. Eighteen of the post-coronary subjects reported that they noticed at least one symptom during sexual activity, and awareness of tachycardia was the most common. The symptoms appeared most often after orgasm, and were usually not severe enough to cause the subject to give up sexual activity. The men reported that the frequency and quality of their sexual activities had improved when they had begun taking part in a physical fitness program, and, after participating, fewer subjects developed symptoms.

Fourteen post-coronary patients who were continuously monitored for two days by a portable ECG and electromagnetic tape recorder provided support for other studies which have indicated that sexual activity does not make excessive physical demands. The equivalent oxygen cost of the average maximum heart rate during sexual activity was less than that of performing a standard single Master two-step test. The mean maximum heart rate during the performance of normal chores at work was 120, with a range of 107 to 130. The mean maximum heart rate during sexual activity was 117, with a range of 90 to 144. The maximum rate lasted only 10 to 15 seconds, and the oxygen cost was equivalent to that of climbing a flight of stairs, or walking briskly.

It is reasonable to proscribe coitus for heart patients during the first four to six weeks of the illness, and usually safe to permit a resumption of sexual activity and normal kinds of employment when the patient can perform exercises at levels of six to eight calories per minute, without accompanying symptoms of abnormal pulse rate, blood pressure or ECG changes. For patients with persisting symptoms, drugs and a physical fitness program can improve sexual and working performance. Abstinence can easily create greater stress and tension than coitus. Anxiety or resentment caused by a partner's negative response can also add to strain on the heart, and spouses should be so advised.

Frequency of coitus should not exceed that which the patient indulged in before the myocardial infarction. The atmosphere in which coitus takes place is important: there should be no tension, pressure, or haste, and coitus is not advisable right after a meal. Many physicians recommend that coitus take place in the morning, when the patient is rested. If intercourse is proscribed masturbation should be also. Masters and Johnson[37] found that cardiac rates in women were higher during masturbation than during coitus.

Physical illness often creates sexual problems and sexual problems are commonly expressed through physical symptoms. A somatic symptom may be the excuse for a patient's visit when the problem is really sexual: a woman who asks for a pelvic examination as a check for cancer may be harboring the concern that she has a problem associated with sexual activity. The symptoms which may signal sexual conflict are similar to those which signal other emotional disturbances and induce chronic fatigue, discomforts which have no reasonable clinical syndrome to connect them, insistence on further evaluation after a short-term problem has been corrected, symptoms out of proportion to the syndrome in question, seductive behavior toward the physician, unexpected therapeutic benefit from a diagnostic procedure, inability to relax during pelvic examination, a minor physical impediment regarded as a major handicap, rapid deterioration at home following successful recovery during hospitalization, and strong reliance on tonics and vitamins. Unfortunately, these symptoms are not diagnostic for sexual problems, even taken as a group. These same complaints arise from a variety of non-sexual etiologies. The physician may find that a direct question about sex will reveal the real complaint, but evasiveness or undue embarrassment on the patient's part may indicate the existence of deep sexual repression.

VENEREAL DISEASES

Venereal diseases by definition are infectious diseases that are acquired by expressions of sexuality through intercourse. Gonorrhea and syphilis are the principal diseases in this category that also includes chancroid, granuloma inguinalae, and lymphogranuloma venereum (lymphopathia venereum). In addition, Trichomonas vaginalis vaginitis, Hemophilus vaginalis vaginitis, and herpes progenitalis are similarly classified as venereal diseases by some authorities.

Gonorrhea exists today in epidemic form, not only in the United States but throughout the world. In this country it is the most common reportable communicable disease even though most treated cases are unreported and many other cases are not recognized or treated. For the calendar year 1970, 600,072 cases were reported, a 12 percent increase over those reported in 1969.[38] The actual number of gonorrhea cases in the United States is estimated at close to 2,000,000, and even though some of these cases may represent repeated infections in the same person, a large and increasing number of people contract gonorrhea each year. Data reported by two states and 25 cities in 1970 indicated that 47 percent of the cases resulted from single exposure to the opposite sex and 32 percent of the cases from multiple exposure to the opposite sex; 15 percent resulted from exposure to a marital partner and the remainder to single and multiple exposures to the same sex.

In 1970, the reported cases showed a preponderance in males with a sex ratio of 3.2 to 1.[39] While the problem of the asymptomatic male is a serious one, it is the asymptomatic female who represents by far the greater problem. It is she who must be identified and treated if the current epidemic of gonorrhea is to be brought under control, because various studies suggest that as many as 50 percent of infected women are asymptomatic carriers of the disease.

The diagnosis of gonorrhea is, in most cases, easier to establish in the male than in the female because of the presence of an acute urethritis with a discharge of pus. The demonstration of gram-negative intracellular diplococci in a microscopic smear (gram stain) will confirm the clinical diagnosis. If the smear examination does not show the organism, a specimen for culture is obtained from the anterior urethra by sterile wire loop or cotton applicator. In homosexuals, a specimen should be collected from the rectum as well.

The diagnosis of gonorrhea in the female is more difficult, for two reasons. In the first place, symptoms of an acute infectious process of the vagina, cervix or urethra, are frequently absent or not distinguishable from the commonly experienced vaginal discharge. In the second place, when gonorrhea is suspected, smear examination alone is totally inadequate for confirmation, since this procedure will miss two-thirds of infected women. Further, a positive smear in the female, ie the finding of gram-negative intracellular diplococci, is too nonspecific to prove the presence of gonorrhea.

It follows then that in every female in whom gonorrhea is suspected, a culture is taken from the cervical canal, and innoculated on Thayer-Martin medium. Occasionally, specimens from the rectum and urethra are also taken.

Until recently, there was no satisfactory transfer media for use in the private physician's office. The recent development of such a medium, called "Transgrow" represents a major breakthrough in the detection of gonorrhea for the practicing physician. This medium, developed by the Public Health Services Center for Disease Control, is currently available from several pharmaceutical houses, and is pre-bottled for instant streaking. Its great advantage lies in its capability of sustaining the specimen for 72 hours, more than ample time for transfer of the medium from the physician's office to the laboratory for further development. Accuracy of diagnosis exceeds 90%. Case rates are highest (1412 per 100,000) in the group 20-24 years of age, the next highest categories being the age group 25-29 (794 per 100,000) and the age group 15-19 (713 per 100,000).[40]

Except for conjunctivitis and vulvovaginitis of pre-adolescent girls, gonorrhea is always contracted sexually. Proctitis due to rectal exposure (anal intercourse) is common and, in males, is almost always due to homosexual activity. It is of interest to note in passing that rectal exposures are occurring with greater frequency among college women, and that prostitutes are also reporting an increased demand for this form of sexual exposure.

Gonorrheal infection also causes gonorrheal arthritis and tenosynovitis, gonoccal meningitis, salpingo-oophritis and pelvic peritonitis (in the female pelvis) and gonorrheal pharyngitis, which is contracted only from fellatio.

Penicillin remains the antibiotic of choice in the treatment of gonorrhea. Current recommendations of the US Public Health Service for the treatment of acute uncomplicated gonorrhea are as follows: In men, aqueous procaine penicillin G, 2.4 million units intramuscularly in one injection. In women, aqueous procaine penicillin G, 4.8 million units intramuscularly in two injection sites in one visit. Or, the combination of equal parts of 1) aqueous procaine penicillin G and 2) procaine penicillin G in oil, with 2% aluminum monostearate, for two separate intramuscular injections of 2.4 million units in each site, given at one visit.

The number of reported cases of syphilis has declined slowing from a peak value of 126,245 in 1962 to 91,382 in 1970. Nevertheless, syphilis was the fourth most common reported infectious disease in the United States in 1970. Primary and secondary syphilis is reported about twice as often in the male as in the female and the "missed" female cases may be a significant reservoir of infection. In 1970, data from 34 states and 102 cities indicated that multiple exposure of the opposite sex accounted for 46 percent of the cases of primary and secondary syphilis, single exposure of the opposite sex 18 percent, and marital partners 12 percent; multiple exposure of the same sex accounted for 15 percent and single exposure of the same sex for 9 percent of the cases.[41] Although the case rates were lower for primary and secondary syphilis, the age distribution in general paralleled that for gonorrhea in 1970 with the highest incidence in the year group 20-24.

The American Medical Association Council on Environmental and Public Health in a statement in April 1971, pointed out that physicians in private practice treat approximately 80 percent of the syphilis and gonorrhea that comes to diagnosis but report to Public Health Departments only one out of every eight cases of syphilis and one out of every nine cases of gonorrhea that they treat.[42] The marked increase in the prevalence of venereal disease, especially gonorrhea, has resulted from a change in the sexual mores of the population, from a reluctance on the part of physicians to report VD cases, from insufficient funds and limited staffs in Public Health Departments that are charged with treating this disease, and from ignorance on the part of the public concerning venereal disease prevention, treatment, and consequences of lack of treatment. Other factors that have led to increased prevalence of venereal disease include changing attitudes toward premarital sex, the presence of asymptomatic gonorrhea especially in the female but also in the male, increasing difficulties in treating penicillin-resistant gonorrhea, and perhaps also to the effect of oral contraceptives in increasing the moisture and alkalinity of the vaginal mucosa which may thereby become a more receptive medium for the growth of the gonococcus. The widespread use of oral contraceptives may have also led to the decreased use of the condom which served to prevent infection as well as pregnancy.

The extent of knowledge by the individual patient of the long-term adverse effects of venereal disease infection may be quite variable. The patient may have acquired reliable information as a result of courses in sex education or venereal disease education in schools or in the military services. On the other hand, the patient may be quite ignorant of these matters which need to be treated by the physician with the same matter-of-fact attitude that he discusses sexual problems with the patient.

Apart from the technical problems of diagnosing and treating venereal diseases as infectious processes with long-term consequences, these diseases pose a number of psychologic and behavioral problems for the physician who may be consulted in these matters. Again, many of these problems result from inadequate knowledge on the part of the patient as a result of deficiencies in venereal disease education. For example, the patient may have fears, some of which may be justifiable, about the sexual consequences of having acquired venereal disease; these fears may relate to impairment of fertility or to effects on potency. The actual discovery of the presence of venereal disease, or the fear of such discovery, may involve enormous feelings of guilt, especially when venereal disease is acquired extra-maritally. This situation may affect marital relations because of fear of transmitting the suspected disease to the spouse. The discovery of venereal disease in a spouse may have disasterous effects on the stability and durability of a marriage. Furthermore, feelings of shame and guilt may lead to unwillingness on the part of the patient to face reality rationally and, consequently, may lead to neglect of appropriate treatment.

In dealing with venereal disease the physician is faced with many professional problems. These include some discussion of the symptoms and consequences of venereal disease when the physician counsels a patient with regard to sexual activity, or in the course of premarital counseling. The physician may be confronted with a positive serological test for syphilis and may have a problem in deciding whether this is a biologically false positive test, especially in connection with a premarital medical examination. The physician must have a high index of diagnostic suspicion with respect to the presence of venereal disease. He should remember that syphilis has been a classic mimic of other diseases, that the female anatomy is such that primary lesions of syphilis may be undetected unless carefully looked for, that the asymptomatic female is one of the principal factors in the current epidemic of gonorrhea, that rectal lesions such as fissures or proctitis may be primary syphilitic lesions especially in male homosexuals, that "any person with a tattoo mark on him is an apt candidate for syphilis, and that any female having a tattoo mark has syphilis until proved otherwise."[43]

Upon making a diagnosis of venereal disease the physician has an immediate problem of deciding whether to assume responsibility for treatment of the disease or for referral elsewhere. In any case, the physician has a legal and moral obligation to report the disease to the public health authorities, who can be depended upon to conduct a discrete and confidential epidemiological inquiry. Apart from the responsibility of reporting the disease, the physician has an enormous commitment to confidentiality, and this includes keeping the information from the family (spouse, or parents in the case of a minor) unless specifically released by the patient. The American Medical Association in December 1968 urged the enactment of state laws that would permit physicians legally to treat venereal disease cases of minors without obtaining parental consent. As of June 30, 1970, 29 states and the District of Columbia had enacted laws permitting minors to give their own consent for venereal disease treatment.

In June 1971 the American Medical Association reaffirmed its position in favor of control of the spread of venereal disease by urging physicians to assist Public Health Departments in the timely reporting of VD cases that they treat, by urging medical societies to support education of patients and the public through more extensive and imaginative use of all available media and through school curricula, by seeking to strengthen in every possible way the research efforts toward the development of vaccines against venereal disease, and by reiterating its support and cooperation with the National Commission on Venereal Disease.

CHAPTER XVII—VARIATIONS OF SEXUAL RESPONSE

Variations from the common patterns of heterosexuality are psychologic in origin, never hereditary, and are most often related to the patient's childhood environment. Many variant sexual responses are traceable to disturbed relationships between the parents and between the parents and the child. Parental failure to provide stable role models is a consistent factor. Relatively few such patients seek the help of a physician, but when they do, the physician's attitude may have a direct bearing on the patient's willingness to pursue treatment. The physician's sympathetic and understanding acceptance of the problem will encourage a patient who is motivated for treatment to accept referral to a specialist for the sexual counseling which is necessary for most of these patients.

Nymphomania, an exaggerated and compulsive sexual desire in a female, is usually an artificial expression of sexuality. Nymphomania may be expressed as a means of avoiding emotional contact, since there is seldom any personal feeling for the sexual partner. Usually, she is either wholly or intermittently non-orgasmic, and her frustration increases her compulsiveness. She may be attractive, but almost always will lead a lonely life, because both men and women feel threatened by her. The nymphomaniac's insatiable demands also may bring out buried anxieties about sexual adequacy in her partners. She is often suicidal, and fairly commonly takes to drugs or heavy drinking.

Satyriasis is an exaggerated sexual desire in a male, and he may or may not derive much pleasure from his compulsive sexual activities. In many cases, the satyr's mother was cold and narcissistic, but seductive. The home environment was often unstable with little loyalty among family members. The child comes to feel that emotional relationships are dangerous, but, lacking love, he also seeks proof of his loveableness. Auerback[44] has written that unconscious incestuous desires, memories of infantile eroticism, and hatred of women commonly appear in cases of satyriasis, but Masters believes that most satyrs simply enjoy coitus and do not harbor fears about their masculinity.

Homosexuality. The male homosexual is unlikely to seek treatment, and when he does, he often wants to become better adjusted without altering his homosexuality. Female homosexuality appears to be more common than many physicians believe. If the lesbian goes to a physician at all, however, she usually goes to a female physician, and she usually avoids gynecologic examination.

Transvestitism is defined as the morbid desire to wear clothes of the opposite sex. The transvestite identifies partly or wholly with the opposite sex, but also prefers a member of the opposite sex as a partner. The condition presents varied problems and it poses a great threat to the security of the transvestite's children. A child who discovers his father dressed in female clothing may develop serious psychologic problems.

Transsexualism is a male's identification of himself as a member of the opposite sex, and he prefers members of his own sex as partners. He cross-dresses, not for sexual stimulation, but because he feels feminine. Psychotherapy for adult transsexuals has been largely ineffective and surgical reassignment of the sex is frequently employed.

Fetishism is a bizarre and compulsive sexual attraction for an object as a substitute for a person. Men are more responsive to visual stimulation and fantasy than women, and fetishism is almost exclusively a male aberration. The object chosen represents an attempt to stave off castration fear. The prospect of cure is not bright but psychotherapy, including psychoanalysis, offers the best hope.

Voyeurism and *exhibitionism* pose only mild threats to society. Voyeurs rarely become rapists; exhibitionists rarely commit more serious crimes. In both cases, distance from the love object is a necessary source of security. The voyeur often masturbates while peeping, and the exhibitionist gets his satisfaction from provoking a strong feminine reaction and recognition of his masculinity. The maker of obscene phone calls is also engaged in sexual activity at a safe distance, but the activity is more aggressive. The telephonist is often trying to shore up a faltering sense of potency by creating awe or fright in a woman while he is in a position of safety; he is usually not a physical menace.

Masochism is deriving sexual pleasure from pain and from playing an acquiescent role, while *sadism* is sexual pleasure from inflicting pain and from domination. Many normal people apparently enjoy biting and being bitten during love-play. Rado[45] noted that people dependent on pain for sexual enjoyment seek advance punishment, so that they may enjoy what they consider a forbidden pleasure without guilt. The pain does not always have to be real, and sadism and masochism are often expressed in staged performances. A criminal manifestation of sadism is lust murder.

Therapy for sadism and masochism is usually directed at helping the patient periodically release rage while receiving love, appreciation and respect, so that the individual can feel respectable and entitled to sexual enjoyment without punishment. The prospects of amelioration seem especially good for women.

Pedophiles, child molesters, are usually passive individuals who feel threatened by other adults, and who are likely to act out their feelings sporadically. Only six to eight percent of first offenders reappear in court. These sex offenders are seldom involved in non-sexual crimes, and seldom pass on to other kinds of sex crimes. Few are drug users, but many are under the influence of alcohol when they commit their crimes, and most have a lower than average sex drive.

Most molestations are committed by an adult known to the child; two studies[46] have found strangers involved in only 12% and 16% of the cases. The most common place of molestation is the home of the child or the molester. The victim often could have avoided the experience, and the child's curiosity about sex is often a contributing factor. Most female victims of molestation are between 5 and 10 years old, most male victims between 7 and 12. The children usually come from homes in which they lack care and attention; they seem to need the attention offered by the adult who eventually molests them. A California study[47] of 71 cases of child molesting assessed 23 as accidental victims and 48 as participating victims. The participating victims were almost universally flirtatious toward the male psychiatrist, and they showed considerable emotional disturbance and a strong need for affection.

Child molesting is viewed with understandable abhorrence by society, but the reaction of both society and the physician can actually harm the victim more than the molestation itself. The physician is often called upon by parents and the police to perform an immediate physical examination in an atmosphere of panic in an emergency room. The child is invariably disturbed; he assumes that what happened must have been terrible to bring on such extreme reactions. Yet if there is no evidence of physical violence, an examination may have been unnecessary and more alarming than the assault. The physician should consider using an anesthetic or not performing the examination at all. In one study[48] of 113 cases of child molestation, there was evidence of physical damage in only four cases——two small vaginal lacerations, and two cases of inflammation of the introitus from digital manipulation.

Most molestations do not by themselves present serious adjustment problems for the child, who may be puzzled by the general alarm. Unfortunately, adults may show more concern about punishing the molester than safeguarding the victim, who is sometimes treated primarily as a witness. Both the child and the parents should receive extensive counseling if the molester is a member of the family.

Sexual assaults on the older child, or overly seductive parental behavior, may result in the same kinds of behavior disturbances that arise from other sources of anxiety: thumb-sucking, nose-picking, sniffling, nail-biting, blinking, enuresis, sleep difficulty, stuttering, and disturbed conduct. Some children who experience parent-child incest during the prepubertal period apparently remain normal; but for some incest is only one among many influences that favor development of psychosis. If seduction is a disguised, hostile invasion of the child's body, the victim may develop a distorted view of his body. Brother-sister incest is often of no further consequence than other forms of childhood sex play.

SEXUAL ASSAULT ON ADULT FEMALES (FORCIBLE RAPE)

Forcible rape is a felony in criminal law, yet the evidence indicates that at least three out of four victims do not report the assault to police. Some women do not even consult a physician.[49] In most jurisdictions a physician is required to report such attacks which come to his attention. As with other categories of violent crime, the incidence of rape is increasing in America. The law requires the physician to determine if the alleged assault occurred. His examination should be aimed at detecting sperm, evidence of force or other medical evidence of an attack. Physicians who may be called on to serve this medical-legal function should make themselves familiar with the laws on rape.

The patient——the victim——requires considerably more of the physician. Rape usually does not result in pregnancy, but the physician may wish to administer estrogen in sufficient quantity to act as a prophylactic measure. During later visits, a serologic test for syphilis should be made and smears or cultures taken for evidence of gonorrhea; the first visit is too soon for these tests to be productive, and they may be emotionally harmful. Whether pregnancy or a venereal disease occurs or not, many women develop a sense of guilt about the attack, and the guilt may create frigidity. Other victims bury feelings which should be uncovered and managed. Counseling should be directed at preventing the development of hatred or fear of men, and it may be helpful to remind the patient specifically of men with whom she has had good relationships.

One study[50] of sex offenders reported on aggressors which had been classified into the following varieties:

Assaultive variety, the most common type, accounted for between 25 and 33% of the study sample. These men find sexual activity alone insufficient without violence or a serious threat of violence. They are generally unknown to their victims, who are selected with little regard for their age, appearance or deportment. In some cases violence substitutes for coitus. This assaultive category included more cases of erectile impotence than the others that follow.

Amoral delinquents tend to ignore social controls and conduct themselves as egocentric hedonists. These men are not sadistic, but when they desire intercourse, they give no consideration to females' wishes; women are seen solely as sexual objects. These men would use force when the situation required it. The study's sample contained 12-16% of this variety of offender.

The *drunken variety* of aggressor is about as common as the amoral delinquent type. Drunks tend to misinterpret situations and, relieved of much of their inhibition by alcohol, may even become violent. Drunkenness is found frequently among all types of aggressors.

The *explosive variety* made up 10-15% of the sample. These men offered no observable indications that they might become aggressors. They appeared average and law-abiding; their aggression appeared suddenly and without warning.

The *double-standard variety* accounted for 10% of the study's subjects. These men see two types of women, good and bad. The "good" women are not his potential victims; he may wish to marry a virgin. "Bad" women he feels are not entitled to consideration; women are judged by their appearance and deportment. He will attempt seduction, but will use whatever force is necessary to satisfy his wish for coitus.

Other types of aggressors were found to be mental defectives, or psychotics, but most of the remainder of the group appeared to be mixtures of the described varieties.

CHAPTER XVIII—REFERRAL AND ALLIED PROFESSIONALS

A sound doctor-patient relationship is not dependent on doctor and patient being of the same sex. The female patient may be initially inclined to tell a male physician only what she wants him to hear or what she thinks he wants to hear, while the male patient is inclined to bolster his ego by painting a flattering picture of himself for a female physician. However, effective counseling will help overcome these problems. Positive transference which is sexually oriented can disrupt therapy but is seldom a major problem.

All physicians encounter patients whom they cannot help. If the physician has been unable to elicit any pertinent information when he strongly suspects a sexual problem, he should encourage a return visit. Also, he should mention the name of a suitable agency or other referral source, since the patient may want to talk about the problem but feel inhibited by him. If a sexual problem is undiminished after approximately six visits, the patient should be referred to another physician.

Numerous sexual problems require psychiatric evaluation and treatment. Otto[51] has listed several symptoms indicative of deep psychologic disturbance which may require psychiatric referral: an obvious or extreme distortion of the patient's perception of his problem; a pattern of inappropriate reaction to past and present family crises; an impaired self-concept; an excessively active and demanding conscience; or the absence of realistic and appropriate feelings of guilt; long-standing and chronic problems or low motivation to enter counseling; an inability to relate to the counselor; and a potentially explosive situation. If one or more of these factors is present, early referral should be considered.

Other sources are of potential assistance to the physician in gathering information and for treatment: clergymen, child care agencies, family service agencies (the Family Service Association of America has marriage counselors in many member agencies), adoption agencies, lawyers, legal aid societies, guidance counselors, and social workers. Before the question of referral arises, the physician should investigate as many of these sources as possible. For example, the American Association of Marriage Counselors, which maintains a referral service, will direct the physician to qualified marriage counselors in his area. The

Association has high standards, and its members have backgrounds in medicine, education, law, the ministry, psychology, or social work. Clinical internship and five years of approved clinical practice are required for membership.

REFERENCES—PART III

1. Masters WH, Johnson VE: *Human Sexual Inadequacy*. Boston, Little Brown & Co, 1970, p 2.

2. Auerback A: Sex vs. the late late show. *Med Aspects Human Sexuality* 2: 38, 1970.

3. Shulman BH: The uses and abuses of sex. *Med Aspects Human Sexuality* 2: 49-51, 1968.

4. Gebhard PH: Factors in marital orgasm. *Med Aspects Human Sexuality* 4: 22-25, 1968.

5. Wallin P, Clark AL, cited by Udry JR: Sex and family life. *Med Aspects Human Sexuality* 2: 77, 1968.

6. Ibid, p 69.

7. Masters WH, Johnson VE: *Human Sexual Response*. Boston, Little Brown & Co, 1966, p 4.

8. Gebhard PH: Factors in marital orgasm. *Med Aspects Human Sexuality* 2: 22-25, 1968.

9. Kinsey AC, Pomeroy WB, Martin CE: *Sexual Behavior in the Human Male*. Philadelphia, WB Saunders Co, 1948, p 580.

10. Masters WH, Johnson VE: *Human Sexual Response*. Boston, Little Brown & Co, 1966, p 65.

11. Kephart WH, cited by Udry JR: Sex and family life. *Med Aspects Human Sexuality* 2: 72, 1968.

12. Masters WH, Johnson VE: *Human Sexual Inadequacy*. Boston, Little Brown & Co, 1970, p 310.

13. Ibid, p 2.

14. Vincent CE: Sources of sexual communication difficulties in marriage, in Vincent CE (ed): *Human Sexuality in Medical Education and Practice*. Springfield, Ill, Charles C Thomas Publisher, 1968, p 453.

15. Nash EM, Louden LM: The premarital medical examination and the Carolina Population Center. *JAMA* 210: 2365-2369, 1969.

16. Simpson SL: Impotence. *Bristish Med J* 1: 692-697, 1950.

17. Masters WH, Johnson VE: *Human Sexual Inadequacy*. Boston, Little Brown & Co, 1970, p 230.

18. Hastings DW: *Impotence and Frigidity*. Boston, Little Brown & Co, 1963, p 78.

19. Masters WH, Johnson VE: *Human Sexual Inadequacy*. Boston, Little Brown & Co, 1970, p 230.

20. Rubin I: Sexual adjustments in relation to pregnancy, illness, surgery, physical handicaps and other unusual circumstances, in Vincent CE (ed): *Human Sexuality in Medical Education and Practice*. Springfield, Ill, Charles C Thomas Publisher, 1968, p 544.

21. Jeffcoate TNA, cited by Kinch RAH: Painful coitus. *Med Aspects Human Sexuality* 1: 8, 1967.

22. Masters WH, Johnson VE: *Human Sexual Inadequacy*. Boston, Little Brown & Co, 1970, p 284.

23. Ibid, pp 288-289.

24. American Medical Association: *AMA Drug Evaluations*, 1971, p 303.

25. Joslin ER, Marbel AF, White P, et al cited by McDowell FH: Sexual Mani-

festations of neurologic disease. *Med Aspects Human Sexuality* 2: 17, 1968.

26. Ellenberg M: Impotence in diabetes: The neurologic factor. *Ann Inter Med* 75: 213-219, 1971.

27. Kolodny RC: Sexual dysfunction in diabetic females. *Diabetes* 20: 557-559, 1971.

28. Bors E. and Comarr A.E.: Neurological disturbances of sexual function with special reference to 529 patients with spinal cord injury, Urol Survey 10: 191, 1960 .

29. Melody GF: Gynecologic illness and sexual behavior. *Med Aspects Human Sexuality* 2: 6-11, 1968.

30. Drellich MG: Sex after hysterectomy. *Med Aspects Human Sexuality* 1: 63, 1967.

31. Sachs BC: This bosom business. *Med Aspects Human Sexuality* 3: 23, 1969.

32. Golden JS: Varieties of sexual problems in obstetrical and gynecological practice, in Wahl CW (ed): *Sexual Problems, Diagnosis and Treatment in Medical Practice.* New York, Free Press, 1967, p 57.

33. Ford AB, Orfirer AP: Sexual behavior and the chronically ill patient. *Med Aspects Human Sexuality* 1: 58, 1968.

34. Ibid, p 57.

35. Tuttle WB, Cook L Jr, Fitch E, cited in Rubin I: *Sexual Life After Sixty.* New York, Signet Books, New American Library Inc, 1965, p 202.

36. Hellerstein HK, Friedman EH: Sexual activity and the post-coronary patient. *Med Aspects Human Sexuality* 3: 70-96, 1969.

37. Masters WH, Johnson VE, cited by Rubin I: Sexual adjustments to pregnancy, illness, surgery, physical handicaps and other unusual circumstances, in Vincent CE (ed): *Human Sexuality in Medical Education and Practice.* Springfield, Ill, Charles C Thomas Publisher, 1968, p 536.

38. Reported incidence of notifiable diseases in the United States, 1970: in *Annual Supplement, Morbidity and Mortality Weekly Report,* Center for Disease Control, Public Health Service, Dept Health, Education and Welfare 19: A. C. 53, 1971.

39. *Today's VD Control Problem —1971:* New York, American Social Health Association, 1971, p 17.

40. Ibid, p 57.

41. Ibid, p 21.

42. Council on Environmental and Public Health: *Statement on Venereal Disease.* Chicago, American Medical Association, 1971.

43. Johnson AN: The venereal disease problem facing the private physician and his patient. *Arch Environ Health* 13: 393-396, 1966.

44. Auerback A: Satyriasis and nymphomania. *Med Aspects Human Sexuality* 2: 40, 1968.

45. Rado S: Common maladaptation: Sexual and social disorders: *Adaptational Psychodynamics: Motivation and Control.* Normal, Ill, Science Publications, 1969, p 207.

46. Mohr JW: A child has been molested. *Med Aspects Human Sexuality* 2: 47, 1968.

47. Ibid, p 48.

48. Ibid, p 43.

49. Sexual assaults on women and girls, editorial. *Ann Intern Med* 72: 277, 1970.

50. Gebhard PH, Gagnon JH, Pomeroy WB, et al: *Sex Offenders.* New York, Harper & Row Inc, 1965, p 197.

51. Otto HA: Evaluating the patient's problem for counseling or referral, in Klemer RH (ed): *Counseling in Marital and Sexual Problems.* Baltimore, Williams & Wilkins Co, 1965, pp 82-84.

PART 4
THE PHYSICIAN, SEX AND SOCIETY

PART IV

THE PHYSICIAN, SEX AND SOCIETY

CHAPTER XIX—SEXUAL STANDARDS

In counseling on problems of human sexuality, the physician is concerned not only with an individual patient, but with a sexual relationship, and with a society of which he himself is a part. Societies determine and enforce the standards of sexual behavior which affect the sexual development and response of every individual in that society. Each person reacts to social standards and pressures somewhat differently, but no one escapes these pressures, and they must be considered by the physician in his assessment of the sexual attitudes of his patients. The physician who discusses sexuality with a patient from the ghetto is dealing with very different social pressures than one who counsels a patient from suburbia.

The sex counselor should not be primarily an advocate of society's standards. Rather, he should be willing to compromise society's admonitions and his own personal views to bring about a satisfactory adjustment of each patient's individual problem.

Although the only approved sexual standard in American society has been that of abstinence until marriage, it has been accepted that most unmarried men engage in coitus. This double standard can be traced far back in our history. Strictures against premarital sexual relations have not prevented violations despite severe penalties; of 200 people baptized in one New England church at the time of the Revolution, 66 confessed that they had had premarital intercourse.[1]

LAWS ON SEX

Many of the most repressive attitudes toward sexuality have been enacted into law, which tells much about society's attitudes toward sexuality. It was observed that in criminal law the laws regarding sexual behavior are unique because the punishment is very nearly inversely proportional to the mischief done. Violent crimes involving sex are more severely punished than are more violent crimes with no sexual component, and sexual aberration is often penalized, while aberrations of power or responsibility are accepted or even rewarded. Sex laws and the punishment exacted of an offender are often based on erroneous concepts and fail to deter the proscribed behavior.

Appendix IV contains a selection of illustrative cases, patient consent forms and articles on law and medicine prepared by the office of the General Counsel of the American Medical Association.

CHANGING STANDARDS IN AMERICA

Many ambiguities are apparent in society's views on sexuality. Children are warned about the dangers of sex, yet they are exposed to sexually oriented material in virtually every advertisement, movie and television show they see. They are led to understand that sex cannot be discussed openly and frankly, only to discover that it is universally used in the promotion of commodities. Society decrees that coitus be confined to marriage, yet many persons engage in premarital and extramarital coitus.

Christensen[2] compared sexual mores and behavior in Denmark with those of a group of Mormons in Utah and a group of midwestern Americans. Among the Danish subjects, more people approved of premarital coitus than had actually engaged in it. In the American samples, however, many more practiced coitus than approved of it. The American groups had far more sexual guilt, fear and anxiety, and the discrepancy between mores and behavior and the percentage of those who felt guilty, remorseful, or frightened were greatest in the highly restrictive Mormon group. In addition, the American samples included marriages at a younger age, and higher divorce rates in association with conceptions prior to marriage.

Recent years have seen important changes in sexual standards in the United States. Reiss[3] has listed four major contemporary premarital sexual standards: 1) abstinence, 2) the double standard, permitting premarital coitus for men but not for women, 3) permissiveness with affection and 4) permissiveness without affection. More and more persons have adopted the standard of permissiveness with affection, in which a stable, affectionate relationship rather than permanence has become the precondition for coitus. Permissiveness also has increased among those whose standards are more conservative. Women who hold to the standard of abstinence are more likely to permit heavy petting, sometimes to orgasm, when they feel affection for the man. Men who hold to the double standard are more likely to condone coitus for single women in love than was true a few years ago.

In summarizing premarital sexual standards Reiss states, "Thus all our premarital sexual codes have been liberalized. Abstinence is still the dominant code for most females and for a sizeable minority of males, particularly those under twenty. The double standard is still the dominant code for many males and females, but permissiveness with affection has today achieved respectability and a sizeable following among both sexes. The choice of a premarital sexual code has become, among young people, a legitimate choice among valid alternatives, and even many of those who accept abstinence defend the right of others to choose permissiveness. The legitimation of choice goes along with the trend toward more permissive sexual attitudes."

Until recently, this change in sexual standards was apparently not accompanied by any appreciable change in premarital sexual behavior. Reiss[4] reported that only 64% of the girls at a midwestern college who said they accepted premarital coitus in principle had actually engaged in premarital coitus, and love was the key motivating factor for most of them. There has also been no evidence that those who accept premarital coitus engage in coitus with more partners or more often than those who do not accept it.

However, many researchers believe that increased acceptance is likely to increase sexually permissive behavior, and this may now be taking place. Thirty years ago, Kinsey found that 51% of male college seniors and 27% of female college seniors were coitally experienced by 21. In recent studies approximately 75% of the male seniors and 50% of the female seniors said that they had had premarital sexual intercourse.

Sexual standards have changed mainly among young people. Reiss[5] found that adults accept petting without affection before they accept coitus with affection, whereas students accept coitus with affection before they accept petting without it. Some of this difference in attitude is traceable to increasing maturity and responsibility; adults' sexual standards are more conservative than those they held when young, and adults with children are more conservative than those without children.

CHAPTER XX—SOCIAL CLASS AND SEXUAL COUNSELING

The physician should keep in mind that if the patient comes from a different level of society than that of the sexual partner, varying attitudes toward sexuality may be complicating the sexual and marital relationship. For example, when a middle class woman complains that her middle class husband is consistently brusque and inconsiderate, the partners require counseling on the importance of consideration and communication in coitus. If, on the other hand, the husband comes from an environment in which women were treated as sexual objects, the physician must consider the life-long conditioning at the root of the husband's attitude and adjust his counseling accordingly. Many subtle but critically important differences in environment and experience can only be uncovered through careful interviewing by the physician.

Similarly, when a physician discusses sexual development with a patient, he should take the patient's environment into consideration. The sexual activities of an adolescent living in a ghetto may not approach the physician's concept of "morality" and it may be difficult for him to give meaningful counseling free of his own sexual values. Nevertheless, nonjudgmental counseling can have a favorable influence on the patient's sexual behavior and later married life. Because of changing mores, the middle class teenage girl may feel socially pressured into accepting coitus in the same way that her mother felt pressured into rejecting it. The physician can help the girl clarify her feelings and make the decision that is most appropriate for her if he counsels wisely within the framework of her environment.

CHAPTER XXI—SEX EDUCATION IN THE COMMUNITY

In discussing sex education in the community, physicians should clearly emphasize that the choice never has been whether to have sex education or not to have it. There has always been sex education on the playground and in family living. The child has been able to observe the attitudes and behavior of the mother and father as man and woman. Physicians, religious, and other counselors, however, testify to the frequent inadequacy of this informal background, as they see its results in the marital problems of the present generation of adults. All professionals who deal with the young are eager to take constructive action to help prevent the development of similar sex-related problems in the next generation. Today we are finally thinking about how sex education can best be presented.

The evasiveness of parents when their children wonder or ask about sex is a major problem (and will continue to be so) for it stems from two sources: adults show an abysmal ignorance of even elementary facts relating to reproduction; parents feel embarrassment discussing these "private" matters with their children. In our society husbands and wives often are unable to communicate freely with each other about their sexuality. Children are constantly exposed to sexual stimuli but are not provided with the balancing factor of sound sexual knowledge given by respected authority figures in their lives.

Teachers, when introducing sex education programs in California, discovered seventh grade children who had received no factual information about sex from their parents. Few children could correctly name their own sex organs, much less those of the opposite sex. A study of 5,000 children,[6] kindergarten through 12th grade, conducted by the Connecticut State Department of Education clearly shows that children want to know about what they instinctively recognize as a universally important part of all life. Coupled with this need as expressed by youth itself, various polls of the past 20 years show that 70% of American adults desire programs of sex education in the schools and clearly indicate a mandate that should be recognized and implemented. At the national level, major professional groups in medicine, health, education, and religion have made policy statements supporting sex education in the school. Thus, the physician is on firm ground when he joins the leaders of his community in a movement towards fulfilling this responsibility.

The American Medical Association and other medical organizations have taken a positive stance regarding the need for the education of children and young people on sexuality in the institutions of the community, particularly the schools:

"Whereas, The traditional sources of sex information and guidance for young people are often inadequate; and Whereas, The local public and parochial schools——as social institutions accessible to all young people, reflecting broad community support and with sufficient intellectual and material resources——can aid substantially in the development of sound individual codes of sexual behavior; therefore be it

Resolved, That the American Medical Association recognizes that the primary responsibility for family life education is in the home, but that the AMA supports in principle the inauguration by State Boards of Education or school districts, whichever is applicable, of a voluntary family life and sex education program at appropriate grade levels:

1. as part of an overall health education program;
2. presented in a manner commensurate with the maturation level of the students;
3. following a professionally developed curriculum foreviewed by representative parents;
4. including ample and continuing involvement of parents and other concerned members of the community;
5. developed around a system of values defined and delineated by representatives comprising physicians, educators, the clergy and other appropriate groups; and
6. utilizing classroom teachers and other professionals who have an aptitude for working with young people and who have received special training; and be it further

Resolved, That local organizations be urged to utilize physicians as consultants, advisors and resource persons in the development and guidance of such curricula and that state and county medical associations be urged to take an active role in this participation."

When the opportunity to contribute to the formulation of sex education plans in the community presents itself, certain basic concepts need to be firmly established at the outset by the physician:

1. Orientation on sex education of school age children has already begun for each child, the child has made observations of critical importance in his own home and the playground has made its own contribution to his views, regardless of the child's age.

2. Sex should not be compartmentalized within the general area of health education. A successful program must maintain sex within the perspective of the whole being.

Experience demonstrates that with a little encouragement from the classroom teacher, students themselves will lead a discussion on sexuality into the areas of interest of their own age group. The responsibility of the teacher lies in maintaining sexuality as a part of the broad area which comprises health education.

In the lower grades, students should be encouraged to discuss the roles and responsibilities of the respective members of the family, even if the family is not traditionally constituted. Discussions such as these are the basis for a rational approach to education on human sexuality.

Students in the middle grades may be introduced to the biologic reproductive system as one aspect of human sexuality and as one system among many in the complex human organism. In some locales the concept of communicable diseases should be introduced at this level; venereal disease has been reported in some students in 5th and 6th grades in some schools. In the upper grades, materials should be addressed to preparing the individual for reproduction. Responsibility is the key word at all levels.

Education on human sexuality should not be approached as a community's insurance policy against venereal disease or premarital pregnancy. A successful program must be planned to aid the child to develop the sexuality component of his being in an orderly and responsible manner.

How the primary institutions of the society, the family, church and school can best serve the needs of the child in the development of the sexual component within his total personality structure is a basic issue confronting our society. Today, accepting that challenge, the physician is clearly one who can and should play a key role.

CHAPTER XXII—THE MULTIPLICITY OF ROLES
OF THE PHYSICIAN

The physician is an educator in the realm of human sexuality whether he wishes to be or not. His position of authority, the knowledge he possesses and his close relationships with people make him a natural source of information. As an educator, he must be sensitive to the needs and views of those he is counseling or addressing, aware of the contribution he can make, and willing to devote the necessary time to studying the subject. It is not easy to fulfill these responsibilities, but the physician can find great satisfaction in fostering a healthy understanding of human sexuality.

The demands on physicians who serve as counselors are likely to grow and may necessitate special planning. Many physicians devote a block of time late in the day, or a half day each week to counseling. The physician may find it especially rewarding at the end of a crowded day to spend time talking in depth with a few patients. In a group practice, the patient with a sexual problem should be seen by the same physician throughout treatment if at all possible. The counselor today also has to acquire much information about the patient which the family physician had as a matter of course, and he should utilize all suitable sources of help. There has been a great increase in the number of allied health workers in recent years and the physician should avail himself of these professionals so that he can most usefully spend his time with his patients.

There are many roles that the physician may play in the development of community sex education programs. He may be a catalyst, an initiator, a consultant, a planner, a regular participant or a guest speaker. He must work out his own participation on the basis of the needs of the community and the time he has available, but his participation in certain aspects is essential.

The role of catalyst is commonly underestimated. The physician has many significant opportunities to discuss and promote adequate programs of sex education, since his own practice is likely to include teachers, administrators, parents, ministers, nurses and community leaders who should take a meaningful interest in the teaching of sexuality. Moreover, these professional people also have many opportunities to exert a beneficial influence. The interested physician can also assist in the training of other potential sex educators including other physicians, health workers, social workers, and nurses. He can emphasize to them the importance of sex education, sensitize them to present needs, show them how to develop their own roles as sex educators and help them to avoid mistakes.

A number of medical schools have instituted speakers bureaus which supply surrounding communities with medical students trained to conduct public discussions on human sexuality. These programs also serve as training grounds for the medical students, who are sent out in teams. One partner conducts the discussion, and another sits in the audience, often with a tape recorder. Fellow students then are given a review of the session or listen to the tape and offer constructive criticisms.

The Sex Education Council of Students at the University of Washington[7] maintains a Speakers Bureau whose medical and nursing students presented more than 225 discussions on sexuality in three years. Programs were presented to grade school, high school and college students, to parent and church groups and in ghetto communities. The standard format for each discussion consisted of a brief talk followed by an extensive period for questions and answers. The topics covered were anatomy, physiology, contraception, disease, and moral and ethical issues, with variations in depth according to the level of sophistication of the group. The emphasis was on self-understanding, the individual's responsibility for intelligent decision-making, the importance of love and affection, and especially with parent groups "the need for communication."

A physician can initiate and even participate in such a program. In 1960, a New England pediatrician attended a White House Conference on Children and returned to his home determined to persuade his community to inaugurate a program of sex education. He told the members of the School Board that he was willing and able to conduct sex education classes for the elementary school. The Board welcomed his offer and he has been conducting courses for children from kindergarten through the sixth grade ever since. Other local physicians followed his lead, and the community now has a broad, continuing program of sex education.

In the physician's role as a consultant, he can answer questions pertaining to such subjects as physiology and venereal diseases, which may be outside the educator's sphere of competence. He can also contribute to the relevancy of the program by discussing problems and attitudes he encounters in his practice. However, in many cases, the physician can accomplish more by acting as an advisor and consultant to teachers than by personally presenting lectures.

Sex education in the schools should be only one part of an overall community approach to sex education. Resources for educating people of all ages should be evaluated, and other types of discussion groups organized, including classes for prenatal care, as needed. The program may be carried out in schools, in churches or both. Some communities include children and parents in these courses; others invite parents and children to participate separately but keep each group aware of what the other is doing. It may take up to two years to develop such a comprehensive program, but the time will be well spent. Hastily devised programs will be inadequate and fail to get the necessary community support. Throughout the planning stage, meetings and press releases should be utilized to keep the public informed of progress. Criticisms should be welcomed and discussed — early critics often turn out to be long-range supporters. Finally, there should be provision for continuing evaluation of the program.

In responding to a request to speak on the subject of human sexuality, the physician should inquire about the nature of the audience, their sophistication and concerns, the format of the meeting, any specific aspect which may be of special interest, and the intended goals of the program. Before accepting the invitation he should be sure he is capable of contributing to the particular meeting. Politicians know that the way one says something is often more important than what one says, and the physician who is uncomfortable, embarrassed or unsure of himself on matters of sexuality will have difficulty communicating. Conversely, one who is relaxed and comfortable with the subject may accomplish much, quite apart from the specifics of his presentation. The American College of Obstetricians and Gynecologists has published a useful pamphlet, "A Guide For Community Action in Family Life Education," which lists considerations for the prospective speaker in detail and gives a selected reading list for preparation.

Many physicians find it helpful to view a presentation to any group on the subject of sexuality not as a lecture, but as a discussion. A single discussion of human sexuality by a knowledgeable physician can benefit any group, but a series of discussions may be even more profitable. Audiences of any age have similar questions regarding sexuality; they want to know something about such aspects as sexual response, pregnancy, delivery, abortion, venereal disease, contraception, and sterilization. The physician should concentrate on areas with which he is familiar and make them more meaningful by discussing clinical examples. Models and illustrations representing anatomical considerations and contraceptive techniques are often helpful. A brief exposition on anatomical facts and reproductive phenomena may often serve as a natural, useful starting point.

The most frequently expressed criticism of programs for teaching human sexuality is that they encourage children to engage in sexual activity. The physician should answer categorically that no such connection between information and undesirable activity exists. He should also emphasize that the informed boy or girl is the least likely to engage in sexual activity out of anxiety or the need for reassurance.

Whatever the format most suitable for the particular group and community, the material should be presented positively, factually, and honestly. Negativism and narrowness have been failings of numerous programs in the past. The rightful goals of sex education are to foster knowledge and understanding and reduce, rather than arouse, fears and anxieties. Some courses in family living have concentrated on such subjects as venereal disease, drug addiction, alcoholism and divorce. Some have been thinly disguised attempts to frighten children away from premarital sexual activity by emphasizing the perils of disease, pregnancy and abortion. Reiss[8] concluded that a number of sex education programs had moralistic and propagandistic overtones, overemphasis on physiology, inadequate teacher training and unclear objectives, and were isolated from other courses. He found repeated references to the value of chastity, the dangers of going steady and the abuses of masturbation. Planning groups may be subjected to pressures to include moralistic advice; these pressures should be resisted. Sexuality is an area of personal decision. Thus, the educator should present and discuss moral considerations in an objective manner without attempting to impose a code of morality.

Margolis has defined sex education as "...education about all the things that affect you or have an impact on you, and the role you play in life, simply because you are born a male or a female." Whether it is conducted in the home, the school, the church or the physician's office, the aim of education on human sexuality is always to create an understanding of human sexual development and response and the broad role which human sexuality plays in the life of every individual.

REFERENCES—PART IV

1. Coombs RH: Acquiring sex attitudes and information in our society, in Vincent CE (ed): *Human Sexuality in Medical Education and Practice.* Springfield, Ill, Charles C Thomas Publisher, 1968, pp 293-294.

2. Christensen HT: Questions of standards and values, in Broderick CB, Bernard J (eds): *The Individual, Sex and Society.* Baltimore, Johns Hopkins Press, 1969, pp 158-164.

3. Reiss IL: Premarital sexual standards and values, in Bernard J (eds): *The Individual, Sex and Society.* Baltimore, Johns Hopkins Press, 1969, pp 111-112.

4. Reiss IL: *The Social Context of Pre-marital Sexual Permissiveness.* New York, Holt Rinehart & Winston Inc, 1967, p 67.

5. Ibid, p 29.

6. Byler, R: *Teach Us What We Want to Know.* Connecticut State Board of Education, Published by the Mental Health Materials Center, Inc, New York, 1969, pp 131-133.

7. Fairbrook D, Bearman D: Methods of sex education. *New Physician* 17: 652, 1970.

8. Reiss IL: Sex education in the public schools: Problem or solution? *Phi Delta Kappan* 50: 52, 1968.

APPENDICES, BIBLIOGRAPHY, GLOSSARY & INDEX

APPENDIX I

Marriage Council of Philadelphia, Inc.
Affiliated with the
Division of Family Study, Department of Psychiatry
University of Pennsylvania School of Medicine
4025 Chestnut Street
Philadelphia, Pennsylvania 19104
BAring 2-7574

SEXUAL PERFORMANCE EVALUATION

(Client will please check answer where indicated)

Case No.   Interviewer
Date Schedule Filled
Filled before ( ) During ( ) or after ( ) counseling on sex adjustment.

1. Are you satisfied with the sexual adjustment in your marriage?
   Do you think your spouse is?

   Yourself   Spouse

   1—Yes   ( )   1—Yes   ( )
   2—No   ( )   2—No   ( )
   3—Mixed feelings ( )   3—Mixed feelings ( )
   4—Do not know   ( )   4—Do not know   ( )

   If not, what is not satisfactory to you?

   If not, what do you think is not satisfactory to your spouse?

2. Have you had any difficulty with any of the following?

                                                        Present
   1—Techniques of petting and foreplay   ( )
   2—Positions   ( )
   3—Wife's inactivity   ( )
   4—Wife does not achieve orgasm   ( )
   5—Husband has difficulty with erection   ( )
   6—Husband has orgasm too quickly   ( )
   7—Painful intercourse   ( )
   8—Fear of pregnancy   ( )
   9—Husband wishes more frequent sexual activity than wife   ( )
   10—Wife wishes more frequent sexual activity than husband   ( )
   11—Differences in attitudes towards sex   ( )
   12—Fatigue   ( )
   13—Lack of privacy   ( )
   14—Interference with sex due to working hours   ( )
   15—Other (specify)
   16—No difficulties

3. Have you been in touch with anyone for assistance with the sexual side of
   your marriage?

                  1—No
                  2—Yes

If yes, how long ago?   Years   or Months

If yes, describe the type of person or agency and whether you were helped.

	Not any help	Received some help	Great deal
Relative	( )	( )	( )
Friend	( )	( )	( )
Doctor	( )	(.)	( )
Psychiatrist	( )	( )	( )
Social Agency	( )	( )	( )
Clinical Psychologist	( )	( )	( )
Clergyman (Minister,			
Priest or Rabbi)	( )	( )	( )
Teacher	( )	( )	( )
Other (specify)	( )	( )	( )

4. How frequently on the average do you and your spouse have intercourse at present? ("Average" means typical or usual)

( ) 1—No intercourse
( ) 2—Less than once a month (specify)
( ) 3—Once or twice a month
( ) 4—Once a week
( ) 5—Twice a week
( ) 6—Three times a week
( ) 7—Four times a week
( ) 8—Five times a week
( ) 9—Six times a week
( ) 10—Seven or more times a week

5. How do you and your spouse feel about frequency?

Self   Spouse
1 ( ) Satisfied   1 ( )
2 ( ) Desire intercourse more frequently   2 ( )
3 ( ) Desire intercourse less frequently   3 ( )
4 ( ) Do not know   4 ( )

6. A. Are any of the following conditions affecting you and your spouse, so that you feel present sex activity is not representative? (Do not include aging or the passage of time.)

1—Pregnancy   ( )   7—Own or partner's health
2—Unusual job situation   (mental or physical)   ( )
3—Separation (not due to   8—Own or partner's interest
    marital friction)   ( )   in other person(s)   ( )
4—Separation (due to   9—Presence of children   ( )
    marital friction)   ( )   10—Personal or family crisis   ( )
5—Marital friction   ( )   11—Other (specify)   ( )
6—Housing   ( )   12—No (ie, present sex activity
                                                  is representative)   ( )

B. If there are such conditions, how do you feel they affect your relationship?

    1. For the better ( ) 2. For the worse ( ) 3. Neither better nor worse ( )

C. Approximately when did these conditions begin to affect it?
                        Months or   Years ago.

D. If you feel there is a more typical frequency of intercourse than reported in Question No. 4, what is it?

    (Use frequencies as in Question No. 4)
    If there is no frequency, check here_____

7. What is the duration of sex play prior to penetration?
    (Be sure to answer even if there is no penetration)

Present			Past (if different)	
1.	( )	No sex play	1.	( )
2.	( )	Less than 10 minutes	2.	( )
3.	( )	10 minutes to less than 20 minutes	3.	( )
4.	( )	20 minutes to less than 30 minutes	4.	( )
5.	( )	30 minutes to less than 45 minutes	5.	( )
6.	( )	45 minutes to an hour	6.	( )
7.	( )	Over one hour	7.	( )

8. How do you and your spouse feel about this duration?

Present				Past (if different)	
Self	Spouse		Self	Spouse	
1. ( )	1. ( )	Satisfied	1. ( )	1. ( )	
2. ( )	2. ( )	Desire longer sex play	2. ( )	2. ( )	
3. ( )	3. ( )	Desire shorter sex play	3. ( )	3. ( )	
4. ( )	4. ( )	Do not know	4. ( )	4. ( )	

9. Average duration of penetration (include time before and after orgasm).

Present			Past (if different)	
1. ( )	No penetration		1. ( )	
2. ( )	Less than 1 minute		2. ( )	
3. ( )	1 minute to less than 5 min.		3. ( )	
4. ( )	5 minutes to less than 10 min.		4. ( )	
5. ( )	10 minutes to 20 min.		5. ( )	
6. ( )	Over 20 minutes (specify)		6. ( )	

10. How do you and your spouse each feel about this duration?

Present			Past (if different)	
Self	Spouse		Self	Spouse
1. ( )	1. ( ) Satisfied		1. ( )	1. ( )
2. ( )	2. ( ) Desire longer time of penetration		2. ( )	2. ( )
3. ( )	3. ( ) Desire shorter time of penetration		3. ( )	3. ( )
4. ( )	4. ( ) Do not know		4. ( )	4. ( )

11. Do you and your spouse have intercourse during menstrual period?

Present		Past (if different)
1. ( )	Usually	1. ( )
2. ( )	Occasionally	2. ( )
3. ( )	Rarely	3. ( )
4. ( )	Never	4. ( )
5. ( )	No menstrual periods	5. ( )

12. How do you each feel about intercourse during menstrual periods?
(Give your feelings whether you have intercourse at this time or not.)

Self	Spouse	
1. ( )	1. ( )	Feel the same as at other times
2. ( )	2. ( )	Dislike intercourse during menstrual periods
3. ( )	3. ( )	Prefer intercourse during menstrual periods
4. ( )	4. ( )	No objections, but believe it harmful
5. ( )	5. ( )	Do not know

13. During your sex activity together, does wife have orgasm?

Present		Past (if different)
1. ( )	Always	1. ( )
2. ( )	Nearly always	2. ( )
3. ( )	About half the time	3. ( )
4. ( )	Seldom	4. ( )
5. ( )	Never	5. ( )
6. ( )	Do not know	6. ( )

14. How do you and your spouse each feel about frequency of wife's orgasm?

Present			Past (if different)	
Self	Spouse		Self	Spouse
1. ( )	1. ( )	Satisfied with frequency	1. ( )	1. ( )
2. ( )	2. ( )	Dissatisfied, but not upset by it	2. ( )	2. ( )
3. ( )	3. ( )	Dissatisfied and upset by it	3. ( )	3. ( )
4. ( )	4. ( )	Do not know	4. ( )	4. ( )

15. Do you have more than one orgasm during a complete sex act (the period from start of arousal to end of activity connected with that arousal)? Does your spouse?

Present			Past (if different)	
Self	Spouse		Self	Spouse
1. ( )	1. ( )	No orgasm	1. ( )	1. ( )
2. ( )	2. ( )	Never more than 1 per act	2. ( )	2. ( )
3. ( )	3. ( )	Occasionally more than 1 per act	3. ( )	3. ( )
4. ( )	4. ( )	Frequently more than 1 per act	4. ( )	4. ( )
5. ( )	5. ( )	Do not know	5. ( )	5. ( )

16. When you or your spouse have orgasm during activity together, does it always occur by penetration?

Present

Self	Spouse		Past (if different)	
			Self	Spouse
1. ( )	1. ( )	Always by penetration	1. ( )	1. ( )
2. ( )	2. ( )	Sometimes by penetration, sometimes by other means	2. ( )	2. ( )
3. ( )	3. ( )	Always by other means	3. ( )	3. ( )
4. ( )	4. ( )	No orgasm	4. ( )	4. ( )

17. If your own orgasm occurs by means other than penetration, how do you and your spouse each feel about it?

Present

Self	Spouse		Past (if different)	
			Self	Spouse
1. ( )	1. ( )	Not achieved by other means	1. ( )	1. ( )
2. ( )	2. ( )	Comfortable	2. ( )	2. ( )
3. ( )	3. ( )	Uncomfortable	3. ( )	3. ( )
4. ( )	4. ( )	Indifferent	4. ( )	4. ( )
5. ( )	5. ( )	Do not know	5. ( )	5. ( )

18. If your spouse's orgasm occurs by means other than penetration, how do you and your spouse each feel about it?

Present

Self	Spouse		Past (if different)	
			Self	Spouse
1. ( )	1. ( )	Not achieved by other means	1. ( )	1. ( )
2. ( )	2. ( )	Comfortable	2. ( )	2. ( )
3. ( )	3. ( )	Uncomfortable	3. ( )	3. ( )
4. ( )	4. ( )	Indifferent	4. ( )	4. ( )
5. ( )	5. ( )	Do not know	5. ( )	5. ( )

19. How frequently does it occur that your spouse desires intercourse and you do not?

Present		Past (if different)
1. ( )	Frequently	1. ( )
2. ( )	Occasionally	2. ( )
3. ( )	Rarely	3. ( )
4. ( )	Never	4. ( )
5. ( )	Do not know when spouse desires intercourse	5. ( )

20. How frequently does it occur that you desire intercourse and your spouse does not?

Present		Past (if different)
1. ( )	Frequently	1. ( )
2. ( )	Occasionally	2. ( )
3. ( )	Rarely	3. ( )
4. ( )	Never	4. ( )
5. ( )	Do not know when spouse desires intercourse	5. ( )

21. If you are not desirous, do you have intercourse to please your spouse?

Present
1. ( ) Frequently
2. ( ) Occasionally
3. ( ) Rarely
4. ( ) Never
5. ( ) Does not apply

Past (if different)
1. ( )
2. ( )
3. ( )
4. ( )
5. ( )

22. If your spouse is not desirous, does he/she have intercourse to please you?

Present
1. ( ) Frequently
2. ( ) Occasionally
3. ( ) Rarely
4. ( ) Never
5. ( ) Does not apply
6. ( ) Do not know

Past (if different)
1. ( )
2. ( )
3. ( )
4. ( )
5. ( )
6. ( )

23. In general, have you and your spouse been using any method of child spacing?

1. ( ) No method
2. ( ) Rhythm method ("safe period")
3. ( ) Withdrawal
4. ( ) Other methods
5. ( ) Do not know

24. Do you and your spouse each feel secure about your method, or lack of method, of child spacing?

Yourself	Spouse	
1. ( )	1. ( )	Feel secure
2. ( )	2. ( )	Feel insecure
3. ( )	3. ( )	Do not know

25. Apart from security, how do you and your spouse each feel about your method, or lack of method, of child spacing?

Yourself	Spouse	
1. ( )	1. ( )	Satisfied
2. ( )	2. ( )	Dissatisfied
3. ( )	3. ( )	Indifferent
4. ( )	4. ( )	Do not know

26. Can you and your spouse each discuss your feelings about sex freely with one another?

Yourself	Spouse	
1. ( )	1. ( )	Yes
2. ( )	2. ( )	No
3. ( )	3. ( )	About some things, not others
4. ( )	4. ( )	Do not know

166

DOES YOUR SEX
ACTIVITY WITH
YOUR SPOUSE
INCLUDE THE
FOLLOWING:

		Frequency:		Satisfaction with Frequency		Feelings about types of activity, whether or not you participate in them:

(a) GENERAL KISSING AND CARESSING

	Present	Past	Self	Spouse	Self	Spouse
1. Always	1	1	1. Satisfied	1	1. Like
2. Usually	2	2	2. Dissatisfied	2	2. Dislike
3. Rarely	3	3	3. Indifferent	3	3. Mixed feelings
4. Never	4	4	4. Do not know	4	4. Indifferent
				5	5. Do not know

(b) DEEP KISS

	Present	Past	Self	Spouse	Self	Spouse
1. Always	1	1	1. Satisfied	1	1. Like
2. Usually	2	2	2. Dissatisfied	2	2. Dislike
3. Rarely	3	3	3. Indifferent	3	3. Mixed feelings
4. Never	4	4	4. Do not know	4	4. Indifferent
				5	5. Do not know

(c) MANUAL MANIPULATION OF WIFE'S BREASTS

	Present	Past	Self	Spouse	Self	Spouse
1. Always	1	1	1. Satisfied	1	1. Like
2. Usually	2	2	2. Dissatisfied	2	2. Dislike
3. Rarely	3	3	3. Indifferent	3	3. Mixed feelings
4. Never	4	4	4. Do not know	4	4. Indifferent
				5	5. Do not know

(d) MOUTH MANIPULATION OF WIFE'S BREASTS

	Present	Past	Self	Spouse	Self	Spouse
1. Always	1	1	1. Satisfied	1	1. Like
2. Usually	2	2	2. Dissatisfied	2	2. Dislike
3. Rarely	3	3	3. Indifferent	3	3. Mixed feelings
4. Never	4	4	4. Do not know	4	4. Indifferent
				5	5. Do not know

(e) MANUAL MANIPULATION OF FEMALE GENITALIA

	Present	Past	Self	Spouse	Self	Spouse
1. Always	1	1	1. Satisfied	1	1. Like
2. Usually	2	2	2. Dissatisfied	2	2. Dislike
3. Rarely	3	3	3. Indifferent	3	3. Mixed feelings
4. Never	4	4	4. Do not know	4	4. Indifferent
				5	5. Do not know

(f) MANUAL MANIPULATION OF MALE GENITALIA

	Present	Past	Self	Spouse	Self	Spouse
1. Always	1	1	1. Satisfied	1	1. Like
2. Usually	2	2	2. Dissatisfied	2	2. Dislike
3. Rarely	3	3	3. Indifferent	3	3. Mixed feelings
4. Never	4	4	4. Do not know	4	4. Indifferent
				5	5. Do not know

(g) ORAL CONTACT WITH FEMALE GENITALIA

	Present	Past	Self	Spouse	Self	Spouse
1. Always	1	1	1. Satisfied	1	1. Like
2. Usually	2	2	2. Dissatisfied	2	2. Dislike
3. Rarely	3	3	3. Indifferent	3	3. Mixed feelings
4. Never	4	4	4. Do not know	4	4. Indifferent
				5	5. Do not know

(h) ORAL CONTACT   Present   Past Self Spouse   Self Spouse
      WITH MALE   1. Always 1   1   1. Satisfied   1 1. Like
      GENITALIA   2. Usually 2   2   2. Dissatisfied 2 2. Dislike
                       3. Rarely   3   3   3. Indifferent   3 3. Mixed feelings
                       4. Never   4   4   4. Do not know 4 4. Indifferent
                                                      5 5. Do not know

(i) ANAL PLAY   Present   Past Self Spouse   Self Spouse
                       1. Always 1   1   1. Satisfied   1 1. Like
                       2. Usually 2   2   2. Dissatisfied 2 2. Dislike
                       3. Rarely   3   3   3. Indifferent   3 3. Mixed feelings
                       4. Never   4   4   4. Do not know 4 4. Indifferent
                                                      5 5. Do not know

(j) OTHER ACTIVITY WITH SPOUSE? (Specify and give frequency and feelings as above)

28. What position(s) do you and your spouse use in intercourse?

          1. Male above usually   ( )
          2. Female above usually   ( )
          3. Male above and female above equally ( )
          4. Side by side   ( )
          5. Usually other positions   ( )

29. To what extent have you and your spouse experimented with positions?

          1. Never   ( )
          2. Occasionally ( )
          3. Frequently   ( )

30. How do you and your spouse each feel about the position(s) you usually use?

         Yourself   Spouse
           ( )   1. Satisfied   ( )
           ( )   2. Dissatisfied ( )
           ( )   3. Indifferent   ( )
           ( )   4. Do not know ( )

31. Who usually takes the initiative in sex activity?

          1. Husband ( )
          2. Wife   ( )
          3. Varies   ( )

32. Are there any questions pertaining to your sexual performance you would like to discuss in person?

               Yes
               No

Portion of a Sample Interview

Sample Interview Provided by Harold I. Lief, M.D.

A 35-year old female patient, married at 17, has been referred to a clinic by her physician after her husband developed secondary impotence.

COMMENT: At first the patient talks about her husband's poor performance, but after a little while it becomes clear that she has had a long-standing inability to reach a climax.

Dr: Tell me more about the problem—not only how long it has been going on but what the problem is and what it means to you and so on.

P: Well, it's frustration on both our parts, I guess—on his part because I don't give in as often as he would like, on my part because I am never satisfied when I do it or else I am completely cold. It is either one way or the other.

Dr: You used the phrase "give in," one moment ago. What do you mean by that?

COMMENT: The therapist senses that a key problem may be the patient's equating of orgasm and submission to her husband. At a conscious level the patient and her husband are in a constant battle over frequency of coitus.

P: Well, there are, I don't know whether you would call it a tug-of-war, but when I said "give in," I meant give in as far as making love.

Dr: Well, that to me has some implication of doing something that you don't want to do.

P: There are times when I don't feel like it and he pursues it, which I think builds up resistance in me, so that it's a vicious cycle. And there are times when I get emotionally involved and then I'm dissatisfied, and he feels that, too.

Dr: Over the last several years, have there been some times when you have had a satisfactory experience?

P: No.

Dr: Not one time over the last several years? When was the last time that you remember?

P: I can't remember.

Dr: Not in eighteen years of marriage?

P: I know it sounds impossible, but I can't remember.

Dr: My goodness, what has your reaction been to this highly unsatisfactory situation?

P: I felt cheated.

Dr: Right from the start?

P: I can't remember from the start whether I felt this way or not. I do know that for quite a few years, I have felt just this way. If I was passionately involved, I was dissatisfied; if not, it was just like doing nothing and then I wasn't dissatisfied after this, so at times I guess I just thought it was safer that way.

Dr: To turn off your feelings?

P: Yes.

The physician inquires into the patient's feelings during the first six months of their marriage. She reports that in the beginning she really did not know what to expect of sex, and, although never feeling fulfilled, was less dissatisfied than during the past six or seven years. Her desire for sexual activity increased notably when her husband became impotent. The physician explains that there are obviously two problems here, and inquires about the husband's impotence. The patient says that the impotence ceased when she was fitted with an IUD, but she still felt no relief of her own tensions. Several events coincided with the development of secondary impotence. Her husband had just recovered from the flu the first time he could not attain erection; he had developed a small bald spot on his neck; they had moved into a new house and their expenses were somewhat higher. But she can pinpoint no change in their relationship at the time. The physician returns to the problem of her responsiveness.

Dr: Let's go back. Now, under what circumstances do you have a climax?

P: I've never had a climax.

Dr: Does this mean that you never had a climax with self-stimulation?

P: Just recently—I've been sort of frantic.

The patient reports that she recently masturbated for the first time after reading in a manual that masturbation was not harmful or wrong and could educate a woman about her own senses. The physician says she seems to have some negative feelings about masturbation, and the patient admits that she may. At this point in her life, she says, she doesn't feel she should have to resort to that. She can't remember what her feelings on the subject were during adolescence, and says she never thought of it. "I guess I was more naive than most," she says.

Dr: Well, the first time you tried, that must have been quite an emotional experience for you.

P: Well, I think the only reason I did try it was because I was feeling frustrated. It wasn't a cold-blooded decision to try. It was a feeling that I was left over from the night before. It was just something that I tried.

Dr: You shake your head meaning that it didn't work. Did you get any greater sense of excitement than with intercourse?

P: No.

Dr: This was what, using your finger?

P: Yes.

Dr: Anything else?

P: No.

COMMENT: The Doctor senses the patient's extreme discomfort, so he shifts the subject to her feelings at that moment.

Dr: How easy is it or difficult for you to talk now?

P: Very difficult.

Dr: You feel embarrassed to go on talking about it?

P: Nervous.

Dr: You feel strange for you to discuss this?

P: That's right.

Dr: With a stranger or with a physician?

P: That's right. I've never discussed this with anybody but my husband.

Dr: I gather that the whole area of sex has been sort of taboo throughout your life, I mean in terms of those discussions with other people.

P: Strangers, right. I never felt as if I was a prude or anything like that, but I always had to know someone fairly well to talk about sex but I never talked about myself and sex to anyone.

Recently, the patient says, she has discussed her problem with a sister. Her sister feels it is very unusual, and that she is right in feeling that she should not have to "have sex" every night. "The more he tries the more I put him off, the more he tries," she says. She becomes aroused during coitus, but "it reaches a certain point and then I am just left there."

P: . . . I know it sounds like I don't love him or want to make love when I say he tries to have sex, but at that time that is the way I feel.

Dr: What is it that you feel?

P: If I am tired and don't feel good, he knows it and instead of just going off to sleep, he doesn't. So he makes me put him off, which I don't like to do.

170

Dr: How do you feel?

P: I feel resentful.

Dr: Well, you feel he is inconsiderate and puts you in an awkward spot of having to say no. And he is angry, too, I suppose—you both go to sleep angry. What happens the next morning?

COMMENT: At times it is worthwhile to put into words the patient's feelings. If the doctor is "on the beam" empathy is increased and the patient feels the doctor understands. If the doctor is in error, the patient has a chance to correct the therapist's misperception.

P: He forgets about it and acts as if nothing has happened, and I don't—I'm resentful and I am still angry.

Near the end of the interview, the physician gives the patient some basic information about female sexual response.

Dr: Let me back up and give you a couple of words of explanation. Basically, there are two major reasons why a woman will not have an orgasm. Either there is some psychic block creating an inhibition of her response, and this is usually because she is frightened, guilty, or angry. One of those emotions inhibits her response. Or there is inadequate preparation, which means that there hasn't been enough body stimulation, both generally over the whole body and locally in the area of the vagina and the clitoris to bring her to a peak of excitation. And sometimes there is a combination of these two reasons so that what I have to do is to ask you very specific questions and, when I see your husband, I would want to know from him what goes on because I have to judge whether you are getting adequate preparation. Many times, it is simply that there is inadequate preparation of the woman. She has to be brought to a peak of excitation generally before penetration, before intercourse, and if this is not accomplished, she will not be able to respond fully. And what I gather so far from talking to you is that there has been some kind of change in you—within you psychologically or some change in your preparation— so that over the last two years you are much more responsive than you were prior to that. So that's why I am asking rather detailed questions, hoping that you will be embarrassed as little as possible by my asking detailed questions. It is only in this way can I know, indeed, whether you are getting adequate preparation, And to help out, I'll show you some pictures, not now, but the next time I see you so that you have a fuller understanding of your own body and what is necessary. Does this make sense?

P: Yes, it does. I guess that stimulation really hasn't been proper because I reach a certain peak and then it becomes painful—the stimulation.

Dr: Actually becomes painful?

P: Yes.

Dr: Tell me more about that.

P: You are talking about the manual stimulation, what do you call it—the clitoris— at that point I guess is when the penetration occurs but at that point also—

Dr: You are already turned off by the pain when he is penetrating.

P: Right.

In answer to a question about use of oral-genital stimulation, the patient says that she has a "revulsion" when her husband stimulates her orally.

Dr: How do you feel about stimulating him?

P: I don't feel adverse to it as long as there is no ejaculation.

Dr: I see. But that is not a reciprocal thing. What feeling do you get?

P: An uneasy feeling. I cannot quite put my finger on it. Just a feeling that I don't want him to do it.

COMMENT: The session ended soon after, after an appointment was made to see the husband alone and then the couple together. If one patient is seen alone, it is usually a good idea to give the couple some time alone, to forestall the feeling that the doctor is taking sides with the original patient.

The patient described here was a markedly inhibited person, not at all comfortable with her own body and with strong taboos against masturbation and oral-genital stimulation. It turned out that her husband, overly concerned about his masculinity, would demand intercourse nightly, leading to sex being a central battleground in the fight over which partner was dominant. Her struggle for power took the form of denying him intercourse; other areas of marital discontent also were fought out in the marital bed Unfortunately, the wife was afraid that if she were to experience an orgasm she would be driven by her need for sexual gratification to submit to her husband's incessant demands, and would be enslaved to him. This is the type of difficult case that should be referred to a psychiatrist or marriage counselor.

CENTER FOR THE STUDY OF SEX EDUCATION IN MEDICINE

SEX KNOWLEDGE AND ATTITUDE TEST
(S. K. A. T.)

A TEST ON KNOWLEDGE ABOUT AND ATTITUDES
CONCERNING SEXUAL BEHAVIOR.

Second Edition
(REVISED 1972)

Division of Family Study
Department of Psychiatry
University of Pennsylvania
School of Medicine
4025 Chestnut Street
Philadelphia, Pennsylvania
19104

HAROLD I. LIEF, M.D.   *DAVID M. REED, Ph.D*
R. KURT EBERT, Ph.D.

Marriage Council of Philadelphia
4025 Chestnut Street
Philadelphia, Pa. 19104

MARITAL PROBLEMS QUESTIONNAIRE

In order to help us obtain a better understanding of your marital situation, please answer the following questions. The questionnaire will then become a part of your confidential file.

Please note there are no "right" answers; the only correct response is the most honest one.

Directions: Circle the appropriate letter according to the following: "(Word or statement) plays a_____part in my marital problems."

A=major part B=large part C=some part D=small part E=no part

1.	Finances	A	B	C	D	E
2.	Children	A	B	C	D	E
3.	Parents	A	B	C	D	E
4.	In-Laws	A	B	C	D	E
5.	Religion	A	B	C	D	E
6.	Race	A	B	C	D	E
7.	Housework	A	B	C	D	E
8.	Job	A	B	C	D	E
9.	Arguments	A	B	C	D	E
10.	Health Problems	A	B	C	D	E
11.	Drugs	A	B	C	D	E
12.	Alcohol	A	B	C	D	E
13.	Different Interests	A	B	C	D	E
14.	Different Background	A	B	C	D	E
15.	Lack of Time Together	A	B	C	D	E
16.	Sexual Relations	A	B	C	D	E
17.	Lack of Communication	A	B	C	D	E
18.	Different Emotional Needs	A	B	C	D	E
19.	Mutual Misunderstanding	A	B	C	D	E
20.	Other (Describe on other side)	A	B	C	D	E

Following the same scale (A=a major part, to E=no part) indicate how the following play a role in your own behavior and that of your spouse.

MY		SPOUSE'S	
1. Drinking	A B C D E	1. Drinking	A B C D E
2. Gambling	A B C D E	2. Gambling	A B C D E
3. Appearance	A B C D E	3. Appearance	A B C D E
4. Temper	A B C D E	4. Temper	A B C D E
5. Detachment	A B C D E	5. Detachment	A B C D E
6. Jealousy	A B C D E	6. Jealousy	A B C D E
7. Impulsiveness	A B C D E	7. Impulsiveness	A B C D E
8. Indecisiveness	A B C D E	8. Indecisiveness	A B C D E
9. Irresponsibility	A B C D E	9. Irresponsibility	A B C D E
10. Lack of Affection	A B C D E	10. Lack of Affection	A B C D E

11. Unfaithfulness	A B C D E	11. Unfaithfulness	A B C D E
12. Lack of		12. Lack of	
Ambition	A B C D E	Ambition	A B C D E
13. Oversensitivity	A B C D E	13. Oversensitivity	A B C D E
14. Flirting	A B C D E	14. Flirting	A B C D E
15. Dependency	A B C D E	15. Dependency	A B C D E
16. Sus-		16. Sus-	
piciousness	A B C D E	piciounesss	A B C D E
17. Indifference	A B C D E	17. Indifference	A B C D E
18. Domineering	A B C D E	18. Domineering	A B C D E
19. Selfishness	A B C D E	19. Selfishness	A B C D E
20. Sloppiness	A B C D E	20. Sloppiness	A B C D E
21. Immaturity	A B C D E	21. Immaturity	A B C D E
22. Laziness	A B C D E	22. Laziness	A B C D E
23. Competi-		23. Competi-	
tiveness	A B C D E	tiveness	A B C D E
24. Other (describe		24. Other (describe	
on back of		on back of	
sheet)	A B C D E	sheet)	A B C D E

Do you have any topic not listed above that you wish to discuss?   YES_____   NO_____

CODING AND GENERAL INSTRUCTIONS

1. Pencils—Use any type of soft lead pencil.
   Do not use an ink or ballpoint pen.
2. All answers are to be recorded on the separate answer sheet.
   Please make no marks on this booklet.
3. Regardless of the number of alternatives provided,
   please mark only one answer per question.

IDENTIFICATION INFORMATION

I.   We strive to maintain complete confidentiality. Some identifying number is necessary simply for the processing of this material. If there is some concern about using your Social Security or Student I.D. number, make up your own *unique* number and retain the key. Identifying numbers are used only for matching information for pre- and post-test comparisons.

II. Please select the *one* alternative that best describes yourself:
     A. High School Student   C. Graduate Student
     B. College Student   D. Non-Student (Skip to VI)

III. Which *one* of the following alternatives best describes your present occupation or field of study:
     A. Medicine   F. Sociology/Anthropology
     B. Theology   G. Humanities

C. Psychology   H. Nursing
D. Education   I. Law
E. Social Work   J. Other

IV. If you are a medical student, intern or resident, please indicate your status:
    A. 1st year student   D. 4th year student or above
    B. 2nd year student   E. Intern
    C. 3rd year student   F. Resident

V. If you are a medical student or a physician, please indicate proposed or present area of specialization:
    A. General Practice   F. Pediatrics
    B. Family Medicine   G. Surgery
    C. Internal Medicine   H. Urology
    D. Obstetrics-Gynecology I. Community Medicine
    E. Psychiatry   J. Other

VI. Are you completing this questionnaire before or after a specific course in sex education?
    A. Pre-instruction   B. Post-instruction   C. Neither

VII. Please mark block A (to identify this as the 1972 version of SKAT).

PART I: ATTITUDES

Please indicate your reaction to each of the following statements on sexual behavior in our culture, using the following alternatives:
        A. Strongly agree
        B. Agree
        C. Uncertain
        D. Disagree
        E. Strongly disagree
Please be sure to answer every question.

1. The spread of sex education is causing a rise in premarital intercourse.
2. Mutual masturbation among boys is often a precursor of homosexual behavior.
3. Extramarital relations are almost always harmful to a marriage.
4. Abortion should be permitted whenever desired by the mother.
5. The possession of contraceptive information is often an incitement to promiscuity.
6. Relieving tension by masturbation is a healthy practice.
7. Premarital intercourse is morally undesirable.
8. Oral-genital sex play is indicative of an excessive desire for physical pleasure.
9. Parents should stop their children from masturbating.

10. Women should have coital experience prior to marriage.
11. Abortion is murder.
12. Girls should be prohibited from engaging in sexual self-stimulation.
13. All abortion laws should be repealed.
14. Strong legal measures should be taken against homosexuals.
15. Laws requiring a committee of physicians to approve an abortion should be abolished.
16. Sexual intercourse should occur only between married partners.
17. The lower-class male has a higher sex drive than others.
18. Society should offer abortion as an acceptable form of birth control.
19. Masturbation is generally unhealthy.
20. A physician has the responsibility to inform the husband or parents of any female he aborts.
21. Promiscuity is widespread on college campuses today.
22. Abortion should be disapproved of under all circumstances.
23. Men should have coital experience prior to marriage.
24. Boys should be encouraged to masturbate.
25. Abortions should not be permitted after the twentieth week of pregnancy.
26. Experiences of seeing family members in the nude arouse curiosity in children.
27. Premarital intercourse between consenting adults should be socially acceptable.
28. Legal abortions should be restricted to hospitals.
29. Masturbation among girls is a frequent cause of frigidity.
30. Lower-class women are typically quite sexually responsive.
31. Abortion is a greater evil than bringing an unwanted child into the world.
32. Mutual masturbation in childhood should be prohibited.
33. Virginity among unmarried girls should be encouraged in our society.
34. Extramarital sexual relations may result in a strengthening of the marriage relationship of the persons involved.
35. Masturbation is acceptable when the objective is simply the attainment of sensory enjoyment.

PART II: KNOWLEDGE

Each of the following statements can be answered either true or false. Please indicate your position on each statement using the following alternatives:

T. True   **F.** False

Be sure to answer every question.

1. Pregnancy can occur during natural menopause (gradual cessation of menstruation).
2. Most religious and moral systems throughout the world condemn premarital intercourse.
3. Anxiety differentially affects the timing of orgasm in men and women.
4. A woman does not have the physiological capacity to have as intense an orgasm as a man.
5. There is no difference between men and women with regard to the age of maximal sex drive.
6. Social class is directly correlated with the frequency of incest.
7. The use of the condom is the most reliable of the various contraceptive methods.
8. The incidence of extramarital intercourse is constant for males between the ages of 21 and 60.
9. Nearly half of all unwed girls in America have sexual intercourse by age 19.
10. There are two kinds of physiological orgastic responses in women, one clitoral and the other vaginal.
11. Impotence is almost always a psychogenic disorder.
12. Tranvestitism (a form of cross-dressing) is usually linked to homosexual behavior.
13. There was as much premarital coitus a generation ago as there is now.
14. Sexual attitudes of children are molded by erotic literature.
15. In some successful marriages sex adjustment can be very poor.
16. Homosexuals are more likely to be exceptionally creative than heterosexuals.
17. A women who has had a hysterectomy (removal of the uterus) can experience orgasm during sexual intercourse.
18. Homosexuality comes from learning and conditioning experiences.
19. In responsive women, non-coital stimulation tends to produce a more intensive physiological orgastic response than does coitus.
20. Those convicted of serious sex crimes ordinarily are those who began with minor sex offenses.
21. One of the immediate results of castration in the adult male is impotence.
22. The body build of most homosexuals lacks any distinguishing features.
23. Masturbation by a married person is a sign of poor marital sex adjustment.
24. Exhibitionists are latent homosexuals.

25. A woman's chances of conceiving are greatly enhanced if she has an orgasm.
26. Only a small minority of all married couples ever experience mouth-genital sex play.
27. Impotence is the most frequent cause of sterility.
28. Certain foods render the individual much more susceptible to sexual stimulation.
29. A high percentage of those who commit sexual offenses against children is made up of the children's friends and relatives.
30. A higher percentage of unmarried white teenage girls than unmarried black teenage girls in the United States have had intercourse with four or more partners.
31. The attitude of the average American male towards premarital intercourse is shaped more by his religious devoutness than by his social class.
32. In teaching their daughters female sex roles, middle-class mothers are more affected by cultural stereotypes than mothers in other social classes.
33. In most instances, the biological sex will override the sex assigned by the child's parents.
34. The onset of secondary impotence (impotence preceded by a period of potency) is often associated with the influence of alcohol.
35. Nursing a baby usually protects the mother from becoming pregnant.
36. In our culture some homosexual behavior is a normal part of growing up.
37. Direct contact between penis and clitoris is needed to produce female orgasm during intercourse.
38. For a period of time following orgasm, women are not able to respond to further sexual stimulation.
39. In some legal jurisdictions artificial insemination by a donor may make a woman liable to suit for adultery.
40. Habitual sexual promiscuity is the consequence of an above-average sex drive.
41. Approximately one out of three adolescent boys has a homosexual experience leading to orgasm.
42. Impotence in men over 70 is nearly universal.
43. Certain conditions of mental and emotional instability are demonstrably caused by masturbation.
44. Women who have had several sex partners before marriage are more likely than others to be unfaithful after marriage.
45. The emotionally damaging consequences of a sexual offense against a child are more often attributable to the attitudes of the adults who deal with the child than to the experience itself.
46. Sexual maladjustment is the major cause of divorce.
47. Direct stimulation of the clitoris is essential to achieving orgasm in the woman.
48. Age affects the sexual behavior of men more than it does women.

49. The circumcized male has more trouble with ejaculatory control than the uncircumcized male.
50. More than a few people who are middle-aged or older practice masturbation.
51. Varied coital techniques are used most often by people in lower socioeconomic classes.
52. Individuals who commit rape have an unusually strong sex drive.
53. The rhythm method (refraining from intercourse during the six to eight days midway between menstrual periods) when used properly is just as effective as the pill in preventing conception.
54. Exhibitionists are no more likely than others to commit sexual assaults.
55. The ability to conceive may be significantly delayed after the menarche (onset of menstruation).
56. Many women erroneously consider themselves to be frigid.
57. Menopause in a women is accompanied by a sharp and lasting reduction in sexual drive and interest.
58. The two most widely used forms of contraception around the world are the condom and withdrawal by the male (coitus interruptus).
59. People in lower socioeconomic classes have sexual intercourse more frequently than those of higher classes.
60. Pornographic materials are responsible for much of today's aberrant sexual behavior.
61. For some women, the arrival of menopause signals the beginning of a more active and satisfying sex life.
62. The sex drive of the male adolescent in our culture is stronger than that of female adolescent.
63. Lower-class couples are generally not interested in limiting the number of children they have.
64. Excessive sex play in childhood and adolescence interferes with later marital adjustment.
65. There is a trend toward more aggressive behavior by women throughout the world in courtship, sexual relations, and coitus itself.
66. Sometimes a child may have cooperated in or even provoked sexual molestation by an adult.
67. LSD usually stimulates the sex drive.
68. Seven out of ten parents desire formal sex education in the schools.
69. For every female that masturbates four males do.
70. Douching is an effective form of contraception.
71. Freshmen medical students know more about sex than other college graduates.

PART III: BACKGROUND

This information will be treated as strictly confidential and will be used for research purposes only. In no way will it be used to reveal anyone's identity. Please mark your responses on Part III of the answer sheet.

1. Age
   - A. 17 or under
   - B. 18—19
   - C. 20—21
   - D. 22—23
   - E. 24—25
   - F. 26—27
   - G. 28—30
   - H. 31—35
   - I. 36 or over

2. Sex
   - A. Male
   - B. Female

3. Race
   - A. White
   - B. Non-white

4. If you have been or are married, age at first marriage?
   - A. 17 or under
   - B. 18—22
   - C. 23—26
   - D. 27—35
   - E. 36 or over

5. If you have been or are married, how long?
   - A. 1 year
   - B. 2 years
   - C. 3 years
   - D. 4 years
   - E. 5 or more years

6. Are you first born?
   - A. yes
   - B. no

7. Father's Occupation:
   - A. Physician
   - B. Clergyman
   - C. Lawyer
   - D. Teacher
   - E. Other professional
   - F. Executive
   - G. Clerical/sales
   - H. Skilled manual
   - I. Semi-skilled
   - J. Unskilled

8. Number of siblings:
   - A. 0
   - B. 1
   - C. 2
   - D. 3
   - E. 4 or more

9. Please indicate the educational status of your *father:*
   - A. Non-high school graduate
   - B. High school graduate
   - C. Attended college but did not graduate
   - D. College graduate
   - E. Attended graduate or professional school but did not graduate
   - F. Holds graduate or professional degree

10. Using the alternatives listed above, please indicate the educational status of your *mother.*

11. Religion:
    - A. Catholic
    - B. Protestant
    - C. Jewish
    - D. Other

12. What was the earliest Church-affiliated sex education you received?
    - A. None
    - B. Elementary (K-6)
    - C. Jr. High   (7-9)
    - D. Sr. High (10-12)
    - E. College

PART IV: EXPERIENCE

It would be helpful if you would fill in the following questions. They refer to levels of experience with sex, and will aid our understanding of relationships between knowledge and attitudes. Please answer honestly, and feel free to omit any question or questions if you find them too personal.

For questions 1-5 indicate how many times you have had the following sexual encounters:

A. Never   **B.** Once   **C.** Two—five   **D.** Over five

1. Dating
2. Going steady
3. Sexual intercourse
4. Intercourse involving the exchange of money
5. Orgasm with partner of the same sex

For questions 6-9 indicate the number of people with whom you have engaged in the following sexual activities:

A. None   **B.** One   **C.** Two—five   **D.** Over five

6. Dating
7. Going steady
8. Sexual intercourse
9. Orgasm with partner of the same sex
10. How do you rate yourself in comparison with your peer group's experience in sex?
    - **A.** Far less experienced than most
    - **B.** Less experienced than most
    - **C.** As experienced as most
    - **D.** More experienced than most
    - **E.** Far more experienced than most
11. How do you rate yourself in comparison with your peer group's knowledge about sex?
    - **A.** Far less knowledgeable than most
    - **B.** Less knowledgeable than most
    - **C.** As knowledgeable as most
    - **D.** More knowledgeable than most
    - **E.** Far more knowledgeable than most
12. How do you rate yourself in comparison with your peer group's sexual adjustment?
    - **A.** Far less adjusted than most
    - **B.** Less adjusted than most
    - **C.** As adjusted as most
    - **D.** More adjusted than most
    - **E.** Far more adjusted than most
13. How would you rate the sexual permissiveness in your home when you were growing up?
    - **A.** Very permissive
    - **B.** Somewhat permissive
    - **C.** Neither permissive nor repressive
    - **D.** Somewhat repressive
    - **E.** Very repressive

For questions 14-17, rate your value system with regard to sex:

- **A.** Not at all
- **B.** Somewhat
- **C.** Definitely
- **D.** Very definitely

14. Is your value system conservative (in favor of traditional standards)?
15. Is your value system liberal (in favor of changing standards)?
16. Is your value system influenced by religion?
17. Is your value system in conflict with your parent's values?
18. Age at which you first began masturbation?
    - **A.** Never masturbated
    - **B.** Under 10
    - **C.** 10–12
    - **D.** 13–15
    - **E.** 16–18
    - **F.** 19 or over

For questions 19-21 indicate the frequency with which you masturbated during the following time periods:
- **A.** Less than once/week
- **B.** Two-three times/week
- **C.** Four-five times/week
- **D.** Six or more times/week

19. Junior High School
20. High School
21. College

For questions 22-26 indicate if you have ever engaged in sexual intercourse using the following birth prevention methods:
- **A.** Yes
- **B.** No

22. I.U.D.
23. Pill
24. Abortion
25. Sterilization
26. "Morning-after" treatment
27. Which *one* of the following contraceptive methods do you prefer?
    - **A.** Rhythm
    - **B.** Douche
    - **C.** Withdrawal
    - **D.** Condom
    - **E.** Foam and/or Diaphragm
    - **F.** I.U.D.
    - **G.** Pill
    - **H.** Sterilization
    - **I.** "Morning-after" treatment
    - **J.** Other

APPENDIX II
SEX EDUCATION

Armstrong, DW: *QUESTIONS BOYS ASK:* Dutton, EP, & Co, Inc, 201 Park Ave S, New York, NY 10003, 1955: $3.75.
  Advice is given on appearance, dating, religion, college and relations with others.

Asimov, Isaac: *THE HUMAN BODY:* Houghton Mifflin Co, 2 Park St, Boston, MA 02107, 1963: $6.95.
  Strictly biological information as to the structure and operation of the human machine.

Baruch, Dorothy W: *NEW WAYS IN SEX EDUCATION:* McGraw-Hill Book Co, 330 W 42 St, New York, NY 10036, 1959: $5.95.
  A guide for parents and teachers.

Bauer: WW: *MOVING INTO MANHOOD:* Doubleday & Co, Inc, 277 Park Ave, New York, NY 10017, 1963: $3.50.
  Answers to questions on dating, going steady, use of tobacco and alcohol, essential facts of sex, in plain language.

Beck, Lester F: *HUMAN GROWTH:* Harcourt Brace Jovanovich, Inc, 757 Third Ave, New York, NY 10017, 1949: $4.95.
  Written for those entering their teens who are curious about physical changes as they grow up.

Bibby, Cyril: *HOW LIFE IS HANDED ON:* Emerson Books, Inc, 251 W 19 St, New York, NY 10011, 1947: $3.95.
  Reproduction processes with animals, birds and human beings, written for the child in middle grades.

Bockner, Ruth: *GROWING YOUR OWN WAY:* Abelard-Schuman, Ltd, Div. of Intext Press, 257 Park Ave S, New York, NY 10010, 1959: $3.50.
  Emotional problems of adolescence, discussed in an informal way.

Boll, Eleanor Stoker: *THE MAN THAT YOU MARRY:* Macrae Smith Co, 225 S 15 St, Philadelphia, PA 19102, 1963: $4.25.
  The complimentary functions of the sexes, addressed to young women.

Boone, CE: *'TWIXT TWELVE AND TWENTY:* Prentice-Hall, Inc, 70 Fifth Ave, New York, NY 10011, 1958: $4.50.
  A light-hearted approach to the questions of the teen.

Bossard, James H and Boll, Eleanor S: *THE GIRL THAT YOU MARRY:* Macrae Smith Co, 225 S 15 St, Philadelphia, PA 19102, 1960: $4.25.
  The distinctive characteristics of women are analyzed, addressed to young men.

Buck, Pearl S: *JOHNNY JACK AND HIS BEGINNINGS:* John Day Co, Inc, Div of Intext Press, 257 Park Ave S, New York, NY 10010, 1954: $3.95.
  A book for children, when they first begin to wonder, "Where did I come from?"

Bundensen, Herman N: *TOWARD MANHOOD:* Lippincott, JB, Co, E Washington Square, Philadelphia, PA 19105, 1951: $5.50.
Designed to give boys an understanding of facts and implications of sex.

Crawford, John and Crawford, Dorothea: *TEENS . . . HOW TO MEET YOUR PROBLEMS:* Morrow Publications, 4163 Market St, San Diego, CA 92101, 1957: $1.45.
Counsel is given to help recognize the problem, then to obtain guidance in helping to solve the problem.

Davis, Maxine: *SEX AND THE ADOLESCENT:* PR Publishing Co, Inc, Meriden, NH 03770, 1968 (reprint of 1958): $.75.
A guide for young people and their parents.

De Schweinitz, Karl: *GROWING UP:* Macmillan, The, Co, Subs. of Crowell Collier & MacMillan, Inc, 866 Third Ave, New York, NY 10022, 1968: $3.95.
The facts of procreation, birth, early growth, written for boys and girls.

Dickerson, Roy E: *INTO MANHOOD:* Assn Press, 291 Broadway, New York, NY 10007, 1954: $2.50.
An introduction to sex and morality for the pre-teen.

Dunbar, Helen Flanders: *YOUR TEENAGER'S MIND AND BODY:* Random House, Inc, Subs. of Radio Corp. of America, 201 E 50 St, New York, NY 10022: $1.25.
A discussion of the behavioral changes from puberty to maturity; how to cope —for parents.

Duvall, Evelyn M: *LOVE AND THE FACTS OF LIFE:* Assn Press, 291 Broadway, New York, NY 10007, 1963: $4.95.
A completely new book replacing the classic Facts of Life and Love for Teen-Agers. Topics as, venereal disease, homosexuality, the pill and pre-marital intimacies are discussed.

Duvall, Evelyn M: *SEX WAYS —IN FACTS AND FAITH:* Monona-Driver Book Co, Box 3222, Madison, WI 53704: $4.95.
Science and the church combine to analyze sex problems, family limitation, teen involvements.

Duvall, Evelyn M: *TODAY'S TEEN-AGERS:* Assn Press, 291 Broadway, New York, NY 10007, 1966: $4.95.
A guide for parents on how to meet concerns of sex, drinking, drugs, et cetera.

Ets, Marie H: *THE STORY OF A BABY:* Viking Press, Inc, 625 Madison Ave, New York, NY 10022, 1939: $3.75.
A life too small to be seen is developed through to birth and beyond — for the young child.

Felsen, Henry Gregor: *LETTERS TO A TEENAGE SON:* Dodd, Mead & Co, 79 Madison Ave, New York, NY 10016, 1962: $3.50.
A personal conversation on many subjects.

Gruenberg, Benjamin C: *THE WONDERFUL STORY OF YOU:* Doubleday & Co, Inc, 277 Park Ave, New York, NY 10017, 1960: $3.95.
An explanation of the how and why of bodily functions for the child.

Gruenberg, Sidonie M: *THE WONDERFUL STORY OF HOW YOU WERE BORN:* Doubleday & Co, Inc, 277 Park Ave, New York, NY 10017, 1970: $3.95.
The mystery of birth and growth, for the young child.

Johnson, Eric W: *HOW TO LIVE THROUGH JUNIOR HIGH SCHOOL:* Lippincott, JB, Co, E Washington Square, Philadelphia, PA 19105, 1959: $4.95.
Two chapters deal with sex education.

Johnson, Eric W: *LOVE AND SEX IN PLAIN LANGUAGE:* Lippincott, JB, Co, E Washington Square, Philadelphia, PA 19105, 1967: $3.95.

Kelly, George A: *THE CATHOLIC YOUTH'S GUIDE TO LIFE AND LOVE:* Random House, Inc, Subs. of Radio Corp. of America, 201 E 50 St, New York, NY 10022, 1960: $6.95.
Practical directives for dealing with critical problems.

Landers, Ann: *TALKS TO TEEN-AGERS ABOUT SEX:* Fawcett World Library, 1 Astor Plaza, New York, NY 10036, 1970: $.60.

Landis, Judson T & Mary G: *TEENAGER'S GUIDE FOR LIVING:* Prentice-Hall, Inc, Englewood Cliffs, NJ 07632, 1957: $4.95.
To help teens decide for themselves.

Leriggo, Marion O & Southard, Helen: *A STORY ABOUT YOU: FACTS YOU WANT TO KNOW ABOUT SEX* (rev): Dutton, EP & Co, Inc, 201 Park Ave S, New York, NY 10003, 1969: $2.95.
For those from nine years to twelve years —differences between male and female and the act of mating.

Leriggo, Marion O: *WHAT'S HAPPENING TO ME?:* Dutton, EP & Co, Inc, 201 Park Ave S, New York, NY 10003, 1969: $2.95.
Physical, mental, emotional changes which occur in boys and girls.

Levine, Milton I and Seligmann, Jean: *BABY IS BORN* (rev): Western Publishing Co, Inc, 1220 Mound Ave, Racine, WI 53404: $2.95, pap. $1.00.
For children six to ten years.

Lorand, Rhoda L: *LOVE, SEX, AND THE TEENAGER:* Macmillan, The, Co, Subs. of Crowell Collier & Macmillan, Inc, 866 Third Ave, New York, NY 10022, 1965: $5.95.
For young adults and their parents.

Maternity Center Association: *BABY IS BORN:* Grossett & Dunlap, Inc, Subs. of National General Corp, 51 Madison Ave, New York, NY 10010, 1964: $3.95.
Picture story.

Menninger, William C: *BLUEPRINT FOR TEENAGE LIVING:* Hale, EM, & Co Pubs, 1201 S Hastings Way, Eau Claire, WI 54701, 1958: $3.54.
A "down-to-earth" guidebook considers petting, alcohol, dating.

Pemberton, Lois: *THE STORK DIDN'T BRING YOU:* Wadsworth Publishing Co, Inc, Belmont, CA 94002, 1966: $3.50.
Facts of life for young adults.

Peters, Donald L: *FOR THINKING TEENS:* Rosen, Richards, Press, Inc, 29 E 21 St, New York, NY 10010, 1967: $3.99.
Special problems: morality, sex, love, et cetera.

Power, Jules: *HOW LIFE BEGINS:* Simon & Schuster, Inc, 630 Fifth Ave, New York, NY 10020, 1968: $1.95.
For the very young — real and thoughtful answers.

Richardson, Frank Howard: *FOR BOYS ONLY:* McKay, David, Co, Inc, 750 Third Ave, New York, NY 10017, 1952: $3.95.
Physical and emotional aspects are discussed.

Richardson, Frank Howard: *FOR GIRLS ONLY:* McKay, David, Co, Inc, 750 Third Ave, New York, NY 10017, 1953: $3.95.
Topics are: petting, friendships with boys, unmarried mothers, et cetera.

Richardson, Frank Howard: *FOR YOUNG ADULTS ONLY:* McKay, David, Co, Inc, 750 Third Ave, New York, NY 10017, 1961: $2.95.

Roosevelt, Eleanor: *YOUR TEENS AND MINE:* Doubleday & Co, Inc, 277 Park Ave, New York, NY 10017: $3.50.
Circumstances may change but people remain the same.

Schimel, John L: *HOW TO BE AN ADOLESCENT AND SURVIVE:* Rosen, Richards, Press, Inc, 29 E 21 St, New York, NY 10010, 1969: $3.99.

Shultz, Gladys Denny: *IT'S TIME YOU KNEW:* Lippincott, JB, Co, E Washington Square, Philadelphia, PA 19105, 1955: $6.95.
For the younger girl: the anatomy of sex and the psychological implications.

Schultz, Gladys Denny: *LETTERS TO JANE:* Lippincott, JB, Co, E Washington Square, Philadelphia, PA 19105, 1960: $4.50.
Frank counseling about sex.

Strain, Frances B: *BEING BORN:* Hawthorne Books, Inc, 70 Fifth Ave, New York, NY 10011, 1970: $4.95.
For young teens, the correct terminology.

Unger, Arthur & Berman, Carmel: *WHAT GIRLS WANT TO KNOW ABOUT BOYS:* Grossett & Dunlap, Inc, Subs. of National General Corp, 51 Madison Ave, New York, NY 10010: $.60.

APPENDIX III
GENETIC COUNSELING UNITS
IN THE UNITED STATES

State	City	Unit	Department
Alabama	Birmingham	Birmingham Southern College	Biology
	Birmingham	University of Alabama Med. Cntr.	*Medical Genetics
Alaska	College	Arctic Health Research Lab.	*Medical Genetics
Arizona	Tempe	Arizona State University	*Birth Defects
Arkansas	Little Rock	Univ. of Arkansas Med. Center	*Pediatrics
California	Berkeley	University of California	*Zoology and Genetics
	Berkeley	Bureau of Maternal and Child Health	Heritable Defects
	Duarte	City of Hope, Medical Center	*Medical Genetics
	Irvine	University of Calif.—Irvine	*Pediatrics
	Los Angeles	University of California	*Pediatrics and Medicine
	Los Angeles	Children's Hospital Medical Center	*Pediatrics and Biochemistry
	Los Angeles	University of Southern California	*Pediatrics
	Martinez	Genetics Consul. and Couns. Serv.	*Health
	Oakland	Children's Hospital Medical Center	*Birth Defects
	Palo Alto	Stanford University Medical School	*Medicine
	Palo Alto	Stanford University Medical School	*Birth Defects
	Pasadena	Pasadena Found. for Medical Res.	Cytogenetics
	Pasadena	California Instit. of Technology	Biology
	Riverside	University of California	Life Sciences
	San Bernardino	St. Bernardine's Hospital	*Pediatrics
	San Francisco	San Francisco General Hospital	Clinical Pathology
	San Francisco	Children's Hospital	*Genetics
	San Francisco	University of California Med. Cntr.	*Pediatrics
	San Francisco	University of California	*Pediatrics
	Stanford	Stanford University Medical School	*Pediatrics
	Stanford	Stanford University Medical School	*Medicine
	Van Nuys	Bio-Science Laboratories	Cytogenetics
Colorado	Boulder	University of Colorado	Psychology
	Denver	University of Colorado Medical Cntr.	Pathology
	Denver	University of Colorado Medical Cntr.	*Pediatrics
	Greeley	Colorado State College	Biology
Connecticut	Hartford	Connecticut Twin Registry	*Health
	New Haven	Yale Medical School	*Pediatrics
	Ridgefield	New England Inst. for Med. Res.	*Cytogenetics
	Storrs	University of Connecticut	Biology
District of Columbia	Washington, D.C.	Howard University College of Med.	*Pediatrics
	Washington, D.C.	Research Foundation, Inc.	Hematology
	Washington, D.C.	American Red Cross	Immunohematology
	Washington, D.C.	Georgetown University Hospital	*Ped. and Obstet.
	Washington, D.C.	Children's Hospital	*Neurology
	Washington, D.C.	George Washington Univ. Hosp.	*Obstet. and Genetics

State	City	Unit	Department
Florida	Miami	University of Miami Child. Dev.	*Pediatrics
	Miami	University of Miami Medical School	Pediatrics
Georgia	Atlanta	Georgia Mental Health Institute	*Psychiatry
	Atlanta	Nat'l. Communicable Disease Cntr.	Genetics
	Augusta	Medical College of Georgia	*Endocrinology
	Augusta	Medical College of Georgia	*Pediatrics
	Milledgeville	Central State Hospital	*Medical Genetics
Hawaii	Honolulu	Kauikeolani Children's Hospital	*Birth Defects
	Honolulu	University of Hawaii School of Med.	Genetics
Idaho	Boise	Mental Retardation Program	*Health
	Boise	Idaho M. R. Program	*Health
Illinois	Chicago	University of Chicago	*Medicine
	Chicago	Michael Reese Research Foundation	*Blood Center
	Chicago	Mt. Sinai Hosp. Medical Cntr.	*Exp. Pathology
	Chicago	Illinois State Pediatric Institute	*Ped.-Mental Health
	Chicago	Veterans Administration Hospital	Hematology
	Chicago	Children's Hospital	*Biochemistry
	Chicago	University of Chicago	*Pediatrics
	Evanston	Evanston Hospital	*Research
	Springfield	Division of Preventive Medicine	*Public Health
Indiana	Indianapolis	Indiana University Medical School	*Medical Genetics
Iowa	Cherokee	Mental Health Institute	
	Des Moines	Des Moines Medical Center	Cytotechnology
	Iowa City	University of Iowa	*Pediatrics
	Iowa City	University of Iowa	St. Serv. Crippled Child.
Kansas	Kansas City	Kansas University Medical Center	*Medicine
	Wichita	Wesley Medical Research Found.	*Clinical Pathology
Kentucky	Lexington	University of Kentucky Med. Cntr.	*Pediatrics
	Louisville	University of Louisville Med. School	*Pediatrics
	Louisville	Child Evaluation Center	*Pediatrics
Louisiana	New Orleans	Tulane University	*Anatomy
Maryland	Baltimore	Johns Hopkins Hospital	*More Clinic
	Baltimore	Sinai Hospital	*Pediatrics
	Baltimore	Baltimore City Hospital	Immunogenetics
	Baltimore	John F. Kennedy Institute	*Pediatrics
	Bethesda	National Institutes of Health	Medical Genetics
	Rockville	National Center for Radiol. Health	Radiation Bio-Effects
	Silver Spring	National Biomedical Res. Found.	Medical Genetics
Massachu-setts	Amherst	University of Massachusetts	Zoology
	Boston	Massachusetts General Hospital	*Pediatrics
	Boston	Massachusetts General Hospital	Medicine
	Boston	Birth Defects Center	*Pediatrics
	Boston	Children's Hospital Medical Center	*Clinical Genetics
	Boston	New England Deaconess Hospital	Cytogenetics
	Boston	New England Med. Cntr. Hosp.	*Hematology

State	City	Unit	Department
	Boston	New England Med. Cntr. Hosp.	Biophysics
	Boston	New England Med. Cntr. Hosp.	*Cytogenetics
Michigan	Ann Arbor	University of Michigan	*Human Genetics
	Detroit	Wayne State University Med. School	Anatomy
	Detroit	University of Detroit	*Biology
	Detroit	Henry Ford Hospital	*Pediatrics
	Grand Rapids	Butterworth Hospital	*Pediatrics, Neurology
	Grand Rapids	Butterworth Hospital	Pathology
	Lansing	Michigan State Hospital	*Zoology
	Northville	Plymouth St. Home & Train. School	*Mental Health
Minnesota	Minneapolis	Minnesota Department of Health	*Human Genetics
	Minneapolis	University of Minnesota Hospital	Laboratory Medicine
	Minneapolis	University of Minnesota	*Dentistry
	Minneapolis	University of Minnesota	*Genetics
Mississippi	Jackson	University of Mississippi Med. Cntr.	*Preventive Medicine
Missouri	Columbia	University of Missouri Medical Cntr.	*Pediatrics
	Columbia	University of Missouri	Med. Res. Farm.
	Kansas City	Kansas City General Hospital	Neurology
	St. Louis	Cardinal Glennon Memorial Hospital for Children	*Pediatrics
	St. Louis	Washington University Med. School	*Medicine
	St. Louis	Children's Hospital	*Pediatrics
	St. Louis	Washington University	*Medical Genetics
Montana	Missoula	University of Montana	Zoology
Nebraska	Omaha	Children's Memorial Hospital	*Birth Defects
	Omaha	Creighton University School of Med.	*Preventive Medicine
	Omaha	University of Nebraska Med. Cntr.	*Pathology
New Hampshire	Hanover	Dartmouth Medical School	*Pathology and Medicine
New Jersey	Camden	Institute for Medical Research	Cytogenetics
	Newark	Newark City Hospital & College of Medicine in New Jersey	*Pediatrics
New Mexico	Albuquerque	Univ. of New Mexico School of Med.	*Pathology
New York	Albany	Birth Defects Institute	*Health
	Bethpage	Mid Island Hospital	Pediatrics
	Brooklyn	The Brookdale Hospital Center	Pathology
	Brooklyn	Maimonides Medical Center	Medicine
	Brooklyn	Alexander S. Wiener, M.D.	*Immuno-hematology
	Brooklyn	Jewish Hospital and Medical Center	*Pediatrics
	Buffalo	Buffalo General Hospital	*Medicine
	Buffalo	Roswell Park Memorial Institute	*Pediatrics
	Buffalo	State University of N.Y. at Buffalo	*Pediatrics
	Buffalo	New York University at Buffalo	*Pediatrics

State	City	Unit	Department
	Jamaica	Creedmoor State Hospital	*Medical Services
	Manhasset	North Shore Hospital	*Genetics Lab.
	New York (Bronx)	Albert Einstein College of Medicine	*Medicine
	New York (Bronx)	Albert Einstein College of Medicine	*Genetics
	New York (Bronx)	Medical College of Yeshiva Univ.	*Genetics
	New York	Columbia University	Biological Sci.
	New York	The New York Hospital-Cornell Medical Center	*Human Genetics
	New York	New York Med. College Metro. Hosp.	*Pathology
	New York	New York University Medical Cntr.	*Pathology
	New York	Rubella Birth Defect Eval. Proj.	Pediatrics
	New York	Beth Israel Hospital	Research Lab.
	New York	The New York Blood Center	*
	New York	Columbia University	Cytogenetics
	New York	St. Luke's Hospital Center	*
	New York	Cornell University Medical College	Pediatrics
	New York	Mount Sinai School of Medicine	*Pediatrics
	New York	New York State Psychiatric Institute	*Medical Genetics
	Rochester	University of Rochester Med. School	*Anatomy, Pediatrics
	Staten Island	Inst. for Basic Res. in Med. Retard.	*Cytogenetics
	Staten Island	Willowbrook State School	Mental Hygiene
	Syracuse	Upstate Medical Center	*Pediatrics
North Carolina	Chapel Hill	Birth Defects Clinic	*Pediatrics
	Chapel Hill	University of North Carolina	Pediatrics
	Durham	Duke Medical Center	Obstetrics, Gynecology
	Morganton	Western Carolina Center	*Birth Defects Eval. Cntr.
North Dakota	Grand Forks	University of North Dakota	Pathology
Ohio	Cincinnati	Children's Hospital Research Found.	*Pediatrics
	Cleveland	Cleveland Metro General Hospital	*Pediatric Neurology
	Cleveland	Cleveland Psychiatric Institute	*Medical Genetics
	Columbus	Children's Hospital	*Pediatrics
	Columbus	University Hospital	*Medicine
	Dayton	Barney Children's Medical Center	*Birth Defects Eval. Cntr.
Oklahoma	Oklahoma City	Children's Hospital	*Pediatrics
Oregon	Eugene	Sacred Heart Hospital	*Pediatrics
	Medford	Rouge Valley Memorial Hospital	Genetics
	Portland	University of Oregon Medical School Crippled Children's Division	*Medical Genetics
Pennsylvania	Danville	Geisinger Medical Center	*Pathology
	Lancaster	Lancaster Cleft Palate Clinic	Research
	Philadelphia	Wistar Institute	Cytogenetics
	Philadelphia	Children's Hospital	*Pediatrics
	Philadelphia	Hahnemann Medical College	*Anatomy
	Philadelphia	Jefferson Hospital	*Medicine
	Pittsburgh	University of Pittsburgh School of Public Health	Biostatics
	Pittsburgh	Children's Hospital	*Pediatrics

State	City	Unit	Department
	Pittsburgh	Magee-Women's Hospital	Medical Cytogenetics
	Pittsburgh	Presbyterian—University Hospital	Radiation Med.
Rhode Island	Providence	Rhode Island Hospital	*Pediatrics, Pathology
South Carolina	Charleston	Medical College of South Carolina	Pathology
Tennessee	Knoxville	University of Tennessee, Memphis Res. Center and Hospital	*Birth Defects Eval. Cntr.
	Memphis	University of Tennessee	*Pediatrics
	Nashville	Vanderbilt Hospital	*Medicine
	Nashville	Meharry Medical College	*Pediatrics
	Nashville	Hubbard Hospital	*Pediatrics
Texas	Austin	University of Texas Genetics Found.	*Human Genetics
	Big Spring	Veterans Administration Hospital	Immunogenetics and Pharmoco-genetics
	Fort Sam Houston	Brooke Army Medical Center	*Pediatrics
	Galveston	University of Texas Medical Branch	*Human Genetics
	Houston	Baylor University College of Medicine	*Pediatrics
	Houston	M.D. Anderson Hospital	*Biology
	Houston	Texas Children's Hospital	Pathology
	Pasadena	Pasadena General Hospital	*Medical Genetics
	Richardson	S.W. Center for Advanced Studies	Biology
	San Antonio	University of Texas Medical School	*Anatomy
Utah	Logan	Utah State University	*Zoology
	Salt Lake City	Primary Children's Hospital	*Birth Defects
	Salt Lake City	University Medical Center	*Internal Med.
Vermont	Burlington	Mary Fletcher Hospital	*Pediatrics
Virginia	Charlottesville	University of Virginia Hospital	*Prev. Med. and Int. Med.
	Charlottesville	University of Virginia School of Med.	*Chromosome Res. Lab.
	Richmond	Medical College of Virginia	*Biology, Genetics
Washington	Seattle	Mason Clinic	Pathology
	Seattle	University of Washington	*Medicine
	Tacoma	Madigan General Hospital	Pediatrics
West Virginia	Morgantown	West Virginia University	*Pediatrics
Wisconsin	Madison	University of Wisconsin Medical School	*Medical Genetics
	Milwaukee	The Milwaukee Children's Hospital	*Cytogenetics & Genetics Clinic

*Offer the services of Genetic Counseling.

For more specific addresses of the foregoing genetics units see the International Directory of Genetic Services published in May, 1968 by the National Foundation, 800 Second Avenue, New York, New York 10017.

APPENDIX IV
SEX AND THE LAW

Sexuality is an important consideration under many aspects of the law, both criminal law and civil law. The scope of this appendix does not permit a detailed analysis of all aspects of the relationship between law and sexuality.

The law is made up of both statutory provisions and common law. Statutes are specific legal enactments of legislative bodies. Common law consists of those legal rules established by the courts, especially those originating prior to the separation of the United States from England. Both are being continually developed and modified by decisional interpretations made by the courts.

Law relating to sexuality is mostly state law. For this reason, this law varies substantially from one state to another. This is especially true with respect to criminal laws regulating sexual activity. Enforcement of the criminal laws is subject to even greater variance. It is also significantly true with respect to law relating to divorce, marital separation and custody of minor children. Because of these variations, it is essential that a competent attorney licensed in the particular state be consulted when legal advice or guidance is required.

Some legal problems in relation to a physician's practice involving guidance of patients in matters of sexuality are less dramatic but of perhaps more practical significance. For guidance of physicians, there are presented here the following discussions of certain practical legal problems that frequently arise.

JANUARY 1973 SUPREME COURT DECISION
ON ABORTION

No. 70-18

Jane Roe et al., Appellants,

v.

Henry Wade.

On Appeal from the United States District Court for the Northern District of Texas.

[January 22, 1973]

MR. JUSTICE BLACKMUN delivered the opinion of the Court.

This Texas federal appeal and its Georgia companion, *Doe* v. *Bolton, post——,* present constitutional challenges to state criminal abortion legislation. The Texas statutes under attack here are typical of those that have been in effect in many States for approximately a century. The Georgia statutes, in contrast, have a modern cast and are a legislative product that, to an extent at least, obviously reflects the influences of recent attitudinal change, of advancing medical knowledge and techniques, and of new thinking about an old issue.

We forthwith acknowledge our awareness of the sensitive and emotional nature of the abortion controversy, of the vigorous opposing views, even among physicians, and of the deep and seemingly absolute convictions that the subject inspires. One's philosophy, one's experiences, one's exposure to the raw edges of human existence, one's religious training, one's attitudes toward life and family and their values, and the moral standards one establishes and seeks to observe, are all likely to influence and to color one's thinking and conclusions about abortion.

In addition, population growth, pollution, poverty, and racial overtones tend to complicate and not to simplify the problem.

Our task, of course, is to resolve the issue by constitutional measurement free of emotion and of predilection. We seek earnestly to do this, and, because we do, we have inquired into, and in this opinion place some emphasis upon, medical and medical-legal history and what that history reveals about man's attitudes toward the abortive procedure over the centuries. We bear in mind, too, Mr. Justice Holmes' admonition in his now vindicated dissent in *Lochner* v. *New York,* 198 U. S. 45, 76 (1905):

> "It [the Constitution] is made for people of fundamentally differing views, and the accident of our finding certain opinions natural and familiar or novel and even shocking ought not to conclude our judgment upon the question whether statutes embodying them conflict with the Constitution of the United States."

I

The Texas statutes that concern us here are Arts. 1191-1194 and 1196 of the State's Penal Code.[1] These make it a crime to "procure an abortion," as therein defined, or to attempt one, except with respect to "an abortion procured or attempted by medical advice for the purpose of saving the life of the mother." Similar statutes are in existence in a majority of the States.[2]

Texas first enacted a criminal abortion statute in 1854. Texas Laws 1854, c. 49, § 1, set forth in 3 Gammel, Laws of Texas, 1502 (1898). This was soon modified into language that has remained substantially unchanged to the present time. See Texas Penal Code of 1857, Arts. 531-536; Paschal's Laws of Texas, Arts. 2192-2197 (1866); Texas Rev. Stat., Arts. 536-541 (1879); Texas Rev. Crim. Stat., Arts. 1071-1076 (1911). The final article in each of these compilations provided the same exception, as does the present Article 1196, for an abortion by "medical advice for the purpose of saving the life of the mother."[3]

[1] "Article 1191. Abortion
"If any person shall designedly administer to a pregnant woman or knowingly procure to be administered with her consent any drug or medicine, or shall use towards her any violence or means whatever externally or internally applied, and thereby procure an abortion, he shall be confined in the penitentiary not less than two nor more than five years; if it be done without her consent, the punishment shall be doubled. By 'abortion' is meant that the life of the fetus or embryo shall be destroyed in the woman's womb or that a premature birth thereof be caused.
"Art. 1192. Furnishing the means
"Whoever furnishes the means for procuring an abortion knowing the purpose intended is guilty as an accomplice.
"Art. 1193. Attempt at abortion
"If the means used shall fail to produce an abortion, the offender is nevertheless guilty of an attempt to produce abortion, provided it be shown that such means were calculated to produce that result, and shall be fined not less than one hundred nor more than one thousand dollars.
"Art. 1194. Murder in producing abortion
"If the death of the mother is occasioned by an abortion so produced or by an attempt to effect the same it is murder.
"Art. 1196. By medical advice
"Nothing in this chapter applies to an abortion procured or attempted by medical advice for the purpose of saving the life of the mother."
The foregoing Articles, together with Art. 1195, comprise Chapter 9 of Title 15 of the Penal Code. Article 1195, not attached here, reads:
"Art. 1195. Destroying unborn child
"Whoever shall during parturition of the mother destroy the vitality or life in a child in a state of being born and before actual birth, which child would otherwise have been born alive, shall be confined in the penitentiary for life or for not less than five years."

[2] Ariz. Rev. Stat. Ann. § 13–211 (1971); Conn. Pub. Act. No. 1 (May 1972 special session) (in 4 Conn. Leg. Serv. 677 (1972), and Conn. Gen. Stat. Rev. §§ 53–29, 53–30 (1968) (or unborn child); Idaho Code § 18–1505 (App. to Supp. 1971); Ill. Rev. Stats. c. 38, § 23–1 (1971); Ind. Code § 35–1–58–1 (1971); Iowa Code § 701.1 (1971); Ky. Rev. Stat. § 436.020 (1963); La. Rev. Stat. § 37: 1285 (6) (1964) (loss of medical license) (but see § 14–87 (1972 Supp.) containing no exception for the life of the mother under the criminal statute); Me. Rev. Stat. Ann. Tit. 17, § 51 (1964); Mass. Gen. Laws Ann. c. 272, § 19 (1970) (using the term "unlawfully," construed to exclude an

abortion to save the mother's life, *Kudish* v. *Bd. of Registration*, 356 Mass. 98, 248 N. E. 2d 264 (1969); Mich. Comp. Laws § 750.14 (1948); Minn. Stat. § 617.18 (1971); Mo. Rev. Stat. § 559.100 (1969); Mont. Rev. Codes Ann. § 94–491 (1961); Neb. Rev. Stat. § 28–405 (1964); Nev. Rev. Stat. § 200:220 (1967); N. H. Rev. Stat. Ann. § 585.13 (1955); N. J. Stat. Ann. § 2A:87–1 (1969) ("without lawful justification"); N. D. Cent. Code §§ 12–25–01, 12–25–02 (1960); Ohio Rev. Code § 2901.16 (1953); Okla. Stat. Ann. Tit. 21, § 861 (1972–1973 Supp.); Pa. Stat. Ann. Tit. 18, §§ 4718, 4719 (1963) ("unlawful"); R. I. Gen. Laws Ann. § 11–3–1 (1969); S. D. Compiled Laws § 22–17–1 (1967); Tenn. Code Ann. §§ 39–301, 39–302 (1956); Utah Code Ann. §§ 76–2–1, 76–2–2 (1953); Vt. Stat. Ann. Tit. 13, § 101 (1958); W. Va. Code Ann. § 61–2–8 (1966); Wis. Stat. § 940.04 (1969); Wyo. Stat. Ann. §§ 6–77, 6–78 (1957).

[3] Long ago a suggestion was made that the Texas statutes were unconstitutionally vague because of definitional deficiencies. The Texas Court of Criminal Appeals disposed of that suggestion peremptorily, saying only,
"It is also insisted in the motion in arrest of judgment that the statute is unconstitutional and void in that it does not sufficiently define or describe the offense of abortion. We do not concur in respect to this question." *Jackson* v. *State*, 55 Tex. Crim. R. 79, 89, 115 S. W. 262, 268 (1908). The same court recently has held again that the State's abortion statutes are not unconstitutionally vague or overboard. *Thompson* v. *State*, — Tex. Crim. App. —. — S. W. 2d — (1971), appeal pending. The court held that "the State of Texas has a compelling interest to protect fetal life"; that Art. 1191 "is designed to protect fetal life"; that the Texas homicide statutes, particularly Art. 1205 of the Penal Code, are intended to protect a person "in existence by actual birth" and thereby implicitly recognize other human life that is not "in existence by actual birth"; that the definition of human life is for the legislature and not the courts; that Art. 1196 "is more definite that the District of Columbia statute upheld in [*United States* v.] *Vuitch*" (402 U. S. 62); and that the Texas statute "is not vague and indefinite or overbroad." A physician's abortion conviction was affirmed.

In n. 2, — Tex. Crim. App., at —, — S. W. 2d, at —, the court observed that any issue as to the burden of proof under the exemption of Art. 1196 "is not before us." But see *Veevers* v. *State*, 172 Tex. Crim. App. 162, 168–169, 354 S. W. 2d 161 (1962). Cf. *United States* v. *Vuitch*, 402 U. S. 62, 69–71 (1971).

II

Jane Roe,[1] a single woman who was residing in Dallas County, Texas, instituted this federal action in March 1970 against the District Attorney of the county. She sought a declaratory judgment that the Texas criminal abortion statutes were unconstitutional on their face, and an injunction restraining the defendant from enforcing the statutes.

Roe alleged that she was unmarried and pregnant; that she wished to terminate her pregnancy by an abortion "performed by a competent, licensed physician, under safe, clinical conditions"; that she was unable to get a "legal" abortion in Texas because her life did not appear to be threatened by the continuation of her pregnancy; and that she could not afford to travel to another jurisdiction in order to secure a legal abortion under safe conditions. She claimed that the Texas statutes were unconstitutionally vague and that they abridged her right of personal privacy, protected by the First, Fourth, Fifth, Ninth, and Fourteenth Amendments. By an amendment to her complaint Roe purported to sue "on behalf of herself and all other women" similarly situated.

James Hubert Hallford, a licensed physician, sought and was granted leave to intervene in Roe's action. In his complaint he alleged that he had been arrested previously for violations of the Texas abortion statutes and that two such prosecutions were pending against him. He described conditions of patients who came to him seeking abortions, and he claimed that for many cases he, as a physician, was unable to determine whether they fell within or outside the exception recognized by Article 1196. He alleged that, as a consequence, the statutes were vague and uncertain, in violation of the Fourteenth Amendment, and that they violated his own and his patients' rights to privacy in the doctor-patient relationship and his own right to practice medicine, rights he claimed were guaranteed by the First, Fourth, Fifth, Ninth, and Fourteenth Amendments.

John and Mary Doe,[5] a married couple, filed a companion complaint to that of Roe. They also named the District Attorney as defendant, claimed like constitutional deprivations, and sought declaratory and injunctive relief. The Does alleged that they were a childless couple; that Mrs. Doe was suffering from a "neuralchemical" disorder; that her physician had "advised her to avoid pregnancy until such time as her condition has materially improved" (although a pregnancy at the present time would not present "a serious risk" to her life); that, pursuant to medical advice, she had discontinued use of birth control pills; and that if she should become pregnant, she would want to terminate the pregnancy by an abortion performed by a competent, licensed physician under safe, clinical conditions. By an amendment to their complaint, the Does purported to sue "on behalf of themselves and all couples similarly situated."

The two actions were consolidated and heard together by a duly convened three-judge district court. The suits thus presented the situations of the pregnant single woman, the childless couple, with the wife not pregnant, and the licensed practicing physician, all joining in the attack on the Texas criminal abortion statutes. Upon the filing of affidavits, motions were made to dismiss and for summary judgment. The court held that Roe and Dr. Hallford, and members of their respective classes, had standing to sue, and presented justiciable controversies, but that the Does had failed to allege facts sufficient to state a present controversy and did not have standing. It concluded that, with respect to the request for a declaratory judgment, abstention was not warranted. On the merits, the District Court held that the "fundamental right of single women and married persons to choose whether to have children is protected by the Ninth Amendment, through the Fourteenth Amendment," and that the Texas criminal abortion statutes were void on their face because they were both unconstitutionally vague and constituted an overbroad infringement of the plaintiffs' Ninth Amendment rights. The court then held that abstention was warranted with respect to the requests for an injunction. It therefore dismissed the Doe complaint, declared the abortion statutes void, and dismissed the application for injunctive relief. 314 F. Supp. 1217 (ND Tex. 1970).

The plaintiffs Roe and Doe and the intervenor Hallford, pursuant to 28 U. S. C. § 1253, have appealed to this Court from that part of the District Court's judgment denying the injunction. The defendant District Attorney has purported to cross appeal, pursuant to the same statute, from the court's grant of declaratory relief to Roe and Hallford. Both sides also have taken protective appeals to the United States Court of Appeals for the Fifth Circuit. That court ordered the appeals held in abeyance pending decision here. We postponed decision on jurisdiction to the hearing on the merits. 402 U. S. 941 (1971).

⁴ The name is a pseudonym.
⁵ These names are pseudonyms.

III

It might have been preferable if the defendant, pursuant to our Rule 20, had presented to us a petition for certiorari before judgment in the Court of Appeals with respect to the granting of the plaintiffs' prayer for declaratory relief. Our decisions in *Mitchell* v. *Donovan*, 398 U. S. 427 (1970), and *Gunn* v. *University Committee*, 399 U. S. 383 (1970), are to the effect that § 1253 does not authorize an appeal to this Court from the grant or denial of declaratory relief alone. We conclude, nevertheless, that those decisions do not foreclose our review of both the injunctive and the declaratory aspects of a case of this kind when it is properly here, as this one is, on appeal under § 1253 from specific denial of injunctive relief, and the arguments as to both aspects are necessarily identical. See *Carter* v. *Jury Commission*, 396 U. S. 320 (1970); *Florida Lime and Avocado Growers, Inc.* v. *Jacobsen*, 362 U. S. 73, 80-81 (1960). It would be destructive of time and energy for all concerned were we to rule otherwise. Cf. *Doe* v. *Bolton, post,*–.

IV

We are next confronted with issues of justiciability, standing, and abstention. Have Roe and the Does established that "personal stake in the outcome of the controversy," *Baker* v. *Carr,* 369 U. S. 186, 204 (1962), that insures that "the dispute sought to be adjudicated will be presented in an adversary context and in a form historically viewed as capable of judicial resolution," *Flast* v. *Cohen,* 392 U. S. 83, 101 (1968), and *Sierra Club* v. *Morton,* 405 U. S. 727, 732 (1972)? And what effect did the pendency of criminal abortion charges against Dr. Hallford in state court have upon the propriety of the federal court's granting relief to him as a plaintiff-intervenor?

A. *Jane Roe.* Despite the use of the pseudonym, no suggestion is made that Roe is a fictitious person. For purposes of her case, we accept as true, and as established, her existence; her pregnant state, as of the inception of her suit in March 1970 and as late as May 21 of that year when she filed an alias affidavit with the District Court; and her inability to obtain a legal abortion in Texas.

Viewing Roe's case as of the time of its filing and thereafter until as late as May, there can be little dispute that it then presented a case or controversy and that, wholly apart from the class aspects, she, as a pregnant single woman thwarted by the Texas criminal abortion laws, had standing to challenge those statutes. *Abele* v. *Markle,* 452 F. 2d 1121, 1125 (CA2 1971); *Crossen* v. *Breckenridge,* 446 F. 2d 833, 838-839 (CA6 1971); *Poe* v. *Menghini,* 339 F. Supp. 986, 990-991 (Kans. 1972). See *Truax* v. *Raich,* 239 U. S. 33 (1915). Indeed, we do not read the appellee's brief as really asserting anything to the contrary. The "logical nexus between the status asserted and the claim sought to be adjudicated," *Flast* v. *Cohen,* 392 U. S., at 102, and the necessary degree of contentiousness, *Golden* v. *Zwickler,* 394 U. S. 103 (1969), are both present.

The appellee notes, however, that the record does not disclose that Roe was pregnant at the time of the District Court hearing on May 22, 1970,[6] or on the following June 17 when the court's opinion and judgment were filed. And he suggests that Roe's case must now be moot because she and all other members of her class are no longer subject to any 1970 pregnancy.

[6] The appellee twice states in his brief that the hearing before the District Court was held on July 22, 1970. Appellee's Brief 13. The docket entries, Appendix, at 2, and the transcript, Appendix, at 76, reveal this to be an error. The July date appears to be the time of the reporter's transcription. See Appendix, at 77.

The usual rule in federal cases is that an actual controversy must exist at stages of appellate or certiorari review, and not simply at the date the action is initiated. *United States* v. *Munsingwear, Inc.,* 340 U. S. 36 (1950); *Golden* v. *Zwickler, supra; SEC* v. *Medical Committee for Human Rights,* 404 U. S. 403 (1972).

But when, as here, pregnancy is a significant fact in the litigation, the normal 266-day human gestation period is so short that the pregnancy will come to term before the usual appellate process is complete. If that termination makes a case moot, pregnancy litigation seldom will survive much beyond the trial stage, and appellate review will be effectively denied. Our law should not be that rigid. Pregnancy often comes more than once to the same woman, and in the general population, if man is to survive, it will always be with us. Pregnancy provides a classic justification for a conclusion of nonmootness. It truly could be "capable of repetition, yet evading review." *Southern Pacific Terminal Co.* v. *ICC,* 219 U. S. 498, 515 (1911). See *Moore* v. *Ogilvie,* 394 U. S. 814, 816 (1969); *Carroll* v. *President and Commissioners,* 393 U. S. 175, 178-179 (1968); *United States* v. *W. T. Grant Co.,* 345 U. S. 629, 632-633 (1953).

We therefore agree with the District Court that Jane Roe had standing to undertake this litigation, that she presented a justiciable controversy, and that the termination of her 1970 pregnancy has not rendered her case moot.

B. *Dr. Hallford.* The doctor's position is different. He entered Roe's litigation as a plaintiff-intervenor alleging in his complaint that he:

"In the past has been arrested for violating the Texas Abortion Laws and at the present time stands charged by indictment with violating said laws in the Criminal District Court of Dallas County, Texas to-wit: (1) *The State of Texas* v. *James H. Hallford,* No. C-69-5307–1H, and (2) *The State of Texas* v. *James H. Hallford,* No. C-69-2524–H. In both cases the defendant is charged with abortion. . . ."

In his application for leave to intervene the doctor made like representations as to the abortion charges pending in the state court. These representations were also repeated in the affidavit he executed and filed in support of his motion for summary judgment.

Dr. Hallford is therefore in the position of seeking, in a federal court, declaratory and injunctive relief with respect to the same statutes under which he stands charged in criminal prosecutions simultaneously pending in state court. Although he stated that he has been arrested in the past for violating the State's abortion laws, he makes no allegation of any substantial and immediate threat to any federally protected right that cannot be asserted in his defense against the state prosecutions. Neither is there any allegation of harassment or bad faith prosecution. In order to escape the rule, articulated in the cases cited in the next paragraph of this opinion, that, absent harassment and bad faith, a defendant in a pending state criminal case cannot affirmatively challenge in federal court the statutes under which the State is prosecuting him, Dr. Hallford seeks to distinguish his status as a present state defendant from his status as a "potential future defendant" and to assert only the latter for standing purposes here.

We see no merit in that distinction. Our decision in *Samuels* v. *Mackell,* 401 U. S. 66 (1971), compels the conclusion that the District Court erred when it granted declaratory relief to Dr. Hallford instead of refraining from so doing. The court, of course, was correct in refusing to grant injuctive relief to the doctor. The reasons supportive of that action, however, are those expressed in *Samuels* v. *Mackell,* *supra,* and in *Younger* v. *Harris,* 401 U. S. 37 (1971); *Boyle* v. *Landry,* 401 U. S. 77 (1971); *Perez* v. *Ledesma,* 401 U. S. 82 (1971); and *Byrne* v. *Karalexis,* 401 U. S. 216 (1971); See also *Dombrowski* v. *Pfister,* 380 U. S. 479 (1965). We note, in passing, that *Younger* and its companion cases were decided after the three-judge District Court decision in this case.

Dr. Hallford's complaint in intervention, therefore, is to be dismissed.[7] He is remitted to his defenses in the state criminal proceedings against him. We reverse the judgment of the District Court insofar as it granted Dr. Hallford relief and failed to dismiss his complaint in intervention.

C. *The Does.* In view of our ruling as to Roe's standing in her case the issue of the Does' standing in their case has little significance. The claims they assert are

[7] We need not consider what different result, if any, would follow if Dr. Hallford's intervention were on behalf of a class. His complaint in intervention does not purport to assert a class suit and makes no reference to any class apart from an allegation that he "and others similarly situated" must necessarily guess at the meaning of Art. 1196. His application for leave to intervene goes somewhat further for it asserts that plaintiff Roe does not adequately protect the interest of the doctor "and the class of people who are physicians . . . and the class of people who are . . . patients . . . ." The leave application, however, is not the complaint. Despite the District Court's statement to the contrary, 314 F. Supp., at 1225, we fail to perceive the essentials of a class suit in the Hallford complaint.

essentially the same as those of Roe, and they attack the same statutes. Nevertheless, we briefly note the Does' posture.

Their pleadings present them as a childless married couple, the woman not being pregnant, who have no desire to have children at this time because of their having received medical advice that Mrs. Doe should avoid pregnancy, and for "other highly personal reasons." But they "fear . . . they may face the prospect of becoming parents." And if pregnancy ensues, they "would want to terminate" it by an abortion. They assert an inability to obtain an abortion legally in Texas and, consequently, the prospect of obtaining an illegal abortion there or of going outside Texas to some place where the procedure could be obtained legally and competently.

We thus have as plaintiffs a married couple who have, as their asserted immediate and present injury, only an alleged "detrimental effect upon [their] marital happiness" because they are forced to "the choice of refraining from normal sexual relations or of endangering Mary Doe's health through a possible pregnancy." Their claim is that sometime, in the future, Mrs. Doe might become pregnant because of possible failure of contraceptive measures, and at that time in the future, she might want an abortion that might then be illegal under the Texas statutes.

This very phrasing of the Does' position reveals its speculative character. Their alleged injury rests on possible future contraceptive failure, possible future pregnancy, possible future unpreparedness for parenthood, and possible future impairment of health. Any one or more of these several possibilities may not take place and all may not combine. In the Does' estimation, these possibilities might have some real or imagined impact upon their marital happiness. But we are not prepared to say that the bare allegation of so indirect an injury is sufficient to present an actual case or controversy. *Younger* v. *Harris,* 401 U. S., at 41-42; *Golden* v. *Zwickler,* 394 U. S., at 109-110 (1969); *Abele* v. *Markle,* 452 F. 2d, at 1124-1125, *Crossen* v. *Breckenridge,* 446 F. 2d, at 839. The Does' claim falls far short of those resolved otherwise in the cases that the Does urge upon us, namely, *Investment Co. Institute* v. *Camp,* 401 U. S. 617 (1971); *Data Processing Service* v. *Camp,* 397 U. S. 150 (1970); and *Epperson* v. *Arkansas,* 393 U. S. 97 (1968). See also *Truax* v. *Raich, supra.*

The Does therefore are not appropriate plaintiffs in this litigation. Their complaint was properly dismissed by the District Court, and we affirm that dismissal.

V

The principal thrust of appellant's attack on the Texas statutes is that they improperly invade a right, said to be possessed by the pregnant woman, to choose to terminate her pregnancy. Appellant would discover this right in the concept of personal "liberty" embodied in the Fourteenth Amendment's Due Process Clause; or in personal, marital, familial, and sexual privacy said to be protected by the Bill of Rights or its penumbras, see *Griswold* v. *Connecticut,* 381 U. S. 479 (1965); *Eisenstadt* v. *Baird,* 405 U. S. 438 (1972); *id.,* at 460 (White, J., concurring); or among those rights reserved to the people by the Ninth Amendment, *Griswold* v. *Connecticut,* 381 U. S., at 486 (Goldberg, J., concurring). Before addressing this claim, we feel it desirable briefly to survey, in several aspects, the history of abortion, for such insight as that history may afford us, and then to examine the state purposes and interests behind the criminal abortion laws.

VI

It perhaps is not generally appreciated that the restrictive criminal abortion laws in effect in a majority of States today are of relatively recent vintage. Those laws, generally proscribing abortion or its attempt at any time during pregnancy except when necessary to preserve the pregnant woman's life, are not of ancient or even of common law origin. Instead, they derive from statutory changes effected, for the most part, in the latter half of the 19th century.

1. *Ancient attitudes.* These are not capable of precise determination. We are told that at the time of the Persian Empire abortifacients were known and that criminal abortions were severely punished.[8] We are also told, however, that abortion was practiced in Greek times as well as in the Roman Era,[9] and that "it was resorted to without scruple."[10] The Ephesian, Soranos, often described as the greatest of the ancient gynecologists, appears to have been generally opposed to Rome's prevailing free-abortion practices. He found it necessary to think first of the life of the mother, and he resorted to abortion when, upon this standard, he felt the procedure advisable.[11] Greek and Roman law afforded little protection to the unborn. If abortion was prosecuted in some places, it seems to have been based on a concept of a violation of the father's right to his offspring. Ancient religion did not bar abortion.[12]

2. *The Hippocratic Oath.* What then of the famous Oath that has stood so long as the ethical guide of medical profession and that bears the name of the great Greek (460(?) 377(?) B. C.), who has been described as the Father of Medicine, the "wisest and the greatest practioner of his art," and the "most important and most complete medical personality of antiquity," who dominated the medical schools of his time, and who typified the sum of the medical knowledge of the past?[13] The Oath varies somewhat according to the particular translation, but in any translation the content is clear: "I will give no deadly medicine to anyone if asked, nor suggest any such counsel; and in like manner I will not give to a woman a pessary to produce abortion,"[14] or "I will neither give a deadly drug to anybody if asked for it, nor will I make a suggestion to this effect. Similarily, I will not give to a woman an abortive remedy."[15]

Although the Oath is not mentioned in any of the principal briefs in this case or in *Doe* v. *Bolton, post,* it represents the apex of the development of strict ethical concepts in medicine, and its influence endures to this day. Why did not the authority of Hippocrates dissuade abortion practice in his time and that of Rome? The late Dr. Edelstein provides us with a theory:[16] The Oath was not uncontested even in Hippocrates' day; only the Pythagorean school of philosophers frowned upon the related act of suicide. Most Greek thinkers, on the other hand, commended abortion, at least prior to viability. See Plato, *Republic,* V, 461; Aristotle, *Politics,* VII, 1335 b 25. For the Pythagoreans, however, it was a matter of dogma. For them the embryo was animate from the moment of conception, and abortion meant destruction of a living being. The abortion clause of the Oath, therefore, "echoes Pythagore-

---

[8] A. Castiglioni, A History of Medicine 84 (2d ed. 1947), E. Krumbhaar, translator and editor (hereinafter "Castiglioni").
[9] J. Ricci, The Genealogy of Gynaecology 52, 84, 113, 149 (2d ed. 1950) (hereinafter "Ricci"); L. Lader, Abortion 75–77 (1966) (hereinafter "Lader"); K. Niswander, Medical Abortion Practices in the United States, in Abortion and the Law 27, 38–40 (D. Smith, editor, 1967); G. Williams, The Sanctity of Life 148 (1957) (hereinafter "Williams"); J. Noonan, An Almost Absolute Value in History, in The Morality of Abortion 1, 3–7 (J. Noonan ed. 1970) (hereinafter "Noonan"); E. Quay, Justifiable Abortion—Medical and Legal Foundations, II, 49 Geo. L. J. 395, 406–422 (1961) (hereinafter "Quay").

[10] L. Edelstein, The Hippocratic Oath 10 (1943) (hereinafter "Edelstein"). But see Castiglioni 227.
[11] Edelstein 12; Ricci 113–114, 118–119; Noonan 5.
[12] Edelstein 13–14.
[13] Castiglioni 148.
[14] *Id.,* at 154.
[15] Edelstein 3.
[16] *Id.,* at 12, 15–18.

an doctrines," and " in no other stratum of Greek opinion were such views held or proposed in the same spirit of uncompromising austerity."[17]

Edelstein then concludes that the Oath originated in a group representing only a small segment of Greek opinion and that it certainly was not accepted by all ancient physicians. He points out that medical writings down to Galen (130-200 A. D.) "give evidence of the violation of almost every one of its injunctions."[18] But with the end of antiquity a decided change took place. Resistance against suicide and against abortion became common. The Oath came to be popular. The emerging teachings of Christianity were in agreement with the Pythagorean ethic. The Oath "became the nucleus of all medical ethics" and "was applauded as the embodiment of truth." Thus, suggests Dr. Edelstein, it is "a Pythagorean manifesto and not the expression of an absolute standard of medical conduct."[19]

This, it seems to us, is a satisfactory and acceptable explanation of the Hippocratic Oath's apparent rigidity. It enables us to understand, in historical context, a long accepted and revered statement of medical ethics.

3. *The Common Law.* It is undisputed that at the common law, abortion performed *before* "quickening"—the first recognizable movement of the fetus *in utero*, appearing usually from the 16th to the 18th week of pregnancy[20]—was not an indictable offense.[21] The absence of a common law crime for pre-quickening abortion appears to have developed from a confluence of earlier philosophical, theological, and civil and canon law concepts of when life begins. These disciplines variously approached the question in terms of the point at which the embryo or fetus became "formed" or recognizably human, or in terms of when a "person" came into being, that is, infused with a "soul" or "animated." A loose consensus evolved in early English law that these events occurred at some point between conception and live birth.[22] This was "mediate animation." Although Christian theology and the canon law came to fix the point of animation at 40 days for a male and 80 days for a female, a view that persisted until the 19th century, there was otherwise little agreement about the precise time of formation or animation. There was agreement, however, that prior to this point the fetus was to be regarded as part of the mother and its destruction, therefore, was not homicide. Due to continued uncertainty about the precise time when animation occurred, to the lack of any empirical basis for the 40-80 day view, and perhaps to Acquinas' definition of movement as one of the two first principles of life, Bracton focused upon quickening as the critical point. The significance of quickening was echoed by later common law scholars and found its way into the received common law in this country.

---

[17] *Id.,* at 18; Lader 76.
[18] Edelstein 63.
[19] *Id.,* at 64.
[20] Dorland's Illustrated Medical Dictionary 1261 (24th ed. 1965).
[21] E. Coke, Institutes III *50 (1648); 1 W. Hawkins, Pleas of the Crown c. 31, § 16 (1762); 1 Blackstone, Commentaries *129–130 (1765); M. Hale, Pleas of the Crown 433 (1778). For discussions of the role of the quickening concept in English common law, see Lader 78; Noonan 223–226; C. Means, The Law of New York Concerning Abortion and the Status of the Foetus, 1664–1968: A Case of Cessation of Constitutionality, 14 N. Y. L. Forum 411, 418–428 (1968) (hereinafter "Means I"); L. Stern, Abortion: Reform and the Law, 59 J. Crim. L. C. & P. S. 84 (1968) (hereinafter "Stern"); Quay 430–432; Williams 152.
[22] Early philosophers believed that the embryo or fetus did not become formed and begin to live until at least 40 days after conception for a male, and 80 to 90 days for a female. See, for example, Aristotle, Hist. Anim. 7.3.583b; Gen. Anim. 2.3.736, 2.5.741; Hippocrates, Lib. de Nat. Puer., No. 10. Aristotle's thinking derived from his three-stage theory of life: vegetable, animal, rational. The vegetable stage was reached at conception, the animal at "animation," and the rational soon after live birth. This theory, together with the 40/80 day view, came to be accepted by early Christian thinkers.

The theological debate was reflected in the writings of St. Augustine, who made a distinction between *embryo inanimatus,* not yet endowed with a soul, and *embryo animatus.* He may have drawn upon Exodus xxi, 22. At one point, however, he expresses the view that human powers cannot determine the point during fetal development at which the critical change occurs. See Augustine, De Origine Animae 4.4 (Pub. Law 44.527). See also Reany, The Creation of the Human Soul, c. 2 and 83–86 (1932); Huser, The Crime of Abortion in Common Law 15 (Catholic Univ. of America, Canon Law Studies No. 162, Washington, D. C. 1942).

Galen, in three treatises related to embryology, accepted the thinking of Aristotle and his followers. Quay 426–427. Later, Augustine on abortion was incorporated by Gratian into the Decretum, published about 1140. Decretum Magistri Gratiani 2.32.2.7 to 2.32.2.10, in 1 Corpus Juris Canonici 1122, 1123 (2d ed. Friedberg ed. 1879). Gratian, together with the decretals that followed, were recognized as the definitive body of canon law until the new Code of 1917.

For discussions of the canon law treatment, see Means I, at 411–412; Noonan, 20–26; Quay 426–430; see also Noonan, Contraception: A History of Its Treatment by the Catholic Theologians and Canonists 18–29 (1965).

Whether abortion of a *quick* fetus was a felony at common law, or even a lesser crime, is still disputed. Bracton, writing early in the 13th century, thought it homicide.[23] But the later and predominant view, following the great common law scholars, has been that it was at most a lesser offense. In a frequently cited passage, Coke took the position that abortion of a woman "quick with childe" is "a great misprision and no murder."[24] Blackstone followed, saying that while abortion after quickening had once been considered manslaughter (though not murder), "modern law" took a less severe view.[25] A recent review of the common law precedents argues, however, that those precedents contradict Coke and that even post-quickening abortion was never established as a common law crime.[26] This is of some importance because while most American courts ruled, in holding or dictum, that abortion of an unquickened fetus was not criminal under their received common law,[27] others followed Coke in stating that abortion of a quick fetus was a "misprision," a term they translated to mean "misdemeanor."[28] That their reliance on Coke on this aspect of the law was uncritical and, apparently in all the reported cases, dictum (due probably to the paucity of common law prosecutions for post-quickening abortion), makes it now appear doubtful that abortion was ever firmly established as a common law crime even with respect to the destruction of a quick fetus.

[23] Bracton took the position that abortion by blow or poison was homicide "if the foetus be already formed and animated, and particularly if it be animated." 2 H. Bracton, De Legibus et Consuetudinibus Angliae 279 (Twiss ed. 1879), or, as a later translation puts it, "if the foetus is already formed or quickened, especially if it is quickened," II Bracton, On the Laws and Customs of England 341 (Thorne ed. 1968). See Quay 431; see also 2 Fleta 60–61 (Book I, c. 23)(Selden Society ed. 1955).

[24] E. Coke, Institutes III *50 (1648).

[25] 1 Blackstone, Commentaries *129–130 (1765).

[26] C. Means, The Phoenix of Abortional Freedom: Is a Penumbral or Ninth-Amendment Right About to Arise from the Nineteenth-Century Legislative Ashes of a Fourteenth-Century Common-Law Liberty?, 17 N. Y. L. Forum 335 (1971) (hereinafter "Means II"). The author examines the two principal precedents cited marginally by Coke, both contrary to his dictum, and traces the treatment of these and other cases by earlier commentators. He concludes that Coke, who himself participated as an advocate in an abortion case in 1601, may have intentionally misstated the law. The author even suggests a reason: Coke's strong feelings about abortion, coupled with his reluctance to acknowledge common law (secular) jurisdiction to assess penalties for an offence that traditionally had been an exclusively ecclesiastical or canon law crime. See also Lader 78–79, who notes that some scholars doubt the common law ever was applied to abortion; that the English ecclesiastical courts seem to have lost interest in the problem after 1527; and that the preamble to the English legislation of 1803, 43 Geo. 3, c. 58, § 1, at 203, referred to in the text, *infra*, states that "no adequate means have been hitherto provided for the prevention and punishment of such offenses."

[27] *Commonwealth* v. *Bangs*, 9 Mass. 387, 388 (1812); *Commonwealth* v. *Parker*, 50 Mass. (9 Met.) 263, 265–266 (1845); *State* v. *Cooper*, 22 N. J. L. 52, 58 (1849); *Abrams* v. *Foshee*, 3 Iowa 274, 278–280 (1856); *Smith* v. *Gaffard*, 31 Ala. 45, 51 (1857); *Mitchell* v. *Commonwealth*, 78 Ky. 204, 210 (1879); *Eggart* v. *State*, 40 Fla. 527, 532, 25 So. 144, 145 (1898); *State* v. *Alcorn*, 7 Idaho 599, 606, 64 P. 1014, 1016 (1901); *Edwards* v. *State*, 79 Neb. 251, 252, 112 N. W. 611, 612 (1907); *Gray* v. *State*, 77 Tex. Crim. R. 221, 224, 178 S. W. 337, 338 (1915); *Miller* v. *Bennett*, 190 Va. 162, 169, 56 S. E. 2d 217, 221 (1949). Contra, *Mills* v. *Commonwealth*, 13 Pa. 631, 633 (1850); *State* v. *Slagle*, 83 N. C. 630, 632 (1880).

[28] See *Smith* v. *State*, 33 Me. 48, 55 (1851); *Evans* v. *People*, 49 N. Y. 86, 88 (1872); *Lamb* v. *State*, 67 Md. 524, 533, 10 A. 208 (1887).

4. *The English statutory law*. England's first criminal abortion statute, Lord Ellenborough's Act, 43 Geo. 3, c. 58, came in 1803. It made abortion of a quick fetus, § 1, a capital crime, but in § 2 it provided lesser penalties for the felony of abortion before quickening, and thus preserved the quickening distinction. This contrast was continued in the general revision of 1828, 9 Geo. 4, c. 31, § 13, at 104. It disappeared, however, together with the death penalty, in 1837, 7 Will. 4 & 1 Vic., c. 85, § 6 at 360, and did not reappear in the Offenses Against the Person Act of 1861, 24 & 25 Vic., c. 100, § 59, at 438, that formed the core of English anti-abortion law until the liberalizing reforms of 1967. In 1929 the Infant Life (Preservation) Act, 19 & 20 Geo. 5, c. 34, came into being. Its emphasis was upon the destruction of "the life of a child capable of being born alive." It made a willful act performed with the necessary intent a felony. It contained a proviso that one was not to be found guilty of the offense "unless it is proved that the act which caused the death of the child was not done in good faith for the purpose only of preserving the life of the mother."

A seemingly notable development in the English law was the case of *Rex* v. *Bourne*, [1939] 1 K. B. 687. This case apparently answered in the affirmative the question whether an abortion necessary to preserve the life of the pregnant woman was excepted from the criminal penalties of the 1861 Act. In his instructions to the jury Judge Macnaghten referred to the 1929 Act, and observed, p. 691, that the Act related to "the case where a child is killed by a willful act at the time when it is being delivered in the ordinary course of nature." *Id.*, at 91. He concluded that the 1861 Act's use of the word "unlawfully," imported the same meaning expressed by the specific proviso in the 1929 Act even though there was no mention of preserving the mother's life in the 1861 Act. He then construed the phrase "preserving the life of the mother" broadly, that is, "in a reasonable sense," to include a serious and permanent threat to the mother's *health*, and instructed the jury to acquit Dr. Bourne if it found he had acted in a good faith belief that the abortion was necessary for this purpose. *Id.*, at 693-694. The jury did acquit.

Recently Parliament enacted a new abortion law. This is the Abortion Act of 1967, 15 & 16 Eliz. 2, c. 87. The Act permits a licensed physician to perform an abortion where two other licensed physicians agree (a) "that the continuance of the pregnancy would involve risk to the life of the pregnant woman, or of injury to the physical or mental health of the pregnant woman or any existing children of her family, greater than if the pregnancy were terminated," or (b) "that there is a substantial risk that if the child were born it would suffer from such physical or mental abnormalities as to be seriously handicapped." The Act also provides that, in making this determination, "account may be taken of the pregnant woman's actual or reasonably foreseeable environment." It also permits a physician, without the concurrence of others, to terminate a pregnancy where he is of the good faith opinion that the abortion "is immediately necessary to save the life or to prevent grave permanent injury to the physical or mental health of the pregnant woman."

5. *The American law*. In this country the law in effect in all but a few States until mid-19th century was the pre-existing English common law. Connecticut, the first State to enact abortion legislation, adopted in 1821 that part of Lord Ellenborough's Act that related to a woman "quick with child."[29] The death penalty was not imposed. Abortion before quickening was made a crime in that State only in 1860.[30] In 1828 New York enacted legislation[31] that, in two respects, was to serve

---

[29] Conn. Stat., Tit. 20, § 14 (1821).
[30] Conn. Pub. Acts, c. 71, § 1 (1860).
[31] N. Y. Rev. Stat., pt. IV, c. I, Tit. II, Art. 1, § 9, at 661, and Tit. VI, § 21, at 694 (1829).

as a model for early anti-abortion statutes. First, while barring destruction of an unquickened fetus as well as a quick fetus, it made the former only a misdemeanor, but the latter second-degree manslaughter. Second, it incorporated a concept of therapeutic abortion by providing that an abortion was excused if it "shall have been necessary to preserve the life of such mother, or shall have been advised by two physicians to be necessary for such purpose." By 1840, when Texas had received the common law,[32] only eight American States had statutes dealing with abortion.[33] It was not until after the War Between the States that legislation began generally to replace the common law. Most of these initial statutes dealt severely with abortion after quickening but were lenient with it before quickening. Most punished attempts equally with completed abortions. While many statutes included the exception for an abortion thought by one or more physicians to be necessary to save the mother's life, that provision soon disappeared and the typical law required that the procedure actually be necessary for that purpose.

Gradually, in the middle and late 19th century the quickening distinction disappeared from the statutory law of most States and the degree of the offense and the penalties were increased. By the end of the 1950's, a large majority of the States banned abortion, however and whenever performed, unless done to save or preserve the life of the mother.[34] The exceptions, Alabama and the District of Columbia, permitted abortion to preserve the mother's health.[35] Three other States permitted abortions that were not "unlawfully" performed or that were not "without lawful justification," leaving interpretation of those standards to the courts.[36] In the past several years, however, a trend toward liberalization of abortion statutes has resulted in adoption, by about one-third of the States, of less stringent laws, most of them patterned after the ALI Model Penal Code, § 230.3,[37] set forth as Appendix B to the opinion in *Doe* v. *Bolton, post—.*

It is thus apparent that at common law, at the time of the adoption of our Constitution, and throughout the major portion of the 19th century, abortion was viewed with less disfavor than under most American statutes currently in effect. Phrasing it

[32] Act of January 20, 1840, § 1, set forth in 2 Gammel, Laws of Texas 177—178 (1898); see *Grigsby* v. *Reib,* 105 Tex. 597, 600, 153 S. W. 1124, 1125 (1913).

[33] The early statutes are discussed in Quay 435—438. See also Lader 85—88; Stern 85—86; and Means II 375—376.

[34] Criminal abortion statutes in effect in the States as of 1961, together with historical statutory development and important judicial interpretations of the state statutes, are cited and quoted in Quay 447—520. See Note, A Survey of the Present Statutory and Case Law on Abortion: The Contradictions and the Problems, 1972 Ill. L. Forum 177, 179, classifying the abortion statutes and listing 25 States as permitting abortion only if necessary to save or preserve the mother's life.

[35] Ala. Code Tit. 14, § 9 (1958); D. C. Code Ann. § 22—201 (1967).

[36] Mass. Gen. Laws Ann., c. 272, § 19 (1970); N. J. Rev. Stat. Ann. 2A:87—1 (1969); Pa. Stat. Ann., Tit. 18, §§ 4718, 4719 (1963).

[37] Fourteen States have adopted some form of the ALI statute. See Ark. Stat. Ann. §§ 41—303 to 41—310 (Supp. 1971); Calif. Health and Safety Code §§ 25950—25955.5 (West Supp. 1972); Colo. Rev. Stats. Ann. §§ 40—2—50 to 40—2—53 (Perm. Cum. Supp. 1967); Del. Code Ann., Tit. 24, §§ 1790—1793 (Supp. 1972); Florida Law of Apr. 13, 1972, c. 72—196, 1972 Fla. Sess. Law Serv., at 380—382; Ga. Code §§ 26—1201 to 26—1203 (1972); Kan. Stat. Ann. § 21—3407 (Supp. 1971); Md. Ann. Code, Art. 43, §§ 137-139 (Repl. 1971); Miss. Code Ann. § 2223 (Supp. 1972); N. M. Stat. Ann. §§ 40A—5—1 to 40A—5—3 (Repl. 1972); N. C. Gen. Stat. § 14—45.1 (Supp. 1971); Ore. Rev. Stat. §§ 435.405 to 435.495 (1971); S. C. Code Ann. §§ 16—82 to 16—89 (Supp. 1971); Va. Code Ann. §§ 18.1—62 to 18.1—62.3 (Supp. 1972). Mr. Justice Clark described some of these States as having "led the way." Religion, Morality and Abortion: A Constitutional Appraisal, 2 Loyola U. (L. A.) L. Rev. 1, 11 (1969).

By the end of 1970, four other States had repealed criminal penalties for abortions performed in early pregnancy by a licensed physician, subject to stated procedural and health requirements. Alaska Stat. § 11.15.060 (1970); Haw. Rev. Stat. § 453—16 (Supp. 1971); N. Y. Penal Code § 125.05 (McKinney Supp. 1972—1973); Wash. Rev. Code §§ 9.02.060 to 9.02.080 (Supp. 1972). The precise status of criminal abortion laws in some States is made unclear by recent decisions in state and federal courts striking down existing state laws, in whole or in part.

another way, a woman enjoyed a substantially broader right to terminate a pregnancy than she does in most States today. At least with respect to the early stage of pregnancy, and very possibly without such a limitation, the opportunity to make this choice was present in this country well into the 19th century. Even later, the law continued for some time to treat less punitively an abortion procured in early pregnancy.

6. *The position of the American Medical Association.* The anti-abortion mood prevalent in this country in the late 19th century was shared by the medical profession. Indeed, the attitude of the profession may have played a significant role in the enactment of stringent criminal abortion legislation during that period.

An AMA Committee on Criminal Abortion was appointed in May 1857. It presented its report, 12 Trans. of the Am. Med. Assn. 73-77 (1859), to the Twelfth Annual Meeting. That report observed that the Committee had been appointed to investigate criminal abortion "with a view to its general suppression." It deplored abortion and its frequency and it listed three causes "of this general demoralization":

> "The first of these causes is a wide-spread popular ignorance of the true character of the crime—a belief, even among mothers themselves, that the foetus is not alive till after the period of quickening.
> "The second of the agents alluded to is the fact that the profession themselves are frequently supposed careless of foetal life . . . .
> "The third reason of the frightful extent of this crime is found in the grave defects of our laws, both common and statute, as regards the independent and actual existence of the child before birth, as a living being. These errors, which are sufficient in most instances to prevent conviction, are based, and only based, upon mistaken and exploded medical dogmas. With strange inconsistency, the law fully acknowledges the foetus in utero and its inherent rights, for civil purposes; while personally and as criminally affected, it fails to recognize it, and to its life as yet denies all protection." *Id.,* at 75—76.

The Committee then offered, and the Association adopted, resolutions protesting "against such unwarrantable destruction of human life," calling upon state legislatures to revise their abortion laws, and requesting the cooperation of state medical societies "in pressing the subject." *Id.,* at 28, 78.

In 1871 a long and vivid report was submitted by the Committee on Criminal Abortion. It ended with the observation, "We had to deal with human life. In a matter of less importance we could entertain no compromise. An honest judge on the bench would call things by their proper names. We could do no less." 22 Trans. of the Am. Med. Assn. 258 (1871). It proffered resolutions, adopted by the Association, *id.,* at 38—39, recommending, among other things, that it "be unlawful and unprofessional for any physician to induce abortion or premature labor, without the concurrent opinion of at least one respectable consulting physician, and then always with a view to the safety of the child—if that be possible," and calling "the attention of the clergy of all denominations to the perverted views of morality entertained by a large class of females—aye, and men also, on this important question."

Except for periodic condemnation of the criminal abortionist, no further formal AMA action took place until 1967. In that year the Committee on Human Reproduction urged the adoption of a stated policy of opposition to induced abortion except when there is "documented medical evidence" of a threat to the health or life of the mother, or that the child "may be born with incapacitating physical deformity or mental deficiency," or that a pregnancy "resulting from legally established statutory or forcible rape or incest may constitute a threat to the mental or physical health of the patient," and two other physicians "chosen because of their recognized professional competence have examined the patient and have concurred

206

in writing," and the procedure "is performed in a hospital accredited by the Joint Commission on Accreditation of Hospitals." The providing of medical information by physicians to state legislatures in their consideration of legislation regarding therapeutic abortion was "to be considered consistent with the principles of ethics of the American Medical Association." This recommendation was adopted by the House of Delegates. Proceedings of the AMA House of Delegates, 40–51 (June 1967).

In 1970, after the introduction of a variety of proposed resolutions, and of a report from its Board of Trustees, a reference committee noted "polarization of the medical profession on this controversial issue"; division among those who had testified; a difference of opinion among AMA councils and committees; "the remarkable shift in testimony" in six months, felt to be influenced "by the rapid changes in state laws and by the judicial decisions which tend to make abortion more freely available"; and a feeling "that this trend will continue." On June 25, 1970, the House of Delegates adopted preambles and most of the resolutions proposed by the reference committee. The preambles emphasized "the best interests of the patient," "sound clinical judgment," and "informed patient consent," in contrast to "mere acquiescence to the patient's demand." The resolutions asserted that abortion is a medical procedure that should be performed by a licensed physician in an accredited hospital only after consultation with two other physicians and in conformity with state law, and that no party to the procedure should be required to violate personally held moral principles.[38] Proceedings of the AMA House of Delegates 221 (June 1970). The AMA Judicial Council rendered a complementary opinion.[39]

7. *The position of the American Public Health Association.* In October 1970, the Executive Board of the APHA adopted Standards for Abortion Services. These were five in number:

"a. Rapid and simple abortion referral must be readily available through state and local public health departments, medical societies, or other nonprofit organizations.

"b. An important function of counseling should be to simplify and expedite the provision of abortion services; it should not delay the obtaining of these services.

"c. Psychiatric consultation should not be mandatory. As in the case of other specialized medical services, psychiatric consultation should be sought for definite indications and not on a routine basis.

"d. A wide range of individuals from appropriately trained, sympathetic volunteers to highly skilled physicians may qualify as abortion counselors.

[38] "Whereas, Abortion, like any other medical procedure, should not be performed when contrary to the best interests of the patient since good medical practice requires due consideration for the patient's welfare and not mere acquiescence to the patient's demand; and

"Whereas, The standards of sound clinical judgment, which, together with informed patient consent should be determinative according to the merits of each individual case; therefore be it

"*RESOLVED,* That abortion is a medical procedure and should be performed only by a duly licensed physician and surgeon in an accredited hospital acting only after consultation with two other physicians chosen because of their professional competency and in conformance with standards of good medical practice and the Medical Practice Act of his State; and be it further

"*RESOLVED,* That no physician or other professional personnel shall be compelled to perform any act which violates his good medical judgment. Neither physician, hospital, nor hospital personnel shall be required to perform any act violative of personally-held moral principles. In these circumstances good medical practice requires only that the physician or other professional personnel withdraw from the case so long as the withdrawal is consistent with good medical practice." Proceedings of the AMA House of Delegates 221 (June 1970).

[39] "The Principles of Medical Ethics of the AMA do not prohibit a physician from performing an abortion that is performed in accordance with good medical practice and under circumstances that do not violate the laws of the community in which he practices.

"In the matter of abortions, as of any other medical procedure, the Judicial Council becomes involved whenever there is alleged violation of the Principles of Medical Ethics as established by the House of Delegates."

"e. Contraception and/or sterilization should be discussed with each abortion patient." Recommended Standards for Abortion Services, 61 Am. J. Pub. Health 396 (1971).

Among factors pertinent to life and health risks associated with abortion were three that "are recognized as important":

"a. the skill of the physician,

"b. the environment in which the abortion is performed, and above all

"c. the duration of pregnancy, as determined by uterine size and confirmed by menstrual history." *Id.,* at 397.

It was said that "a well-equipped hospital" offers more protection "to cope with unforeseen difficulties than an office or clinic without such resources. . . . The factor of gestational age is of overriding importance." Thus it was recommended that abortions in the second trimester and early abortions in the presence of existing medical complications be performed in hospitals as inpatient procedures. For pregnancies in the first trimester, abortion in the hospital with or without overnight stay "is probably the safest practice." An abortion in an extramural facility, however, is an acceptable alternative "provided arrangements exist in advance to admit patients promptly if unforeseen complications develop." Standards for an abortion facility were listed. It was said that at present abortions should be performed by physicians or osteopaths who are licensed to practice and who have "adequate training." *Id.,* at 398.

8. *The position of the American Bar Association.* At its meeting in February 1972 the ABA House of Delegates approved, with 17 opposing votes, the Uniform Abortion Act that had been drafted and approved the preceding August by the Conference of Commissioners on Uniform State Laws. 58 A. B. A. J. 380 (1972). We set forth the Act in full in the margin.[40] The Conference has appended an enlightening Prefatory Note.[41]

[40]   "UNIFORM ABORTION ACT
"SECTION 1. [*Abortion Defined; When Authorized.*]
"(a) 'Abortion' means the termination of human pregnancy with an intention other than to produce a live birth or to remove a dead fetus.
"(b) An abortion may be performed in this state only if it is performed:
"(1) by a physician licensed to practice medicine [or osteopathy] in this state or by a physician practicing medicine [or osteopathy] in the employ of the government of the United States or of this state, [and the abortion is performed [in the physician's office or in a medical clinic, or] in a hospital approved by the [Department of Health] or operated by the United States, this state, or any department, agency, or political subdivision of either;] or by a female upon herself upon the advice of the physician, and
"(2) within [20] weeks after the commencement of the pregnancy [or after [20] weeks only if the physician has reasonable cause to believe (i) there is a substantial risk that continuance of the pregnancy would endanger the life of the mother or would gravely impair the physical or mental health of the mother, (ii) that the child would be born with grave physical or mental defect, or (iii) that the pregnancy resulted from rape or incest, or illicit intercourse with a girl under the age of 16 years of age].
"SECTION 2. [*Penalty.*] Any person who performs or procures an abortion other than authorized by this Act is guilty of a [felony] and, upon conviction thereof, may be sentenced to pay a fine not exceeding [$1,000] or to imprisonment [in the state penitentiary] not exceeding [5 years], or both.
"SECTION 3. [*Uniformity of Interpretation.*] This Act shall be construed to effectuate its general purpose to make uniform the law with respect to the subject of this Act among those states which enact it.
"SECTION 4. [*Short Title.*] This Act may be cited as the Uniform Abortion Act.
"SECTION 5. [*Severability.*] If any provision of this Act or the application thereof to any person or circumstance is held invalid, the invalidity does not affect other provisions or applications of this Act which can be given effect without the invalid provision or application, and to this end the provisions of this Act are severable.
"SECTION 6. [*Repeal.*] The following acts and parts of acts are repealed:
"(1)
"(2)
"(3)

"SECTION 7. [*Time of Taking Effect.*] This Act shall take effect_____."

[41] "This Act is based largely upon the New York abortion act following a review of the more recent laws on abortion in several states and upon recognition of a more liberal trend in laws on this subject. Recognition was given also to the several decisions in state and federal courts which show a further trend toward liberalization of abortion laws, especially during the first trimester of pregnancy.

"Recognizing that a number of problems appeared in New York, a shorter time period for 'unlimited' abortions was advisable. The time period was bracketed to permit the various states to insert a figure more in keeping with the different conditions that might exist among the states. Likewise, the language limiting the place or places in which abortions may be performed was also bracketed to account for different conditions among the states. In addition, limitations on abortions after the initial 'unlimited' period were placed in brackets so that individual states may adopt all or any of these reasons, or place further restrictions upon abortions after the initial period.

"This Act does not contain any provision relating to medical review committees or prohibitions against sanctions imposed upon medical personnel refusing to participate in abortions because of religious or other similar reasons, or the like. Such provisions, while related, do not directly pertain to when, where, or by whom abortions may be performed; however, the Act is not drafted to exclude such a provision by a state wishing to enact the same."

VII

Three reasons have been advanced to explain historically the enactment of criminal abortion laws in the 19th century and to justify their continued existence.

It has been argued occasionally that these laws were the product of a Victorian social concern to discourage illicit sexual conduct. Texas, however, does not advance this justification in the present case, and it appears that no court or commentator has taken the argument seriously.[42] The appellants and *amici* contend, moreover, that this is not a proper state purpose at all and suggest that, if it were, the Texas statutes are overbroad in protecting it since the law fails to distinguish between married and unwed mothers.

A second reason is concerned with abortion as a medical procedure. When most criminal abortion laws were first enacted, the procedure was a hazardous one for the woman.[43] This was particularly true prior to the development of antisepsis. Antiseptic techniques, of course, were based on discoveries by Lister, Pasteur, and others first announced in 1867, but were not generally accepted and employed until about the turn of the century. Abortion mortality was high. Even after 1900, and perhaps until as late as the development of antibiotics in the 1940's, standard modern techniques such as dilation and curettage were not nearly so safe as they are today. Thus it has been argued that a State's real concern in enacting a criminal abortion law was to protect the pregnant woman, that is, to restrain her from submitting to a procedure that placed her life in serious jeopardy.

Modern medical techniques have altered this situation. Appellants and various *amici* refer to medical data indicating that abortion in early pregnancy, that is, prior to the end of first trimester, although not without its risk, is now relatively safe. Mortality rates for women undergoing early abortions, where the procedure is legal, appear to be as low as or lower than the rates for normal childbirth.[44]

[42] See, for example, *YWCA* v. *Kugler*, 342 F. Supp. 1048, 1074 (N. J. 1972); *Abele* v. *Markle*, 342 F. Supp. 800, 805–806 (Conn. 1972) (Newman, J., concurring), appeal pending; *Walsingham* v. *Florida*, 250 So. 2d 857, 863 (Ervin, J., concurring) (Fla. Supp. 1972); *State* v. *Gedicke*, 43 N. J. L. 86, 80 (Sup. St. 1881); Means II, at 381–382.

[43] See C. Haagensen & W. Lloyd, A Hundred Years of Medicine 19 (1943).

[44] Potts, Postconception Control of Fertility, 8 Int'l J. of G. & O. 957, 967 (1970) (England and Wales); Abortion Mortality, 20 Morbidity and Morality, 208, 209 (July 12, 1971) (U. S. Dept. of HEW, Public Health Service) (New York City); Tietze, United States: Therapeutic Abortions, 1963–1968, 59 Studies in Family Planning 5, 7 (1970); Tietze, Mortality with Contraception and Induced Abortion, 45 Studies in Family Planning 6 (1969) (Japan, Czechoslovakia, Hungary); Tietze & Lehfeldt, Legal Abortion in Eastern Europe, 175 J. A. M. A. 1149, 1152 (April 1961). Other sources are discussed in Lader 17–23.

Consequently, any interest of the State in protecting the woman from an inherently hazardous procedure, except when it would be equally dangerous for her to forgo it, has largely disappeared. Of course, important state interests in the area of health and medical standards do remain. The State has a legitimate interest in seeing to it that abortion, like any other medical procedure, is performed under circumstances that insure maximum safety for the patient. This interest obviously extends at least to the performing physician and his staff, to the facilities involved, to the availability of after-care, and to adequate provision for any complication or emergency that might arise. The prevalence of high mortality rates at illegal "abortion mills" strengthens, rather than weakens, the State's interest in regulating the conditions under which abortions are performed. Moreover, the risk to the woman increases as her pregnancy continues. Thus the State retains a definite interest in protecting the woman's own health and safety when an abortion is proposed at a late stage of pregnancy.

The third reason is the State's interest—some phrase it in terms of duty—in protecting prenatal life. Some of the argument for this justification rests on the theory that a new human life is present from the moment of conception.[45] The State's interest and general obligation to protect life then extends, it is argued, to prenatal life. Only when the life of the pregnant mother herself is at stake, balanced against the life she carries within her, should the interest of the embryo or fetus not prevail. Logically, of course, a legitimate state interest in this area need not stand or fall on acceptance of the belief that life begins at conception or at some other point prior to live birth. In assessing the State's interest, recognition may be given to the less rigid claim that as long as at least *potential* life is involved, the State may assert interests beyond the protection of the pregnant woman alone.

Parties challenging state abortion laws have sharply disputed in some courts the contention that a purpose of these laws, when enacted, was to protect prenatal life.[46] Pointing to the absence of legislative history to support the contention, they claim that most state laws were designed solely to protect the woman. Because medical advances have lessened this concern, at least with respect to abortion in early pregnancy, they argue that with respect to such abortions the laws can no longer be justified by any state interest. There is some scholarly support for this view of original purpose.[47] The few state courts called upon to interpret their laws in the late 19th and early 20th centuries did focus on the State's interest in protecting the woman's health rather than in preserving the embryo and fetus.[48] Proponents of this view point out that in many States, including Texas,[49] by statute or judicial interpretation, the pregnant woman herself could not be prosecuted for self-abortion or for cooperating in an abortion performed upon her by another.[50] They claim that adoption of the "quickening" distinction through received common law and state statutes tacitly recognizes the greater health hazards inherent in late abortion and impliedly repudiates the theory that life begins at conception.

It is with these interests, and the weight to be attached to them, that this case is concerned.

[45] See Brief of Amicus National Right to Life Foundation; R. Drinan, The Inviolability of the Right to Be Born, in Abortion and the Law 107 (D. Smith, editor, 1967); Louisell, Abortion, The Practice of Medicine, and the Due Process of Law, 16 UCLA L. Rev. 233 (1969); Noonan I.

[46] See, e. g., Abele v. Markle, 342 F. Supp. 800 (Conn. 1972), appeal pending.

[47] See discussions in Means I and Means II.

[48] See, e. g., State v. Murphy, 27 N. J. L. 112, 114 (1858).

[49] Watson v. State, 9 Tex. App. 237, 244–245 (1880); Moore v. State, 37 Tex. Crim. R. 552, 561, 40 S. W. 287, 290 (1897); Shaw v. State, 73 Tex. Crim. R. 337, 339, 165 S. W. 930, 931 (1914); Fondren v. State, 74 Tex. Crim. R. 552, 557, 169 S. W. 411, 414 (1914); Gray v. State, 77 Tex. Crim. R. 221, 229, 178 S. W. 337, 341 (1915). There is no immunity in Texas for the father who

is not married to the mother. *Hammett* v. *State*, 84 Tex. Crim. R. 635, 209 S. W. 661 (1919); *Thompson* v. *State*, — Tex. Crim. R. — (1971), appeal pending.

[50] See *Smith* v. *State*, 33 Me. 48, 55 (1851); *In re Vince*, 2 N. J. 443, 450, 67 A. 2d 141, 144 (1949). A short discussion of the modern law on this issue is contained in the Comment to the ALI's Model Penal Code § 207.11, at 158 and nn. 35–37 (Tent. Draft No. 9, 1959).

VIII

The Constitution does not explicitly mention any right of privacy. In a line of decisions, however, going back perhaps as far as *Union Pacific R. Co.* v. *Botsford*, 141 U. S. 250, 251 (1891), the Court has recognized that a right of personal privacy, or a guarantee of certain areas or zones of privacy, does exist under the Constitution. In varying contexts the Court or individual Justices have indeed found at least the roots of that right in the First Amendment, *Stanley* v. *Georgia*, 394 U. S. 557, 564 (1969); in the Fourth and Fifth Amendments, *Terry* v. *Ohio*, 392 U. S. 1, 8–9 (1968), *Katz* v. *United States*, 389 U. S. 347, 350 (1967), *Boyd* v. *United States*, 116 U. S. 616 (1886), see *Olmstead* v. *United States*, 277 U. S. 438, 478 (1928) (Brandeis, J. dissenting); in the penumbras of the Bill of Rights, *Griswold* v. *Connecticut*, 381 U. S. 479, 484–485 (1965); in the Ninth Amendment, *id.*, at 486 (Goldberg, J., concurring); or in the concept of liberty guaranteed by the first section of the Fourteenth Amendment, see *Meyer* v. *Nebraska*, 262 U. S. 390, 399 (1923). These decisions make it clear that only personal rights that can be deemed "fundamental" or "implicit in the concept of ordered liberty," *Palko* v. *Connecticut*, 302 U. S. 319, 325 (1937), are included in this guarantee of personal privacy. They also make it clear that the right has some extension to activities relating to marriage, *Loving* v. *Virginia*, 388 U. S. 1, 12 (1967), procreation, *Skinner* v. *Oklahoma*, 316 U. S. 535, 541–542 (1942), contraception, *Eisenstadt* v. *Baird*, 405 U. S. 438, 453–454 (1972); *id.*, at 460, 463–465 (White, J., concurring), family relationships, *Prince* v. *Massachusetts*, 321 U. S. 158, 166 (1944), and child rearing and education, *Pierce* v. *Society of Sisters*, 268 U. S. 510, 535 (1925), *Meyer* v. *Nebraska, supra*.

This right of privacy, whether it be founded in the Fourteenth Amendment's concept of personal liberty and restrictions upon state action, as we feel it is, or, as the District Court determined, in the Ninth Amendment's reservation of rights to the people, is broad enough to encompass a woman's decision whether or not to terminate her pregnancy. The detriment that the State would impose upon the pregnant woman by denying this choice altogether is apparent. Specific and direct harm medically diagnosable even in early pregnancy may be involved. Maternity, or additional offspring, may force upon the woman a distressful life and future. Psychological harm may be imminent. Mental and physical health may be taxed by child care. There is also the distress, for all concerned, associated with the unwanted child, and there is the problem of bringing a child into a family already unable, psychologically and otherwise, to care for it. In other cases, as in this one, the additional difficulties and continuing stigma of unwed motherhood may be involved. All these are factors the woman and her responsible physician necessarily will consider in consultation.

On the basis of elements such as these, appellants and some *amici* argue that the woman's right is absolute and that she is entitled to terminate her pregnancy at whatever time, in whatever way, and for whatever reason she alone chooses. With this we do not agree. Appellants' arguments that Texas either has no valid interest at all in regulating the abortion decision, or no interest strong enough to support any limitation upon the woman's sole determination, is unpersuasive. The Court's decisions recognizing a right of privacy also acknowledge that some state regulation in areas protected by that right is appropriate. As noted above, a state may properly assert important interests in safe-guarding health, in maintaining medical standards, and in protecting potential life. At some point in pregnancy, these respective interests become sufficiently compelling to sustain regulation of the factors that govern the abortion decision. The privacy right involved, therefore, cannot be said to be absolute. In fact, it is not clear to us that the claim asserted by some *amici* that one has an unlimited right to do with one's body as one pleases bears a close relationship to the right of privacy previously articulated in the Court's decisions. The Court has refused to recognize an unlimited right of this kind in the past. *Jacobson* v. *Massachusetts,* 197 U. S. 11 (1905) (vaccination); *Buck* v. *Bell,* 274 U. S. 200 (1927) (sterilization).

We therefore conclude that the right of personal privacy includes the abortion decision, but that this right is not unqualified and must be considered against important state interests in regulation.

We note that those federal and state courts that have recently considered abortion law challenges have reached the same conclusion. A majority, in addition to the District Court in the present case, have held state laws unconstitutional, at least in part, because of vagueness or because of overbreadth and abridgement of rights. *Abele* v. *Markle,* 342 F. Supp. 800 (Conn. 1972), appeal pending; *Abele* v. *Markle,* —— F. Supp. —— (Conn. Sept. 20, 1972), appeal pending; *Doe* v. *Bolton,* 319 F. Supp. 1048 (ND Ga. 1970), appeal decided today, *post* ——; *Doe* v. *Scott,* 321 F. Supp. 1385 (ND Ill. 1971), appeal pending; *Poe* v. *Menghini,* 339 F. Supp. 986 (Kan. 1972); *YWCA* v. *Kugler,* 342 F. Supp. 1048 (NJ 1972); *Babbitz* v. *McCann,* 310 F. Supp. 293 (ED Wis. 1970), appeal dismissed, 400 U. S. 1 (1970); *People* v. *Belous,* 71 Cal. 2d 954, 458 P. 2d 194 (1969), cert. denied, 397 U. S. 915 (1970); *State* v. *Barquet,* 262 S. 2d 431 (Fla. 1972).

Others have sustained state statutes. *Crossen* v. *Attorney General,* 344 F. Supp. 587 (ED Ky. 1972), appeal pending; *Rosen* v. *Louisiana State Board of Medical Examiners,* 318 F. Supp. 1217 (ED La. 1970), appeal pending; *Corkey* v. *Edwards,* 322 F. Supp. 1248 (WDNC 1971), appeal pending; *Steinberg* v. *Brown,* 321 F. Supp. 741 (ND Ohio 1970); *Doe* v. *Rampton,* —— F. Supp. —— (Utah 1971), appeal pending; *Cheaney* v. *Indiana,* —— Ind. ——, 285 N. E. 2d 265 (1972); *Spears* v. *State,* 257 So. 2d 876 (Miss. 1972); *State* v. *Munson,* —— S. D. ——, 201 N. W. 2d 123 (1972), appeal pending.

Although the results are divided, most of these courts have agreed that the right of privacy, however based, is broad enough to cover the abortion decision; that the right, nonetheless, is not absolute and is subject to some limitations; and that at some point the state interests as to protection of health, medical standards, and prenatal life, become dominant. We agree with this approach.

Where certain "fundamental rights" are involved, the Court has held that regulation limiting these rights may be justified only by a "compelling state interest," *Kramer* v. *Union Free School District,* 395 U. S. 621, 627 (1969); *Shapiro* v. *Thompson,* 394 U. S. 618, 634 (1969), *Sherbert* v. *Verner,* 374 U. S. 398, 406 (1963), and that legislative enactments must be narrowly drawn to express only the legitimate state interests at stake. *Griswold* v. *Connecticut,* 381 U. S. 479, 485 (1965); *Aptheker* v. *Secretary of State,* 378 U. S. 500, 508 (1964); *Cantwell* v. *Connecticut,* 310 U. S. 296, 307–308 (1940); see *Eisenstadt* v. *Baird,* 405 U. S. 438, 460, 463–464 (1972) (White, J., concurring).

In the recent abortion cases, cited above, courts have recognized these principles. Those striking down state laws have generally scrutinized the State's interest in protecting health and potential life and have concluded that neither interest justified broad limitations on the reasons for which a physician and his pregnant patient might decide that she should have an abortion in the early stages of pregnancy. Courts sustaining state laws have held that the State's determinations to protect health or prenatal life are dominant and constitutionally justifiable.

IX

The District Court held that the appellee failed to meet his burden of demonstrating that the Texas statute's infringement upon Roe's rights was necessary to support a compelling state interest, and that, although the defendant presented "several compelling justifications for state presence in the area of abortions," the statutes outstripped these justifiications and swept "far beyond any areas of compelling state interest." 314 F. Supp., at 1222–1223. Appellant and appellee both contest that holding. Appellant, as has been indicated, claims an absolute right that bars any state imposition of criminal penalties in the area. Appellee argues that the State's determination to recognize and protect prenatal life from and after conception constitutes a compelling state interest. As noted above, we do not agree fully with either formulation.

A. The appellee and certain *amici* argue that the fetus is a "person" within the language and meaning of the Fourteenth Amendment. In support of this they outline at length and in detail the well-known facts of fetal development. If this suggestion of personhood is established, the appellant's case, of course, collapses, for the fetus' right to life is then guaranteed specifically by the Amendment. The appellant conceded as much on reargument.[51] On the other hand, the appellee conceded on reargument[52] that no case could be cited that holds that a fetus is a person within the meaning of the Fourteenth Amendment.

[51] Tr. of Rearg. 20–21.
[52] Tr. of Rearg. 24.

The Constitution does not define "person" in so many words. Section 1 of the Fourteenth Amendment contains three references to "person." The first, in defining "citizens," speaks of "persons born or naturalized in the United States." The word also appears both in the Due Process Clause and in the Equal Protection Clause. "Person" is used in other places in the Constitution: in the listing of qualifications for representatives and senators, Art. I, § 2, cl. 2, and § 3, cl. 3; in the Apportionment Clause, Art. I, § 2, cl. 3;[53] in the Migration and Importation provision, Art. I, § 9, cl. 1; in the Emolument Clause, Art. I, § 9, cl. 8; in the Electors provisions, Art. II, § 1, cl. 2, and the superseded cl. 3; in the provision outlining qualifications for the office of President, Art. II, § 1, cl. 5; in the Extradition provisions, Art. IV, § 2, cl. 2, and the superseded Fugitive Slave cl. 3; and in the Fifth, Twelfth, and Twenty-second Amendments as well as in §§ 2 and 3 of the Fourteenth Amendment. But in nearly all these instances, the use of the word is such that it has application only postnatally. None indicates, with any assurance, that it has any possible pre-natal application.[54]

[53] We are not aware that in the taking of any census under this clause, a fetus has ever been counted.

[54] When Texas urges that a fetus is entitled to Fourteenth Amendment protection as a person, it faces a dilemma. Neither in Texas nor in any other State are all abortions prohibited. Despite broad proscription, an exception always exists. The exception contained in Art. 1196, for an abortion procured or attempted by medical advice for the purpose of saving the life of the mother, is typical. But if the fetus is a person who is not to be deprived of life without due process of law, and if the mother's condition is the sole determinant, does not the Texas exception appear to be out of line with the Amendment's command?

There are other inconsistencies between Fourteenth Amendment status and the typical abortion statute. It has already been pointed out, n. 49, *supra*, that in Texas the woman is not a principal or an accomplice with respect to an abortion upon her. If the fetus is a person, why is the woman not a principal or an accomplice? Further, the penalty for criminal abortion specified by Art. 1195 is significantly less than the maximum penalty for murder prescribed by Art. 1257 of the Texas Penal Code. If the fetus is a person, may the penalties be different?

All this, together with our observation, *supra*, that throughout the major portion of the 19th century prevailing legal abortion practices were far freer than they are today, persuades us that the word "person," as used in the Fourteenth Amendment, does not include the unborn.[55] This is in accord with the results reached in those few cases where the issue has been squarely presented. *McGarvey* v. *Magee Womens Hospital*, 340 F. Supp. 751 (WD Pa. 1972); *Byrn* v. *New York City Health & Hospitals Corp.*, 31 N. Y. 2d 194, 286 N. E. 2d 887 (1972), appeal pending; *Abele* v. *Markle*, —— F. Supp. —— (Conn. Sept. 20, 1972), appeal pending. Compare *Cheaney* v. *Indiana*, —— Ind. ——, 285 N. E. 265, 270 (1972); *Montana* v. *Rogers*, 278 F. 2d 68, 72 (CA7 1960), aff'd *sub nom. Montana* v. *Kennedy*, 366 U. S. 308 (1961); *Keeler* v. *Superior Court*, —— Cal. ——, 470 P. 2d 617 (1970); *State* v. *Dickinson*, 23 Ohio App. 2d 259, 275 N. E. 2d 599 (1970). Indeed, our decision in *United States* v. *Vuitch*, 402 U. S. 62 (1971), inferentially is to the same effect, for we would not have indulged in statutory interpretation favorable to abortion in specified circumstances if the necessary consequence was the termination of life entitled to Fourteenth Amendment protection.

This conclusion, however, does not of itself fully answer the contentions raised by Texas, and we pass on to other considerations.

[55] Cf. the Wisconsin abortion statute, defining "unborn child" to mean "a human being from the time of conception until it is born alive," Wis. Stat. § 940.04 (6) (1969), and the new Connecticut statute, Public Act No. 1, May 1972 Special Session, declaring it to be the public policy of the State and the legislative intent "to protect and preserve human life from the moment of conception."

B. The pregnant woman cannot be isolated in her privacy. She carries an embryo and, later, a fetus, if one accepts the medical definitions of the developing young in the human uterus. See Dorland's Illustrated Medical Dictionary, 478–479, 547 (24th ed. 1965). The situation therefore is inherently different from marital intimacy, or bedroom possession of obscene material, or marriage, or procreation, or education, with which *Eisenstadt, Griswold, Stanley, Loving, Skinner, Pierce,* and *Meyer* were respectively concerned. As we have intimated above, it is reasonable and appropriate for a State to decide that at some point in time another interest, that of health of the mother or that of potential human life, becomes significantly involved. The woman's privacy is no longer sole and any right of privacy she possesses must be measured accordingly.

Texas urges that, apart from the Fourteenth Amendment, life begins at conception and is present throughout pregnancy, and that, therefore, the State has a compelling interest in protecting that life from and after conception. We need not resolve the difficult question of when life begins. When those trained in the respective disciplines of medicine, philosophy, and theology are unable to arrive at any consensus, the judiciary, at this point in the development of man's knowledge, is not in a position to speculate as to the answer.

It should be sufficient to note briefly the wide divergence of thinking on this most sensitive and difficult question. There has always been strong support for the view that life does not begin until live birth. This was the belief of the Stoics.[56] It appears to be the predominant, though not the unanimous, attitude of the Jewish faith.[57] It may be taken to represent also the position of a large segment of the Protestant community, insofar as that can be ascertained; organized groups that have taken a formal position on the abortion issue have generally regarded abortion as a matter for the conscience of the individual and her family.[58] As we have noted, the common law found greater significance in quickening. Physicians and their scientific colleagues have regarded that event with less interest and have tended to focus either upon conception or upon live birth or upon the interim point at which the fetus becomes "viable," that is, potentially able to live outside the mother's womb, albeit with artificial aid.[59] Viability is usually placed at about seven months (28 weeks) but may occur earlier, even at 24 weeks.[60] The Aristotelian theory of "mediate animation," that held sway throughout the Middle Ages and the Renaissance in Europe, continued to be official Roman Catholic dogma until the 19th century, despite opposition to this "ensoulment" theory from those in the Church who would recognize the existence of life from the moment of conception.[61] The latter is now, of course, the official belief of the Catholic Church. As one of the briefs *amicus* discloses, this is a view strongly held by many non-Catholics as well, and by many physicians. Substantial problems for precise definition of this view are posed, however, by new embryological data that purport to indicate that conception is a "process" over time, rather than an event, and by new medical techniques such as menstrual extraction, the "morning-after" pill, implantation of embryos, artificial insemination, and even artificial wombs.[62]

In areas other than criminal abortion the law has been reluctant to endorse any theory that life, as we recognize it, begins before live birth or to accord legal rights to the unborn except in narrowly defined situations and except when the rights are contingent upon live birth. For example, the traditional rule of tort law had denied recovery for prenatal injuries even though the child was born alive.[63] That rule has been changed in almost every jurisdiction. In most states recovery is said to be permitted only if the fetus was viable, or at least quick, when the injuries were sustained, though few courts have squarely so held.[64] In a recent development, generally opposed by the commentators, some states permit the parents of a stillborn child to maintain an action for wrongful death because of prenatal injuries.[65] Such an action, however, would appear to be one to vindicate the parents' interest and is thus consistent with the view that the fetus, at most, represents only the potentiality of life. Similarly, unborn children have been recognized as acquiring rights or interests by way of inheritance or other devolution of property, and have been represented by guardians *ad litem*.[66] Perfection of the interests involved, again, has generally been contingent upon live birth. In short, the unborn have never been recognized in the law as persons in the whole sense.

---

[56] Edelstein 16.
[57] Lader 97–99; D. Feldman, Birth Control in Jewish Law 251–294 (1968). For a stricter view, see I. Jakobovits, Jewish Views on Abortion, in Abortion and the Law 124 (D. Smith ed. 1967).
[58] Amicus Brief for the American Ethical Union et al. For the position of the National Council of Churches and of other denominations, see Lader 99–101.
[59] L. Hellman & J. Pritchard, Williams Obstetrics 493 (14th ed. 1971); Dorland's Illustrated Medical Dictionary 1689 (24th ed. 1965).
[60] Hellman & Pritchard, *supra*, n. 58, at 493.
[61] For discussions of the development of the Roman Catholic position, see D. Callahan, Abortion: Law, Choice and Morality 409–447 (1970); Noonan 1.
[62] See D. Brodie, The New Biology and the Prenatal Child, 9 J. Fam. L. 391, 397 (1970); R. Gorney, The New Biology and the Future of Man, 15 UCLA L. Rev. 273 (1968); Note, Criminal Law–Abortion–The "Morning-After" Pill and Other Pre-Implantation Birth-Control Methods and the Law, 46 Ore. L. Rev. 211 (1967); G. Taylor, The Biological Time Bomb 32 (1968); A. Rosenfeld, The Second Genesis 138–139 (1969); G. Smith, Through a Test Tube Darkly: Artificial Insemination and the Law, 67 Mich. L. Rev. 127 (1968); Note, Artificial Insemination and the Law, U. Ill. L. F. 203 (1968).
[63] Prosser, Handbook of the Law of Torts 335–338 (1971); 2 Harper & James, The Law of Torts 1028–1031 (1956); Note, 63 Harv. L. Rev. 173 (1949).
[64] See cases cited in Prosser, *supra*, n. 62, at 336–338; Annotation, Action for Death of Unborn Child, 15 A. L. R. 3d 992 (1967).
[65] Prosser, *supra*, n. 62, at 338; Note, The Law and the Unborn Child, 46 Notre Dame Law. 349, 354–360 (1971).

[66] D. Louisell, Abortion, The Practice of Medicine, and the Due Process of Law, 16 UCLA L. Rev. 233, 235–238 (1969); Note, 56 Iowa L. Rev. 994, 999–1000 (1971); Note, The Law and the Unborn Child, 46 Notre Dame Law. 349, 351–354 (1971).

X

In view of all this, we do not agree that, by adopting one theory of life, Texas may override the rights of the pregnant woman that are at stake. We repeat, however, that the State does have an important and legitimate interest in preserving and protecting the health of the pregnant woman, whether she be a resident of the State or a nonresident who seeks medical consultation and treatment there, and that it has still *another* important and legitimate interest in protecting the potentiality of human life. These interests are separate and distinct. Each grows in substantiality as the woman approaches term and, at a point during pregnancy, each becomes "compelling."

With respect to the State's important and legitimate interest in the health of the mother, the "compelling" point, in the light of present medical knowledge, is at approximately the end of the first trimester. This is so because of the now established medical fact, referred to above at p. 34, that until the end of the first trimester mortality in abortion is less than mortality in normal childbirth. It follows that, from and after this point, a State may regulate the abortion procedure to the extent that the regulation reasonably relates to the preservation and protection of maternal health. Examples of permissible state regulation in this area are requirements as to the qualifications of the person who is to perform the abortion; as to the licensure of that person; as to the facility in which the procedure is to be performed, that is, whether it must be a hospital or may be a clinic or some other place of less-than-hospital status; as to the licensing of the facility; and the like.

This means, on the other hand, that, for the period of pregnancy prior to this "compelling" point, the attending physician, in consultation with his patient, is free to determine, without regulation by the State, that in his medical judgment the patient's pregnancy should be terminated. If that decision is reached, the judgment may be affectuated by an abortion free of interference by the State.

With respect to the State's important and legitimate interest in potential life, the "compelling" point is at viability. This is so because the fetus then presumably has the capability of meaningful life outside the mother's womb. State regulation protective of fetal life after viability thus has both logical and biological justifications. If the State is interested in protecting fetal life after viability, it may go so far as to proscribe abortion during that period except when it is necessary to preserve the life or health of the mother.

Measured against these standards, Art. 1196 of the Texas Penal Code, in restricting legal abortions to those "procured or attempted by medical advice for the purpose of saving the life of the mother," sweeps too broadly. The statute makes no distinction between abortions performed early in pregnancy and those performed later, and it limits to a single reason, "saving" the mother's life, the legal justification for the procedure. The statute, therefore, cannot survive the constitutional attack made upon it here.

This conclusion makes it unnecessary for us to consider the additional challenge to the Texas statute asserted on grounds of vagueness. See *United States* v. *Vuitch*, 402 U. S. 62, 67–72 (1971).

XI

To summarize and to repeat:

1. A state criminal abortion statute of the current Texas type, that excepts from criminality only a *life saving* procedure on behalf of the mother, without regard to

pregnancy stage and without recognition of the other interests involved, is violative of the Due Process Clause of the Fourteenth Amendment.

(a) For the stage prior to approximately the end of the first trimester, the abortion decision and its effectuation must be left to the medical judgment of the pregnant woman's attending physician.

(b) For the stage subsequent to approximately the end of the first trimester, the State, in promoting its interest in the health of the mother, may, if it chooses, regulate the abortion procedure in ways that are reasonably related to maternal health.

(c) For the stage subsequent to viability the State, in promoting its interest in the potentiality of human life, may, if it chooses, regulate, and even proscribe, abortion except where it is necessary, in appropriate medical judgment, for the preservation of the life or health of the mother.

2. The State may define the term "physician," as it has been employed in the preceding numbered paragraphs of this Part XI of this opinion, to mean only a physician currently licensed by the State, and may proscribe any abortion by a person who is not a physician as so defined.

In *Doe* v. *Bolton, post,* procedural requirements contained in one of the modern abortion statutes are considered. That opinion and this one, of course, are to be read together.[67]

[67] Neither in this opinion nor in *Doe* v. *Bolton, post,* do we discuss the father's rights, if any exist in the constitutional context, in the abortion decision. No paternal right has been asserted in either of the cases, and the Texas and the Georgia statutes on their face take no cognizance of the father. We are aware that some statutes recognize the father under certain circumstances. North Carolina, for example, 1B N. C. Gen. Stat. § 14–45.1 (Supp. 1971), requires written permission for the abortion from the husband when the woman is a married minor, that is, when she is less than 18 years of age, 41 N. C. A. G. 489 (1971); if the woman is an unmarried minor, written permission from the parents is required. We need not now decide whether provisions of this kind are constitutional.

This holding, we feel, is consistent with the relative weights of the respective interests involved, with the lessons and example of medical and legal history, with the lenity of the common law, and with the demands of the profound problems of the present day. The decision leaves the State free to place increasing restrictions on abortion as the period of pregnancy lengthens, so long as those restrictions are tailored to the recognized state interests. The decision vindicates the right of the physician to administer medical treatment according to his professional judgment up to the points where important state interests provide compelling justifications for intervention. Up to those points the abortion decision in all its aspects is inherently, and primarily, a medical decision, and basic responsibility for it must rest with the physician. If an individual practitioner abuses the privilege of exercising proper medical judgment, the usual remedies, judicial and intra-professional, are available.

XII

Our conclusion that Art. 1196 is unconstitutional means, of course, that the Texas abortion statutes, as a unit, must fall. The exception of Art. 1196 cannot be stricken separately, for then the State is left with a statute proscribing all abortion procedures no matter how medically urgent the case.

Although the District Court granted plaintiff Roe declaratory relief, it stopped short of issuing an injunction against enforcement of the Texas statutes. The Court has recognized that different considerations enter into a federal court's decision as to declaratory relief, on the one hand, and injunctive relief, on the other. *Zwickler* v. *Koota,* 389 U. S. 241, 252–255 (1967); *Dombrowski* v. *Pfister,* 380 U. S. 479 (1965). We are not dealing with a statute that, on its face, appears to abridge free expression, an area of particular concern under *Dombrowski* and refined in *Younger* v. *Harris,* 401 U. S., at 50.

We find it unnecessary to decide whether the District Court erred in withholding injunctive relief, for we assume the Texas prosecutorial authorities will give full credence to this decision that the present criminal abortion statutes of that State are unconstitutional.

The judgment of the District Court as to intervenor Hallford is reversed, and Dr. Hallford's complaint in intervention is dismissed. In all other respects the judgment of the District Court is affirmed. Costs are allowed to the appellee.

It is so ordered.

MR. JUSTICE STEWART, concurring.

In 1963, this Court, in *Ferguson* v. *Skrupa,* 372 U. S. 726, purported to sound the death knell for the doctrine of substantive due process, a doctrine under which many state laws had in the past been held to violate the Fourteenth Amendment. As Mr. Justice Black's opinion for the Court in *Skrupa* put it: "We have returned to the original constitutional proposition that courts do not substitute their social and economic beliefs for the judgment of legislative bodies, who are elected to pass laws." *Id.,* at 730.[1]

Barely two years later, in *Griswold* v. *Connecticut,* 381 U. S. 479, the Court held a Connecticut birth control law unconstitutional. In view of what had been so recently said in *Skrupa,* the Court's opinion in *Griswold* understandably did its best to avoid reliance on the Due Process Clause of the Fourteenth Amendment as the ground for decision. Yet, the Connecticut law did not violate any provision of the Bill of Rights, nor any other specific provision of the Constitution.[2] So it was clear to me then, and it is equally clear to me now, that the *Griswold* decision can be rationally understood only as a holding that the Connecticut statute substantively invaded the "liberty" that is protected by the Due Process Clause of the Fourteenth Amendment.[3] As so understood, *Griswold* stands as one in a long line of pre-*Skrupa* cases decided under the doctrine of substantive due process, and I now accept it as such.

"In a Constitution for a free people, there can be no doubt that the meaning of 'liberty' must be broad indeed." *Board of Regents* v. *Roth,* 408 U. S. 564, 572. The Constitution nowhere mentions a specific right of personal choice in matters of marriage and family life, but the "liberty" protected by the Due Process Clause of the Fourteenth Amendment covers more than those freedoms explicitly named in the Bill of Rights. See *Schware* v. *Board of Bar Examiners,* 353 U. S. 232, 238–239; *Pierce* v. *Society of Sisters,* 268 U. S. 510, 534–535; *Meyer* v. *Nebraska,* 262 U. S. 390, 399–400. Cf. *Shapiro* v. *Thompson,* 394 U. S. 618, 629–630; *United States* v. *Guest,* 383 U. S. 745, 757–758; *Carrington* v. *Rash,* 380 U. S. 89, 96; *Aptheker* v. *Secretary of State,* 378 U. S. 500, 505; *Kent* v. *Dulles,* 357 U. S. 116, 127; *Bolling* v. *Sharpe,* 347 U. S. 497, 499–500; *Truax* v. *Raich,* 239 U. S. 33, 41.

---

[1] Only Mr. Justice Harlan failed to join the Court's opinion, 372 U. S., at 733.

[2] There is no constitutional right of privacy, as such. "[The Fourth] Amendment protects individual privacy against certain kinds of governmental intrusion, but its protections go further, and often have nothing to do with privacy at all. Other provisions of the Constitution protect personal privacy from other forms of governmental invasion. But the protection of a person's *general* right to privacy—his right to be let alone by other people—is, like the protection of his property and of his very life, left largely to the law of the individual States." *Katz* v. *United States,* 389 U. S. 347, 350–351 (footnotes omitted).

[3] This was also clear to Mr. Justice Black, 381 U. S., at 507 (dissenting opinion); to Mr. Justice Harlan, 381 U. S., at 499 (opinion concurring in the judgment). See also Mr. Justice White, 381 U. S., at 502 (opinion concurring in the judgment). See also Mr. Justice Harlan's thorough and thoughtful opinion dissenting from dismissal of the appeal in *Poe* v. *Ullman,* 367 U. S. 497, 522.

As Mr. Justice Harlan once wrote: "The full scope of the liberty guaranteed by the Due Process Clause cannot be found in or limited by the precise terms of the specific guarantees elsewhere provided in the Constitution. This 'liberty' is not a series of isolated points picked out in terms of the taking of property; the freedom of speech, press, and religion; the right to keep and bear arms; the freedom from unreasonable searches and seizures; and so on. It is a rational continuum which, broadly speaking, includes a freedom from all substantial arbitrary impositions and purposeless restraints, . . . and which also recognizes, what a reasonable and sensitive judgment must, that certain interests require particularly careful scrutiny of the state needs asserted to justify their abridgment." *Poe* v. *Ullman,* 367 U. S. 497, 543 (opinion dissenting from dismissal of appeal) (citations omitted). In the words of Mr. Justice Frankfurter, "Great concepts like . . . 'liberty' . . . were purposely left to gather meaning from experience. For they relate to the whole domain of social and economic fact, and the statesmen who founded this Nation knew too well that only a stagnant society remains unchanged." *National Mutual Ins. Co.* v. *Tidewater Transfer Co., Inc.,* 337 U. S. 582, 646 (dissenting opinion).

Several decisions of this Court make clear that freedom of personal choice in matters of marriage and family life is one of the liberties protected by the Due Process Clause of the Fourteenth Amendment. *Loving* v. *Virginia,* 388 U. S. 1, 12; *Griswold* v. *Connecticut, supra; Pierce* v. *Society of Sisters, supra; Meyer* v. *Nebraska, supra.* See also *Prince* v. *Massachusetts,* 321 U. S. 158, 166; *Skinner* v. *Oklahoma,* 316 U. S. 535, 541. As recently as last Term, in *Eisenstadt* v. *Baird,* 405 U. S. 438, 453, we recognized "the right of the *individual,* married or single, to be free from unwarranted governmental intrusion into matters so fundamentally affecting a person as the decision whether to bear or beget a child." That right necessarily includes the right of a woman to decide whether or not to terminate her pregnancy. "Certainly the interests of a woman in giving of her physical and emotional self during pregnancy and the interests that will be affected throughout her life by the birth and raising of a child are of a far greater degree of significance and personal intimacy than the right to send a child to private school protected in *Pierce* v. *Society of Sisters,* 268 U. S. 510 (1925), or the right to teach a foreign language protected in *Meyer* v. *Nebraska,* 262 U. S. 390 (1923)." *Abele* v. *Markle,* —— F. Supp. ——, —— (Conn. 1972).

Clearly, therefore, the Court today is correct in holding that the right asserted by Jane Roe is embraced within the personal liberty protected by the Due Process Clause of the Fourteenth Amendment.

It is evident that the Texas abortion statute infringes that right directly. Indeed, it is difficult to imagine a more complete abridgment of a constitutional freedom than that worked by the inflexible criminal statute now in force in Texas. The question then becomes whether the state interests advanced to justify this abridgment can survive the "particularly careful scrutiny" that the Fourteenth Amendment here requires.

The asserted state interests are protection of the health and safety of the pregnant woman, and protection of the potential future human life within her. These are legitimate objectives, amply sufficient to permit a State to regulate abortions as it does other surgical procedures, and perhaps sufficient to permit a State to regulate abortions more stringently or even to prohibit them in the late stages of pregnancy. But such legislation is not before us, and I think the Court today has thoroughly demonstrated that these state interests cannot constitutionally support the broad abridgment of personal liberty worked by the existing Texas law. Accordingly, I join the Court's opinion holding that that law is invalid under the Due Process Clause of the Fourteenth Amendment.

————

Mr. Justice Rehnquist, dissenting.

The Court's opinion brings to the decision of this troubling question both extensive historical fact and a wealth of legal scholarship. While its opinion thus commands my respect, I find myself nonetheless in fundamental disagreement with those parts of it which invalidate the Texas statute in question, and therefore dissent.

I

The Court's opinion decides that a State may impose virtually no restriction on the performance of abortions during the first trimester of pregnancy. Our previous decisions indicate that a necessary predicate for such an opinion is a plaintiff who was in her first trimester of pregnancy at some time during the pendency of her law suit. While a party may vindicate his own constitutional rights, he may not seek vindication for the rights of others. *Moose Lodge* v. *Irvis*, 407 U. S. 163 (1972); *Sierra Club* v. *Morton*, 405 U. S. 727 (1972). The Court's statement of facts in this case makes clear, however, that the record in no way indicates the presence of such a plaintiff. We know only that plaintiff Roe at the time of filing her complaint was a pregnant woman; for aught that appears in this record, she may have been in her *last* trimester of pregnancy as of the date the complaint was filed.

Nothing in the Court's opinion indicates that Texas might not constitutionally apply its proscription of abortion as written to a woman in that stage of pregnancy. Nonetheless, the Court uses her complaint against the Texas statute as a fulcrum for deciding that States may impose virtually no restrictions on medical abortions performed during the *first* trimester of pregnancy. In deciding such a hypothetical lawsuit the Court departs from the longstanding admonition that it should never "formulate a rule of constitutional law broader than is required by the precise facts to which it is to be applied." *Liverpool, New York and Philadelphia Steamship Co.* v. *Commissioners of Emigration,* 113 U. S. 33, 39 (1885). See also *Ashwander* v. *TVA,* 297 U. S. 288, 345 (1936) (Brandeis, concurring).

II

Even if there were a plaintiff in this case capable of litigating the issue which the Court decides, I would reach a conclusion opposite to that reached by the Court. I have difficulty in concluding, as the Court does, that the right of "privacy" is involved in this case. Texas by the statute here challenged bars the performance of a medical abortion by a licensed physician on a plaintiff such as Roe. A transaction resulting in an operation such as this is not "private" in the ordinary usage of that word. Nor is the "privacy" which the Court finds here even a distant relative of the freedom from searches and seizures protected by the Fourth Amendment to the Constitution which the Court has referred to as embodying a right to privacy. *Katz* v. *United States,* 389 U. S. 347 (1967).

If the Court means by the term "privacy" no more than that the claim of a person to be free from unwanted state regulation of consensual transactions may be a form of "liberty" protected by the Fourteenth Amendment, there is no doubt that similar claims have been upheld in our earlier decisions on the basis of that liberty. I agree with the statement of Mr. Justice Stewart in his concurring opinion that the "liberty," against deprivation of which without due process the Fourteenth Amendment protects, embraces more than the rights found in the Bill of Rights. But that liberty is not guaranteed absolutely against deprivation, but only against deprivation without due process of law. The test traditionally applied in the area of social and economic legislation is whether or not a law such as that challenged has a rational relation to a valid state objective. *Williamson* v. *Lee Optical Co.,* 348 U. S. 483, 491 (1955). The Due Process Clause of the Fourteenth Amendment undoubtedly does place a limit on legislative power to enact laws such as this, albeit a broad one. If the Texas statute were to prohibit an abortion even where the mother's life is in jeopardy, I have little doubt that such a statute would lack a rational relation to a valid state objective under the test stated in *Williamson, supra.* But the Court's sweeping invalidation of any restrictions on abortion during the first trimester is impossible to justify under that standard, and the conscious weighing of competing factors which the Court's opinion apparently substitutes for the established test is far more appropriate to a legislative judgment than to a judicial one.

The Court eschews the history of the Fourteenth Amendment in its reliance on the "compelling state interest" test. See *Weber* v. *Aetna Casualty & Surety Co.,* 406 U. S. 164, 179 (1972) (dissenting opinion). But the Court adds a new wrinkle to this test by transposing it from the legal considerations associated with the Equal Protection Clause of the Fourteenth Amendment to this case arising under the Due Process Clause of the Fourteenth Amendment. Unless I misapprehend the consequences of this transplanting of the "compelling state interest test," the Court's opinion will accomplish the seemingly impossible feat of leaving this area of the law more confused than it found it.

While the Court's opinion quotes from the dissent of Mr. Justice Holmes in *Lochner* v. *New York,* 198 U. S. 45 (1905), the result it reaches is more closely attuned to the majority opinion of Mr. Justice Peckham in that case. As in *Lochner* and similar cases applying substantive due process standards to economic and social welfare legislation, the adoption of the compelling state interest standard will inevitably require this Court to examine the legislative policies and pass on the wisdom of these policies in the very process of deciding whether a particular state interest put forward may or may not be "compelling." The decision here to break the term of pregnancy into three distinct terms and to outline the permissible restrictions the State may impose in each one, for example, partakes more of judicial legislation than it does of a determination of the intent of the drafters of the Fourteenth Amendment.

The fact that a majority of the States, reflecting after all the majority sentiment in those States, have had restrictions on abortions for at least a century seems to me as strong an indication there is that the asserted right to an abortion is not "so rooted in the traditions and conscience of our people as to be ranked as fundamental," *Snyder* v. *Massachusetts,* 291 U. S. 97, 105 (1934). Even today, when society's views on abortion are changing, the very existence of the debate is evidence that the "right" to an abortion is not so universally accepted as the appellants would have us believe.

To reach its result the Court necessarily has had to find within the scope of the Fourteenth Amendment a right that was apparently completely unknown to the drafters of the Amendment. As early as 1821, the first state law dealing directly with abortion was enacted by the Connecticut legislature. Conn. Stat. Tit. 22, §§ 14, 16 (1821). By the time of the adoption of the Fourteenth Amendment in 1868 there were at least 36 laws enacted by state or territorial legislatures limiting abortion.[1] While many States have amended or updated their laws, 21 of the laws on the books in 1868 remain in effect today.[2] Indeed, the Texas statute struck down today was, as the majority notes, first enacted in 1857 and "has remained substantially unchanged to the present time." *Ante,* at ——.

[1] States having enacted abortion laws prior to the adoption of the Fourteenth Amendment in 1868:
1. Alabama—Ala. Acts, c. 6, § 2 (1840—1841).
2. Arizona—Howell Code, c. 10, § 45 (1865).
3. Arkansas—Ark. Rev. Stat., c. 44, div. III, Art. II, § 6 (1838).
4. California—Cal. Sess. Stats., c. 99, § 45, at 233 (1849—1850).
5. Colorado (Terr.)—Colo. Gen. Laws of Terr. of Colo., 1st Sess., § 42, at 296—297 (1861).
6. Connecticut—Conn. Stat. Tit. 22, §§ 14, 16, at 152, 153 (1821).
By 1868 this statute had been replaced by another abortioi law. Conn. Pub. Acts, c. LXXI, §§ 1, 2, at 65 (1860).
7. Florida—Fla. Acts 1st Sess., c. 1637, III, § 10, § 11, VIII, § 9, § 10, § 11, as amended now in Fla. Stat. Ann. §§ 782.09, 782.10, 797.01, 797.02, 782.16 (1944).
8. Georgia—Ga. Pen. Code §§ 56, 57, 58, 67, 68, 69 (1833).
9. Kingdom of Hawaii—Hawaii Pen. Code §§ 1, 2, 3 (1850).
10. Idaho (Terr.)—Idaho (Terr.) Laws §§ 33, 34, 42, at 435 (1863).
11. Illinois—Ill. Rev. Code §§ 40, 41, 46, at 130, 131 (1827). By 1868 this statute had been replaced by a subsequent enactment. Ill. Pub. Laws §§ 1, 2, 3, at 89 (1867).
12. Indiana—Ind. Rev. Stat. §§ 1, 3, at 224 (1838). By 1868 this statute had been superseded by a subsequent enactment. Ind. Laws c. LXXXI, § 2 (1859).
13. Iowa (Terr.)—Iowa (Terr.) Stat. 1st Legis., 1st Sess., § 18, at 145 (1838). By 1868 this statute had been superseded by a subsequent enactment. Iowa (Terr.) Rev. Stat. §§ 10, 13 (1843).
14. Kansas (Terr.)—Kan. (Terr.) Stat. c. 48, §§ 9, 10, 39 (1855). By 1868 this statute had been superseded by a subsequent enactment. Kan. Gen. Laws c. 28, §§ 9, 10 (1859).
15. Louisiana—La. Rev. Stat. § 24, at 138 (1856).
16. Maine—Me. Rev. Stat. c. 160, §§ 11, 12, 13, 14 (1840).
17. Maryland—Md. Laws c. 179, § 2, at 318 (1868).
18. Massachusetts—Mass. Acts & Resolves c. 27 (1845).
19. Michigan—Mich. Rev. Stat. c. 153, §§ 32, 33, 34, at 662 (1846).
20. Minnesota (Terr.)—Minn. (Terr.) Rev. Stat. c. 100, §§ 10, 11, at 493 (1851).
21. Mississippi—Miss. Code §§ 8, 9, at 958 (1848).
22. Missouri—Mo. Rev. Stat. Art. II, §§ 9, 10, 36, at 168 (1835).
23. Montana (Terr.)—Mont. (Terr.) Laws § 41, at 184 (1864).
24. Nevada (Terr.)—Nev. (Terr.) Laws c. 28, § 42, at 63 (1861).
25. New Hampshire—N. H. Laws c. 743, § 1, at 708 (1848).
26. New Jersey—N. J. Laws, at 266 (1849).
27. New York—N. Y. Rev. Stat. pt. IV, c. I, Tit. II, §§ 8, 9, at 550 (1828). By 1868 this statute had been superseded by subsequent enactments. N. Y. Laws c. 260, §§ 1, 2, 3, 4, 5, 6, at 285 (1845); N. Y. Laws c. 22, § 1, at 19 (1846).
28. Ohio—Ohio Gen. Stat. §§ 111 (1), 112 (2), at 252 (1841).
29. Oregon—Ore. Gen. Laws Crim. Code, c. 43, § 509, at 528 (1845—1864).
30. Pennsylvania—Pa. Laws No. 374, §§ 87, 88, 89 (1860).
31. Texas—Tex. Gen. Stat. Dig. c. VII, Arts. 531—536, at 524 (Oldham & White 1859).
32. Vermont—Vt. Acts No. 33, § 1 (1846). By 1868 this statute had been amended by a subsequent enactment. Vt. Acts No. 57, §§ 1, 3 (1867).
33. Virginia—Va. Acts Tit. II, c. 3, § 9, at 96 (1848).
34. Washington (Terr.)—Wash. (Terr.) Stats. c. II, §§ 37, 38, at 81 (1854).
35. West Virginia—Va. Acts Tit. II, c. 3, § 9, at 96 (1848).
36. Wisconsin—Wis. Rev. Stat. c. 133, §§ 10, 11 (1849). By 1868 this statute had been superseded by a subsequent enactment. Wis. Rev. Stat. c. 164, §§ 10, 11; c. 169, §§ 58, 59 (1858).

[2] Abortion laws in effect in 1868 and still applicable as of August 1970:

1. Arizona (1865).
2. Connecticut (1860).
3. Florida (1868).
4. Idaho (1863).
5. Indiana (1838).
6. Iowa (1843).
7. Maine (1840).
8. Massachusetts (1845).
9. Michigan (1846).
10. Minnesota (1851).
11. Missouri (1835).
12. Montana (1864).
13. Nevada (1861).
14. New Hampshire (1848).
15. New Jersey (1849).
16. Ohio (1841).
17. Pennsylvania (1860).
18. Texas (1859).
19. Vermont (1867).
20. West Virginia (1848).
21. Wisconsin (1858).

There apparently was no question concerning the validity of this provision or of any of the other state statutes when the Fourteenth Amendment was adopted. The only conclusion possible from this history is that the drafters did not intend to have the Fourteenth Amendment withdraw from the States the power to legislate with respect to this matter.

III

Even if one were to agree that the case which the Court decides were here, and that the enunciation of the substantive constitutional law in the Court's opinion were proper, the actual disposition of the case by the Court is still difficult to justify. The Texas statute is struck down *in toto,* even though the Court apparently concedes that at later periods of pregnancy Texas might impose these selfsame statutory limitations on abortion. My understanding of past practice is that a statute found to be invalid as applied to a particular plaintiff, but not unconstitutional as a whole, is not simply "struck down" but is instead declared unconstitutional as applied to the fact situation before the Court. *Yick Wo* v. *Hopkins,* 118 U. S. 356 (1886); *Street* v. *New York,* 394 U. S. 576 (1969).

For all of the foregoing reasons, I respectfully dissent.

No. 70–40

Mary Doe et al., Appellants,

     v.

Arthur K. Bolton, as Attorney General of the State of Georgia, et al.

On Appeal from the United States District Court for the Northern District of Georgia.

[January 22, 1973]

MR. JUSTICE BLACKMUN delivered the opinion of the Court.

In this appeal the criminal abortion statutes recently enacted in Georgia are challenged on constitutional grounds. The statutes are §§ 26–1201 through 26–1203 of the State's Criminal Code, formulated by Georgia Laws, 1968 Session, 1249, 1277–1280. In *Roe* v. *Wade, ante* ––, we today have struck down, as constitutionally defective, the Texas criminal abortion statutes that are representative of provisions long in effect in a majority of our States. The Georgia legislation, however, is different and merits separate consideration.

I

The statutes in question are reproduced as Appendix A, *post* ––.[1] As the appellants acknowledge,[2] the 1968 statutes are patterned upon the American Law Institute's Model Penal Code, § 230.3 (Proposed Official Draft, 1962), reproduced as Appendix B, *post* ––. The ALI proposal has served as the model for recent legislation in approximately one-fourth of our States.[3] The new Georgia provisions replaced statutory law that had been in effect for more than 90 years. Georgia Laws 1876, No. 130, § 2, at 113.[4] The predecessor statute paralleled the Texas legislation considered in *Roe* v. *Wade, ante,* and made all abortions criminal except those necessary "to preserve the life" of the pregnant woman. The new statutes have not been tested on constitutional grounds in the Georgia state courts.

Section 26–1201, with a referenced exception, makes abortion a crime, and § 26–1203 provides that a person convicted of that crime shall be punished by imprisonment for not less than one nor more than 10 years. Section 26–1202 (a) states the

[1] The portions italicized in Appendix A are those held unconstitutional by the District Court.
[2] Appellants' Brief 25 n. 5; Tr. of Oral Arg. 9.
[3] See *Roe* v. *Wade, ante* –– n. 37.
[4] The active provisions of the 1876 statute were:
"Section I. *Be it enacted, etc.,* That from and after the passage of this Act, the wilful killing of

an unborn child, so far developed as to be ordinarily called 'quick,' by any injury to the mother of such child, which would be murder if it resulted in the death of such mother, shall be guilty of a felony, and punishable by death or imprisonment for life, as the jury trying the case may recommend.

"Section II. *Be it further enacted,* That every person who shall administer to any woman pregnant with a child, any medicine, drug, or substance whatever, or shall use or employ any instrument or other means, with intent thereby to destroy such child, unless the same shall have been necessary to preserve the life of such mother, or shall have been advised by two physicians to be necessary for such purpose, shall, in case the death of such child or mother be thereby produced, be declared guilty of an assault with intent to murder.

"Section III. *Be it further enacted,* That any person who shall wilfully administer to any pregnant woman any medicine, drug or substance, or anything whatever, or shall employ any instrument or means whatever, with intent thereby to procure the miscarriage or abortion of any such woman, unless the same shall have been necessary to preserve the life of such woman, or shall have been advised by two physicians to be necessary for that purpose, shall, upon conviction, be punished as prescribed in section 4310 of the Revised Code of Georgia."

It should be noted that the second section, in contrast to the first, makes no specific reference to quickening. The section was construed, however, to possess this line of demarcation. *Taylor* v. *State,* 105 Ga. 846, 33 S. E. 190 (1899).

exception and removes from § 1201's definition of criminal abortion, and thus makes noncriminal, an abortion "performed by a physician duly licensed" in Georgia when, "based upon his best clinical judgment . . . an abortion is necessary because

"(1) A continuation of the pregnancy would endanger the life of the pregnant woman or would seriously and permanently injure her health, or

"(2) The fetus would very likely be born with a grave, permanent, and irremediable mental or physical defect, or

"(3) The pregnancy resulted from forcible or statutory rape."[5]

Section 26–1202 also requires, by numbered subdivisions of its subsection (b), that, for an abortion to be authorized or performed as a noncriminal procedure, additional conditions must be fulfilled. These are (1) and (2) residence of the woman in Georgia; (3) reduction to writing of the performing physician's medical judgment that an abortion is justified for one or more of the reasons specified by § 26–1202 (a), with written concurrence in that judgment by at least two other Georgia-licensed physicians, based upon their separate personal medical examinations of the woman; (4) performance of the abortion in a hospital licensed by the State Board of Health and also accredited by the Joint Commission on Accreditation of Hospitals; (5) advance approval by an abortion committee of not less than three members of the hospital's staff; (6) certifications in a rape situation; and (7), (8), and (9) maintenance and confidentiality of records. There is a provision (subsection (c)) for judicial determination of the legality of a proposed abortion on petition of the judicial circuit law officer or of a close relative, as therein defined, of the unborn child, and for expeditious hearing of that petition. There is also a provision (subsection (e)) giving a hospital the right not to admit an abortion patient and giving any physician and any hospital employee or staff member the right, on moral or religious grounds, not to participate in the procedure.

II

On April 16, 1970, Mary Doe,[6] 23 other individuals (nine described as Georgia-licensed physicians, seven as nurses registered in the State, five as clergymen, and two as social workers), and two nonprofit Georgia corporations that advocate abortion reform, instituted this federal action in the Northern District of Georgia against the State's attorney general, the district attorney of Fulton County, and the chief of police of the city of Atlanta. The plaintiffs sought a declaratory judgment that the Georgia abortion statutes were unconstitutional in their entirety.

[5] In contrast with the ALI model, the Georgia statute makes no specific reference to pregnancy resulting from incest. We were assured by the State at reargument that this was because the statute's reference to "rape" was intended to include incest. Tr. of Rearg. 32.

[6] Appellants by their complaint, Appendix 7, allege that the name is a pseudonym.

224

They also sought injunctive relief restraining the defendants and their successors from enforcing the statutes.

Mary Doe alleged:

"(1) She was a 22-year-old Georgia citizen, married, and nine weeks pregnant. She had three living children. The two older ones had been placed in a foster home because of Doe's poverty and inability to care for them. The youngest, born July 19, 1969, had been placed for adoption. Her husband had recently abandoned her and she was forced to live with her indigent parents and their eight children. She and her husband, however, had become reconciled. He was a construction worker employed only sporadically. She had been a mental patient at the State Hospital. She had been advised that an abortion could be performed on her with less danger to her health than if she gave birth to the child she was carrying. She would be unable to care for or support the new child.

"(2) On March 25, 1970, she applied to the Abortion Committee of Grady Memorial Hospital, Atlanta, for a therapeutic abortion under § 26–1202. Her application was denied 16 days later, on April 10, when she was eight weeks pregnant, on the grounds that her situation was not one described in § 26–1202 (a).[7]

"(3) Because her application was denied, she was forced either to relinquish 'her right to decide when and how many children she will bear' or to seek an abortion that was illegal under the Georgia statutes. This invaded her rights of privacy and liberty in matters related to family, marriage, and sex, and deprived her of the right to choose whether to bear children. This was a violation of rights guaranteed her by the First, Fourth, Fifth, Ninth, and Fourteenth Amendments. The statutes also denied her equal protection and procedural due process and, because they were unconstitutionally vague, deterred hospitals and doctors from performing abortions. She sued 'on her own behalf and on behalf of all others similarly situated.'"

[7] In answers to interrogatories Doe stated that her application for an abortion was approved at Georgia Baptist Hospital on May 5, 1970, but that she was not approved as a charity patient there and had no money to pay for an abortion. Appendix 64.

The other plaintiffs alleged that the Georgia statutes "chilled and deterred" them from practicing their respective professions and deprived them of rights guaranteed by the First, Fourth, and Fourteenth Amendments. These plaintiffs also purported to sue on their own behalf and on behalf of others similarly situated.

A three-judge district court was convened. An offer of proof as to Doe's identity was made, but the court deemed it unnecessary to receive that proof. The case was then tried on the pleadings and interrogatories.

The District Court, *per curiam,* 319 F. Supp. 1048 (ND Ga. 1970), held that all the plaintiffs had standing but that only Doe presented a justiciable controversy. On the merits, the court concluded that the limitation in the Georgia statute of the "number of reasons for which an abortion may be sought," *id.,* at 1056, improperly restricted Doe's rights of privacy articulated in *Griswold* v. *Connecticut,* 381 U. S. 479 (1965), and of "personal liberty," both of which it thought "broad enough to include the decision to abort a pregnancy," *id.,* at 1055. As a consequence, the court held invalid those portions of §§ 26–1202 (a) and (b) (3) limiting legal abortions to the three situations specified; § 26–1202 (b) (6) relating to certifications in a rape situation; and § 26–1202 (c) authorizing a court test. Declaratory relief was granted accordingly. The court, however, held that Georgia's interest in protection of health, and the existence of a *"potential* of independent human existence" (emphasis in original), *id.,* at 1055, justified state regulation of "the manner of performance as well as the quality of the final decision to abort," *id.,* at 1056, and it refused to strike down the other provisions of the statutes. It denied the request for an injunction, *id.,* at 1057.

Claiming that they were entitled to an injunction and to broader relief, the plaintiffs took a direct appeal pursuant to 28 U. S. C. § 1253. We postponed decision on jurisdiction to the hearing on the merits. 402 U. S. 941 (1971). The defendants also purported to appeal, pursuant to § 1253, but their appeal was dismissed for want of jurisdiction. 402 U. S. 936 (1971). We are advised by the defendant-appellees, Brief 42, that an alternative appeal on their part is pending in the United States Court of Appeals for the Fifth Circuit. The extent, therefore, to which the District Court decision was adverse to the defendants, that is, the extent to which portions of the Georgia statutes were held to be unconstitutional, technically is not now before us.[8] *Swarb* v. *Lennox,* 405 U. S. 191, 201 (1972).

[8] What we decide today obviously has implications for the issues raised in the defendants' appeal pending in the Fifth Circuit.

III

Our decision in *Roe* v. *Wade, ante* ——, establishes (1) that, despite her pseudonym, we may accept as true, for this case, Mary Doe's existence and her pregnant state on April 16, 1970; (2) that the constitutional issue is substantial; (3) that the interim termination of Doe's and all other Georgia pregnancies in existence in 1970 has not rendered the case moot; and (4) that Doe presents a justiciable controversy and has standing to maintain the action.

Inasmuch as Doe and her class are recognized, the question whether the other appellants—physicians, nurses, clergymen, social workers, and corporations—present a justiciable controversy and have standing is perhaps a matter of no great consequence. We conclude, however, that the physician-appellants, who are Georgia-licensed doctors consulted by pregnant women, also present a justiciable controversy and do have standing despite the fact that the record does not disclose that any one of them has been prosecuted, or threatened with prosecution, for violation of the State's abortion statutes. The physician is the one against whom these criminal statutes directly operate in the event he procures an abortion that does not meet the statutory exceptions and conditions. The physician-appellants, therefore, assert a sufficiently direct threat of personal detriment. They should not be required to await and undergo a criminal prosecution as the sole means of seeking relief. *Crossen* v. *Breckenridge,* 446 F. 2d 833, 839—840 (CA 6 1971); *Poe* v. *Menghini,* 339 F. Supp. 986, 990—991 (Kans. 1972).

In holding that the physicians, while theoretically possessed of standing, did not present a justiciable controversy, the District Court seems to have relied primarily on *Poe* v. *Ullman,* 367 U. S. 497 (1961). There a sharply divided Court dismissed an appeal from a state court on the ground that it presented no real controversy justifying the adjudication of a constitutional issue. But the challenged Connecticut statute, deemed to prohibit the giving of medical advice on the use of contraceptives, had been enacted in 1879, and, apparently with a single exception, no one had ever been prosecuted under it. Georgia's statute, in contrast, is recent and not moribund. Furthermore, it is the successor to another Georgia abortion statute under which, we are told,[9] physicians were prosecuted. The present case, therefore, is closer to *Epperson* v. *Arkansas,* 393 U. S. 97 (1968), where the Court recognized the right of a school teacher, though not yet charged criminally, to challenge her State's anti-evolution statute. See also *Griswold* v. *Connecticut,* 381 U. S., at 481.

The parallel claims of the nurse, clergy, social worker, and corporation-appellants are another step removed and as to them, the Georgia statutes operate less directly. Not being licensed physicians, the nurses and the others are in no position to render medical advice. They would be reached by the abortion statutes only in their capacity as accessories or as counselor-conspirators. We conclude that we

226

need not pass upon the status of these additional appellants in this suit, for the issues are sufficiently and adequately presented by Doe and the physician-appellants, and nothing is gained or lost by the presence or absence of the nurses, the clergymen, the social workers, and the corporations. See *Roe* v. *Wade, ante,* at ——.

[9] Tr. of Oral Arg. 21–22.

IV

The appellants attack on several grounds those portions of the Georgia abortion statutes that remain after the District Court decision: undue restriction of a right to personal and marital privacy; vagueness; deprivation of substantive and procedural due process; improper restriction to Georgia residents; and denial of equal protection.

A. *Roe v. Wade, ante* ——, sets forth our conclusion that a pregnant woman does not have an absolute constitutional right to an abortion on her demand. What is said there is applicable here and need not be repeated.

B. The appellants go on to argue, however, that the present Georgia statutes must be viewed historically, that is, from the fact that prior to the 1968 Act an abortion in Georgia was not criminal if performed to "preserve the life" of the mother. It is suggested that the present statute, as well, has this emphasis on the mother's rights, not on those of the fetus. Appellants contend that it is thus clear that Georgia has given little, and certainly not first, consideration to the unborn child. Yet it is the unborn child's rights that Georgia asserts in justification of the statute. Appellants assert that this justification cannot be advanced at this late date.

Appellants then argue that the statutes do not adequately protect the woman's right. This is so because it would be physically and emotionally damaging to Doe to bring a child into her poor "fatherless"[10] family, and because advances in medicine and medical techniques have made it safer for a woman to have a medically induced abortion than for her to bear a child. Thus, "a statute which requires a woman to carry an unwanted pregnancy to term infringes not only on a fundamental right of privacy but on the right to life itself." Brief 27.

The appellants recognize that a century ago medical knowledge was not so advanced as it is today, that the techniques of antisepsis were not known, and that any abortion procedure was dangerous for the woman. To restrict the legality of the abortion to the situation where it was deemed necessary, in medical judgment, for the preservation of the woman's life was only a natural conclusion in the exercise of the legislative judgment of that time. A State is not to be reproached, however, for a past judgmental determination made in the light of then-existing medical knowledge. It is perhaps unfair to argue, as the appellants do, that because the early focus was on the preservation of the woman's life, the State's present professed interest in the protection of embryonic and fetal life is to be downgraded. That argument denies the State the right to readjust its views and emphases in the light of the advanced knowledge and techniques of the day.

C. Appellants argue that § 26–1202 (a) of the Georgia statute, as it has been left by the District Court's decision, is unconstitutionally vague. This argument centers in the proposition that, with the District Court's having stricken the statutorily specified reasons, it still remains a crime for a physician to perform an abortion except when, as § 26–1202 (a) reads, it is "based upon his best clinical judgment that an abortion is necessary." The appellants contend that the word "necessary" does not warn the physician of what conduct is proscribed; that the statute is wholly without objective standards and is subject to diverse interpretation; and that doctors

[10] Appellants' Brief 25.

will choose to err on the side of caution and will be arbitrary.

The net result of the District Court's decision is that the abortion determination, so far as the physician is concerned, is made in the exercise of his professional, that is, his "best clinical" judgment in the light of *all* the attendant circumstances. He is not now restricted to the three situations originally specified. Instead, he may range farther afield wherever his medical judgment, properly and professionally exercised, so dictates and directs him.

The vagueness argument is set at rest by the decision in *United States* v. *Vuitch,* 402 U. S. 62, 71–72 (1971), where the issue was raised with respect to a District of Columbia statute making abortions criminal "unless the same were done as necessary for the preservation of the mother's life or health and under the direction of a competent licensed practitioner of medicine." That statute has been construed to bear upon psychological as well as physical well-being. This being so, the Court concluded that the term "health" presented no problem of vagueness. "Indeed, whether a particular operation is necessary for a patient's physical or mental health is a judgment that physicians are obviously called upon to make routinely whenever surgery is considered." 402 U. S., at 72. This conclusion is equally applicable here. Whether, in the words of the Georgia statute, "an abortion is necessary," is a professional judgment that the Georgia physician will be called upon to make routinely.

We agree with the District Court, 319 F. Supp., at 1058, that the medical judgment may be exercised in the light of all factors—physical, emotional, psychological, familial, and the woman's age—relevant to the well-being of the patient. All these factors may relate to health. This allows the attending physician the room he needs to make his best medical judgment. And it is room that operates for the benefit, not the disadvantage, of the pregnant woman.

D. The appellants next argue that the District Court should have declared unconstitutional three procedural demands of the Georgia statute: (1) that the abortion be performed in a hospital accredited by the Joint Commission on Accreditation of Hospitals;[11] (2) that the procedure be approved by the hospital staff abortion committee; and (3) that the performing physician's judgment be confirmed by the independent examinations of the patient by two other licensed physicians. The appellants attack these provisions not only on the ground that they unduly restrict the woman's right of privacy, but also on procedural due process and equal protection grounds. The physician-appellants also argue that, by subjecting a doctor's individual medical judgment to committee approval and to confirming consultations, the statute impermissibly restricts the physician's right to practice his profession and deprives him of due process.

[11] We were advised at reargument, Tr. of Rearg. 10, that only 54 of Georgia's 159 counties have a JCAH accredited hospital.

1. *JCAH Accreditation.* The Joint Commission on Accreditation of Hospitals is an organization without governmental sponsorship or overtones. No question whatever is raised concerning the integrity of the organization or the high purpose of the accreditation process.[12] That process, however, has to do with hospital standards generally and has no present particularized concern with abortion as a medical or surgical procedure.[13] In Georgia there is no restriction of the performance of non-abortion surgery in a hospital not yet accredited by the JCAH so long as other requirements imposed by the State, such as licensing of the hospital and of the operating surgeon, are met. See Georgia Code §§ 88–1901 (a) and 88–1905 (1971) and 84–907 (Supp. 1971). Furthermore, accreditation by the Commission is not

granted until a hospital has been in operation at least one year. The Model Penal Code, § 230.3, Appendix B hereto, contains no requirement for JCAH accreditation. And the Uniform Abortion Act (Final Draft, August 1971),[14] approved by the American Bar Association in February 1972, contains no JCAH accredited hospital specification.[15] Some courts have held that a JCAH accreditation requirement is an overbroad infringement of fundamental rights because it does not relate to the particular medical problems and dangers of the abortion operation. *Poe* v. *Menghini*, 339 F. Supp. 986, 993–994 (Kan. 1972); *People* v. *Barksdale*, 96 Cal. Rptr. 265, 273–274 (Cal. App. 1971).

[12] Since its founding, JCAH has pursued the "elusive goal" of defining the "optimal setting" for "quality of service in hospitals." JCAH, Accreditation Manual for Hospitals, Foreward (Dec. 1970). The Manual's Introduction states the organization's purpose to establish standards and conduct accreditation programs that will afford quality medical care "to give patients the optimal benefits that medical science has to offer." This ambitious and admirable goal is illustrated by JCAH's decision in 1966 "to raise and strengthen the standards from their present level of minimum essential to the level of optimum achievable . . . ." Some of these "optimum achievable" standards required are: disclosure of hospital ownership and control; a dietetic service and written dietetic policies; a written disaster plan for mass emergencies; a nuclear medical services program; facilities for hematology, chemistry, microbiology, clinical microscopy, and sero-immunology; a professional library and document delivery service; a radiology program; a social services plan administered by a qualified social worker; and a special care unit.
[13] "The Joint Commission neither advocates nor opposes any particular position with respect to elective abortions." Letter dated July 9, 1971, from John L. Brewer, M. D., Commissioner, JCAH, to the Rockefeller Foundation. Brief for *amici*, American College of Obstetricians and Gynecologists, et al., p. A–3.
[14] See *Roe* v. *Wade*, *ante* ——, n. 49.
[15] Some state statutes do not have the JCAH accreditation requirement. Alaska Stat. § 11.15.060 (1970); Hawaii Rev. Stat. § 453.16 (Supp. 1971); N. Y. Penal Code § 125.05.3 (McKinney Supp. 1972–1973). Washington has the requirement but couples it with the alternative of "a medical facility approved . . . by the state board of health." Wash. Rev. Code § 9.02.070 (Supp. 1972). Florida's new statute has a similar provision. Law of Apr. 13, 1972, c. 72–196, § 1 (2). Others contain the specification. Ark. Stat. Ann. §§ 41–303 to 41–310 (Supp. 1971); Cal. Health and Safety Code §§ 25950–25955.5 (West Supp. 1972); Colo. Rev. Stats. Ann. §§ 40–2–50 to 40–2–53 (Perm. Cum. Supp. 1967); Kan. Stat. Ann. § 21–3047 (Supp. 1971); Md. Ann. Code Art. 43, §§ 137–139 (Repl. 1971). Cf. Del. Code Ann. §§ 1790–1793 (Supp. 1970) specifying "a nationally recognized medical or hospital accreditation authority," § 1790 (a).

We hold that the JCAH accreditation requirement does not withstand constitutional scrutiny in the present context. It is a requirement that simply is not "based on differences that are reasonably related to the purposes of the Act in which it is found." *Morey* v. *Doud*, 354 U. S. 457, 465 (1957).

This is not to say that Georgia may not or should not, from and after the end of the first trimester, adopt standards for licensing all facilities where abortions may be performed so long as those standards are legitimately related to the objective the State seeks to accomplish. The appellants contend that such a relationship would be lacking even in a lesser requirement that an abortion be performed in a licensed hospital, as opposed to a facility, such as a clinic, that may be required by the State to possess all the staffing and services necessary to perform an abortion safely (including those adequate to handle serious complications or other emergency, or arrangements with a nearby hospital to provide such services). Appellants and various *amici* have presented us with a mass of data purporting to demonstrate that some facilities other than hospitals are entirely adequate to perform abortions if they possess these qualifications. The State, on the other hand, has not presented persuasive data to show that only hospitals meet its acknowledged interest in insuring the quality of the operation and the full protection of the patient. We feel compelled to agree with appellants that the State must show more than it has in order to prove that only the full resources of a licensed hospital, rather than those of some other appropriately licensed institution, satisfy these health interests. We hold that the hospital requirement of the Georgia law, because it fails to exclude the first trimester of pregnancy, see *Roe* v. *Wade ante* ——, p. ——, is also invalid. In so holding we naturally express no opinion on the medical judgment involved in any particular case, that is, whether the patient's situation is such that an abortion should be performed in a hospital rather than in some other facility.

2. *Committee Approval.* The second aspect of the appellants' procedural attack relates to the hospital abortion committee and to the pregnant woman's asserted lack of access to that committee. Relying primarily on *Goldberg* v. *Kelly,* 397 U. S. 254 (1970), concerning the termination of welfare benefits, and *Wisconsin* v. *Constantineau,* 400 U. S. 433 (1971), concerning the posting of an alcoholic's name, Doe first argues that she was denied due process because she could not make a presentation to the committee. It is not clear from the record, however, whether Doe's own consulting physician was or was not a member of the committee or did or did not present her case, or, indeed, whether she herself was or was not there. We see nothing in the Georgia statute that explicitly denies access to the committee by or on behalf of the woman. If the access point alone were involved, we would not be persuaded to strike down the committee provision on the unsupported assumption that access is not provided.

Appellants attack the discretion the statute leaves to the committee. The most concrete argument they advance is their suggestion that it is still a badge of infamy "in many minds" to bear an illegitimate child, and that the Georgia system enables the committee members' personal views as to extramarital sex relations, and punishment therefor, to govern their decisions. This approach obviously is one founded on suspicion and one that discloses a lack of confidence in the integrity of physicians. To say that physicians will be guided in their hospital committee decisions by their predilections on extramarital sex unduly narrows the issue to pregnancy outside marriage. (Doe's own situation did not involve extramarital sex and its product.) The appellants' suggestion is necessarily somewhat degrading to the conscientious physician, particularly the obstetrician, whose professional activity is concerned with the physical and mental welfare, the woes, the emotions, and the concern of his female patients. He, perhaps more than anyone else, is knowledgeable in this area of patient care, and he is aware of human frailty, so-called "error," and needs. The good physician—despite the presence of rascals in the medical profession, as in all others, we trust that most physicians are "good"—will have a sympathy and an understanding for the pregnant patient that probably is not exceeded by those who participate in other areas of professional counseling.

It is perhaps worth noting that the abortion committee has a function of its own. It is a committee of the hospital and it is composed of members of the institution's medical staff. The membership usually is a changing one. In this way its work burden is shared and is more readily accepted. The committee's function is protective. It enables the hospital appropriately to be advised that its posture and activities are in accord with legal requirements. It is to be remembered that the hospital is an entity and that it, too, has legal rights and legal obligations.

Saying all this, however, does not settle the issue of the constitutional propriety of the committee requirement. Viewing the Georgia statute as a whole, we see no constitutionally justifiable pertinence in the structure for the advance approval by the abortion committee. With regard to the protection of potential life, the medical judgment is already completed prior to the committee stage, and review by a committee once removed from diagnosis is basically redundant. We are not cited to any other surgical procedure made subject to committee approval as a matter of state criminal law. The woman's right to receive medical care in accordance with her licensed physician's best judgment and the physician's right to administer it are substantially limited by this statutorily imposed overview. And the hospital itself is otherwise fully protected. Under § 26–1202 (e) the hospital is free not to admit a patient for an abortion. It is even free not to have an abortion committee. Further, a physician or any other employee has the right to refrain, for moral or religious reasons, from participating in the abortion procedure. These provisions obviously are in the statute in order to afford appropriate protection to the individual and to the denominational hospital. Section 26–1202 (e) affords adequate protection to the hospital and little more is provided by the committee prescribed by § 26–1202 (b) (5).

We conclude that the interposition of the hospital abortion committee is unduly restrictive of the patient's rights and needs that, at this point, have already been medically delineated and substantiated by her personal physician. To ask more serves neither the hospital nor the State.

3. *Two-Doctor Concurrence.* The third aspects of the appellants' attack centers on the "time and availability of adequate medical facilities and personnel." It is said that the system imposes substantial and irrational roadblocks and "is patently unsuited" to prompt determination of the abortion decision. Time, of course, is critical in abortion. Risks during the first trimester of pregnancy are admittedly lower than during later months.

The appellants purport to show by a local study[16] of Grady Memorial Hospital (serving indigent residents in Fulton and DeKalb Counties) that the "mechanics of the system itself forced . . . discontinuation of the abortion process" because the median time for the workup was 15 days. The same study shows, however, that 27% of the candidates for abortion were already 13 or more weeks pregnant at the time of application, that is, they were at the end of or beyond the first trimester when they made their applications. It is too much to say, as appellants do, that these particular persons "were victims of [a] system over which they [had] no control." If higher risk was incurred because of abortions in the second rather than the first trimester, much of that risk was due to delay in application, and not to the alleged cumbersomeness of the system. We note, in passing, that appellant Doe had no delay problem herself; the decision in her case was made well within the first trimester.

It should be manifest that our rejection of the accredited hospital requirement and, more important, of the abortion committee's advance approval eliminates the major grounds of the attack based on the system's delay and the lack of facilities. There remains, however, the required confirmation by two Georgia-licensed physicians in addition to the recommendation of the pregnant woman's own consultant (making under the statute, a total of six physicians involved, including the three on the hospital's abortion committee). We conclude that this provision, too, must fall.

The statute's emphasis, as has been repetitively noted, is on the attending physician's "best clinical judgment that an abortion is necessary." That should be sufficient. The reasons for the presence of the confirmation step in the statute are perhaps apparent, but they are insufficient to withstand constitutional challenge. Again, no other voluntary medical or surgical procedure for which Georgia requires confirmation by two other physicians has been cited to us. If a physician is licensed by the State, he is recognized by the State as capable of exercising acceptable clinical judgment. If he fails in this, professional censure or deprivation of his license are available remedies. Required acquiescence by co-practitioners has no

---

[16] L. Baker & M. Freeman, Abortion Surveillance at Grady Memorial Hospital Center for Disease Control (June and July 1971) (U. S. Dept. of HEW, PHS).

rational connection with a patient's needs and unduly infringes on the physician's right to practice. The attending physician will know when a consultation is advisable —the doubtful situation, the need for assurance when the medical decision is a delicate one, and the like. Physicians have followed this routine historically and know its usefulness and benefit for all concerned. It is still true today that "reliance must be placed upon the assurance given by his license, issued by an authority competent to judge in that respect, that he [the physician] possesses the requisite qualifications." *Dent* v. *West Virginia,* 129 U. S. 114, 122–123 (1889). See *United States* v. *Vuitch,* 402 U. S., at 71.

E. The appellants attack the residency requirement of the Georgia law, §§ 26–1202 (b)(1) and (b)(2), as violative of the right to travel stressed in *Shapiro* v. *Thompson,* 394 U. S. 618, 629–631 (1969), and other cases. A requirement of this kind, of course, could be deemed to have some relationship to the availability of post-procedure medical care for the aborted patient.

Nevertheless, we do not uphold the constitutionality of the residence require-ment. It is not based on any policy of preserving state-supported facilities for Georgia residents, for the bar also applies to private hospitals and to privately retained physicians. There is no intimation, either, that Georgia facilities are utilized to capacity in caring for Georgia residents. Just as the Prvileges and Immunities Clause, Const. Art. IV, § 2, protects persons who enter other States to ply their trade, *Ward* v. *Maryland,* 79 U. S. (12 Wall.) 418, 430 (1870); *Blake* v. *McClung,* 172 U. S. 239, 248–256 (1898), so must it protect persons who enter Georgia seeking the medical services that are available there. See *Toomer* v. *Witsell,* 334 U. S. 385, 396–397 (1948). A contrary holding would mean that a State could limit to its own residents the general medical care available within its borders. This we could not approve.

F. The last argument on this phase of the case is one that often is made, namely, that the Georgia system is violative of equal protection because it discriminates against the poor. The appellants do not urge that abortions should be performed by persons other than licensed physicians, so we have no argument that because the wealthy can better afford physicians, the poor should have non-physicians made available to them. The appellants acknowledged that the procedures are "non-discriminatory in . . . express terms" but they suggest that they have produced invidious discriminations. The District Court rejected this approach out of hand. 319 F. Supp., at 1056. It rests primarily on the accreditation and approval and confirmation requirements, discussed above, and on the assertion that most of Georgia's counties have no accredited hospital. We have set aside the accreditation, approval, and confirmation requirements, however, and with that, the discrimina-tion argument collapses in all significant aspects.

V

The appellants complain, finally, of the District Court's denial of injunctive relief. A like claim was made in *Roe* v. *Wade, ante.* We declined decision there insofar as injunctive relief was concerned, and we decline it here. We assure that Georgia's prosecutorial authorities will give full recognition to the judgment of this Court.

In summary, we hold that the JCAH accredited hospital provision and the re-quirements as to approval by the hospital abortion committee, as to confirmation by two independent physicians, and as to residence in Georgia are all violative of the Fourteenth Amendment. Specifically, the following portions of § 26–1202 (b), re-maining after the District Court's judgment, are invalid:

(1) Subsections (1) and (2).

(2) That portion of Subsection (3) following the words "such physician's judg-ment is reduced to writing."

(3) Subsections (4) and (5).

The judgment of the District Court is modified accordingly and, as so modified, is affirmed. Costs are allowed to the appellants.

APPENDIX A

Criminal Code of Georgia

(The italicized portions are those held unconstitutional by the District Court)

CHAPTER 26–12. ABORTION.

26–1201. Criminal Abortion. Except as otherwise provided in section 26–1202, a person commits criminal abortion when he administers any medicine, drug or other substance whatever to any woman or when he uses any instrument or other means whatever upon any woman with intent to produce a miscarriage or abortion.

26–1202. Exception. (a) Section 26–1201 shall not apply to an abortion performed by a physician duly licensed to practice medicine and surgery pursuant to Chapter 84–9 or 84–12 of the Code of Georgia of 1933, as amended, based upon his best clinical judgment that an abortion is necessary *because:*

(1) A continuation of the pregnancy would endanger the life of the pregnant woman or would seriously and permanently injure her health; or

(2) The fetus would very likely be born with a grave, permanent, and irremediable mental or physical defect; or

(3) The pregnancy resulted from forcible or statutory rape.

(b) No abortion is authorized or shall be performed under this section unless each of the following conditions is met:

(1) The pregnant woman requesting the abortion certifies in writing under oath and subject to the penalties of false swearing to the physician who proposes to perform the abortion that she is a bona fide legal resident of the State of Georgia.

(2) The physician certifies that he believes the woman is a bona fide resident of this State and that he has no information which should lead him to believe otherwise.

(3) Such physician's judgment is reduced to writing and concurred in by at least two other physicians duly licensed to practice medicine and surgery pursuant to Chapter 84–9 of the Code of Georgia of 1933, as amended, who certify in writing that based upon their separate personal medical examinations of the pregnant woman, the abortion is, in their judgment, necessary *because of one or more of the reasons enumerated above.*

(4) Such abortion is performed in a hospital licensed by the State Board of Health and accredited by the Joint Commission on Accreditation of Hospitals.

(5) The performance of the abortion has been approved in advance by a committee of the medical staff of the hospital in which the operation is to be performed. This committee must be one established and maintained in accordance with the standards promulgated by the Joint Commission on the Accreditation of Hospitals, and its approval must be by a majority vote of a membership of not less than three members of the hospital's staff; the physician proposing to perform the operation may not be counted as a member of the committee for this purpose.

(6) If the proposed abortion is considered necessary because the woman has been raped, the woman makes a written statement under oath, and subject to the penalties of false swearing, of the date, time and place of the rape and the name of the rapist, if known. There must be attached to this statement a certified copy of any report of the rape made by any law enforcement officer or agency and a statement by the solicitor general of the judicial circuit where the rape occurred or allegedly occurred that, according to his best information, there is probable cause to believe that the rape did occur.

(7) Such written opinions, statements, certificates, and concurrences are maintained in the permanent files of such hospital and are available at all reasonable times to the solicitor general of the judicial circuit in which the hospital is located.

(8) A copy of such written opinions, statements, certificates, and concurrences is filed with the Director of the State Department of Public Health within ten (10) days after such operation is performed.

(9) All written opinions, statements, certificates, and concurrences filed and maintained pursuant to paragraphs (7) and (8) of this subsection shall be confidential records and shall not be made available for public inspection at any time.

(c) Any solicitor general of the judicial circuit in which an abortion is to be performed under this section, or any person who would be a relative of the child within the second degree of consanguinity, may petition the superior court of the county in which the abortion is to be performed for a declaratory judgment whether the performance of such abortion would violate any constitutional or other legal rights of the fetus. Such solicitor general may also petition such court for the purpose of taking issue with compliance with the requirements of this section. The physician who proposes to perform the abortion and the pregnant woman shall be respondents. The petition shall be heard expeditiously and if the court adjudges that such abortion would violate the constitutional or other legal rights of the fetus, the court shall so declare and shall restrain the physician from performing the abortion.

(d) If an abortion is performed in compliance with this section, the death of the fetus shall not give rise to any claim for wrongful death.

(e) Nothing in this section shall require a hospital to admit any patient under the provisions hereof for the purpose of performing an abortion, nor shall any hospital be required to appoint a committee such as contemplated under subsection (b) (5). A physician, or any other person who is a member of or associated with the staff of a hospital, or any employee of a hospital in which an abortion has been authorized, who shall state in writing an objection to such abortion on moral or religious grounds shall not be required to participate in the medical procedures which will result in the abortion, and the refusal of any such person to participate therein shall not form the basis of any claim for damages on account of such refusal or for any disciplinary or recriminatory action against such person.

26–1203. Punishment. A person convicted of criminal abortion shall be punished by imprisonment for not less than one nor more than 10 years.

APPENDIX B
American Law Institute
MODEL PENAL CODE

Section 230.3. Abortion.

(1) *Unjustified Abortion.* A person who purposely and unjustifiably terminates the pregnancy of another otherwise than by a live birth commits a felony of the third degree or, where the pregnancy has continued beyond the twenty-sixth week, a felony of the second degree.

(2) *Justifiable Abortion.* A licensed physician is justified in terminating a pregnancy if he believes there is substantial risk that continuance of the pregnancy would gravely impair the physical or mental health of the mother or that the child would be born with grave physical or mental defect, or that the pregnancy resulted from rape, incest, or other felonious intercourse. All illicit intercourse with a girl below the age of 16 shall be deemed felonious for purposes of this subsection. Justifiable abortions shall be performed only in a licensed hospital except in case of emergency when hospital facilities are unavailable. [Additional exceptions from the requirement of hospitalization may be incorporated here to take account of situations in sparsely settled areas where hospitals are not generally accessible.]

(3) *Physicians' Certificates; Presumption from Non-Compliance.* No abortion shall be performed unless two physicians, one of whom may be the person performing the abortion, shall have certified in writing the circumstances which they believe to justify the abortion. Such certificate shall be submitted before the abortion to the hospital where it is to be performed and, in the case of abortion following felonious intercourse, to the prosecuting attorney or the police. Failure to comply with any of the requirements of this Subsection gives rise to a presumption that the abortion was unjustified.

(4) *Self-Abortion.* A woman whose pregnancy has continued beyond the twenty-sixth week commits a felony of the third degree if she purposely terminates her own pregnancy otherwise than by a live birth, or if she uses instruments, drugs or violence upon herself for that purpose. Except as justified under Subsection (2), a person who induces or knowingly aids a woman to use instruments, drugs or violence upon herself for the purpose of terminating her pregnancy otherwise than by a live birth commits a felony of the third degree whether or not the pregnancy has continued beyond the twenty-sixth week.

(5) *Pretended Abortion.* A person commits a felony of the third degree if, representing that it is his purpose to perform an abortion, he does an act adapted to cause abortion in a pregnant woman although the woman is in fact not pregnant, or the actor does not believe she is. A person charged with unjustified abortion under Subsection (1) or an attempt to commit that offense may be convicted thereof upon proof of conduct prohibited by this Subsection.

(6) *Distribution of Abortifacients.* A person who sells, offers to sell, possesses with intent to sell, advertises, or displays for sale anything specially designed to terminate a pregnancy, or held out by the actor as useful for that purpose, commits a misdemeanor, unless:

(a) the sale, offer or display is to a physician or druggist or to an intermediary in a chain of distribution to physicians or druggists; or

(b) the sale is made upon prescription or order of a physician; or

(c) the possession is with intent to sell as authorized in paragraphs (a) and (b); or

(d) the advertising is addressed to persons named in paragraph (a) and confined to trade or professional channels not likely to reach the general public.

(7) *Section Inapplicable to Prevention of Pregnancy.* Nothing in this Section shall be deemed applicable to the prescription, administration or distribution of drugs or other substances for avoiding pregnancy, whether by preventing implantation of a fertilized ovum or by any other method that operates before, at or immediately after fertilization.

Nos. 70—18 AND 70—40
———

MR. CHIEF JUSTICE BURGER, concurring.

I agree that, under the Fourteenth Amendment to the Constitution, the abortion statutes of Georgia and Texas impermissably limit the performance of abortions necessary to protect the health of pregnant women, using the term health in its broadest medical context. See *Vuitch* v. *United States,* 402 U. S. 62, 71–72 (1971). I am somewhat troubled that the Court has taken notice of various scientific and medical data in reaching its conclusion; however, I do not believe that the Court has exceeded the scope of judicial notice accepted in other contexts.

In oral argument, counsel for the State of Texas informed the Court that early abortive procedures were routinely permitted in certain exceptional cases, such as nonconsensual pregnancies resulting from rape and incest. In the face of a rigid and narrow statute, such as that of Texas, no one in these circumstances should be placed in a posture of dependence on a prosecutorial policy or prosecutorial discretion. Of course, States must have broad power, within the limits indicated in the opinions, to regulate the subject of abortions, but where the consequences of state intervention are so severe, uncertainty must be avoided as much as possible. For my part, I would be inclined to allow a State to require the certification of two physicians to support an abortion, but the Court holds otherwise. I do not believe that such a procedure is unduly burdensome, as are the complex steps of the Georgia statute, which require as many as six doctors and the use of a hospital certified by the JCAH.

I do not read the Court's holding today as having the sweeping consequences attributed to it by the dissenting Justices; the dissenting views discount the reality that the vast majority of physicians observe the standards of their profession, and act only on the basis of carefully deliberated medical judgments relating to life and health. Plainly, the Court today rejects any claim that the Constitution requires abortion on demand.

————

MR. JUSTICE DOUGLAS, concurring.

While I join the opinion of the Court,[1] I add a few words.

The questions presented in the present cases go far beyond the issues of vagueness, which we considered in *United States* v. *Vuitch,* 402 U. S. 62. They involve the right of privacy, one aspect of which we considered in *Griswold* v. *Connecticut,* 381 U. S. 479, 484, when we held that various guarantees in the Bill of Rights create zones of privacy.[2]

The *Griswold* case involved a law forbidding the use of contraceptives. We held that law as applied to married people unconstitutional:

> "We deal with a right of privacy older than the Bill of Rights—older than our political parties, older than our school system. Marriage is a coming together for better or for worse, hopefully enduring and intimate to the degree of being sacred." *Id.,* 486.

The District Court in *Doe* held that *Griswold* and related cases "establish a constitutional right to privacy broad enough to encompass the right of a woman to terminate an unwanted pregnancy in its early stages, by obtaining an abortion." 319 F. Supp., at 1054.

The Supreme Court of California expressed the same view in *People* v. *Belous,*[3] 71 Cal. 2d 954, 963.

The Ninth Amendment obviously does not create federally enforceable rights. It merely says, "The enumeration in the Constitution of certain rights shall not be construed to deny or disparage others retained by the people." But a catalogue of these rights includes customary, traditional, and time-honored rights, amenities, privileges, and immunities that come within the sweep of "the Blessings of Liberty" mentioned in the preamble to the Constitution. Many of them in my view come within the meaning of the term "liberty" as used in the Fourteenth Amendment.

First is the autonomous control over the development and expression on one's intellect, interests, tastes, and personality.

---

[1] I disagree with the dismissal of Dr. Hallford's complaint in intervention in *Roe* v. *Wade,* because my disagreement with *Younger* v. *Harris,* 401 U. S. 37, revealed in my dissent in that case, still persists and extends to the progeny of that case.

[2] There is no mention of privacy in our Bill of Rights but our decisions have recognized it as one of the fundamental values those amendments were designed to protect. The fountainhead case is *Boyd* v. *United States*, 116 U. S. 616, holding that a federal statute which authorized a court in tax cases to require a taxpayer to produce his records or to concede the Government's allegations offended the Fourth and Fifth Amendments. Justice Bradley, for the Court, found that the measure unduly intruded into the "sanctity of a man's home and the privacies of life." *Id.*, 630. Prior to *Boyd*, in *Kilbourn* v. *Thompson*, 103 U. S. 168, 195, Mr. Justice Miller held for the Court that neither House of Congress "possesses the general power of making inquiry into the private affairs of the citizen." Of *Kilbourn* Mr. Justice Field later said, "This case will stand for all time as a bulwark against the invasion of the right of the citizen to protection in his private affairs against the unlimited scrutiny of investigation by a congressional committee." *In re Pacific Ry. Comm'n*, 32 F. 231, 253 (cited with approval in *Sinclair* v. *United States*, 279 U.S. 263, 293). Mr. Justice Harlan, also speaking for the Court, in *Interstate Commerce Comm'n* v. *Brimson*, 154 U. S. 447, 478, thought the same was true of administrative inquiries, saying the Constitution did not permit a "general power of making inquiry into the private affairs of the citizen." In a similar vein were *Harriman* v. *Interstate Commerce Comm'n*, 211 U. S. 407; *United States* v. *Louisville & Nashville R. R.*, 236 U. S. 318, 335; and *Federal Trade Comm'n* v. *American Tobacco Co.*, 264 U. S. 298.

[3] The California abortion statute, held unconstitutional in the *Belous* case made it a crime to perform or help perform an abortion "unless the same is necessary to preserve [the mother's] life." 71 Cal. 2d, at 959.

These are rights protected by the First Amendment and in my view they are absolute, permitting of no exceptions. See *Terminiello* v. *Chicago*, 337 U. S. 77; *Roth* v. *United States*, 354 U. S. 476, 508 (dissent); *Kingsley Pictures Corp.* v. *Regents*, 360 U. S. 684, 697 (concurring); *New York Times Co.* v. *Sullivan*, 376 U. S. 254, 293 (Black, J., concurring in which I joined). The Free Exercise Clause of the First Amendment is one facet of this constitutional right. The right to remain silent as respects one's own beliefs, *Watkins* v. *United States*, 354 U. S. 178, 196–199, is protected by the First and the Fifth. The First Amendment grants the privacy of first-class mail. *United States* v. *Van Leeuwen*, 397 U. S. 249, 253. All of these aspects of the right of privacy are "rights retained by the people" in the meaning of the Ninth Amendment.

Second is freedom of choice in the basic decisions of one's life respecting marriage, divorce, procreation, contraception, and the education and upbringing of children.

These rights, unlike those protected by the First Amendment, are subject to some control by the police power. Thus the Fourth Amendment speaks only of "unreasonable searches and seizures" and of "probable cause." These rights are "fundamental" and we have held that in order to support legislative action the statute must be narrowly and precisely drawn and that a "compelling state interest" must be shown in support of the limitation. *E. g., Kramer* v. *Union Free School Dist.*, 395 U. S. 621 (1969); *Shapiro* v. *Thompson*, 394 U. S. 618 (1969); *Carrington* v. *Rash*, 380 U. S. 89 (1965); *Sherbert* v. *Verner*, 374 U. S. 398 (1963); *NAACP* v. *Alabama ex rel. Patterson*.

The liberty to marry a person of one's own choosing. *Loving* v. *Virginia*, 388 U. S. 1; the right of procreation. *Skinner* v. *Oklahoma*, 316 U. S. 535; the liberty to direct the education of one's children. *Pierce* v. *Society of Sisters*, 268 U. S. 510, and the privacy of the marital relation. *Griswold* v. *Connecticut*, *supra*,[4] are in this

[4] My Brother Stewart, writing in the present cases, says that our decision in *Griswold* reintroduced substantive due process that had been rejected in *Ferguson* v. *Skrupa*, 372 U. S. 726. *Skrupa* involved legislation governing a business enterprise; and the Court in that case, as had Mr. Justice Holmes on earlier occasions, rejected the idea that "liberty" within the meaning of the Due Process Clause of the Fourteenth Amendment was a vessel to be filled with one's personal choices of values, whether drawn from the *laissez faire* school, from the socialistic school, or from the technocrats. *Griswold* involved legislation touching on the marital relation and involving the conviction of a licensed physician for giving married people information concerning contraception. There is nothing specific in the Bill of Rights that covers that item. Nor is there anything

in the Bill of Rights that in terms protects the right of association or the privacy in one's association. Yet we found those rights in the periphery of the First Amendment, *NAACP v. Alabama*, 357 U. S. 449, 462. Other peripheral rights are the right to educate one's children as one chooses. *Pierce v. Society of Sisters*, 268 U. S. 510, and the right to study the German language, *Meyer v. Nebraska*, 262 U. S. 390. These decisions, with all respect, have nothing to do with substantive due process. One may think they are not peripheral rights to other rights that are expressed in the Bill of Rights. But that is not enough to bring into play the protection of substantive due process.

There are of course those who have believed that the reach of due process in the Fourteenth Amendment included all of the Bill of Rights but went further. Such was the view of Mr. Justice Murphy and Mr. Justice Rutledge. See *Adamson v. California*, 332 U. S. 46, 123, 124 (dissenting). Perhaps they were right; but it is a bridge that neither I nor those who joined the Court opinion in *Griswold* crossed.

category. Only last Term in *Eisenstadt v. Baird*, 405 U. S. 438, another contraceptive case, we expanded the concept of *Griswold* by saying:

> "It is true that in *Griswold* the right of privacy in question inhered in the marital relationship. Yet the marital couple is not an independent entity with a mind and heart of its own, but an association of two individuals each with a separate intellectual and emotional makeup. If the right of privacy means anything, it is the right of the *individual*, married or single, to be free from unwarranted government intrusion into matters so fundamentally affecting a person as the decision whether to bear or beget a child."

This right of privacy was called by Mr. Justice Brandeis the right "to be let alone." *Olmstead v. United States*, 277 U. S. 438, 478. That right includes the privilege of an individual to plan his own affairs, for, "outside of areas of plainly harmful conduct, every American is left to shape his own life as he thinks best, do what he pleases, go where he pleases." *Kent v. Dulles*, 357 U. S. 116, 126.

Third is the freedom to care for one's health and person, freedom from bodily restraint or compulsion, freedom to walk, stroll, or loaf.

These rights, though fundamental, are likewise subject to regulation on a showing of "compelling state interest." We stated in *Papachristou v. City of Jacksonville*, 405 U. S. 156, 164, that walking, strolling, and wandering "are historically part of the amenities of life as we have known them." As stated in *Jacobson v. Massachusetts*, 197 U. S. 11, 29:

> "There is, of course, a sphere within which the individual may assert the supremacy of his own will and rightfully dispute the authority of any human government, especially of any free government existing under a written constitution, to interfere with the exercise of that will."

In *Union Pac. Ry. Co. v. Botsford*, 141 U. S. 250, 252, the Court said,

> "The inviolability of the person is as much invaded by a compulsory stripping and exposure as by a blow."

In *Terry v. Ohio*, 392 U. S. 1, 8–9, the Court in speaking of the Fourth Amendment stated:

> "This inestimable right of personal security belongs as much to the citizen on the streets of our cities as to the Governor closeted in his study to dispose of his secret affairs."

Katz v. United States, 389 U. S. 347, 350, emphasizes that the Fourth Amendment:

> "protects individual privacy against certain kinds of governmental intrusion."

In *Meyer v. Nebraska*, 262 U. S. 390, 399, the Court said:

> "Without doubt, it [liberty] denotes not merely freedom from bodily restraint but also the right of the individual to contract, to engage in any of the common occupations of life, to acquire useful knowledge, to marry, establish a home and bring up children, to worship God according to the dictates of his own

conscience, and generally to enjoy those privileges long recognized at common law as essential to the orderly pursuit of happiness by free men."

The Georgia statute is at war with the clear message of these cases—that a woman is free to make the basic decision whether to bear an unwanted child. Elaborate argument is hardly necessary to demonstrate that childbirth may deprive a woman of her preferred life style and force upon her a radically different and undesired future. For example, rejected applicants under the Georgia statute are required to endure the discomforts of pregnancy; to incur the pain, higher mortality rate, and aftereffects of childbirth; to abandon educational plans; to sustain loss of income; to forgo the satisfactions of careers; to tax further mental and physical health in providing childcare; and, in some cases, to bear the lifelong stigma of unwed motherhood, a badge which may haunt, if not deter, later legitimate family relationships.

Such a holding is, however, only the beginning of the problem. The State has interests to protect. Vaccinations to prevent epidemics are one example, as *Jacobson* holds. The Court held that compulsory sterilization of imbeciles afflicted with hereditary forms of insanity or imbecility is another. *Buck* v. *Bell,* 274 U. S. 200. Abortion affects another. While childbirth endangers the lives of some women, voluntary abortion at any time and place regardless of medical standards would impinge on a rightful concern of society. The woman's health is part of that concern; as is the life of the fetus after quickening. These concerns justify the State in treating the procedure as a medical one.

One difficulty is that this statute as construed and applied apparently does not give full sweep to the "psychological as well as physical well-being" of women patients which saved the concept "health" from being void for vagueness in *United States* v. *Vuitch, supra,* at 72. But apart from that, Georgia's enactment has a constitutional infirmity because, as stated by the District Court, it "limits the number of reasons for which an abortion may be sought." I agree with the holding of the District Court, "This the State may not do, because such action unduly restricts a decision sheltered by the Constitutional right to privacy." 319 F. Supp., at 1056.

The vicissitudes of life produce pregnancies which may be unwanted, or which may impair "health" in the broad *Vuitch* sense of the term, or which may imperil the life of the mother, or which in the full setting of the case may create such suffering, dislocations, misery, or tragedy as to make an early abortion the only civilized step to take. These hardships may be properly embraced in the "health" factor of the mother as appraised by a person of insight. Or they may be part of a broader medical judgment based on what is "appropriate" in a given case, though perhaps not "necessary" in a strict sense.

The "liberty" of the mother, though rooted as it is in the Constitution, may be qualified by the State for the reasons we have stated. But where fundamental personal rights and liberties are involved, the corrective legislation must be "narrowly drawn to prevent the supposed evil," *Cantwell* v. *Connecticut,* 310 U. S. 296, 307, and not be dealt with in an "unlimited and indiscriminate" manner. *Shelton* v. *Tucker,* 364 U. S. 479, 490. And see *Talley* v. *California,* 362 U. S. 60. Unless regulatory measures are so confined and are addressed to the specific areas of compelling legislative concern, the police power would become the great leveller of constitutional rights and liberties.

There is no doubt that the State may require abortions to be performed by qualified medical personnel. The legitimate objective of preserving the mother's health clearly supports such laws. Their impact upon the woman's privacy is minimal. But the Georgia statute outlaws virtually all such operations—even in the earliest stages of pregnancy. In light of modern medical evidence suggesting that an early abortion is safer healthwise than childbirth itself, it cannot be seriously urged that so comprehensive a ban is aimed at protecting the woman's health.[5] Rather, this expansive proscription of all abortions along the temporal spectrum can rest only on a public goal of preserving both embryonic and fetal life.

[5] Many studies show that it is safer for a woman to have a medically induced abortion than to bear a child. In the first 11 months of operation of the New York abortion law, the mortality rate associated with such operations was six per 100,000 operations. Abortion Mortality, 20 Morbidity and Mortality 208, 209 (1971) (U. S. Department of Health, Education and Welfare, Public Health Service). On the other hand, the maternal mortality rate associated with childbirths other than abortions was 18 per 100,000 live births. Tietze, Mortality with Contraception and Induced Abortion, 45 Studies in Family Planning 6 (1969). See also C. Tietze & H. Lehfeldt, Legal Abortion in Eastern Europe 175 J. A. M. A. 1149, 1152 (1961); V. Kolblova, Legal Abortion in Czechoslovakia, 196 J. A. M. A. 371 (1966); Mehland, Combating Illegal Abortion in the Socialist Countries of Europe, 13 World Med. J. 84 (1966).

The present statute has struck the balance between the woman and the State's interests wholly in favor of the latter. I am not prepared to hold that a State may equate, as Georgia has done, all phases of maturation preceding birth. We held in *Griswold* that the States may not preclude spouses from attempting to avoid the joinder of sperm and egg. If this is true, it is difficult to perceive any overriding public necessity which might attach precisely at the moment of conception. As Mr. Justice Clark has said:[6]

"To say that life is present at conception is to give recognition to the potential, rather than the actual. The unfertilized egg has life, and if fertilized, it takes on human proportions. But the law deals in reality, not obscurity—the known rather than the unknown. When sperm meets egg, life may eventually form, but quite often it does not. The law does not deal in speculation. The phenomenon of life takes time to develop, and until it is actually present, it cannot be destroyed. Its interruption prior to formation would hardly be homicide, and as we have seen, society does not regard it as such. The rites of Baptism are not performed and death certificates are not required when a miscarriage occurs. No prosecutor has ever returned a murder indictment charging the taking of the life of a fetus.[7] This would not be the case if the fetus constituted human life."

In summary, the enactment is overbroad. It is not closely correlated to the aim of preserving pre-natal life. In fact, it permits its destruction in several cases, including pregnancies resulting from sex acts in which unmarried females are below the statutory age of consent. At the same time, however, the measure broadly proscribes aborting other pregnancies which may cause severe mental disorders. Additionally, the statute is overbroad because it equates the value of embryonic life immediately after conception with the worth of life immediately before birth.

III

Under the Georgia Act the mother's physician is not the sole judge as to whether the abortion should be performed. Two other licensed physicians must concur in his judgment.[8] Moreover, the abortion must be performed in a licensed hospital;[9] and the abortion must be approved in advance by a committee of the medical staff of that hospital.[10]

Physicians, who speak to us in *Doe* through an *amicus* brief, complain of the Georgia Act's interference with their practice of their profession.

[6] Religion, Morality and Abortion: A Constitutional Appraisal, 2 Loy. U. (L. A.) L. Rev. 1, 10 (1969).
[7] In *Keeler* v. *Superior Court*, 2 Cal. 3d 619, 470 P. 2d 617, the California Supreme Court held in 1970 that the California murder statute did not cover the killing of an unborn fetus, even though the fetus be "viable" and that it was beyond judicial power to extend the statute to the killing of an unborn. It held that the child must be "born alive before a charge of homicide can be sustained." 2 Cal. 3d, at 639.
[8] See § 26–1202 (b) (3).
[9] See § 26–1202 (b) (4).
[10] Section 26–1202 (b) (5).

The right of privacy has no more conspicuous place than in the physician-patient relationship, unless it be in the priest-penitent relation.

It is one thing for a patient to agree that her physician may consult with another physician about her case. It is quite a different matter for the State compulsorily to impose on that physician-patient relationship another layer or, as in this case, still a third layer of physicians. The right of privacy—the right to care for one's health and person and to seek out a physician of one's own choice protected by the Fourteenth Amendment—becomes only a matter of theory not a reality, when a multiple physician approval system is mandated by the State.

The State licenses a physician. If he is derelict or faithless, the procedures available to punish him or to deprive him of his license are well known. He is entitled to procedural due process before professional disciplinary sanctions may be imposed. See *In re Ruffalo,* 390 U. S. 544. Crucial here, however, is state-imposed control over the medical decision whether pregnancy should be interrupted. The good-faith decision of the patient's chosen physician is overridden and the final decision passed on to others in whose selection the patient has no part. This is a total destruction of the right of privacy between physician and patient and the intimacy of relation which that entails.

The right to seek advice on one's health and the right to place his reliance on the physician of his choice are basic to Fourteenth Amendment values. We deal with fundamental rights and liberties, which, as already noted, can be contained or controlled only by discretely drawn legislation that preserves the "liberty" and regulates only those phases of the problem of compelling legislative concern. The imposition by the State of group controls over the physician-patient relation is not made on any medical procedure apart from abortion, no matter how dangerous the medical step may be. The oversight imposed on the physician and patient in abortion cases denies them their "liberty," *viz.,* their right of privacy, without any compelling, discernable state interest.

Georgia has constitutional warrant in treating abortion as a medical problem. To protect the woman's right of privacy, however, the control must be through the physician of her choice and the standards set for his performance.

The protection of the fetus when it has acquired life is a legitimate concern of the State. Georgia's law makes no rational, discernible decision on that score.[11] For under the Act the developmental stage of the fetus is irrelevant when pregnancy is the result of rape or when the fetus will very likely be born with a permanent defect or when a continuation of the pregnancy will endanger the life of the mother or permanently injure her health. When life is present is a question we do not try to resolve. While basically a question for medical experts, as stated by Mr. Justice Clark,[12] it is, of course, caught up in matters of religion and morality.

In short, I agree with the Court that endangering the life of the woman or seriously and permanently injuring her health are standards too narrow for the right of privacy that are at stake.

I also agree that the superstructure of medical supervision which Georgia has erected violates the patient's right of privacy inherent in her choice of her own physician.

[11] See Rochat, Tyler, and Schoenbucher, An Epidemiological Analysis of Abortion in Georgia, 61 Am. J. of Public Health 541 (1971).

[12] Religion, Morality and Abortion: A Constitutional Appraisal, 2 Loy. U. (L. A.) L. Rev. 1, 10 (1969).

MR. JUSTICE WHITE, with whom MR. JUSTICE REHNQUIST joins, dissenting.

At the heart of the controversy in these cases are those recurring pregnancies that pose no danger whatsoever to the life or health of the mother but are nevertheless unwanted for any one or more of a variety of reasons—convenience, family planning, economies, dislike of children, the embarrassment of illegitimacy, etc. The common claim before us is that for any one of such reasons, or for no reason at all, and without asserting or claiming any threat to life or health, any woman is entitled to an abortion at her request if she is able to find a medical advisor willing to undertake the procedure.

The Court for the most part sustains this position: During the period prior to the time the fetus becomes viable, the Constitution of the United States values the convenience, whim or caprice of the putative mother more than the life or potential life of the fetus; the Constitution, therefore, guarantees the right to an abortion as against any state law or policy seeking to protect the fetus from an abortion not prompted by more compelling reasons of the mother.

Within all due respect, I dissent. I find nothing in the language or history of the Constitution to support the Court's judgment. The Court simply fashions and announces a new constitutional right for pregnant mothers and, with scarcely any reason or authority for its action, invests that right with sufficient substance to override most existing state abortion statutes. The upshot is that the people and the legislatures of the 50 States are constitutionally disentitled to weigh the relative importance of the continued existence and development of the fetus on the one hand against a spectrum of possible impacts on the mother on the other hand. As an exercise of raw judicial power, the Court perhaps has authority to do what it does today; but in my view its judgment is an improvident and extravagant exercise of the power of judicial review which the Constitution extends to this Court.

The Court apparently values the convenience of the pregnant mother more than the continued existence and development of the life or potential life which she carries. Whether or not I might agree with that marshalling of values, I can in no event join the Court's judgment because I find no constitutional warrant for imposing such an order of priorities on the people and legislatures of the States. In a sensitive area such as this, involving as it does issues over which reasonable men may easily and heatedly differ, I cannot accept the Court's exercise of its clear power of choice by interposing a constitutional barrier to state efforts to protect human life and by investing mothers and doctors with the consitutionally protected right to exterminate it. This issue, for the most part, should be left with the people and to the political processes the people have devised to govern their affairs.

It is my view, therefore, that the Texas statute is not constitutionally infirm because it denies abortions to those who seek to serve only their convenience rather than to protect their life or health. Nor is this plaintiff, who claims no threat to her mental or physical health, entitled to assert the possible rights of those women whose pregnancy assertedly implicates their health. This, together with *United States* v. *Vuitch,* 402 U. S. 62 (1971), dictates reversal of the judgment of the District Court.

Likewise, because Georgia may constitutionally forbid abortions to putative mothers who, like the plaintiff in this case, do not fall within the reach of § 26–1202 (a) of its criminal code, I have no occasion, and the District Court had none, to consider the constitutionality of the procedural requirements of the Georgia statute as applied to those pregnancies posing substantial hazards to either life or health. I would reverse the judgment of the District Court in the Georgia case.

No. 70–40

MR. JUSTICE REHNQUIST, dissenting.

The holding in *Roe* v. *Wade, ante* ——?, that state abortion laws can withstand constitutional scrutiny only if the States can demonstrate a compelling state interest apparently compels the Court's close scrutiny of the various provisions in Georgia's abortion statute. Since, as indicated by my dissent in *Wade,* I view the compelling state interest standard as an inappropriate measure of the constitutionality of state abortion laws, I respectfully dissent from the majority's holding.

No. 70–18

SARAH WEDDINGTON, Austin, Tex. (ROY LUCAS, NORMAN DORSEN, LINDA N. COFFEE, ROY L. MERRILL, JR., and DAUGHERTY, BRUNER, LASTELICK & ANDERSON, with her on the brief) for appellants; ROBERT C. FLOWERS, Assistant Attorney General, State of Texas (CRAWFORD C. MARTIN, Attorney General, NOLA WHITE, First Assistant Attorney General, ALFRED WALKER, Executive Assistant Attorney General, JAY FLOYD, Assistant Attorney General, HENRY WADE, Dallas Cty. District Attorney, and JOHN B. TOLLE, Assistant District Attorney, with him on the brief) for appellees; EUGENE J. McMAHON filed brief for Women for the Unborn, four other organizations, and various individuals, as amici curiae, seeking affirmance; CHARLES E. RICE filed brief for Americans United for Life, as amicus curiae, seeking affirmance; JOSEPH P. WITHERSPOON, JR. filed brief for Assn. of Texas Diocesan Attorneys, as amicus curiae, seeking affirmance; DENNIS J. HORAN, JEROME A. FRAZEL, JR., THOMAS M. CRISHAM, DOLORES B. HORAN, and JOHN D. GORBY filed brief for certain physicians, professors, and fellows of the American College of Obstetricians and Gynecologists, as amici curiae, seeking affirmance; ROBERT E. DUNNE filed brief for Robert L. Sassone, as amicus curiae, seeking affirmance; ALFRED L. SCANLAN, MARTIN J. FLYNN, ROBERT M. BYRN, JUAN J. RYAN, JOSEPH V. GARTLAN, JR., and SHEA & GARDNER filed brief for National Right to Life Commitee, as amicus curiae, seeking affirmance and reversal; HARRIET F. PILPEL, NANCY F. WECHSLER, RUTH ZANE ZUCKERMAN, MICHAEL KENNETH BROWN, and GREENBAUM, WOLFF & ERNST filed brief for Planned Parenthood Federation of America, Inc. and American Assn. of Planned Parenthood Physicians, as amici curiae, seeking affirmance and reversal; ALAN F. CHARLES and SUSAN GROSSMAN ALEXANDER filed brief for National Legal Program on Health Problems of the Poor, National Welfare Rights Organization, and American Public Health Assn., as amici curiae, seeking reversal; CAROL RYAN, J. ROBERT WILSON, KEITH P. RUSSELL, and WARREN E. MAGEE filed brief for American College of Obstetricians and Gynecologists, three other organizations, and a group of 178 physicians, as amici curiae, seeking reversal; HELEN L. BUTTENWIESER and BONNIE P. WINAWER filed brief for American Ethical Union and nine other organizations, as amici curiae, seeking reversal; NORMA G. ZARKY filed brief for American Assn. of University Women, six other organizations, and various individuals, as amici curiae, seeking reversal; MARRTIE L. THOMPSON and MARCIA LOWRY filed brief for State Communities Aid Assn., as amicus curiae; NANCY STEARNS filed brief for New Women Lawyers, Women's Health and Abortion Project, Inc., and National Abortion Action Coalition, as amici curiae; JOAN K. BRADFORD filed brief for California Committee to Legalize Abortion, Zero Population Growth, Inc., and three other organizations and individuals, as amici curiae.

No. 70—40

MARGIE PITTS HAMES, Atlanta, Ga. (ELIZABETH ROEDIGER RIND-SKOPF, GALE M. SIEGEL, TOBIANE SCHWARTZ, REBER F. BOULT, JR., and CHARLES MORGAN, JR., with her on the brief) for appellants; DOROTHY T. BEASLEY, Assistant Attorney General, State of Georgia (ARTHUR K. BOL-TON, Attorney General, HAROLD N. HILL, JR., Executive Assistant Attorney General, COURTNEY WILDER STANTON, Assistant Attorney General, JOEL FELDMAN, HENRY L. BOWDEN, and RALPH H. WITT, with her on the brief) for appellees; DENNIS J. HORAN, JEROME A. FRAZEL, JR., THOMAS M. CRISHAM, DOLORES B. HORAN, and JOHN D. GORBY filed brief for certain physicians, professors, and fellows, of the American College of Obstetricians and Gynecologists, as amici curiae, seeking affirmance; ROBERT E. DUNNE filed brief for Robert L. Sassone, as amicus curiae, seeking affirmance; FERDINAND BUCK-LEY, JAMES A. EICHELBERGER, and HUGH ROBINSON, JR. filed brief for Ferdinand Buckley, as amicus curiae, seeking affirmance; ALFRED L. SCANLAN, MARTIN J. FLYNN, ROBERT M. BYRN, JUAN J. RYAN, JOSEPH V. GARTLAN, JR., and SHEA & GARDNER filed brief for National Right to Life Committee, as amicus curiae, seeking affirmance and reversal; HARRIET F. PILPEL, NANCY F. WECHSLER, RUTH JANE ZUCKERMAN, MICHAEL KENNETH BROWN, and GREENBAUM, WOLFF & ERNST filed brief for Planned Parenthood Federation of America, Inc. and American Assn. of Planned Parenthood Physicians, as amici curiae, seeking affirmance and reversal; ALAN F. CHARLES and SUSAN GROSSMAN ALEXANDER filed brief for National Legal Program on Health Problems of the Poor, National Welfare Rights Organization, and American Public Health Assn., as amici curiae, seeking reversal; HELEN L. BUTTENWIESER and BONNIE P. WINAWER filed brief for American Ethical Union and nine other organizations, as amici curiae, seeking reversal; NORMA G. ZARKY filed brief for American Assn. of University Women, six other organizations, and various individuals, as amici curiae, seeking reversal; MARRTIE L. THOMPSON and MARCIA LOWRY filed brief for State Communities Aid Assn., as amicus curiae; NANCY STEARNS filed brief for New Women Lawyers, Women's Health and Abortion Project, Inc., and National Abortion Action Coalition, as amici curiae.

LAW AND MEDICINE

Liability for Unsuccessful Birth Control

"This case may well be the first case tried in the United States wherein the 'birth control' pill was at issue as contrasted to the vasectomy or sterilization operation." So said an Iowa trial court in a recent malpractice action against a physician by a wife who had borne a child despite taking birth control pills prescribed by the physician (*Maley vs Armstrong,* Dist Ct, Linn Co, Docket No 83195, Jan 1967).

In ordering a directed verdict in favor of the physician, the Iowa court applied rules laid down in cases involving surgical sterilization. Since there were no adverse medical effects as a result of the pregnancy and childbirth, the court concluded that the parents had suffered no damage in the normal birth of a normal child. "This is a situation," the court said, "where the plaintiffs bargained for lead and received gold."

Vasectomy

In reaching its decision, the Iowa court relied principally upon three cases, each involving the birth of a child to the wife after the husband had undergone a vasectomy. The three cases quoted by the court are *Ball vs Mudge* (391 P 2d 201 Wash, 1964); *Corman vs Anderson* (Super Ct, Los Angeles, No 701, 588 —memorandum trial court decision, Nov 16, 1960); and *Shaheen vs Knight* (6 Lyc 19, 11 Pa Dist & Co R 2nd 4 1957).

In all three of the cases, it was stated or assumed that a contract to perform a sterilization operation was not, in itself, illegal or contrary to public policy, even where the sterilization was undertaken for reasons of convenience, rather than for medical reasons. The *Corman* and *Shaheen* cases involved sterilization of convenience, while in the *Ball* case sterilization was sought, not only for economic reasons, but also because the wife had undergone three cesarean sections.

In each of the three cases, the issues of negligence in performing the operation and breach of contract in failing to achieve a promised result were recognized. However, in the *Ball* and *Corman* cases it was held that neither negligence nor breach of warranty had been proved. In the *Shaheen* case, no breach of warranty was found, and for the alleged negligence the court concluded that no damages were recoverable, on the ground that it would be against public policy to allow damages for the normal birth of a normal child. There was no discussion as to whether a different conclusion might have been reached had the child been abnormal or stillborn, or had the birth or pregnancy adversely affected the mother's health, or resulted in a miscarriage or in the death of the mother. In the *Ball* case, the jury had found in favor of the physician, and the Supreme Court of Washington, in reviewing the case, refused to rule on the question of whether the issue of damages should have gone to the jury or been barred as a matter of law.

Surgical Sterilization of Wife

At about the same time as the decision on the *Maley* case was handed down, a Washington trial court, in a case involving a pregnancy and childbirth after a sterilization operation on the wife rather than on the husband, held in favor of the physician on the ground that there was no proof of negligence in performing the operation since recanalization of the tubes might have occurred in the absence of negligence (*Nichol vs Komarniski,* Super Ct, King C, Docket No 634, 423, Dec 14, 1966). However, even if there had been negligence, the court said, no damages were allowable for the normal birth of a normal child. "A claim which asks damages for the birth of a normal, healthy child seems in many respects to be repugnant to the basic principles of our society and certain goals of the law," the court said. Referring to damage which might ensue to the child in later years upon discovering that he was un- wanted, the court declared: "I am of the opinion that the policy of the law should be that in a case such as this and under the evidence introduced in this case that a mother should be estopped from claiming damages, under these circumstances, on the grounds of decency, morality, and public policy."

A few months later, in a case also involving a pregnancy and childbirth after a sterilization operation on the wife, a federal trial court in West Virginia took an opposite view (*Bishop vs Byrne,* 265 F Supp 460, 1967). Holding that it was common knowledge that pregnancy and childbirth would cause some physical and mental pain and suffering, the court ruled that if the physician had been negligent in failing to perform the sterilization operation successfully, he would be liable for such pain and suffering. In the *Bishop* case, it was alleged that the operation had been sought in order to safeguard the health of the wife. Some 17 months after the operation was performed, the wife became pregnant and was later delivered of a child by cesarean section. At the time of the birth, one of her fallopian tubes was found to be intact. There was no contention that the child was abnormal or that the birth was an unusual cesarean section. In the absence of an express warranty that the operation would result in sterility, the court found as a matter of law that there was no breach of warranty. However, if the wife could prove that the sterilization operation was negligently performed, she could recover for any pain and suffering resulting from the pregnancy and childbirth. The amount of mental or physical suffering, if any, was a matter of fact and was for the jury to determine, the court said. Therefore, the physician's mo- tions to dismiss the case were overruled.

In arriving at the decision in the *Bishop* case, the federal court relied on the ruling handed down in the case of *West vs Underwood* (40 A 2d 610, NJ, 1945). That case raised the question of a physician's liability for failing to carry out an alleged agreement to sterilize a patient at the time he performed a cesarean operation on her. The court in the *West* case held that the jury could find that the physician had undertaken to perform a sterilization operation and had failed to do so, apparently through oversight, and thus the patient and her husband would be entitled to recover for all pain and suffering, mental and physical, together with loss of services and any other loss or damages prox- imately resulting from the negligence.

Birth Control Pills

In the *Maley* case, where the physician prescribed birth control pills, the court held that it was not clear that there was sufficient legal consideration to support a specific agreement to prevent pregnancy, so that an action for breach of warranty would not lie. On the issue of negligence, the court refused to send the case to the jury, on the ground that public policy barred recovery of damages. Admitting that birth control is "clearly not against public policy," the court nevertheless held that a cause of action for the birth of a normal and loved child, with the mother's health unimpaired, should be allowed only if sanctioned by the legislature after complete public debate. "A decision of this nature involving conflicting mores and far flung social ramifications should not depend upon the personal, religious and social views of a particular judge or jury," the court said. In the absence of direction by the state supreme court or by a legislative act or by judicial fiat, the court said that it would not consider, as compensable items of damage, such elements of childbirth as mental depression of the wife and temporary loss of consortium by the husband if attributable to pregnancy.

Problems of "The Pill"

As the decision on the *Maley* case demonstrates, childbirth following the taking of birth control pills raises a question identical to that in case of childbirth following a sterilization operation upon either the husband or the wife: that is, even if the failure to achieve sterility is the result of negligence on the part of the physician or of some other third party, are damages recoverable by one or both parents for the normal birth of a normal child?

In virtually all other respects, however, the problems presented in cases involving the pill differ widely from those encountered in surgical sterilization cases. Proof of postoperative fertility would, for example, in cases of surgical sterilization, be a strong factor in a suit against a physician for negligence. In the case of birth control pills, however, it is difficult to see in what way a physician could be considered negligent in prescribing the pills, unless, perhaps, he may have negligently given the patient incorrect instructions as to dosage or as to the days on which the pills were to be taken. Moreover, while a sterilization operation is under the sole control of the physician, the taking of birth control pills requires the cooperation of the patient, so that failure of the pill to cause temporary sterility might as easily be due to the negligence of the patient in failing to take the pills in the prescribed manner as to any negligence on the part of the physician prescribing them.

Another important difference between cases involving surgical sterilization cases and cases involving the pill is the possibility of suits for negligence against parties other than the physician, as, for example, the manufacturer of the pills, or the distributor or retailer. In fact, the court in the *Maley* case suggested that in certain situations an action might lie against the manufacturer of the pills under a doctrine of implied warranty of fitness for a particular purpose. Similarly, a druggist might be liable for negligence if he supplied the wrong pills in filling a prescription for birth control pills.

Undecided Questions of Liability

Still unexplored is the whole area of liability for unsuccessful sterilization, either by surgery or medication, in cases where an ensuing pregnancy or childbirth results in impairment of the mother's health, birth of an abnormal child, or death of the mother or the child. Even in the case of the normal birth of a normal child, the courts are divided. It may be, as the court in the *Maley* case suggested, an area in which general principles and policies will have to be set for each state "by the duly elected legislature after complete public debate." Until then, the resolution of the issues in cases of unsuccessful sterilization will be on a case-by-case basis, at least in states where the state supreme court has not yet ruled. —*VERONICA M. O'HERN*

Reprint from the Journal of the American Medical Association, October 16, 1967, Vol. 202, Adv. Pages 269 and 270, Copyright 1964, American Medical Association.

LAW AND MEDICINE
Minors and Contraception

According to the report of the Family Law Section of the American Bar Association presented in 1968 (published as "Family Planning and the Law," *Family Law Quart,* Dec 1967, pp 103-108), one out of every 19 babies born in this country is illegitimate. More than 40% of the mothers are under 19 years old and "a substantial number" are under 15 years of age. The effects of illegitimacy and its inherent problems constitute a national social problem and great tragedy for all individuals involved. In recent years, particularly since the advent of "the pill," more and more physicians are being asked for contraceptives by unmarried teenaged girls. Does the physician run any risk of legal liability if he accedes to this request without the knowledge of the girl's parents? Unlike the problems raised by treating a minor for venereal disease, the physician in this case does not deal with "illness" and he may also be afraid of criminal as well as civil liability.

Constitutional Aspects

Most restrictions on giving contraceptives to married women fell in 1965, when the United States Supreme Court decided *Griswold vs Connecticut* (381 US 479). The Court held that the Connecticut statute prohibiting the use of contraceptives violated the right of privacy of the individuals involved. It not only interfered with the marital relationship but with the physician's right to treat his patient as he thought best. Since this decision, it is now clear that a married minor is certainly entitled to contraceptive advice and it is no more the state's business if her physician gives it than if he treats her for tonsillitis. Within the past few months, the US Circuit Court (First Circuit) struck down a Massachusetts statute banning delivery of contraceptives to unmarried people. The court held that such a statute was violative of the 14th Amendment's guarantees of equal protection of the laws. Chief Judge Aldrich's opinion, after declaring that the state does have the right to protect the health of its citizens, declared "if the legislature is fully concerned with deterring fornication, it may increase the statutory penalty to mark the measure of its concern. It may not, however, do so by making the penalty a personally and socially undesired pregnancy," (*Baird vs Eisenstadt,* CCA 1, July 6, 1970). In the March 1969 *American Bar Association Journal,* (pp 223-225), Federal District Judge Don J. Young suggested in his article "Court Ordered Contraception" that a juvenile court is constitutionally empowered to *order* that a sexually active juvenile have an intrauterine contraceptive device implanted whether she wants it or not.

Criminal Liability

Neither the *Griswold* case nor the *Baird* case specifically dealt with the legal difference between minors and adults. Many physicians may believe that they run a risk of being arrested for "contributing to the delinquency of a minor." While this may be hypothetically possible, no case can be found where it actually occurred. (Baird's arrest followed a public speech he made on contraception during which he gave a device to an unmarried girl as part of the presentation.) The Ohio Supreme Court decided in 1965 that these "contributing" statutes did not apply to the mother of a 16-year-old girl who was arrested for instructing her daughter in the use of contraceptives (*Ohio vs McLaughlin,* 212 NE 2d 635). The conviction was reversed on the grounds

248

that it violated the mother's freedom of speech. This appears to be the only case in which any attempt was made to bring criminal charges against anyone for giving contraceptive advice to minors.

While some physicians may feel personally that giving contraceptives to teenagers is "condoning immorality," it seems highly unlikely that prosecution would ever occur. Refusing a request for birth control is much more likely to result in pregnancy than deterring sexual activity. As the ABA report put it:

> In view of the impulsiveness of adolescence as well as the lack of foresight and trust to luck against pregnancy observed among sexually mature teenagers, the availability of birth control cannot be thought the determinant of whether or not they engage in sex relations. The development of a youthful standard of sexual morality is a matter for the home, the church and the community; it cannot be maintained through ignorance of the availability of birth control.

Presumably the teenager who requests contraceptives is already sexually active. Any physician who feels that, in his professional judgment, a pregnancy would cause physical or emotional harm to the minor, would undoubtedly have an adequate defense to any criminal charge. It should be reiterated, however, that it is unlikely that a criminal charge would arise.

Civil Liability

The historical common law rule was that a minor could not be treated on his or her own say-so except in an emergency. The doctrine of "emancipation" however, has meant that married minors or those living away from home and self-supporting did not need parental consent. Furthermore, the doctrine is now developing that a "mature minor" who is not legally emancipated, but who "understands and appreciates the consequences of the treatment" is also able to consent. No cases can be located in which a physician has been found liable to the parent for treating a minor of 14 years or over where the minor gave his consent.

In regard to contraception, it should be noted that the ABA report among other sources indicates that some college health services are providing contraceptives to women students whether or not they have passed their 21st birthday. The number has undoubtedly increased in the three years since that report.

It should be noted that a minor who has borne an illegitimate child has the legal authority to surrender it for adoption (*In re Brock*, 25 So 2d 659, Fla 1946; *Petition of Gonzales*, 46 NW 2d 453, Mich 1951; *Matter of Presler*, 171 Misc 559, NY 1939). It should also be noted that she can consent to an abortion in New York under the new abortion statute. The Health and Hospitals Corporation, which takes care of New York City municipal hospitals, has stated that they will perform abortions on minors without parental consent if the patient is "married, emancipated, or at least 17 years old (or) . . . if in the opinion of the attending physician the seeking of parental consent would endanger the physical or mental health of the patient." This being the case, it would appear unlikely that a physician could be found liable if he enables the girl to avoid the alternatives of adoption or abortion, to both of which she can consent. However, there are no cases in which the matter has ever been adjudicated.

As the excellent and exhaustive study of Harriet F. Pilpel and Nancy F. Wechsler on "Birth Control, Teenagers and the Law" (*Family Planning Perspect* 1:29, 1969 puts it:

> On the basis of the recent developments in the law, it would seem, then, that there are many tenable rationales available to a physician who, after

weighing all the circumstances, responsibly prescribes contraception for the sexually active minor. Certainly, the trend seems to be in favor of his doing what his professional obligation requires.

The authors of that article do suggest, however, that when dealing with a minor, the following practices be observed: (1) Inquiry should always be made as to the feasibility of parental consent. (2) Full case histories should be obtained and maintained. The physician should then consider the total situation of the patient. (3) A record should be kept of "emergency" need and the judgment of the physician that pregnancy would constitute a serious health hazard —one more serious than the possible disadvantage of the prescription. (4) The minor should be clearly aware of the problems presented and the nature and consequences of the procedure suggested. She should be required to sign a consent form so indicating. (5) Where follow-up care is indicated, it should be insisted upon. These precautions will undoubtedly minimize the possible adverse legal consequences of minors. The physician will, of course, have the same risks of liability for negligence that he would have in advising or caring for adult patients in relation to birth control.

Conclusion

Many physicians undoubtedly do not want to give contraceptives to their unmarried minor patients. Their objections may be medical or ethical, or they may just feel that it is "not the best thing to do." This view should most certainly be accorded the utmost respect and there should never be the slightest suggestion made that they are obliged to do so or are remiss in any way if they do not. However, if the reluctance is based solely on a fear that either civil or criminal liability is likely to ensue, the possibility would appear to be remote. The courts in this as in all other aspects of the law involving physicians respect the use of his best professional judgment. Good faith use of that judgment for the best interest of his patient in giving contraceptive advice or in any other sort of medical treatment will avoid legal problems. The problems for a child raised by a mother who is too immature to care for him properly, of a girl who is caught in a cycle of repeated pregnancies, and of a society which suffers from an appalling number of both must be solved in some way. Sociologically, these cases are usually "disaster areas." When the alternatives are contraception, abortion, adoption, or a grim life for the mother and child, the legal problem of the minor's right to consent can be seen in its true perspective. —*ANGELA RODDEY HOLDER, JD*

Reprinted from the Journal of the American Medical Association, June 21, 1971, Vol. 216, Copyright 1971, American Medical Association.

LAW AND MEDICINE

Treating a Minor for Venereal Disease

The startling increase in the number of cases of venereal disease (VD) in this country in recent years presents a particular legal problem for the physician, occasioned by the fact that a very large number of these patients are minors. May the physician treat them without parental consent if they refuse to tell their parents that treatment is necessary? What liability, if any, might the physician encounter?

At common law, it technically constituted assault and battery for a physician to treat a minor patient without parental consent. This rule applied without regard to whether the minor was 2 years old or 18 (eg, *Bonner vs Moran,* 126 F 2d 121, DC, 1941; *Zaman vs Schultz,* 19 Pa D &C 309, 1933). In general, unless abrogated by statute, this is probably still the rule. However, exceptions to this doctrine have always been recognized and the requirement of parental consent was dispensed with in certain cases.

Emergencies

Nowhere is a physician liable for treating a child or a youth in an emergency without the consent of his parents (eg, *Luka vs Lowrie,* 136 NW 1106, Mich 1912; *Sullivan vs Montgomery,* 279 NYS 575, NY 1935). Although this rule has usually been applied to victims of accidents and the like, it is at least strongly arguable that the patient with VD constitutes a medical emergency. This view may be based not only on the consequences of nontreatment to the patient himself but on the likelihood that the untreated infection will spread to others. Apparently with this view in mind, the following statement appeared in the *AMA News* of April 17, 1967, p 4:

> The inability to obtain parental consent to treat a minor for venereal disease should not cause a physician to withhold treatment if, in his professional judgment, treatment is immediately required.
>
> This applies even though such action might appear to make the physician liable to a technical charge of assault and battery.
>
> It is, of course, better if the physician can persuade the minor to inform his parents and thereby provide the necessary consent. But where this is impossible and it appears that without the physician's promise of confidentiality the youth will probably delay seeking treatment, the youth's health is paramount to any other consideration.

Thus it would appear that a physician is entirely justified in applying the doctrine of emergency treatment to this situation and considering a minor with venereal disease to be as much of an urgent case as one who had been involved in an automobile accident.

Emancipation

The common law has for many years recognized the doctrine of "emancipation." This means that the parent has surrendered his parental duties and responsibilities and all his rights to custody of the minor. A married minor is considered emancipated by law and may consent to medical treatment (eg, *Bach vs Long Island Jewish Hospital,* 267 NYS 2d 289, 1966). Other situations in which a minor is considered emancipated and thus capable of independent consent include service in the military (*Swenson vs Swenson,* 227 SW 2d 103, Mo 1950) or where he is otherwise self-supporting. In any case, an emancipated minor has the full legal right to consent to medical treatment without consulting his parents (eg, *Smith vs Seibly,* 431 P 2d 719, Wash 1967).

Quite a few states have enacted special legislation specifically permitting an emancipated minor to consent to medical or surgical treatment. Mississippi's very comprehensive statute, in fact, not only gives this right to married or emancipated minors but to unemancipated minors of "sufficient intelligence to understand and appreciate the consequences of the proposed treatment" (Miss Code Ann § 7129-81 et seq). Other states with such legislation include Arizona (Rev Stat § 44-132, 44-133), California (Civ Code Ann § 34.5), Indiana (Inc Stat Ann § 35-4407), Nevada (Rev Stat § 129.030), New Mexico (Stat Ann § 12-12-1, et seq), and there was a very recent enactment in Pennsylvania. It is also clear that the common law observes this doctrine in the absence of special legislation. Where these factual circumstances are applicable, the physician should have no reluctance to treat his patient for any disease, including VD.

The Mature Minor

It appears that a concept is developing that a "mature minor," although not emancipated in the strict legal sense, also has the right to consent to medical treatment by himself. For example in *The Law of Medical Practice* by Shartel and Plant (Springfield, Ill, Charles C Thomas Publisher, 1959) at section 1-10 (p 26) the authors conclude:

> Parental consent should only be omitted (a) if the patient is of the age of discretion (15-20), (b) if the medical measures are taken for the patient's own benefit, (c) if the measures can be justified as necessary by conservative medical opinion, and (d) if there is some good reason why parental consent cannot be obtained.

All of these factors would appear to be present when the patient's illness is venereal disease. There have been several decisions in which this concept has been accepted in situations involving nonemergency surgery or other medical procedures. For example, in *Gulf and Ship Island Railway vs Sullivan* (119 So, Miss 1928), it was held that a 17-year-old boy could consent to being vaccinated without consulting his parents, since he was "of sufficient intelligence to understand and appreciate the consequences." In *Lacey vs Laird* (139 NE 2d 25, Ohio 1956) the same rule was applied to cosmetic surgery on an 18-year-old girl's nose. This rule has applied in Michigan since the 1906 decision of *Bakker vs Welsh* (108 NW 94) and the 1921 decision of *Bishop vs Shurly* (211 NW 75).

It should be noted also that a careful search has located *no* decisions at all in which any physician has been held liable for treating a minor of 14 years or older without parental consent when the minor has himself consented.

Special Statutes

As a result of the dilemma posed by this very question, numerous states have enacted special statutes permitting a minor to consent to the treatment of VD by himself. New York and Pennsylvania have, for example, done so quite recently. A full list of these statutes, their provisions and citations as well as statutes providing for the minor's right to consent to treatment in general and statutes dealing with contraception for minors appears in the excellent and comprehensive article "Birth Control, Teenagers and the Law" (which also discusses the question of venereal disease) by Pilpel and Wechsler in *Family Planning Perspectives* (1:29, 1969). According to the authors of that study, the following states specifically allow minors to consent to treatment of VD without parental consent: California (1968 Reg Sess Ch 417), Colorado (Rev Stat 66-9-2), Connecticut (Gen Stat Ann 19-89a), Maryland (Code Ann § 149D), Massachusetts (Gen Laws Ann § 117), Nebraska (Rev Stat § 71-1119, 71-1120), New Jersey (Stat Ann 9:17-A-5), and Rhode Island (Gen Laws § 23-11-11). The list of states which are enacting these laws will undoubtedly increase quite rapidly in the near future.

Conclusion

The question of the minor's rights and responsibilities in regard to the treatment of VD is an extremely fast-moving area of the law. The massive proportions of the problem of the increase in the rate of infection in our society has presented new questions in terms of the physician's liability. To date,there are no cases which specifically confront the problem directly and so there are no absolute guidelines which apply to states other than those which have adopted statutes. It appears, however, that the likelihood of litigation in this situation is extremely remote. The physician who does treat a minor with venereal disease without parental consent probably runs less risk of a suit brought by the parents in this situation than a great many other risks of suit which he accepts as an inevitable part of the practice of medicine. Among other things, if the parents discover that treatment has been undertaken without their consent, it is quite likely that due to the nature of the illness they would be most reluctant to publicize the child's disease to the extent necessary to bring the action. Therefore, even if no special statute exists in the state where the physician practices, it is highly unlikely that his good faith attempts to help his patient will result in legal difficulties for him.

Furthermore, the physician has a professional responsibility in this situation which is undeniable. The tragic consequences of untreated venereal disease are so enormous, both to the patient himself and to society in general, that common sense would require the physician to take the view that "something has to be done." As the statement in the AMA News pointed out, of course it is infinitely preferable that the parents be informed. Wise counseling of the young person may lead him to agree that perhaps "they will understand" after all, but if he refuses, the physician should remember that the medical welfare of the patient should be his first consideration. While a wise lawyer no more guarantees to his client that no legal difficulty will ever arise in a given situation than a wise physician promises a patient that he will cure even a minor disease, it does appear that the calculated risk in this situation is very small.
—ANGELA RODDEY HOLDER, JD

LAW AND MEDICINE

The Illegitimate and His Father

The father of an illegitimate child may legally acknowledge his paternity in a variety of different ways. In many jurisdictions, illegitimate children may be legitimatized under statutory provisions for acknowledgment by the father. Some states require the father's acknowledgment to be in writing while others permit recognition by public conduct. Earlier decisions normally involved suits brought by the child or his mother against the father's estate in order for the child to inherit as if he had been born in wedlock. Others involved suits for support by a mother against a living father who denied paternity but who was alleged to have satisfied the requirements of the acknowledgment at some prior time, hence rendering him legally liable for his economic responsibilities. Only in the past few years, apparently, have men who have fathered illegitimate children begun to bring legal actions in opposition to the children's mothers to seek custody or control of the children.

Paternity Suits

Only one case can be located in which a father sued to have himself declared as such under the statute in New York which allows a parent (meaning mothers, here-to-fore) to seek a decree of filiation. In Crane vs Battle (307

NYS 2d 355, 1970), the mother was married, but had been geographically separated from her husband for seven years. The child's actual father sued for a declaration of paternity and the court held that although the statute in question was designed to provide a mother with the means of obtaining support from the father of her child, to deny the father the same right would be to deny him equal protection of the laws as required by the 14th Amendment to the US Constitution. Obviously, fathers of illegitimate children are not going to besiege the courts in great numbers to bring these actions, but where they do arise, the same principle will doubtless apply in other jurisdictions.

Custody

Another increasingly frequent legal situation arises when the father of an illegitimate child seeks custody. Since almost all courts apply the rule that the best interest of the child is the sole consideration, more and more jurisdictions are allowing fathers to have custody (eg, *Guardianship of Leland Smith*, 265 P 2d 888, 37 ALR 2d 867, Cal 1954). Most states now agree that the father of an illegitimate child does have standing to sue for custody (eg, *Dellinger vs Bollinger*, 89 SE 2d 592, NC 1955; *Torres vs Gonzales*, 450 P 2d 921, NM 1969).

The general rule appears to be that the mother has a higher right to custody of an illegitimate child than the father does, but that the father has a right superior to all other persons. For example, in *Cornell vs Hartley* (283 NYS 2d 318, NY 1967), the child lived with his father for some time but the father agreed to let him return to his mother. When the father later tried to regain custody, the court held that the mother had a prior right to the child, but awarded liberal visitation rights to the father.

Of course, it should always be remembered that any court has the power to place a child where the child will receive the best environment possible; therefore, no rigid rules can be made.

For example, in *Dellinger vs Bollinger* a father was allowed to bring an action to remove the child from its mother when he charged that the mother's neglect of the child rendered her unfit. On the other hand, in *State ex rel Smith vs Superior Court* (161 P 2d 188, Wash 1945), the children were awarded, after their mother's death, to the maternal aunt and uncle in opposition to the father, whom the court declared to be "cruel and depraved." Therefore, the essential criteria of any child custody action's determination will be the child's best interests regardless of any theoretical abstract legal principles.

Visitation Rights

In general, courts ruling on applications for visitation rights by putative fathers allowed the privilege unless it can be demonstrated that it would be detrimental to the child (eg, *Ex parte Hendrix*, 100 P 2d 444, Okla 1944; *People ex rel Francois vs Ivanova*, 221 NYS 2d 75, 1961; *Baker vs Baker*, 85 Atl 816, NJ 1913). As the court said in *Mixon vs Mize* (198 So 2d 373, Fla 1967):

> The weight of authority in this country appears to be that where a putative father acknowledges his relationship to an illegitimate child, manifests a genuine interest in the child's welfare and provides it with support, such a father should be granted the right to visit the child at reasonable times unless such visits are shown to be detrimental to the child's welfare.

Again, however, the best interest of the child is the governing criterion, in spite of the fact of illegitimacy or the preferences of the parents. Courts do recognize that these children are more in need of emotional support than other children (*Commonwealth vs Rozanski,* 213 A 2d 155, Pa 1965).

A few cases have held that the father may have visitation rights even though he does not support the child (*Bagwell vs Powell,* 99 So 2d 195, Ala 1957). However, most courts appear to feel that except in case of acute financial need, a father who makes no effort to support his child, legitimate or otherwise, under most circumstances is not evidencing much interest in the child's welfare.

Generally speaking, then, the father of an illegitimate child has visitation rights if he is interested in the child, since forbidding this contract will deprive the child of love (*Anonymous vs Anonymous,* 289 NYS 2d 792, NY 1968). Courts can always change visitation or custody orders if the relationship has an adverse effect on the child.

It should be noted, however, that Illinois courts have held that the father has no legal right to visit his illegitimate child (*DePhillips vs DePhillips,* 219 NE 2d 465, Ill 1965; *Wallace vs Wallace,* 210 NE 2d 4, Ill 1965).

An interesting recent Pennsylvania decision held that a father does not have to submit to a blood test in order to visit a child he claims as his. The mother of the child had been married at the time the child was born to the man who asked for visitation rights. She claimed, however, that the child was really that of her second husband. The first husband claimed that the child was a legitimate issue of his marriage but refused to submit to a blood test. The lower court held that the refusal voided his rights to ask for visitation, but this ruling was reversed on appeal. The appellate court's decision reiterated the rule that fathers may not be deprived of the right to visit their children unless such visits would be detrimental to the best interests of their child. This is the sole criterion unless the mother in this case could provide evidence that the man was not the father (*Pennsylvania ex rel Meta vs Cinello,* 268 A 2d 135, 1970).

Conclusion

Courts are aware that illegitimate children inevitably suffer hardships, psychological and otherwise, which do not beset other children, even those of divorced parents. The "best interest" rule always applies to custody or visitation of any child, but courts are especially aware of the special needs of the illegitimate child. He has, in the view of most judges, enough troubles already without depriving him of contact with some male figure. Of course, in the hypothetical case where the mother has remarried and the current husband is in the house with the child and fulfilling the father role, the child is not in as great need of attention from his actual father as would otherwise be the case. In that situation, however, courts still seem to award the natural father the right to see the child. No decision could be found which discussed the possible outcome of an application for visitation where the mother, now married to another man, has never told the child that he is not her current husband's child. In actual practice, this occurs more often than one might imagine. While it is doubtless unwise as it is also a mistake not to tell a child he is adopted, the reasons for doing it are perfectly obvious and easy to understand. Given that set of facts, where a happy child is growing up attached to a man whom he believes to be his "Daddy," a court would probably not be as eager to interject a second male onto the scene. No actual instance where this has happened can be located. In conflicts between children's interests and the interests of the adults involved, however, it is clear that the child's will prevail in every jurisdiction in the country.

Physicians are, of course, constantly consulted about family problems, either directly because the patient does not know where else to turn or because this kind of conflict provides a setting for the development of physical ills. In this instance, of course, the wise physician will send the patient to a lawyer for legal advice and not attempt to help with the problem himself other than providing emotional support and understanding for his patient. However, when these situations occur, the physician ought to have some basic knowledge of the probabilities and alternatives which are likely to occur so that he will not inadvertently get his patient's hopes up or dash them to pieces by a chance remark or a well-meant but injudicious statement.

—ANGELA RODDEY HOLDER, JD

Reprinted from The Journal of the American Medical Association, June 14, 1971, Vol. 216, Copyright 1971, American Medical Association.

LAW AND MEDICINE
The Sexual Psychopath

There is no branch of law which medicine, particularly psychiatry, serves so importantly as the criminal law. This is because of the immediate interest which society has, and the direct part it plays, in a criminal prosecution. The principal areas of the criminal law which are dependent upon medical science are legal insanity, criminal mental incompetency, and sexual psychopathy. It is the last-named subject which this communication will treat.

The "Typical" Sexual Psychopath Law

A sexual psychopath law is not a typical type of statute as it does not exist in most states. But in the states having such a law it typically provides that a person charged with a sex offense may be psychiatrically examined by at least two court-appointed psychiatrists, a report as to the examination be prepared and submitted to the court, a hearing be held to determine whether such person is a sexual psychopath, a finding be made pursuant to such hearing, and dispositioned accordingly, with a finding of sexual psychopathy resulting in an automatic and immediate commitment to the state department of mental health.

Sex Offenses

Typical sex offenses are rape, deviate sexual assault, indecent liberties with a child, contributing to the sexual delinquency of a child, indecent solicitation of a child, adultery, fornication, public indecency, aggravated incest, incest, bigamy, marrying a bigamist, prostitution, soliciting for a prostitute, pandering, keeping a place of prostitution, patronizing a prostitute, pimping, and obscenity. Any of these offenses against children, plus deviate sexual assault, public indecency, aggravated incest, and incest manifest a pathological bent.

Excluding rape, due to its extreme seriousness and consequent life or even death maximum punishment, the average minimum and maximum for first convictions of the other eighteen named offenses, in Illinois, for example, are one year or less and five years, respectively.

256

The Report

According to Henry A. Davidson, MD:

> Five psychiatric syndromes embrace the great majority of sex offenders. These are: (1) mental defectives, (2) psychotics, (3) psychoneurotics, (4) alcoholics, and (5) psychopaths. If the psychiatrist finds the existence of any one of these, the report first highlights this basic psychiatric category (Davidson, H.A.: *Forensic Psychiatry,* New York: The Ronald Press Co., ed 2, 1965).

The Examination

The psychiatric examination customarily is required to be conducted by at least two psychiatrists appointed by the court. Illinois, for example, requires that the examination be made by two psychiatrists who are licensed in Illinois and who have practiced their specialty for not less than five years (Illinois Revised Statutes 1966, chapter 38, sections 105-4 and 105-4.01).

The Trial and Its Aftermath

At the trial the public prosecutor and the defense counsel may introduce their own expert medical witnesses. Depending on the resources of the respondent (the person alleged to be a criminal sexual psychopath), there may be a so-called battle of the experts by a so-called small army of experts, the number permitted being discretionary with the court, with an implied maximum of 25 for each side in Illinois, for example. The weight of the expert testimony adduced, rather than the number of experts produced by each side, is the legally recognized criterion.

In Illinois, for example, once a petition and a report by two qualified psychiatrists of at least five years' standing are filed, the trial will be held. A jury will be impaneled only if the respondent asks for it. At the trial, evidence of all prior crimes of whatever nature committed by the respondent is admissible. The trial is a civil proceeding subject to civil rules of evidence.

If the respondent is found to be a sexually dangerous person, the court shall appoint the Director of Public Safety as his guardian. The Department of Mental Health must examine the patient if requested to do so by the Department of Public Safety. The Director of Public Safety may place the patient in the Psychiatric Division of the Illinois State Penitentiary at Menard, Ill, or, with the consent of its Director, in the care and treatment of the Department of Mental Health.

The application alleging that the patient has fully recovered may be filed by any party in interest but only in the committing court. The disposition of the application may result in continued detention, conditional release (if the court finds it impossible to determine with certainty under conditions of institutional care that the patient has fully recovered) or absolute discharge. A patient conditionally released might be described as a "parolee-outpatient." With the view of obtaining the absolute discharge of a conditionally released patient, the application alleging full recovery may be filed by any interested party in the committing court. If any of the terms prescribed as to conditional release are violated by the patient, the court must revoke such conditional release and recommit the patient, and no hearing as to such revocation is required. An absolute discharge effects the quashing of every outstanding information and indictment, the basis of which was the reason for the detention.

A second type of petition, which may allege only partial recovery, may be filed in the committing court only by the Director of Public Safety, and its disposition may result in only continued detention or conditional release, with the same provision governing as to the effect of a violation of the terms prescribed for such conditional releases. While a patient is out on conditional release as a result of such action, any interested party, including the Director of Public Safety, may file a recovery application.

Value of the Legislation

The principal value of this type of legislation lies in regarding the sexual psychopath as a mentally ill person instead of a criminal and in prescribing treatment rather than punishment. As Jerome D. Frank, MD, observes, "... sexual deviates are clearly sick in the sense that they are caught up in behavior patterns they cannot control" (Frank, J.D.: *Persuasion and Healing —A Comparative Study of Psychotherapy,* Baltimore: Johns Hopkins Press, 1961, p 9).

And Winfred Overholser, MD, points out:

> Many of the persistent sexual offenders, notably those who engage in so-called paraphilic ("perverted") practices such as homosexuality or exhibitionism or who make sexual advances to young children of either sex, are mentally abnormal, the bulk of them probably suffering from a neurotic fixation. Furthermore, a measurable share of them are amenable to treatment.... The significant feature pointing toward the future is the fact that here is a recognition by the law that there are persons who stand between the shade of "insanity" and the sunlight of sanity, that there is a middle ground which calls for special handling and for an indeterminate period of segregation, during which treatment can be attempted, or who, treatment failing, may be continued in confinement (Overholser, W.: *The Psychiatrist and the Law,* New York: Harcourt, Brace & World, Inc., 1953, pp 49, 50).

Criticism of the Legislation

Two of the primary arguments advanced and accepted for the passage of sexual psychopath laws are that sex offenders have an unusually high rate of recidivism and that the sex criminal usually first commits a relatively minor offense such as public indecency and goes on eventually to commit an extremely serious offense such as rape. This is simply not borne out by the facts. Manfred S. Guttmacher, MD, notes:

> Most people have a mistaken concept of recidivism in sex offenses. . . . In the table on recidivism in the Uniform Crime Reports, rape was twenty-fourth and "other sex offenses" twenty-fifth in order of recidivism among the 26 offenses listed . . . our investigations, as well as others, indicate first, that there is a low degree of recidivism among sexual offenders, and second, that there is no basis for the common belief that sex criminals engage in sexual crime of progressive malignancy (Guttmacher, M.S., *Sex Offenses —The Problem, Causes and Prevention,* New York: W. W. Norton & Co., Inc., 1951, pp 113, 114).

Another fallacy lies in the bland and naive assumption that because treatment is prescribed, rather than punishment imposed, for the adjudicated sexual psychopath, that such person will actually be the recipient of effective and beneficial treatment. Frank T. Lindman and Donald M. McIntyre, Jr., in their splendid *The Mentally Disabled and the Law,* interject the following much-needed note of realism:

> Serious questions have been raised about the ability of medical science to cure or substantially improve the vast majority of sexual psychopaths. . . .

Quite often the only treatment recommended is institutional care. . . . The lack of treatment is a basic condemnation of the sex deviate laws, since the philosophy behind such legislation is that these offenders should be treated rather than punished. Lack of treatment destroys any otherwise valid reason for differential consideration of the sexual psychopath. It would appear that the law is looking to medical knowledge for solutions to problems in this area only to find that such knowledge is as yet nonexistent or imprecise (Lindman, F.T., and McIntyre, D. M., Jr.: *The Mentally Disabled and the Law,* Chicago: American Bar Foundation, 1961, pp 307, 308).

And, according to Dr. Guttmacher and Henry Weihofen:

A criticism that can be leveled against all sexual psychopath laws is that they are based on a fallacious premise in assuming that sex offenders are a distinct type, more recidivistic than other criminals, and that they can be treated by special techniques. Actually recidivism among sex offenders varies widely . . . and the available statistics give little support to the idea that as a group they are more recidivistic than other criminals. The causes of their behavior are likely to be similar to those motivating non-sexual criminality (Guttmacher, M. S., and Weihofen, H.: *Psychiatry and the Law,* New York: W. W. Norton & Co., Inc., 1952, p. 132). — *HOWARD N. MORSE*

Reprinted from The Journal of the American Medical Association, April 24, 1967, Vol. 200, Adv. pp. 57 and 58, Copyright 1967, by American Medical Association.

LAW AND MEDICINE
Changing Sex on Birth Certificates

Society and the law recognize only two sexes. Physicians assign a sex at birth from the appearance of the external genitalia, which usually is the sex in which the individual is reared.

At the present time with improved understanding of transsexualism, many lawyers continue to assume that at least the terms "male" and "female" are changeless and may be accepted without further definition or investigation. In fact the legal dictionaries take this attitude and supply little additional information. Furthermore, many of the states seem to show little interest in the subject of intersex. The statutes of several provide that words importing the masculine gender shall include females. However, at least eight criteria may be employed in determining sex: chromosomal sex, gonadal sex, hormone pattern, internal sex organs, external genitalia, habitus, sex of rearing, and gender role and orientation. Thus it is reasonable to understand that errors of judgment and diagnosis may occur. A patient designated as a male at birth because of external genitalia, at age 5, was shown to be endowed with ovaries, tubes and a uterus. The criteria of sex in this instance were five for male and three for female identification. Another patient raised as a male had five female criteria, two male criteria, and one ambiguous. Another, a female, had four criteria for female, one not determined, and two male criteria. Although the physician had stated male at birth, the mother disagreed and raised the patient as a female.

Medicolegal problems arise because of these circumstances in connection with (1) domestic and matrimonial law, (2) criminal law, (3) law of wills and inheritance, and (4) problems of vital statistics.

1. A female was born with certain male organs. These were removed when she was 19 years old and an artificial vagina was constructed. Her husband

knew these facts prior to marriage. Could his suit for divorce be granted on the ground that there could be no proper consummation of the marriage under these circumstances?

2. Could such a wife be a party to an adulterous relationship or could one who sexually assaulted her argue that she was not really a female?

3. An individual raised as a female later became quite masculine, took a male name and lived as a male thereafter. Her father's will left $5,000 to his eldest daughter. Assuming there were other "real" girls born later, would the money go to the intersex person or to the oldest of the "real" girls?

4. Can a vital statistic birth record be changed if an original assignment of sex is later found to be wrong? More particularly, what if the change in apparent sex is the result of convertive surgery?

Transsexualism

Transsexualism has been defined as a striking disturbance of gender role and gender orientation —a disorder of the harmony and uniformity of the psychosexual personality —a split between the psychological and the morphological sex. Transsexuals differ among themselves as much as normal persons do among themselves, and the extent of social rejection of a transsexual is in direct ratio to the degree of affliction.

Convertive Surgery

At present, ten states have permitted a change of sex on the birth certificate of a transsexual who has undergone convertive surgery (Alabama, California, Hawaii, Illinois, Maryland, New Jersey, North Carolina, Pennsylvania, Tennessee, and Virginia). New York has held differently. In *Anonymous vs Weiner* (270 NYS 2d 319, New York, 1966), the question was whether the state judiciary would compel the municipal executive to change the sex on the birth certificate of a transsexual upon whom convertive surgery had been performed.

The petitioner instituted a proceeding, in the nature of a mandamus, for an order directing the appropriate official of the municipal executive department to change the sex on the petitioner's birth certificate from male to female, to change the given name thereon to one assumed by the petitioner subsequent to birth, and to issue a new certificate. The petitioner had undergone convertive surgery and assumed the name and role of a female in society. The petitioner's request was submitted to the Director of the Bureau of Records and Statistics but was held in abeyance pending the consideration and determination by the Board of Health of the general subject of change of birth certificates of transsexuals.

The Board of Health, in recognition of the serious consequences attendant upon a decision, initiated an exhaustive inquiry into the subject and called upon the New York Academy of Medicine to study the problem and to submit its recommendations to the board. This recognition of the need for full exploration of the problem reflected the board's awareness of its obligation to society to insure the accuracy of public records. It also indicated its deep concern for the individual, the transsexual.

The New York Academy, through its Committee on Public Health issued a report entitled "Change of Sex on Birth Certificates for Transsexuals." The report stated:

Because of the complexity of the subject which cuts across biology and medicine and projects into the domain of law, the Committee called on a group of specialists in several fields to study the problem. This group included gynecologists, endocrinologists, cytogeneticists, psychiatrists and a lawyer.

After a detailed analysis of the many facts and ramifications of the change of sex on birth certificates the committee report concluded:

1. Male-to-female transsexuals are still chromosomal males while ostensibly females.
2. It is questionable whether laws and records such as the birth certificate should be changed and thereby used as a means to help psychologically ill persons in their social adaptation.
3. The committee is therefore opposed to a change of sex on birth certificates in transsexualism.
4. The desire of concealment of a change of sex by the transsexual is outweighed by the public interest for protection against fraud.

On Oct. 13, 1965, the Board of Health passed the following resolution:

Resolved, that in view of all the evidence considered, including the report of the Committee on Public Health of the New York Academy of Medicine, it is the sense of the Board of Health that the Health Code not be amended to provide for a change of sex on birth certificates in cases of transsexuals.

At the same meeting, the Board of Health, by unanimous vote, decided to:

go on record as generally favoring the recommendations of the Committee on Public Health of the Academy of Medicine, and, in effect, stating that an individual born once one sex cannot be changed for reasons proposed by the request which was made to us. Sex can be changed where there is an error, of course, but not when there is a later attempt to change the psychological orientation of the patient and including . . . surgery.

The Board of Health therefore denied the petitioner's request for the amendment or issuance of a new certificate.

On appeal, the New York Supreme Court stated that the issue before it was whether or not the Board of Health had acted arbitrarily in deciding that the petitioner did not establish that the evidence submitted showed the true facts and in deciding that an error was made at the time of preparing and filing of the certificate and, accordingly, in denying the application for amendment and issuance of a new certificate.

It found that the petitioner did not establish that the evidence submitted showed that an error had been made at the time of preparing and filing the original certificate. The board did not act arbitrarily in refusing to change what was not error. The court also said it was not at liberty to substitute its views for those of the board.

"In its role as ultimate arbiter of the legality of administrative action, the judiciary may not arrogate to itself the power of a super Board of Health to weigh the wisdom of respondent's acts."

The New York Supreme Court, in conclusion, deferred to the opinion of the board members with their specialized training and skill and also denied the petitioner's request.

Conclusion

Physicians should be aware of problems of patients with ambisexual development. As early in the person's life as possible, the physician should decide the sex, based on cytological, endocrinological, and physical findings.

The law must rely strongly on medicine in assignment of sex. Cooperation between medicine and law in cases of intersexuality is necessary and important, but the law cannot accept classifications of sex that are inconsistent with the practical relationships of everyday life. On the other hand, the law must exhibit concern for all its citizens, even those who are transsexuals. In *Anonymous vs Weiner,* the Board of Health convinced itself that it was exhibiting such a concern. There might be some doubt as to the sincerity of such concern, however, when the law requires one who, for valid physical, not merely psychiatric, reasons, feels obligated to live as a female (and has undergone convertive surgery to assist her) to present a birth certificate of a male when she wants to marry or qualify for social security or other government or insurance benefits. —*HOWARD N. MORSE AND GEORGE E. HALL*

Reprint from the Journal of the American Medical Association, August 5, 1968, Vol. 205, Adv Pg 289 and 290, Copyright 1968, by American Medical Association.

ARTIFICIAL INSEMINATION

If recent literature is to be believed, physicians are more and more being asked to perform, and are performing, artificial insemination procedures. Artificial insemination may be performed using the semen of the woman's husband or the semen of a donor who is, or should be, unknown to both the woman and her husband and who, conversely, should not know either of them. If the semen of the woman's husband is used, the procedure is known as AIH (artificial insemination homologous). If the semen of some other man is used, it is known as AID (artificial insemination donor). In all probability, AIH poses few, if any, legal problems inasmuch as the child is actually the biological offspring of the husband and wife.

In *Doornbos vs Doornbos,* the trial court in a declaratory judgment proceeding said that AIH "is not contrary to public policy and good morals, and does not present any difficulty from the legal point of view." But of AID, the court said, "Heterologous Artificial Insemination * * * with or without the consent of husband, is contrary to public policy and good morals, and constitutes adultery on the part of the mother. A child so conceived is not a child born in wedlock and therefore illegitimate. As such it is the child of the mother and the father has no right or interest in said child." In a similar New York case, a child resulting from AID which had been performed with the consent of the husband was held not to be illegitimate and the husband was given the right of visitation. It was stated, as dictum, in a Canadian divorce case that artificial insemination, without the consent of the husband, is adultery on the part of the wife. In two recent cases, the courts ordered the divorced husband to support the children who were the products of artificial insemination. In *People vs Sorensen,* the court held that, since the husband consented to the procedure, he must support the child. In a New York divorce case, *Anonymous vs Anonymous,* the husband had given his written consent to the procedure. While not ruling on the legitimacy of the children, the court held that the husband's written consent to the procedure contained an implied promise to support the children. Two states have adopted statutes declaring that a child resulting from artificial insemination is legitimate. These statutes also set forth requirements under which the procedure must be performed.

As is the case with other medical procedures, the physician cannot free himself from the obligation to use due care and skill in the performance of artificial insemination. The agreement with the parties should cover the points set forth below.

(1) The wife should consent in writing to the procedure because otherwise its accomplishment would constitute an assault and battery.

(2) The written consent of the husband should be obtained because the procedure seriously affects and involves the marital relationship.

(3) The donor should consent in writing to the unrestricted use of the semen he supplies and should certify that he will make no effort to ascertain the identity of the husband and wife involved.

(4) Although the possibility of suit by her is remote, the written consent of the donor's wife to the giving of the semen may also be desirable inasmuch as her marital interests are affected.

(5) The physician should have permission to use his own best judgement in selecting the outside donor.

The law has not as yet delineated the responsibilities of the physician on the score, but it would seem that he would be obligated to use reasonable care in selecting a healthy donor who has no knowable transmissible disease.

There are certain other desirable precautions which the physician should observe. The physician should establish to his own satisfaction that, from the medical point of view, the husband is sterile.

Reprinted from Medicolegal Forms With Legal Analysis, pp. 99-100, Copyright 1973, by American Medical Association.

LAW AND MEDICINE

Infringement of Conjugal Rights

A physician who is charged with depriving a married couple of their conjugal rights or making sex less pleasurable for them need not fear that he will be forced to pay heavy damages solely because a hysterectomy or sterilization operation was followed by bad results. True, the courts wax poetic in such cases, as did the California intermediate court in *Gist vs French* (288 P2d 1003, 1955), by saying: "There is no amount of sentiment or of gold that is so effective in preserving the comfort, the tranquility, and the happiness of a man and woman united in wedlock for lifetime as does their conjugal relationship," but in all such cases the physician will be exonerated if he shows that he treated the patients with the standard of care practiced in the community or in his best judgment in the patient's interest.

In the *French* case, a 37-year-old wife secured a $70,000 judgment for malpractice, and her husband a $9,000 damage claim for loss of her services and consortium. The woman visited her physician at his clinic and complained of a pain in her right side. After a complete physical examination, he advised her that a tumor had to be removed. She returned to the clinic for the operation later that day after conferring with her husband. The physician, without the aid of an assistant surgeon, administered a spinal anesthetic, and without any preoperative tests or a biopsy, removed her uterus, cervix, and appendix. He then left town and during the ten days of her hospitalization she was seen by substitute physicians who noted that she suffered backache, nausea, insomnia, dizziness, fever, abnormal pulse rate, crackling in her ears, a drop in her red and white blood cell counts, and a drop in the hemoglobin level from 11.7 to 9.1 gm/100 cc. The woman returned to the physician's clinic, three days after her discharge, because of heavy vaginal bleeding. At this time, with an assistant surgeon, the physician removed the left tube and ovary and part of the broad ligament.

The physician was held professionally liable, primarily for failing to tie off the vaginal branch of the uterine artery in the first delicate operation, as a result of which her ovary was unnecessarily removed and her vagina shortened in the second operation.

While the physician objected strenuously to the testimony of out-of-town experts as to the standards of care he should have followed, it was held that the expert who had been educated in the same medical school that defendant had attended, was competent to testify as to the propriety of the defendant's conduct even though the witness practiced elsewhere. The court refused to define "standards of the community" narrowly to include only the area where the defendant's clinic was located, but expanded it to "an area as is governed by the same laws, and the people are unified by the same sovereignty and customs."

The court also noted that information relative to the treatment of diseases and injuries was disseminated to the medical world in "attractive journals, whereby practitioners are equipped immediately to utilize the new remedies. ... If a surgeon in a coast town does not maintain the same ethical standards as do surgeons of the ... more populous cities, it is not because the standards have not been established there, but rather because of his lack of interest in his work, or he is negligent in performance."

Failure to Adhere to One's Own Standard

Just as a physician may be held professionally liable for failure to adhere to the recognized standards of care within the community, so may he be liable for failure to pursue a different course of treatment than that which he intended but did not perform. This is illustrated in the Tennessee case of *Wooten vs Curry* (362 SW2d 820, 1961).

The patient's vagina "grew together" so that it was almost completely closed after a hysterectomy. She was sent home nine days after the operation and was instructed to return for a check-up at the end of six weeks. When she kept her check-up appointment, the physician gave her some medication for cleansing her "female" organs without physically examining her. The woman found that it was impossible for her to use the medication as directed, and with her husband and daughter in tow returned to the physician's office. At this time the physician examined the patient and allegedly told her daughter that "if he had examined her sooner he would have seen it" and told the husband that the condition could have been avoided had he checked on her "as he should."

At the close of the couple's suit, the lower court directed a verdict in favor of the physician but this judgment was reversed on the basis that the physician's statements in the absence of any explanation made a prima facie case of negligence and provided the proximate cause of injury.

The appellate court held that there was no fixed rule in the area where the physician practiced as to whether a patient should be manually examined after a hysterectomy. However, the physician's admissions to the patient's daughter and husband that her condition would probably have been different had he examined her earlier as he "should" have done, indicated that in his best judgment proper post-operative treatment would have been to manually examine her notwithstanding that this was not the prevailing standard of the community. His failure to adhere to this standard indicated that his course of treatment was not that which he intended to follow, and his own comments laid the basis for the case going back for trial before a jury on the question of professional liability.

264

Issue of Marriage Not Proof of Negligence

In 1964, the Supreme Court of Washington (*Ball vs Mudge*, 391 P2d 201) held that a couple to whom was delivered a fourth child who was normal, healthy, loved, and whom they would not consider placing for adoption, and would not sell for $50,000, had no basis upon which to appeal a jury verdict finding a physician not professionally liable in failing to successfully sterilize the husband and innocent of charges of fraud and deceit in connection with the operation.

The couple consulted the physician for a vasectomy after the wife was advised by her obstetrician that it would be unwise for her to have any more children by Caesarean section. She had had three children by Caesarean section in as many years. The vasectomy was done in November 1957, and the husband was told that he could resume sexual relations four to six weeks after the operation. A year later the wife became pregnant and the child was delivered in August 1959, without any extraordinary adverse effect upon her health.

The couple asked for damages for expenses of delivery of the fourth child, care, maintenance, and support of such child, their pain, suffering, and mental anguish, and the loss of the wife's services, society, companionship, and consortium by the husband. Contraceptives were not used by the couple.

During the trial the couple made much of the physician's failure to advise of the necessity of a postoperative test of semen to determine if the husband was producing sperm and his failure to make such a test. A urologist testified as an expert witness that there was no accepted standard in the Seattle area for mandatory postoperative testing after vasectomies.

All of the expert witnesses testified that a surgeon could not prevent recanilization, which rarely occurred, but which could not be absolutely ruled out to have happened in the husband's case. The theory of recanilization was strengthened by consideration of the husband's high fertility before the operation, and his sperm counts 1½ and 4½ years after the operation.

The couple also charged that the physician had assured them that sterility would be insured by his method of cutting and suturing rather than simply tying the cord.

Among the assignments of errors on appeal, the couple asserted that they were prejudiced by the trial court's refusal to instruct the jury that they could, on the basis of their common knowledge, determine if the physician was so grossly negligent in doing the vasectomy that they need not rely on the testimony of expert witnesses. The court upheld the refusal of the lower court to so charge the jury on the succinct ground that the required skill in the performance of a successful vasectomy and the necessity for postoperative tests did not lie within the common knowledge of laymen.

Another case involving a sterilization operation is noteworthy for it was held that there was no abuse of discretion by the lower court in denying a motion to amend a complaint against a physician in which the plaintiff sought to add three additional counts to her complaint four days before the physician was scheduled to move for judgement in his favor.

In this Florida case, *Dunn vs Campbell* (166 So2d 217, 1964), the husband died after a sterilization operation done in the physician's office. Bleeding in the scrotum with consequent hematoma and infection resulted in his death. The wife filed a wrongful-death action in a single-count complaint, and the physician answered denying professional liability and asserting among his defenses the assumption of risk by the parties.

The physician in his defense brought out that the parties were advised of the advantages of hospital surgery in that bleeding could be controlled but that office surgery was elected instead, and that both parties signed requisite consent forms to the operation. The court held that as upon trial the wife could present all of her evidence, the proceedings need not be delayed by amendment of the complaint.

Conclusions

A woman whose sexual capacities are impaired following surgery is acutely aware that her condition may not be corrected even if she were willing to submit to further operations. If she and her husband decide to sue the physician whom they hold responsible for their embarrassment, their demand for damages is apt to be high since their emotional need for the restoration of conjugal happiness is great enough for them to bare in court delicate details of their married life. If the husband discovers that his operation for sterilization was unsuccessful, the couple is unaware that other means of contraception may be practiced by them in the future, and they are less likely to sue. In either case, if the suit goes to actual trial, the physician may be assured of dramatics in the courtroom. —*NICK G. ONYCHUK*

Reprint from the Journal of the American Medical Association, May 16, 1966, Vol. 196, Adv. pp. 237 and 238, Copyright 1966, American Medical Association.

STERILIZATION

Statutes in twenty-eight states provide for the eugenic sterilization of various classes of persons such as the feeble-minded, the mentally ill, sexual deviates, and habitual criminals. Such statutes have been declared to be a constitutionally valid exercise of the police power of the state. In these states the physician authorized to perform the operation incurs no personal liability if the operation is performed in accordance with a valid law and without negligence. This holds true even over the objection of the person upon whom he operates.

In Connecticut and Utah it is a crime, by statute to sterilize any person without therapeutic or eugenical justification. The statutes in these states do not distinguish between a therapeutic sterilization to preserve the life or health of a woman whose life would be endangered by pregnancy, and sterilization that is the incidental result of medical or surgical treatment for a diseased condition. However, it is clear that sterilization solely for reasons of convenience constitutes a crime in these states. Statutes in Georgia, North Carolina, Oregon, and Virginia authorize sterilization for convenience.

From the standpoint of the religious and moral beliefs of many people, sterilization of convenience is comparable to non-therapeutic abortion. However, until declared illegal by the legislature or the courts in the physician's state, non-therapeutic sterilization is largely a matter of individual conscience and principle.

With regard to civil damages, sterilization has not presented any greater exposure to liability than other medical and surgical procedures alleged to have been negligently performed. In an early California case, *Corman vs Anderson,* subsequent to the performance of a vasectomy upon the plaintiff, the plaintiff's wife became pregnant and he became the father of a child. The plaintiff sued the defendant physician for malpractice and breach of contract. The operation was performed solely for the convenience of the couple who wanted no more children. Finding neither negligence nor breach of contract, the court held for the defendant doctor. Neither party challenged the legality of non-therapeutic sterilization. But Judge Samuel R. Blake said:

Admittedly there is no statutory prohibition in California against sterilization as such, with consent, and it is legally recognized, although there are other states in which this particular operation is regulated. California recognizes sterilization in mental defectives and mentally deficient persons under the Health and Welfare Code as well as in the Penal Code for certain crimes under Section 645. In other words, it is not like an operation which is prohibited and unlawful, and there is no judicial or legislative announcement of public policy against sterilization as such, with the consent of the husband and wife, although in some states of the Union there is a prohibition against such an operation except where it is medically required.

In a Pennsylvania case, *Shaheen vs Knight,* a father contracted with a physician for a vasectomy because he believed it to be necessary to limit the size of his family for economic reasons. Seventeen months after the operation, the plaintiff's wife gave birth to another child, whereupon the plaintiff brought suit for breach of contract, seeking damages for the expense of rearing and educating the child. The plantiff alleged a special contract in which the physician agreed to make the plaintiff permanently sterile and guaranteed the results. The court said:

> We are of the opinion that a contract to sterilize a man is not void as against public policy and public morals. . . . It is only when a given policy is so obviously for or against the public health, safety, morals or welfare that there is a virtual unanimity of opinion in regard to it, that a court may constitute itself the voice of the community in declaring such policy void. . . .
>
> It is the faith of some that sterilization is morally wrong whether to keep wife from having children or for any other reason. Many people have no moral compunctions against sterilization. Others are against sterilization, except when a man's life is in danger, when a person is low mentally, when a person is an habitual criminal. There is no virtual unanimity of opinion regarding sterilization. . . .
>
> However, on the issue of damages, the court was of the opinion that to allow damages for the normal birth of a normal child is foreign to the universal public sentiment of the people. . . . Many people would be willing to support this child were they given the right of custody and adoption, but according to plaintiff's statement, plaintiff does not want such. He wants to have the child and wants the doctor to support it. In our opinion to allow such damages would be against public policy.

It is interesting to speculate as to what might have been the court's decision if the child had been crippled or an imbecile or if the mother had suffered severe injury or even death during childbirth.

In *Ball vs Mudge,* after his wife had delivered three children by Caesarean section, a man underwent a vasectomy. His wife later became pregnant and delivered a normal child by another Caesarean section. The couple sued the physician, seeking damages for the expenses of the delivery of the child, for their pain, suffering and mental anguish, for the loss of the services, society, companionship and consortium of the wife, and for the care, maintenance and support of the child. Affirming the judgement for the physician, the Washington Supreme Court held that the jury may well have concluded that the parents "suffered no damage in the birth of a normal, healthy child, whom they dearly love . . . and that the cost incidental to such birth was far outweighed by the blessing of a cherished child, albeit an unwanted child at the time of conception."

However, a different conclusion was reached in *Bishop vs Byrne.* In this case a woman underwent a sterilization operation. She later became pregnant and delivered a normal child by Caesarean section. At the time of this birth, one of her Fallopian tubes was found to be intact. The parents sued the physician for negligence and breach of warranty, claiming damages for the expenses incurred in the delivery of the child and for the anguish and suffering endured by the woman during pregnancy.

Refusing to dismiss the parents' claim, the court ruled that the physician may be held liable for the delivery expenses and for the woman's anguish and suffering if they resulted from his negligence.

The possible liability exposure of a physician in such cases was further expanded in *Custodio vs Bauer*. A woman with nine children underwent a sterilization operation. She later became pregnant. Prior to the birth of the child, she and her husband sued the physician, claiming damages for the medical costs of the pregnancy, for mental, physical and nervous pain and suffering, for fraud and deceit, and for the costs and expenses to properly care for and raise the child to the age of maturity. Relying upon earlier decisions, the physician contended that pregnancy, the ensuing birth of a child, and the costs and expenses of the delivery and rearing of a child are not legally recognized injuries. The appellate court said:

> The crux of this case is whether or not plaintiffs are precluded from showing any damage even though it be assumed that defendants were negligent, or that they made negligent or intentional misrepresentations, or that they contracted for and warranted performance which they failed to effect. . . . If plaintiffs establish a violation of duty by the defendants, they should at least be reimbursed for any outlay for the unsuccessful operation . . . If by amendment or supplemental complaint they can show physical complications and mental, physical and nervous pain and suffering which the operation was designed to prevent, they should be able to recover. . . .
>
> If the mother dies in childbirth from foreseeable complications of the proscribed pregnancy, the defendants may be charged therewith. . . . If she survives but is crippled . . . the physicians would have to compensate her for her injuries, and her husband for loss of her services and for medical expenses . . . The propriety of further damages must be established . . . as the facts may be developed.

In *Jackson vs Anderson,* a Florida appellate court noted that a child born after sterilization operation was not unwanted or unloved, but was unplanned. The court did not rule on the amount of damages, as this was a question for the jury.

In jurisdictions where sterilization of convenience is a crime or contravenes public policy, a patient who voluntarily submits to the procedure could be barred from recovering damages for a bad result on the ground that the patient is in pari delicto in an illegal transaction. This has been the holding in many cases seeking civil damages arising out of criminal abortions but some jurisdictions have permitted recovery in such cases.

In a Minnesota case, *Christensen vs Thornby,* the therapeutic justification for a vasectomy was that further pregnancies would be dangerous to the health of the plaintiff's wife. The operation was performed on the plaintiff's husband because the operation for the sterilization of a male is simpler and less dangerous than that for the sterilization of a female. This was held to be not contrary to public policy. There is language in the opinion to support the conclusion that consent alone is sufficient to permit a sterilization operation in Minnesota.

In the case where the physician neglects to obtain the consent of the patient's spouse to a non-therapeutic sterilization operation, the physician may be liable for a successful operation. The question has not been litigated, but an argument could be made that husband and wife have a mutual interest in each other's powers of procreation and the consent of both is therefore essential before the ability of either to procreate is terminated for non-medical reasons.

Reprinted from Medicolegal Forms With Legal Analysis, pp. 48-53, Copyright 1973, by American Medical Association.

MEDICOLEGAL FORMS

CONSENT TO ARTIFICIAL INSEMINATION

Date_____Time_____
A.M.
P.M.

We,_____and_____,
being husband and wife and both of legal age, authorize Dr._____ and such assistants as he may designate, to inseminate the wife artificially, and to use the semen of (the husband) (the husband and a donor or donors) (a donor or donors) for this purpose. We authorize him to employ such assistants he may desire to assist him.

We understand that even though the insemination may be repeated as often as recommended by Dr._____, there is no guarantee on his part or assurance that pregnancy or full term pregnancy will result.

We agree to rely upon the sole discretion of Dr._____ in the selection of qualified donors and never to seek to discover the identity of any donor. We agree that following the insemination, Dr._____ may destroy all records and information concerning the identity of the donor or donors.

We, and each of us, do hereby agree to support the child which is artificially conceived until said child reaches majority.

We understand that if pregnancy shall result, there is the possibility of complications of childbirth or delivery, or the birth of an abnormal infant or infants, or undesirable hereditary tendencies of such issue, or other adverse consequences.

(CROSS OUT ANY WORDS ABOVE WHICH DO NOT APPLY)

Signed_____
(Husband)

Signed_____
(Wife)

Witness_____

OFFER TO SERVE AS A DONOR OF SEMEN

Date_____Time_____
A.M.
P.M.

To Dr._____:

    1. I offer my services as donor of semen with the understanding that the identity of any recipient shall not be disclosed to me, nor shall you voluntarily reveal my identity to any recipient.

    2. To the best of my knowledge:

        (a) I am in good health; I have no communicable disease; and I do not now, nor have I ever suffered from any physical or mental impairment or disability, whether inherited or as a result of any disease or ailment, except as follows:
_____

        (b) I am not now nor have I ever been afflicted with syphilis or any other venereal disease, except as follows:_____
_____

        (c) None of my grandparents, parents, brothers, sisters, or children, if any, nor their lineal descendants, have ever been afflicted with emotional illness or any inherited mental or physical disabilities or disease, except as follows:___
_____

    3. For the purpose of determining whether I am acceptable as a donor of semen, I consent to a physical examination, including the taking of blood and other body fluids, by you or any other physician whom you may designate.

Signed_____
(Donor)

Witness_____

CONSENT OF WIFE OF DONOR

Date_____

To Dr._____:

    1. I have read my husband's offer to serve as a donor of semen and to the best of my knowledge the statements he has made are true.

    2. If my husband is accepted as a donor, I understand that it is your intention to use his semen for purposes of artificial insemination, but not with respect to myself.

    3. I know that artificial insemination is a medical procedure intended to cause pregnancy through the use of semen introduced by means other than sexual intercourse.

    4. I agree that I shall not attempt to discover the identity of any recipient of my husband's semen.

    5. In serving as a donor of semen, I know that my husband may become the father of a child or children of which I am not the mother, but I nevertheless consent to the performance of such services by him.

Signed_____

Witness_____

270

REQUEST FOR PRESCRIPTION
OF ORAL CONTRACEPTIVES

A.M.
Date_____Time_____P.M.

    I hereby acknowledge that I have received from_____, M.D., a booklet containing information on the use, effectiveness, and known hazards of oral contraceptives, including   (insert name of product) , and that I have been informed by said_____, M.D., of the possible serious side-effects of such oral contraceptives, including but not limited to phlebitis, thromboembolism, breakthrough bleeding and hepatic disease and informed of alternative methods of contraception. I further acknowledge that I understand such information and warnings.

    I understand that such oral contraceptives are prescribed for the intended purpose of preventing future pregnancies, but no guarantees or assurances of the results of the use of such oral contraceptives have been given by anyone. I, nevertheless, request_____ _____, M.D., to prescribe for me, or for   (insert name and relationship) , the oral contraceptive   (insert name of product)

Signed_____

(Patient or person authorized)

Witness_____

REQUEST AND CONSENT FOR PLACEMENT
OF INTRAUTERINE CONTRACEPTIVE DEVICE

    I acknowledge that _____, M.D., has informed me of the nature and purpose of intrauterine contraceptive devices, including   (insert name of device). I understand that such device is placed in the uterus of a female patient for the intended purpose of preventing future pregnancies, but that it is not invariably effective in preventing pregnancy. I further acknowledge that no guarantee or assurance has been given by anyone as to the results to be obtained from the placement and use of such device within the uterus.

    I have been informed by _____, M.D., of alternative methods of contraception and of the risks and possible complications which may arise from the placement and use of such intrauterine contraceptive device, including but not limited to perforation of the uterus by the device, expulsion of the device, infection, pain and cramps.

    I, nevertheless, request and consent to the placement of such intrauterine contraceptive device within my uterus or the uterus of _____(insert name and relationship)_____by _____, M.D.

Signed_____

(Patient or person authorized
to consent for the patient)

Witness_____

STATEMENT OF NEED FOR THERAPEUTIC ABORTION

Date_____Time_____ A.M.
                                           P.M.

We find from observation and examination of _____
that she is pregnant and that she is suffering from the following ailment or condition: _____
_____
Further progress of her pregnancy would gravely endanger or imperil her life. Therefore, we
are of the opinion that it is medically necessary to perform a therapeutic abortion upon her.

(1)_____
(2)_____
(3)_____
(Duly licensed physicians)

AUTHORIZATION TO TREAT CONDITION OF RECENT OR PARTIAL ABORTION

Date_____Time_____ A.M.
                                           P.M.

I authorize Dr. _____ to treat me for the condition set forth in the
following history:_____
_____
_____
_____
_____
This condition occurred prior to the time that I visited Dr._____ for
treatment.

Signed_____

Witness_____

RELEASE FOR RITUAL CIRCUMCISION

Date_____Time_____
A.M.
P.M.

We request Dr._____, the attending physician, and_____
Hospital to permit our son to be circumcised by_____
(person to perform circumcision)
whom we have selected as a person qualified in the ritual of our faith and by experience to
perform this procedure. We assume full responsibility and release the attending physician,
that hospital and its staff from liability for any adverse results that may occur.

Signed_____
(Father)

Signed_____
(Mother)

Witness_____

CONSENT TO TREATMENT

Date_____Time_____
A.M.
P.M.

I have been fully informed by Dr._____of the risks, possible alternative methods of treatment, and possible consequences involved in treatment by means of
_____
_____

for relief of _____. Nevertheless, I authorize Dr._____
to administer such treatment to me.

Signed_____
(Patient or person authorized
to consent for patient)

Witness_____

ACKNOWLEDGEMENT OF EMERGENCY TREATMENT

Date_____Time_____A.M.
P.M.

I acknowledge that the medical care which (was) (is about to be) furnished to_____
_____by Dr._____ (was) (will be) limited solely to emergency treatment. I understand that it will be necessary to select another physician and make immediate arrangements with him for a complete diagnosis and continuation of treatment.

(CROSS OUT INAPPROPRIATE WORDS)

Signed_____

(Patient or person authorized
to consent for patient)

Witness_____

REQUEST FOR STERILIZATION

Date_____Time_____A.M.
P.M.

1. I authorize the performance upon myself of the following operation_____
(State name
_____ to be performed by or under the direction of Dr. _____.
of operation)

2. It has been explained to me that this operation is intended to result in my sterility, but no such result has been guaranteed.

3. I understand that a sterile person is NOT capable of becoming a parent.

4. I understand that if the operation proves successful the results will be permanent and it will thereafter be physically impossible for me to inseminate, or to conceive or bear children.

5. The nature of this operation, the possible consequences, the possibility that the operation may be unsuccessful, and the possibility of complications have been fully explained to me by Dr._____and by_____.

Signed_____

Witness_____

I have read the above REQUEST FOR STERILIZATION and do hereby consent to the operation under the terms therein set forth as the spouse of _____.

Signed_____

Date_____Time_____

274

REQUEST FOR STERILIZATION

A.M.
Date_____Time_____P.M.

We, the undersigned husband and wife, each being more than twenty-one years of age and of sound mind, request Dr._____, and assistants of his choice, to perform upon_____the following
(name of patient)
operation:_____.
(state nature and extent of operation)

It has been explained to us that this operation is intended to result in sterility although this result has not been guaranteed. We understand that a sterile person is NOT capable of becoming a parent.

We voluntarily request the operation and understand that if it proves successful the results will be permanent and it will thereafter be physically impossible for the patient to inseminate, or to conceive or bear children.

Signed_____
(Husband)

Signed_____72
(Wife)

Witness_____

GLOSSARY

This glossary has been prepared for the convenience of those readers who have not had formal medical training.

ADRENAL GLANDS —A pair of glands located atop the kidneys composed of an inner core, the medulla, which produces epinephrine (adrenalin) and norepinephrine, and an outer cortex, which produces a number of hormones including sex hormones and cortisone.

AMENORRHEA —The absence of menstruation.

AMNIOCENTESIS —A technique in which an instrument is introduced through the abdomen into the pregnant uterus for withdrawal of a sample of amniotic fluid.

AMPULLA OF THE VAS DEFERENS —The widened portion of the vas deferens before it is joined by the seminal vesicle.

OF THE FALLOPIAN TUBE —The section of the fallopian tube between the funnel-shaped portion nearest the ovary and the narrow portion joining the uterus.

ANASTOMOSIS —A communication between two vessels; the formation of a passage between any two normally distinct spaces or organs.

ANDROGEN —A male hormone produced by the testes and, to a lesser extent, by the adrenal cortex in both sexes which is responsible for development of characteristics associated with maleness.

ANLAGE —The earliest discernable indication during embryonic development of an organ or part.

ANTIBODY —A protein (globulin) produced by the body in response to a foreign substance (an antigen).

APAREUNIA —The absence of, or the inability to have, coitus.

APHRODISIAC —A drug or food which is claimed to stimulate sexual desire.

AREOLA —The circular area of darker color surrounding the nipple.

ARTIFICIAL INSEMINATION —Introduction of semen into the female reproductive tract without sexual contact.

ATRESIA —The absence or closure of a normal body opening or passage.

ATROPHY —The wasting away or diminution in the size of a cell, tissue, organ, or part.

AUTONOMIC NERVOUS SYSTEM —The portion of the nervous system concerned with regulation of activity of cardiac muscle, smooth muscle, and glands and greatly influenced by hormones.

AUTOSOMES —Chromosomes other than the sex (X and Y) chromosomes.

BIOLOGIC SEX —The internal and external reproductive structure of the individual as determined by the chromosomes, the sex glands, and the hormones and their effect on the end organs.

CASTRATE —To remove the ovaries or testes.

CEREBROVASCULAR ACCIDENT —The shutting off of the blood supply to a portion of the brain due to hemorrhage or occlusion of a cerebral blood vessel.

CERVIX —The lower, narrowed end of the uterus.

CHANCROID —A venereal disease caused by a bacterium (Haemophilus), and characterized by many soft ulcers on the external genitalia.

CHROMATIN-POSITIVE —Containing a dark-staining body (sex chromatin) in the cell nucleus, characteristic of cells in the normal female.

CHROMOSOMES —Those structures in the nucleus of a cell that carry the genetic material, DNA.

COITUS —Sexual union; intercourse.

COITUS INTERRUPTUS —Coitus in which the penis is withdrawn from the vagina before ejaculation.

COLOSTOMY —The surgical creation of a new opening of the colon on the surface of the body.

CONDOM —A cover for the penis, worn during coitus to prevent impregnation or infection.

CORONA GLANDIS —The rounded proximal border of the glans penis.

CORONARY OCCLUSION —An obstruction of the blood flow through an artery supplying the heart muscle as a result of the presence of a thrombus (clot) or narrowing of the vessel due to arteriosclerosis.

CORTICOSTEROIDS —Hormones produced by the adrenal cortex which include those that influence sodium and water balance or carbohydrate metabolism, and sex hormones.

CROSS GENDER BEHAVIOR —Behavior including avoidance of play and clothing typical of the individual's biologic sex, and an openly stated wish to be the opposite sex.

CRYPTORCHIDISM —A developmental defect in which the testes fail to descend into the scrotum.

CULDOSCOPY —Visual examination of the internal reproductive organs of the female by means of an optical instrument introduced into the pelvic cavity by way of the vagina.

CUNNILINGUS —Oral stimulation of the vulva or clitoris.

CYSTITIS —Inflammation of the urinary bladder.

DIAPHRAGM —A device of molded rubber or other soft plastic material that is fitted over the cervix to prevent entrance of sperm.

DYSGENESIS, GONADAL —Defective development of ovaries or testes.

DYSPAREUNIA —Difficult or painful coitus.

ECTOPIC PREGNANCY —The implantation of the ovum and development of the fetus outside the uterus, usually in the fallopian tube.

ENDOMETRIOSIS —Growth of cells that normally line the uterus in body cavities outside of the uterus, usually in the pelvis.

ENDOSCOPY —Inspection of any cavity of the body by means of an endoscope.

EPIGASTRIUM —The upper region of the abdomen between the end of the breast bone and the umbilicus.

EPIPHYSIS —The end of a long bone, usually wider than the shaft, composed entirely or in part of cartilage at which growth occurs.

EPISIOTOMY —A surgical incision made to enlarge the orifice of the vagina during birth of the fetus.

EPITHELIUM —The layer of tissue covering the external surfaces of the body, and some of the body's internal surfaces.

EROGENOUS AREAS —Zones of the body sensitive to sexual stimulation.

EROTIC —Tending to arouse sexual desire.

ESTROGENS —Hormones produced by the ovary (and the placenta) which influence the development of secondary sex characteristics, the function of the reproductive and menstrual cycles, and the metabolism.

EUNUCH —A male deprived of the testes.

EXHIBITIONISM —The display of one's body for the purpose, conscious or unconscious, of attracting sexual interest.

EXPANDED FAMILY —Grandparents, aunts, uncles, and close family friends.

FALLOPIAN TUBES —Slender tubes that extend from the upper angle of the uterus to the region of the ovaries through which the ovum passes to the uterus.

FELLATIO —Oral stimulation or manipulation of the penis.

FERTILE —Capable of reproducing.

FERTILIZATION —Union of a sperm and an ovum to begin the development of a new individual.

FETUS —A term applied to the unborn young from the second month after fertilization to birth.

FETISHISM —A compulsive sexual attraction to an inanimate object or body part.

FRIGIDITY —The abnormal lack of sexual desire in the female.

GENDER IDENTITY —The sense of masculinity or femininity.

GENITALIA —The internal and external reproductive organs.

GENOTYPE —The genetic makeup (assortment of genes) of an individual.

GESTATION —The period of development of the young from time of fertilization of the ovum to birth.

GLANS —The erectile tissue at the top of the clitoris; the head or tip of the penis.

GONAD —The ovary or testis.

GONORRHEA —An infectious disease transmitted by sexual contact and affecting the external genitalia and urethra but capable of spreading to other parts of the body if untreated.

GRANULOMA INGUINALE —A venereal disease characterized by deep pus-producing ulcers of the skin of the external genitalia, prevalent in the tropics of North and South America and India, affecting especially dark-skinned people.

GYNECOMASTIA —Excessive development of the male mammary glands, even to the functional state.

HERMAPHRODITE —An individual possessing both male and female gonadal tissue.

HETEROSEXUAL —An individual who is sexually attracted to persons of the opposite sex.

HOMOSEXUAL —An individual who is sexually attracted to persons of the same sex.

HORMONE —A chemical substance produced in the body, which regulates the rate of cellular processes.

HYMEN —The membranous fold which partially or wholly occludes the outer opening of the vagina.

HYPERPLASIA —The abnormal increase in the number of normal cells, in normal arrangement, in a tissue.

HYPOGONADOTROPIC EUNUCHOIDISM —The lack of development of the testes and secondary sex characteristics due to the failure of secretion of anterior pituitary gonad-stimulating hormones.

HYPOTHALAMUS —The portion of the forebrain which integrates the various automatic functions of the body.

HYSTERECTOMY —The operation of removing the uterus.

IMPOTENCE —The inability in the male to have an erection. *Primary impotence:* the condition of males who have never been able to achieve an erection. *Secondary impotence:* the condition of males who have lost their ability to achieve erection because of some physical or psychologic impairment.

INCEST —Sexual intercourse between persons so closely related that marriage is illegal or forbidden.

INGUINAL —Pertaining to the groin.

INTEGUMENT —The skin.

INTERCOURSE —Sexual union; coitus.

INTERSEXUALITY —Having characteristics of both sexes, including physical form, reproductive organs, and sexual behavior as a result of some flaw in embryonic development.

INTRA-UTERINE DEVICE —A metal or plastic object designed to act as a contraceptive when inserted into the uterus.

INTROITUS —The external opening to the female reproductive tract.

INTROMISSION —The insertion of the penis into the vagina.

KARYOTYPE —An arrangement of the chromosomes of a single cell typical of an individual.

LABIA —The inner and outer fleshy folds of the genital region of the female.

LACTATION —The secretion of milk.

LAPAROSCOPY —Examination of the interior of the abdomen by means of a laparoscope, an optical instrument inserted through the abdominal wall.

LAPAROTOMY —Surgical opening of the abdomen.

LATENT HOMOSEXUALITY —Concealed or not yet manifested homosexuality.

LESBIANISM —Homosexuality between women.

LEYDIG'S CELLS —Interstitial cells; the cells in the testes which produce androgens.

LIBIDO —Sexual desire.

LYMPHOGRANULOMA VENEREUM —A venereal disease caused by a virus and producing a sore on the external genitalia followed by swelling of the lymph nodes of the groin.

MASOCHISM —Deriving sexual pleasure from being subjected to abuse or physical pain.

MASTECTOMY —Surgical removal of a breast.

MASTURBATION —Production of orgasm by self-manipulation of the genitals.

MENARCHE —The onset of menstruation occurring in adolescence.

MENOPAUSE —Cessation of menstruation occurring usually between the ages of 46 and 50.

MONS —A pad of fatty tissue over the symphysis pubis.

MOSAIC —An individual having two or more cell populations derived from a single fertilized egg, each population having a different chromosomal composition.

MÜLLERIAN DUCTS —A pair of ducts in the embryo which develop into the reproductive tract in the female and have no function in the male.

MULTIPARA —A woman who has given birth to two or more children.

MYOCARDIAL INFARCTION —Degeneration of muscle tissue of the heart because the blood supply was interrupted, as in coronary thrombosis.

MYOMA —A tumor made up of muscular tissue.

NEUROGENIC BLADDER —Dysfunction of the urinary bladder produced by the interference with normal conduction of nerve impulses over one or more of the nerve tracts.

NOCTURNAL EMISSION —Emission of semen during sleep.

NUCLEAR FAMILY —Immediate family with whom a person lives.

NULLIPARA —A women who has not given birth to a living child.

NYMPHOMANIA —An exaggerated and compulsive sexual desire in a female.

OEDIPAL —Libidinal feeling of a child toward the parent of the opposite sex.

ORCHITIS —Inflammation of a testis.

ORGASM —The climax of sexual excitement.

OVARY —The sex gland in the female in which the ova are formed.

OVUM —The reproductive cell (egg) produced in the female.

PERINEORRHAPHY —Surgery to repair or reconstruct the perineum, which is the group of tissues forming the floor of the pelvis.

PERITONEAL CAVITY —The space in the abdominal region of the body below the diaphragm.

PERIURETHRAL —Occurring around the urethra; the tube leading from the bladder to the exterior of the body.

PHENOTYPE —The outward, visible expression of the hereditary constitution of an organism.

PITUITARY GONADOTROPINS —Hormones produced in the pituitary gland which stimulate the gonads (ovaries or testes).

POSTPARTUM —Occurring after childbirth.

POTENCY —The ability of the male to have sexual intercourse.

PRECOCIOUS PUBERTY —Development of pubertal changes before the age at which they normally would occur.

PREMATURE EJACULATION —Expulsion of semen during or almost immediately after intromission.

PRIMIGRAVIDA —A woman pregnant for the first time.

PRIMIPARA —A woman who has given birth to one living child.

PROCTITIS —Inflammation of the rectum.

PROGESTAGEN —A hormone produced by the ovary (and the placenta) which prevents ovulation and is necessary for preparing the uterine lining for the fertilized ovum and for maintaining pregnancy.

PROMISCUOUS —Having indiscriminate sexual relations.

PSEUDOHERMAPHRODITE —An individual whose gonads are of one sex but who possesses some outward characteristics of the opposite sex.

PUBERTY —The period of time during which the reproductive system matures and secondary sex characteristics appear.

PUBESCENT —Reaching the age of puberty.

Rh FACTOR —An antigenic substance on the surface of the red blood cells of 85% of the population (Rh positive); if Rh negative individuals are given Rh positive blood, they will produce antibodies that will destroy the Rh positive red blood cells.

SADISM —Deriving sexual pleasure from inflicting pain on others.

SALPINGO-OOPHORECTOMY —Surgical removal of the fallopian tube and ovary.

SALPINGOSCOPY —Inspection of the fallopian tube with an optical instrument.

SATYRIASIS —An exaggerated sexual desire in a male.

SEMINAL VESICLE —An outpocketing of the vas deferens which secretes a substance which makes up part of the semen.

SEMINIFEROUS TUBULES —The small tubules of the testis which produce sperm.

SIBLING —A brother or sister.

SODOMY —As described in some laws, anal and oral intercourse and intercourse with animals.

SOMATIC —Pertaining to the body; pertaining to cells of the body other than those producing sperm and ova.

SPERMATOZOA —The reproductive cells (sperm) produced by the male.

STERILIZE —To render incapable of reproduction.

SYPHILIS —A highly infectious disease caused by a spirochete and transmitted by sexual contact. If untreated, syphilis can involve the skin, blood vessels, heart, liver, central nervous system and other organs.

TABES DORSALIS —A degenerative wasting away of a portion of the spinal cord and of the sensory nerve trunks, as a complication of syphilis.

TACHYCARDIA —Excessively rapid heartbeat.

TESTIS —The sex gland in the male in which sperm are produced.

TESTOSTERONE —One of the androgens produced by the testes (and the adrenal cortex).

TOXEMIA OF PREGNANCY —A variety of complications in pregnancy which includes severe vomiting, liver and kidney disease, high blood pressure, and edema.

TRANSVESTITE —An individual with a morbid desire to wear clothes of the opposite sex.

TRIMESTER —A period of three months, one-third the duration of pregnancy.

TUBAL LIGATION —Surgical sterilization by cutting and tying off both fallopian tubes.

URETHRA —The canal which conveys urine from the bladder to the exterior of the body.

UROGENITAL —Pertaining to the urinary and reproductive organs.

UTERUS —The pear-shaped structure of the female reproductive tract which maintains the developing fetus.

VAGINAL ATRESIA —Absence or closure of the vagina.

VAGINISMUS —Painful spasm of the vagina.

VAS DEFERENS —The canal that conveys sperm extending from the testis to the prostate; together with its blood vessels and nerves, it is called the spermatic cord.

VASECTOMY —Surgical sterilization by removing the vas deferens, or a portion of it.

VASOCONGESTION —Excessive or abnormal accumulation of blood in a vessel.

VENEREAL DISEASE —A disease transmitted by sexual contact.

VIRILIZATION —The development of male secondary sex characteristics, especially the induction of such changes in the female.

VOYEUR —A person who derives sexual gratification from observing the genital organs and sexual acts of others.

VULVA —The external genital organs of the female.

VULVITIS —Inflammation of the vulva.

WOLFFIAN DUCT —A structure in the embryo which forms parts of the male reproductive tract and parts of the urinary bladder in both male and female.

BIBLIOGRAPHY

Books

Ard BN, Ard CC (eds): *Handbook of Marriage Counseling.* Palo Alto, Calif, Science & Behavior Books Inc, 1969. ($12.95)
> The methods of marriage counseling evaluated by marriage counselors and physicians. Among the subjects covered are the assumptions of marriage counseling, values and moral issues in marital counseling, male and female roles in marital counseling, conjoint therapy, group therapy, premarital counseling, contraception for the unmarried, sexual inadequacy in marriage, gynecological diagnosis, and divorce.

Belliveau F, Richter L: *Understanding Human Sexual Inadequacy.* Boston — Toronto, Little, Brown and Company, 1970. ($6.95)
> A clear, simple and complete explanation of Dr. William H. Masters and Virgina B. Johnson's pioneering new study, *Human Sexual Inadequacy,* based on their research in sexual functioning and on patient care studies. Written in easy-to-understand language, it is the only analysis authorized by Masters and Johnson.

Brecher R, Brecher E (eds): *An Analysis of Human Sexual Response.* New York, The New American Library, 1966. (paperback $1.25)
> A summary of the Masters and Johnson report, Human Sexual Response, including methods and findings, with additional chapters on other sex research and the applications of the findings.

Broderick CB, Bernard J (eds): *The Individual, Sex and Society: A SIECUS Handbook for Teachers and Counselors.* Baltimore, The Johns Hopkins Press, 1969. ($4.50)
> A collection of views of human sexuality, with special attention to teaching, standards and values, normal functioning, and problems. There are individual chapters dealing with normal socio-sexual development, sexual behavior in a Negro ghetto, sexual behavior among the poor, premarital sexual standards, human reproduction, human sexual response, family planning, sex errors of the body, masturbation, and sexual deviations.

Ellis A, Abarbanel A: *Aspects of Sexuality* (Star Series) Original Title: *Encyclopedia of Sexual Behavior.* New York, Ace Publishing Corp, 1969. (paperback $0.95)
> This 1,072 page collection deals with varied aspects of human sexuality among American Indians, aphrodisiacs, sex and art, sex and religion, sexual techniques, deviations, customs, divorce, marriage, illegitimacy, love, nutrition, sex life in Polynesia, and reproduction.

Group for the Advancement of Psychiatry: *Normal Adolescence: Its Dynamics and Impact.* New York, Charles Scribner's Sons, 1968. (hardcover $4.95; paperback $1.65)
> A short history of normal sexual and social development during adolescence, with special attention to the environment of adolescence, rapid social change as an adolescent problem, the role of childhood experience, and the development of pre-, early, and late adolescence.

Hastings DW: *Impotence and Frigidity.* Boston, Little Brown & Co, 1963. ($6.00)

This book is designed for the practicing physician to aid him in understanding several common sexual problems. Topics discussed are: intercourse, impotence, premature ejaculation, frigidity, treatment and homosexuality.

Israel LS, Rubin I: *Sexual Relations During Pregnancy and the Post-Delivery Period.* SIECUS Study Guide No. 6. SIECUS Publications, 1967. ($.50)
The question of sexual relations during pregnancy and after birth is examined, and the validity of its interdiction for long periods is questioned. Also gives information as to other forms of sexual expression during these periods.

Kinsey AC, Pomeroy WB, Martin CE, Gebhard PH: *Sexual Behavior in the Human Female.* Philadelphia, WB Saunders Co, 1953. (hardcover $10.25) New York, Pocket Books Inc. (paperback $1.65)
This volume is the result of a fifteen-year "fact-finding survey in which an attempt was made to discover what people do sexually, what factors may account for their patterns of sexual behavior, how their sexual experiences have affected their lives, and what social significance there may be in each type of behavior." The book includes chapters on the sample and its statistical analysis and the source of data as well as the results of the survey.

Kinsey AC, Pomeroy WB, Martin CE: *Sexual Behavior in the Human Male.* Philadelphia, WB Saunders Co, 1948. ($10.25)
This volume is the result of a nine-year survey which was aimed at discovering "what people do sexually, and what factors account for differences in sexual behavior among individuals, and among various segments of the population." The book includes chapters on interviewing techniques, statistical problems and validity of the data as well as the results of the survey.

Klemer RH (ed): *Counseling in Marital and Sexual Problems: A Physician's Handbook.* Baltimore, Williams & Wilkins Co, 1965. ($11.00)
A collection of articles about the methods and problems of marriage counseling. Individual chapters deal with changes in American marriages, counseling techniques, considerations of diagnosis and treatment, the physical examination, referral, male and female sexual conditioning, discussing sexual problems, deviations, infidelity, sexual communication, parent-child problems, divorce, widowhood, family planning, and premarital counseling.

Lidz T: *Person: His Development Throughout the Life Cycle.* New York, Basic Books Inc, 1968. ($10.00)
An examination of emotional and sexual development and reaction throughout the life cycle, with chapters on infancy, the Oedipal period, childhood integration, adolescence, the young adult, marital and occupational choice, marriage, parenthood, the middle years, old age, and death.

Masters WH, Johnson VE: *Human Sexual Inadequacy.* Boston, Little Brown & Co, 1970. ($12.50)
Results of a program designed to treat both the husband and wife of a sexually dysfunctional marriage. Sexual inadequacies treated were: pre-

mature ejaculation, ejaculatory incompetence, primary impotence, secondary impotence, orgasmic dysfunction, vaginismus, dyspareunia, and sexual
inadequacy in the aging male and female. The bibliography has about
1000 references.

Masters WH, Johnson VE: *Human Sexual Response.* Boston, Little Brown &
Co, 1966. ($12.50)
A comprehensive report of the sexual response of men and women as
observed during laboratory studies over a period of ten years. The book
includes detailed descriptions of sexual physiology and sexual response
during coitus, masturbation, artificial masturbation, pregnancy, and aging.

Pilpel HF, Zavin T: *Your Marriage and the Law.* New York, Macmillan Co,
1964. (paperback $0.95)
A discussion of laws affecting marriage and marital sexuality, including
such problems as illegitimacy, abortion, birth control, sterilization,criminal
law, and divorce.

Rado S: *Adaptational Psychodynamics.* Jameson J, Klein H (eds), New York,
Science House, 1969. ($12.50)
This collection is based on a series of lectures given by the author between 1945 and 1955 and constitutes a psychiatrist's analysis of human
emotional and sexual development. Chapters on sexuality deal with sexual
behavior, love, sex and marriage, sexual development, and sexual disorders.

Reiss IL: *Premarital Sexual Standards in America.* New York, The Free Press,
1960. ($7.50)
This work discusses premarital sexual standards, including permissiveness
with affection, permissiveness without affection, the double standard, and
abstinence.

Reiss IL: *The Social Context of Premarital Permissiveness.* New York, Holt
Rinehart & Winston Inc, 1967. ($8.25)
A study of changes in sexual attitudes, premarital sexual standards in
America, and the relationship between permissiveness and race, social
class, family relations, with details of the study methods, findings, and the
author's conclusions.

Rubin I: *Sexual Life After Sixty.* New York, Basic Books Inc, 1965. ($6.95)
A study of sexuality and aging, with emphasis on the myths and mis-
understandings about sex and old age. Chapters deal with the available
research, sexual response, sexual aging in men and women, common and
uncommon problems, the effects of surgery, and sexual activity after
heart disease.

Sex Information and Education Council of the U.S.: *Sexuality and Man.* New
York, Charles Scribner's Sons, 1970. (hardcover $6.95; paperback $2.65)
This book is based largely on the SIECUS Study Guides Numbers 1-12.
The chapters consider the different aspects of human sexuality. The topics
include: sexual response, premarital sexual standards, sexual relations
during pregnancy, masturbation, homosexuality, sexual life in the later
years, sex education. There is an annotated list of film resources for sex
education programs.

Sex Information and Education Council of the U.S. Study Guides:
(1) Kirkendall A: Sex Education; (2) Rubin I: Homosexuality; (3) Johnson W: Masturbation; (4) Pomeroy W, Christenson C: Characteristics of Male and Female Sexual Response; (5) Reiss I: Premarital Sexual Standards; (6) Israel S, Rubin I: Sexual Relations During Pregnancy and Post-Delivery Period; (7) Film Resources for Sex Education; (8) Kirkendall A, Rubin I: Sexuality and the Life Cycle; (9) Christensen HT: Sex, Science, and Values; (10) Rubin I: The Sex Educator and Moral Values; (11) Gagnon JH, Simon W: Sexual Encounters Between Adults and Children; (12) Rubin I: Sexual Life in the Later Years; (13) Brown TE: Concerns of Parents about Sex Education; (14) Sarrel PM: Teenage Pregnancy: Prevention and Treatment. New York, Sex Information and Education Council of the U.S. Publications Office, 1965-1971.

Each of the 14 study guides is about 20 pages. The guides are simple, forthright, and informative.

Slovenko R (ed): *Sexual Behavior and the Law.* Springfield, III, Charles C Thomas Publisher, 1965. ($19.50)

An encyclopedic treatment of sexual problems and laws governing sexuality. The book contains an overview of sexual behavior and the law, and chapters on marriage, divorce, abortion, deviations, prostitution, sexual components of non-sexual crimes, treatment of sex offenders, and the laws on the dissemination of sexual information.

Trainer JB: *Psychologic Foundations for Marriage Counseling.* St. Louis, CV Mosby Co, 1965. ($10.50)

A physician's evaluation of sexual development, marriage, and the physician's role in sexual and marital counseling. Chapters discuss the institution of marriage, male and female hormones, human mating, pregnancy, genetics and developmental defects, contraception, infertility, abortion, premarital examinations, and the special problems of sexuality within marriage.

Van De Velde TH: *Ideal Marriage: Its Physiology and Techniques,* rev ed. New York, Random House Inc, 1965. ($7.95)

A marriage manual which includes an explanation of the physiology of sex and human anatomy, an examination of marriage and the techniques of intercourse.

Vincent CE (ed): *Human Sexuality in Medical Education and Practice.* Springfield, III, Charles C Thomas Publisher, 1968. ($18.75)

This collection includes chapters on the teaching of human sexuality in medical education, sexual problems in medical practice, sexual attitudes and standards of society, the physiology of sexuality, sexual learning and socialization, male and female sexual response, sexual deviations, the physician's role in marital and sexual problems, illegitimate pregnancy, masturbation, sexual activity during pregnancy, sexuality among the aging, sexual adjustments and illness, and a list of available written and filmed resources.

Vincent CE: *Unmarried Mothers.* New York, The Free Press, 1961. (hardcover $6.95; paperback $2.45)

This volume contains the results of a survey of over one thousand unwed mothers in California. Factors taken into account in the survey were: attitudes of society and the unwed mother, social and economic background, unwed mothers and their partners, psychological and familial factors, and adoption.

Wahl CW (ed): *Sexual Problems: Diagnosis and Treatment in Medical Practice.* New York, The Free Press, 1967. ($8.50)
A study of human sexual problems, with chapters on the taking of a sexual history, physical symptoms which hide sexual problems, sexual relations in marriage, contraception, abortion, sexual problems of children, impotence and premature ejaculation, the intersexed patient, sexual deviations, the doctor's attitude toward sexual problems, and sexual problems of the chronically ill.

Williams RH (ed): *Textbook of Endocrinology,* ed 4. Philadelphia, WB Saunders Co, 1968. ($24.00)
The major role of genetic factors in the endocrinopathies is considered in this book.

INDEX

Abnormal Development see
DEVELOPMENT
ABORTION 5, 49, 54, 57-58, 67-
71, 157
Complications following 70
Deaths, Maternal 71
Gestation Period 70
Induced 69
Spontaneous 74
Texas statute 68
Therapeutic 57
U.S. Supreme Court
decision 68-69
ABSTINENCE 41, 72, 77, 128,
148-149
ADOLESCENCE 28, 39, 58, 81,
148
see also BOY'S ROLE;
GIRL'S ROLE; TEENAGER
Management of problems
in puberty 51
Physician, Role of 44-59
Precocious 46
Sexual Development 39-59
ADOPTION 38, 54, 58, 75, 141
ADRENAL CORTICOSTEROID
THERAPY 36
ADRENAL FUNCTION 65
ADRENAL HYPERPLASIA 35-
36, 47
ADULTHOOD
Early 60-75, 108
sexual development 65-75,
management of problems
74-80
variant sexual development
61-63
Late 81-84, 127
management of problems
83-85
normal sexual development
81-82
AFFECTION 15, 26, 33, 118
Permissiveness with 46
AGING 81, 84, 127
Fears 82
Physiologic 81
Psychologic 81
ALCOHOL AND ALCOHOLISM
44, 111, 122, 137, 139, 157
ALLEN, E. D. 17

AMENORRHEA 47-48
AMERICAN ACADEMY of
FAMILY PHYSICIANS 53
AMERICAN ACADEMY of
PEDIATRICS 53
AMERICAN ASSOCIATION OF
MARRIAGE COUNSELORS
141
AMERICAN COLLEGE OF
OBSTETRICIANS AND
GYNECOLOGISTS 53, 64,
156
AMERICAN MEDICAL
ASSOCIATION
Committee on Human
Reproduction 72
Council on Environmental
and Public Health 132
General Council 148
Policy statement on pregnancy
51-52
Position on venereal diseases
134
Resolutions on family life
education 152-153
AMNIOCENTESIS 76
ANDREWS, W. C. 64
ANDROGENS 25
Deficiency 30
Stimulation 31
Therapy 36
ANXIETIES 6-7, 12, 16, 21, 29,
34, 77, 82-84, 91-92, 104-108,
119, 148, 157
APHRODISIACS 122
Arousal see FOREPLAY;
MASTURBATION, PETTING
ARTIFICIAL INSEMINATION 37,
76
ASSAULT, SEXUAL 4, 118, 138-
140
ATTITUDES TOWARD SEX
Denmark 148
Family 15, 23, 75, 151
Healthy 3, 26, 93
Husband 73-74, 108-110
Mature 29
Norms 3
Patient 11, 15
Physician 8-12
Society 5, 41, 147-150

Wife   108-110, 117-122
AUERBACK, A.   92, 135

BEHAVIOR
    Adolescence   38-59
    Antisocial   27
    Extra-marital   15, 62, 68,
        73-74, 77-80, 82, 131
    Gynecologic considerations
        124
    Mimetic   25
    Non-marital   77-80
    Seductive   12, 26, 129,
        135-136
    Suicidal   135
"BERDACHE"   41
BENE, E.   58
BIEBER, I.   77
BILATERAL SALPINGO-
    OOPHORECTOMY   125
BIOLOGIC SEX   4, 24-26, 37
BIRTH   45, 90
    New York City   90
    Premature   73
    West Virginia City   90
BIRTH CONTROL   41, 43, 58
BLOOD
    Antibodies   75
    Bleeding   62, 73
    Pressure   65, 100, 123
    Rh factor   75
BOREDOM   77-78, 92
BOY'S ROLE   26, 29, 39, 42, 45,
    51, 53
    see also ADOLESCENCE;
        TEENAGER
BREAST   96, 103, 108
    Adolescence   39, 40, 45-48
    Cancer   126
    Pain   73
BREAST FEEDING   74
Breathing
    see COITUS, Respiration
BRODERICK, C. B.   26, 29
BRYANT, F. T.   29
BUCCAL SMEAR   37, 48
BURNAP, D. W.   9
BYLER, R.   151

CARCINOMAS   121, 124, 126, 129
Cardiac Rate   see COITUS
CASTELNUOVO-TEDESCO, P.   13
CASTRATION   123
    Fear   136

CEREBELLUM, DISEASE   123
CEREBRAL ARTERIES   65
    Cerebrovascular accidents
        127
CERVIX   73-74
CHASTITY   157
CHEZ, R. A.   13
CHILDREN   71, 148, 151-153, 155
    Development   28-38
    Of unwed mother   59
    Seduction   61, 137-138
    Transvestite   134
CHRISTENSEN, H. T.   148
CHROMOSOMES   24, 25, 30, 37
    Abnormalities   30, 31
    Analysis   48
CLARK, A. L.   93
CLERGY   151-162
CLITORIS   25, 81, 84, 96, 99-100,
    109, 121
COCAINE   122
COITUS   3-4, 7-8, 15, 39, 43,
    49-51, 67, 73, 76, 84, 95-102
    103-105, 109-110, 112-114,
    122, 124, 126-129, 135,
    137-140, 147-148, 150
    Abstinence   41, 67, 73, 128,
        147-149
    Adolescence   42, 43, 49-51,
        148
    Adulthood   60, 77, 81-84
    Anal   131
    Blood pressure   99-100
    Cardiac rate   99-100, 128-129
    Conception   75
    Divorcee   78
    Dyspareunia   see
        DYSPAREUNIA
    Extra-marital   15, 61, 74,
        77-79, 133
    Foreplay   92, 101
    Homosexuals   61
    Lateral position   104-105
    Marital   60, 74, 82, 90-92
    Menstruation   102
    Methods   103-105, 121-122
    Non-marital sexual behavior
        78-80
    Oral-genital contact   4, 44,
        61, 92, 103, 122
    Petting   83
    Physiology   95-102
    Positions   75, 103-105
    Post-coronary   128

Post-marital 78
Pregnancy 73-74
Pre-marital 15, 49-54, 71, 132, 147, 148
Pulse rate 99-100
Respiration 99-100
Side by side position 105
Surgical sterilization 70-71
COITUS INTERRUPTUS 67
COLOSTOMY 125
COLPORRHAPHY 120
Complaints, Sexual see
    PROBLEMS, MANAGEMENT OF
CONDOM 53, 67, 69, 76, 120, 133
CONJUNCTIVITIS 131
CONNECTICUT DEPT. OF EDUCATION 151
CONTRACEPTIVES 4, 23, 43, 51-53, 57, 63, 65-67, 70-71, 79, 108, 155, 157
    see also COITUS INTERRUPTUS
    American Medical Association recommendations 51-52
    Chemicals 119
    Condom 53, 67, 69, 76, 120, 132
    Counseling 49-50, 63-67, 106
    Diaphragm 51, 53, 66-67, 120
    Douche 67
    Intra-uterine devices 65-66
    Oral 51-53, 64-65, 132
    Rhythm 67
    Spermatocidal vaginal foams 67
CORE GENDER 24-25
CORONARY OCCLUSIONS 3, 7, 127, 128
COUNSELING
    Family 57-58
    Genetic 76
    Marriage see MARRIAGE COUNSELING
    Physician see PHYSICIANS-COUNSELING
    Pre-marital 49, 71, 108, 110
    Psychiatrist see PSYCHOTHERAPY
CRYPTORCHIDISM 47
CUBER, J. F. 10
CULDOSCOPY 75

DENMARK 148
DEPRESSION 65, 122
DEVELOPMENT, SEXUAL
    Adolescent 39-40
    Adulthood
        early 60-61
        late 81-82
    Childhood 28-30
    Normal 28-30
    Precocious 46
DIABETES 61, 111, 123
Diaphragm see CONTRACEPTIVES
DISEASE 121-124, 131, 153, 157
    see also specific disease
DIVORCE 57, 60-61, 71, 79-80, 148, 157
DOUBLE STANDARDS 139-140, 148
DOUCHE 67, 75, 121
DREAMS 116
DRUGS 128, 135
    Addiction 157
    Androgens 36
    Anti-estrogens 46
    Cocaine 122
    Estrogens 36, 39, 40, 46, 48, 64, 81, 84, 120, 125, 139
    Heroin 122
    LSD 122
    Marijuana 122
    Norethindrone 35
    Penicillin 129
    Progestogens 31, 35-36
    Tranquilizers 115
DUCTS 31
    Genital 36
    Mullerian 24-25
    Wolffian 24-25
DYSFUNCTION, SEXUAL 17, 21, 119, 125, 127 197,
DYSPAREUNIA 7, 80, 83, 120-121

Education, Sex see FAMILY LIFE EDUCATION
EMOTIONS see
    AFFECTION
    ANXIETIES
    FEAR
    FEELING, SEXUAL
    GUILT
    LOVE

EJACULATION 84, 91, 96, 104
114-118, 124
Premature 7, 15, 91, 106,
111, 114-116, 118
ENCEPHALOMYELITIS 46
ENDOMETRIAL BIOPSY 75
ENDOMETRIOSIS 118, 120, 121,
124
Erections, Penile see PENIS
ESTROGENS 37, 39-40, 46, 48
64, 84, 121, 125
Deficiency 124
Therapy 84
EUNUCH 47
EXHIBITIONISM 136
Extra-Marital Encounters
see BEHAVIOR, EXTRA-
MARITAL

FALLOPIAN TUBES 25
Sterilization 71-72
FAMILY 12, 21-22, 53, 153
see also RELATIONSHIPS;
PARENT-CHILD MODEL
Planning 72-73, 106
Pre-adolescents 39
Problems 12, 56, 92-93,
122, 150
FAMILY LIFE EDUCATION
57-58, 72-73, 151-158
Adolescence 44, 53, 58, 152
Children 151-153
Community 151-153
Definition 157-158
Parental 29, 34, 49,
149-152, 154-156
Schools 151-153, 156
FAMILY SERVICE ASSOCIATION
OF AMERICA 141
Father-Daughter Relationship
see RELATIONSHIPS
Father-Son Relationship see
RELATIONSHIPS
FEAR 7, 10, 30, 51, 62, 106-108
111, 114, 116, 120-126, 131,
139, 148, 157
FEELING, SEXUAL 40-41
Adolescence 30, 40-41
Father-daughter 42, 62, 117
Neurotic suppression 41, 120
see also GUILT
FELLATIO 9, 131
FEMALE ROLE 23, 25-26, 39, 44
129, 148

see also GIRL'S ROLE
Americans 61
Arousal, sexual 93-102, 106
Coital positions 103-15
Contraception 64-67
Counseling 106
see also PHYSICIANS,
COUNSELING
Love 43
Masturbation see
MASTURBATION
Femininity see FEMALE ROLE;
GIRL'S ROLE
FERNANDEZ, F. L. see PUGH,
W. E.
FERTILITY 30, 38, 65, 71, 74, 76,
80-81, 133
see also STERILITY
FETISHISM 136
FETUS 24, 31, 75
FINCH, S. M. 33
FORD, A. B. 126
FOREPLAY 96, 106
see also COITUS
FREEMAN, J. T. 83
FREUD, S. 28, 112
FRIEDMAN, E. H. 128
FRIGIDITY 7, 13, 17, 81,
106, 117, 139

GEBHARD, P. H. 93, 100
GENDER IDENTITY 24, 27,
34, 38
GENETICS
Counseling 76
Defects 76
GENITALIA 5, 16, 25, 28,
31, 36-37, 45, 108, 114
see also GONADS
Examination 17, 39
External 38
Infections 124
Infantile 47
Masculinization 31
GENOTYPE 24
GERBIE, A. G. see NADLER,
H. L.
GIRL'S ROLE 26, 30, 39, 41-42
45, 50-53
see also ADOLESCENCE;
TEENAGER
GLUCOSE TOLERANCE TEST 65
GOLDEN, J. S. 7, 9, 10, 126
GONADAL DYSGENESIS

(TURNER'S) SYNDROME
31, 38, 48
GONADOTROPINS 47-48
GONADS 24, 37, 46-47
see also HYPOGONADISM;
OVARY; TESTIS
Defects 31, 46
Development 30
Failure 82
Precocious puberty 46
Tissue heterologous 37
GONORRHEA 67, 75, 121, 129-
134, 139
Treatment 131
GOODE, WILLIAM
"After Divorce" 79
GREENSON, P. R. 23
GROUP FOR THE
ADVANCEMENT OF
PSYCHIATRY 41
GRUMBACH, M. M. 32
GUILT 9-10, 13-14, 16, 26, 30,
40-41, 55-56, 106, 109-112,
117, 126, 133, 139, 141, 148
Adolescence 40-41
unwed 55-56, 59
Adulthood 77-78
Childhood 26, 30
Divorce 79-80, 112
Moral code 60
Patient 9-10, 16
GYNECOLOGIC DISORDERS
120, 123-125, 132-133
Examination 134
GYNECOMASTIA 30, 40

HAIRGROWTH 39-40, 46, 47
HASTINGS, D. W. 117
HEADACHES 65
Heart Rate see COITUS,
cardiac rate
HEDONIST 139
HEGAR DILATORS 120
HELLERSTEIN, H. K. 128
HERMAPHRODITE 25, 31, 38
HEROIN 122
HETEROLOGOUS GONADAL
TISSUE 38
HISTORY, SEXUAL 14, 17, 63
see also PHYSICIAN
COUNSELING
HOMOSEXUALITY 9, 15-16
26-27, 48-49, 63, 76-77;
111, 113, 118, 120, 130,

132, 135-136
Adolescence 48-49
Adulthood 61-63, 135-136
early 76-77
Childhood seduction 61
Episodes 43-44
History 118
Latent 62
Parent-child relationship
27, 48
HORMONES 39, 122
Adrenal hyperplasia 37, 47
Derangement 123
Therapy 38, 47, 84
HUGO, VICTOR 83
HUSBANDS AND WIVES
Communication 91-92, 151
Relationship 15
HUTTON, L. 40
HYDROCEPHALUS 46
HYMEN 113, 121
HYPERPLASIA
Congenital Adrenal 36-37, 47
HYPERTENSION 65
HYPOGONADISM 48
HYPOGONADOTROPIC
EUNUCHOIDISM 47
HYPOTHALAMUS 46, 123
HYSTERECTOMY 4, 7, 81,
125-126
HYSTEROSALPINGOGRAPHY 75

IDENTITY, SEXUAL 3, 24, 25,
33, 48
IMPOTENCE 7, 10, 13, 15, 17,
91, 106, 111-114, 120, 123-
127
Homosexuals 61
Primary 111-113
Secondary 111-112
INDIANS, PLAINS-AMERICA 41
INFERTILITY 74-76
INFIDELITY 76-79
INTELLIGENCE 46-47
Intercourse see COITUS
INTERSEXUALITY, DIAGNOSIS
33
INTERVIEWING see HISTORY,
SEXUAL
INTRA-UTERINE DEVICE (IUD)
65-66
INTROITUS 81-82, 100, 120,
138

JEFFCOATE, T. N. S.   120
Johnson, V. E.   see MASTERS,
   W. H. and JOHNSON, V. E.
JOSLIN, E. R.   123

KARYOTYPE   48
KEPHART, W. H.   100
KINSEY, A. C.   27-28, 41-44, 62,
   79, 95, 101, 149
KINSEY INSTITUTE   39
KIRKENDALL, L. A.   81
KLEEGMAN, S.   82
KLINEFELTER'S SYNDROME
   30, 37, 47, 81

LABIA MAJORA   81, 96
LABIA MINORA   96, 99
LANSING, C.   13
LAPAROSCOPY   75
LATENCY PERIOD   28
LAWS ON SEX   5, 136, 147-148
LESBIANISM   15, 62-63, 135
   see also HOMOSEXUALITY
LESIONS
   Intracranial   46
LEYDIG CELLS   39, 47, 82
LIBERTINE   78
LIBIDINAL DRIVE   28, 81-82
   120-121
LIDZ, T.   40, 42
LIEF, H. I.   8, 17, 54
LOEB, M. B.   27
LONELINESS   44, 50
LOVE   43, 50, 109, 115, 137
LSD   122
"LUST MURDER"   137

MACE, D. R.   78
MAGIC MODEL   11
MALE ROLE   23, 26, 39, 43-44,
   91
   See also BOY'S ROLE
   Aging   81
   Coital position   103-105
   Homosexual   61
   Impotency   82
   Love   43
   Older, arousal   106
   Physical examination   72
   Single-contraceptives   63
MARGOLIS, F. J.   30, 157-158
MARIJUANA   122
MARRIAGE   8, 12, 28, 43, 54-56,
   59, 72, 80

American   60-61, 148
Attitudes, sexual   92-93
Counseling   14, 72-73, 105-
   108
Early   59, 61
Relationships   29, 117-118
Remaining together after
   sixty   61
   problems   78-90
Unwed mother   59
MARRIAGE COUNCIL OF
   PHILADELPHIA   92
Masculinity   see BOY's ROLE
   MALE ROLE
MASOCHISM   106, 136-137
Mastectomy   see BREAST
   CANCER
MASTERS, W. H. and JOHNSON,
   V. E.   73, 75, 81-82, 91, 93,
   95, 101-102, 104, 106,
   108, 112, 114-115, 118,
   119, 129
MASTURBATION   4, 40-42,
   44-45, 103, 111-117, 119,
   129, 157
   Adolescence   40-42, 44-45
   Adulthood   60, 103, 111-117,
   113, 129
   Aged   85
   Cardiac rate   129
   Voyeurism   136
   Women   60, 101
MATHIS, J. E.   9
MEAD, M.   23
MEASLES   46
MELODY, F. G.   124
MENINGITIS   131
MENOPAUSE   4, 7, 81, 118
MENSTRUATION   30, 39, 45-46
   65-67, 81, 102
MONEY, J.   25, 26, 28
MORALS   4, 8, 10, 150,
   Advise   157
   Code   150, 157
MORES, SEXUAL
   American   21, 23, 41-43,
   147-150
   Denmark   148
   Indians, Plains   41
   Samoan Islands   41
   Western cultures   60
MORMONS   148
Mother-Daughter Relationship
   see RELATIONSHIPS

Mother-Son Relationship   see
    RELATIONSHIPS
MYOCARDIAL INFARCTION   129
MYOMA 66
MUMPS 75

NADLER, H. L. and GERBIE,
    A. B.   76
NATIONAL COMMISSION ON
    VENEREAL DISEASE   134
NEUROLOGIC DISORDERS
    123-124
Neuroses, Sex   see ANXIETIES,
    FEARS, GUILT
    Neurologic disorders   123-124
    Neurotic suppression of
    sexual feelings   41, 122
NEW HAVEN CONN., YOUNG
    MOTHERS PROGRAM   57-58
NEWMAN, G.   83
NEW YORK (CITY)
    Abortions —statistics   69-71
    Blackout 90
    Bureau of Maternity Services
    and Family Planning   69
    Complications following
    abortions —statistics   70
    Deaths, maternal —statistics
    71
    Memorial Hospital study   126
NICHOLS, C. R.   83
NON-MARITAL BEHAVIOR   see
    BEHAVIOR, NON-MARITAL
NON-ORGASMIC RESPONSE
    117-119, 135
NORETHINDRONE   36
Normal Development   see
    DEVELOPMENT
NUDITY   29
NULLIPAROUS WOMEN   66,
    96, 99
NUTRITION   47, 123
NYMPHOMANIA   135

OBSTETRICIAN-GYNECOLOGIST
    7, 64, 72-74, 113
OEDIPAL CONFLICT   28, 40
    see also ASSAULT, SEXUAL
Oral Contraceptives   see
    CONTRACEPTIVES
ORAL-GENITAL CONTACT
    4, 44, 61, 92, 103, 122
ORCHIECTOMY   125
ORFIRER, A. P.   126

ORGASM   4-5, 7, 15, 23, 28, 41,
    44, 74, 82, 93, 99-102, 106,
    109-113, 118-119, 124, 128,
    148
    Non-orgasmic response
    117-120
    Secondary orgasmic
    dysfunction   123
OTTO, H. A.   141
OVARY   24, 31, 39, 80, 125
    Atrophy   81
    Deficiency   65
    Granulosa cell tumor   46
    Hypofunction   48
    Lesions   124
    Tumors   47
OVUM   24
    Extra-ovular   66
OVULATION   39, 47, 67, 102

PAKTER, J.   69
PAPANICOLAOU SMEAR   17
PARAPLEGIA   114, 124
PARENT-CHILD MODEL   11
PAROUS WOMEN   97
PEDIATRICIAN   7, 72, 142
PEDOPHILIA   137-138
PEER MODEL   11
PELVIS
    Congestion   101, 121
    Examination   17, 45, 120-121
    Inflammatory disease
    118, 120-121
PENICILLIN   131
PENIS   25, 37, 39-40, 121
    Erections   28, 82-84, 95,
    111-116, 122, 124-125
    139
PENNSYLVANIA, UNIVERSITY OF
    Marriage Council of
    Philadelphia   92
PERINEORRHAPHY SCARS   83
PERITONITIS, PELVIC   131
PETTING   43, 103, 124
    see also COITUS
PEYRONIE'S DISEASE   121
PHARMACEUTICAL
    MANUFACTURERS
    ASSOCIATION   64
PHARYNGITIS   131
PHENOTYPE
    Female   31
    Male   30, 37, 47
PHIMOSIS   121

PHYSICAL EXAMINATION 17
see also GENITALIA,
PELVIS
PHYSICIAN, ATTITUDE AND
PERSONALITY 9-10
Preparation for
counseling 8, 17
PHYSICIANS-COUNSELING
Adolescent 44-49
Adolescent, management
of problems 46-59
Adulthood
early 63-69, 108-110
late 81, 106-110
late, management of
problems 83-85, 111-
120
late, normal sexual
development 81-83
Children 35-36
Children, management of
Community 151-158
problems 36-38
Parent 33-36
Pre-marital 46, 49-54, 72,
74, 108-110
PITUITARY GONADOTROPIC
HORMONES 39, 46-47
POTENCY 82, 84, 112, 123-125
PREGNANCY 4, 23, 30-31, 38,
46, 55-59, 68, 72, 74, 84, 118,
131, 139, 157
AMA policy statement 51-52
Decrease 61
Ectopic 124
Extra-ovular 66
Fear 60
Lactation during 74
Non-marital 54, 59
Pre-marital 43, 52-54
Rape 139
Sexual adjustment 73-74
Teenage 42, 52-59
PRE-MARITAL
Counseling 49-54, 72-74,
108-110
Examination 17, 72, 108-110
Sexual encounters 15, 132
147-148
Standards 148-149
PREPUBERTAL CASTRATE
SYNDROME 48
PROBLEMS, MANAGEMENT OF
Adolescence 49-59

Adulthood
early 63-79
late 81-85
Childhood 36-38
Physician's role 7-8
PROCTITIS 131, 134
PROGESTERONE 39
PROGESTOGENS 31, 36-37
PROSTATECTOMY 7, 81, 121-
122
PROSTITUTES 111-112, 114, 132
PSEUDOHERMAPHRODITE 25,
31, 37, 40
PSYCHIATRY 133
see also MENTAL DISORDERS
PSYCHOBIOLOGIC SEX 24
PSYCHOLOGICAL DISTURBANCE
25, 133, 141
PSYCHOSEXUAL DISTURBANCES
see also ADOLESCENCE,
PUBERTY
Illness 126, 129
PSYCHOTHERAPY 38, 122
Complaints, sexual 106
Fetishism 136
Homosexual-adolescence 49
Homosexual-adulthood, early
61, 76-77
Transexualism 136
Unwed teenager 55-59
PUBERTY 17, 35-34
Precocious 46-48
Precocious pseudopuberty 46
PUGH, W. E. and FERNANDEZ,
F. L. 74
Pulse Rate
see COITUS

RADO, S. 136
RAPE see ASSAULT, SEXUAL
see also PREGNANCY
RECTOSIGMOID SUPPURATIVE
PROCESS 124
RECTUM
Inflammation 132
Lesions 134
Smears 130-131
REED, D. M. 17-18
REFERRALS 141
REISS, I. L. 49, 60, 148-149, 157
RELATIONSHIPS
Adolescence, sexual 27, 30,
46-47, 51, 55

Father-daughter 30, 42, 62, 117
Father-son 30, 33, 45
Husbands and wives 15, 72-74, 91-92
Interpersonal 118-119
Mother-daughter 30, 62
Mother-son 26, 62, 135
RELIGION 22, 111, 120, 151
  Activities 91
  Christianity 44
  Judaism 44
REPRODUCTIVE ORGANS 17, 24-45
Respiration see COITUS
RESPONSE, SEXUAL 7, 16, 75-76, 78, 91-102
  Anatomy and Physiology 95-100, 197
  Excitation phase 96
  Female 117-122
  Male 111-116
  Non-orgasmis phase 75, 99-102
  Orgasmic phase 75, 99-102
  Plateau phase 75, 96-97
  Pregnancy 73-74
  Resolution phase 100
  Temporary failures 6, 91
  Variations 135-140
RETIREMENT 92
RHYTHM 67
ROE, JANE 68
RUBIN, I. 61, 81

SACHS, B. C. 126
SADISM 136-137
SALPINGO-OOPHORECTOMY 125
SALPINGO-OOPHRITIS 131
SAMOAN ISLANDS 41
SARREL, P. M. 57, 73
SATYR 135
SCHOFIELD, M. 27
SCROTUM 39, 100
SECONDARY SEX CHARACTERISTICS 39-40, 46-48
Seduction see BEHAVIOR
SELF-HELP MODEL 11
Self Stimulation see MASTURBATION
SEMEN 36, 71, 76
SEMINIFEROUS TUBULE 39

Dysgenesis 31
SEMMENS, J. P. 113
SEROLOGIC TEST 139
Sex Education see FAMILY LIFE EDUCATION
SEX ERRORS, OF THE BODY 30-31, 36-38, 46-48, 76
SEXUAL DRIVES 15, 60, 93, 121, 125
  Adolescence 42, 45
  Adulthood
    early 60
    late 81-83
  Female 60
SEXUAL STANDARDS 147-150
SHULMAN, B. H. 93
SMEARS 139
  Buccal 37, 54
  Cervical canal 131
  Gram-negative intracellular diplococci 130
  Oral mucosal 31
  Papanicolaou 17
  Rectum 130-131
  Urethra 130-131
"SPANISH FLY" see APHRODISIACS
SPERM 138
  Spermatocidal vaginal foams 67
  Spermatogenesis 39, 82
  Spermatozoa 24, 71, 96
SPINAL CORD LESION 124
SPINAL REFLEXES 124
STATE AND COUNTY MEDICAL ASSOCIATIONS, ROLE 152
STERILITY 10, 30, 38, 75
  Female 10, 75
  Male 30, 38, 75
STERILIZATION 157
  Surgical 71
  Tubal 71-72
  Vasectomy 71
SURGICAL CORRECTIONS 37, 113
  Bilateral salpingo-oophorectomy 125
  Colostomy 125
  Exploration 37
  Hysterectomy 4, 7, 81, 119, 125-126
  Orchiectomy 125
  Procedures 125-126
  Rectum 120, 125

Sex reassignment 38
Sterilization 71
    tubal 71-72
    vasectomy 4, 71
SYPHILIS 129-134, 139

TABES DORSALIS 123
TACHYCARDIA 128
TEENAGER 27, 42, 51, 150
    See also ADOLESCENCE:
        BOY'S ROLE; GIRL'S ROLE
    Brides 42
    Education 53
    Pregnancy 42, 51-59
TEMPORAL LOBE LESIONS 124
TENOSYNOVITIS 131
TESTICULAR FEMINIZING
    SYNDROME 31, 36-37
TESTES 24, 31, 74, 96, 100
    Absence 47
    Atrophy 47
    Fetal 25
    Function 30
    Mosaicism 31, 47
    Tumors 47
TESTOSTERONE
    Production 82
    Treatment 47
TEXAS
    Abortion statute 68
THAYER MARTIN MEDIUM 131
THROMBOEMBOLISM 64
TOMBOY 26, 39-49
TOUCHING 107-108
TRANQUILIZERS 115
TRANSEXUAL 26, 33, 136
"TRANSGROW" 131
TRANSVESTITE 26, 136
TUMORS 46-48
    Granulosa cell 46
    Ovarian tumors 46, 47
    Pituitary tumors 123
    Testicular tumors 47
Turner's Syndrome see
    GONADAL DYSGENESIS
    (TURNER'S) SYNDROME
URETHRA 45, 100, 103
URINARY
    Bladder 24
    17-ketosteroids 37
    Tract infections 124
U. S. FOOD AND DRUG
    ADMINISTRATION
    Oral Contraceptives 64

U. S. PUBLIC HEALTH SERVICE,
    CENTER FOR DISEASE
        CONTROL 131
U. S. SUPREME COURT 68-69
UTERUS 74, 81, 96, 100, 125
    Atrophy 81
    Bleeding 73
    Cavity 66
    Prolapse 120
    Retrodisplacement of 124
    Vaginal canal 24
    Wall-perforation 66
VAGINA
    Atresia 83
    Dyspareunia see
        DYSPAREUNIA
    Enlargement 96-100
    Vaginitis 83
    Vulvitis 83
VARIANT SEXUAL
    DEVELOPMENT 30-31,
        36-38, 46-48, 76
VARIANT SEXUAL IDENTITY
    31-33, 38, 135-136
VAS DEFERENS 71
VASECTOMY 4, 7, 71, 125
VASOCONGESTION 93, 96-97
VENEREAL DISEASE 13, 45, 53,
    67, 129-134, 139, 153
    see also GONORRHEA;
        SYPHILIS
    National Commission on
        Venereal Disease 134
VINCENT C. E. 26, 51, 55-56, 79
VOICE
    Boy 39
    High pitch 47
VOYEURISM 136
VULVOVAGINITIS 120, 131

WADE, HENRY 68
WAHL, C. W. 15-16-77
WALLIN, P. 93
WASHINGTON UNIVERSITY OF
    SEX EDUCATION COUNCIL
    OF STUDENTS 155
"WHAT YOU SHOULD KNOW
    ABOUT 'THE PILL'" 64
WHITE, P. 121
WHITE HOUSE CONFERENCE
    ON CHILDREN 155
WIDOW AND WIDOWER 79
Withdrawal see COITUS
    INTERRPUTUS

Wives   see HUSBANDS AND
    WIVES

YOUNG MOTHERS PROGRAM,
    NEW HAVEN   57-58

American Medical Association.
    Committee on Human Sexuality.